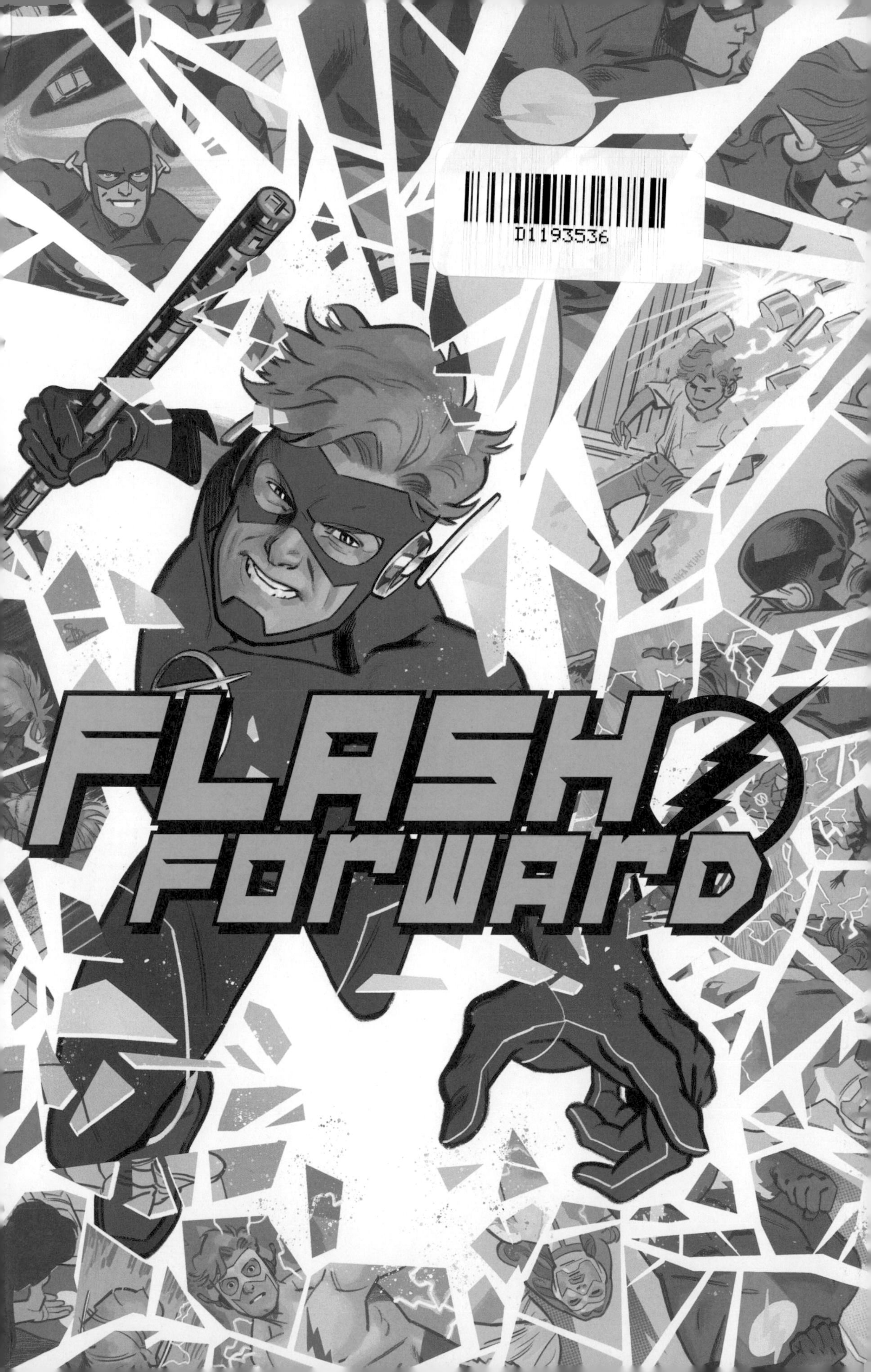
FLASH
FORWARD

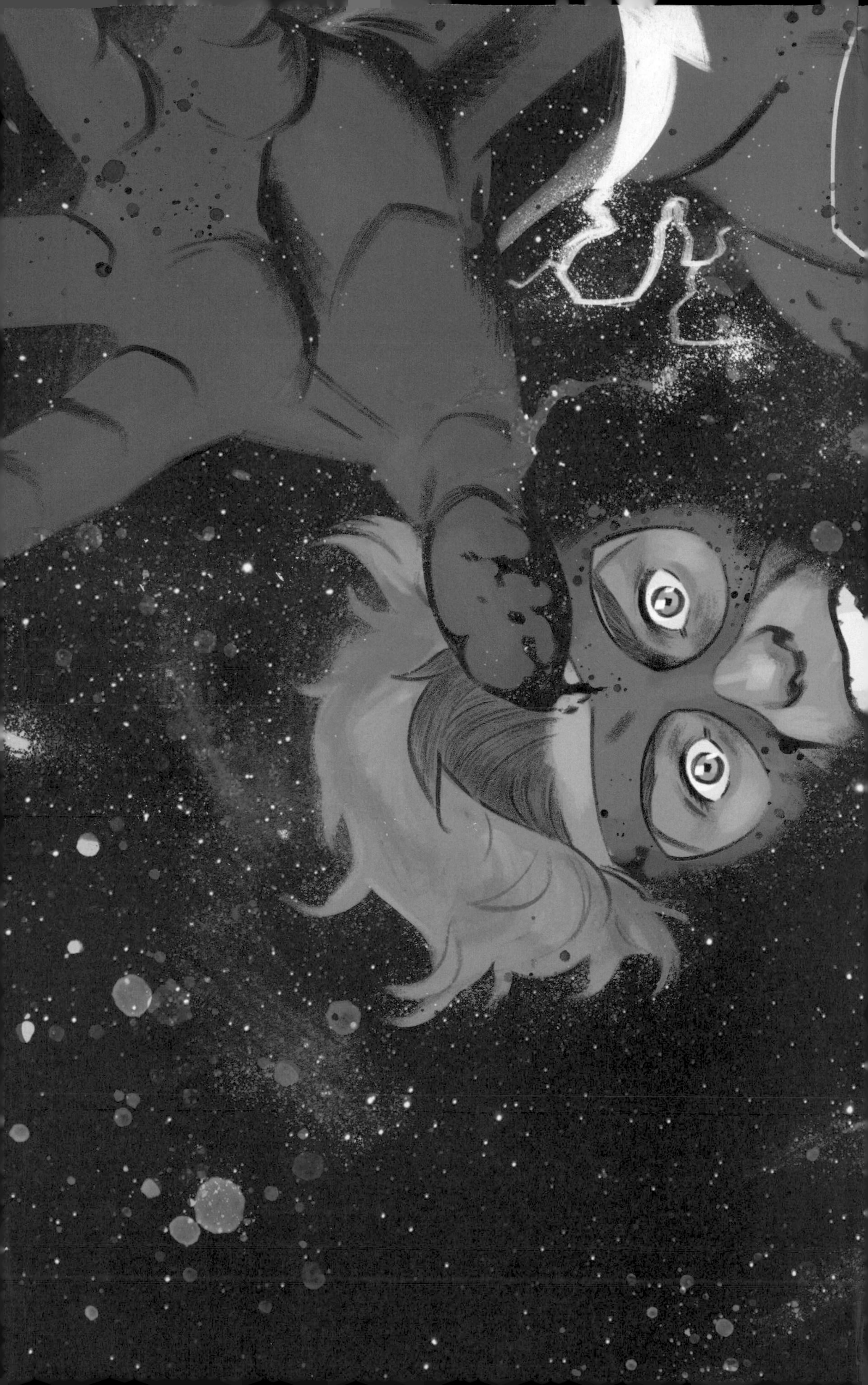

FLASH FORWARD

SCOTT LOBDELL writer

BRETT BOOTH penciller

NORM RAPMUND inker

LUIS GUERRERO colorist

ALW'S TROY PETERI letterer

BRETT BOOTH, NORM RAPMUND,
and **LUIS GUERRERO** collection cover artists

EVAN "DOC" SHANER original series cover artist

SUPERMAN created by
JERRY SIEGEL and **JOE SHUSTER**
By special arrangement with
the JERRY SIEGEL family

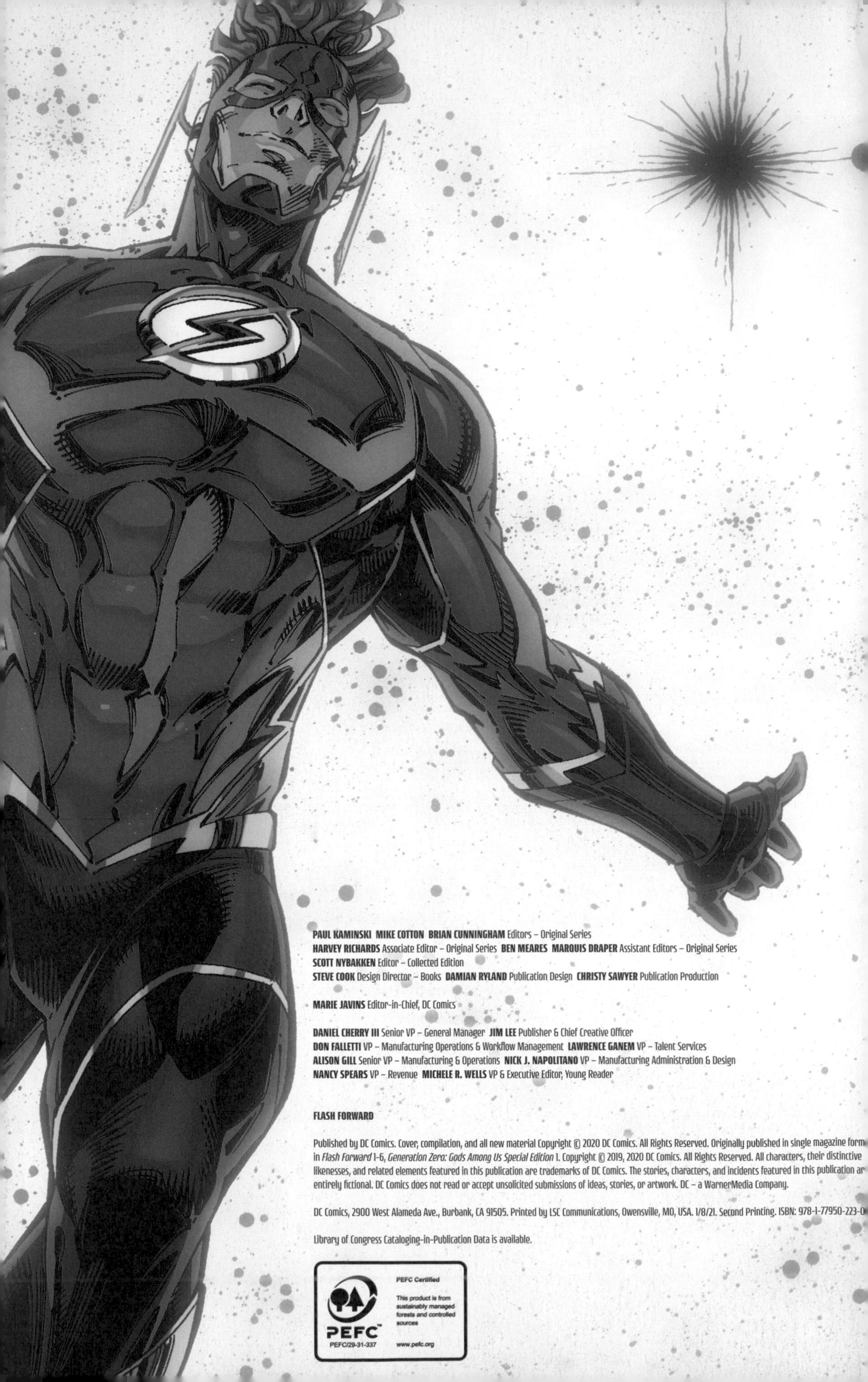

PAUL KAMINSKI MIKE COTTON BRIAN CUNNINGHAM Editors – Original Series
HARVEY RICHARDS Associate Editor – Original Series **BEN MEARES MARQUIS DRAPER** Assistant Editors – Original Series
SCOTT NYBAKKEN Editor – Collected Edition
STEVE COOK Design Director – Books **DAMIAN RYLAND** Publication Design **CHRISTY SAWYER** Publication Production

MARIE JAVINS Editor-in-Chief, DC Comics

DANIEL CHERRY III Senior VP – General Manager **JIM LEE** Publisher & Chief Creative Officer
DON FALLETTI VP – Manufacturing Operations & Workflow Management **LAWRENCE GANEM** VP – Talent Services
ALISON GILL Senior VP – Manufacturing & Operations **NICK J. NAPOLITANO** VP – Manufacturing Administration & Design
NANCY SPEARS VP – Revenue **MICHELE R. WELLS** VP & Executive Editor, Young Reader

FLASH FORWARD

DC Comics, 2900 West Alameda Ave., Burbank, CA 91505. Printed by LSC Communications, Owensville, MO, USA. 1/8/21. Second Printing. ISBN: 978-1-77950-223-0

Library of Congress Cataloging-in-Publication Data is available.

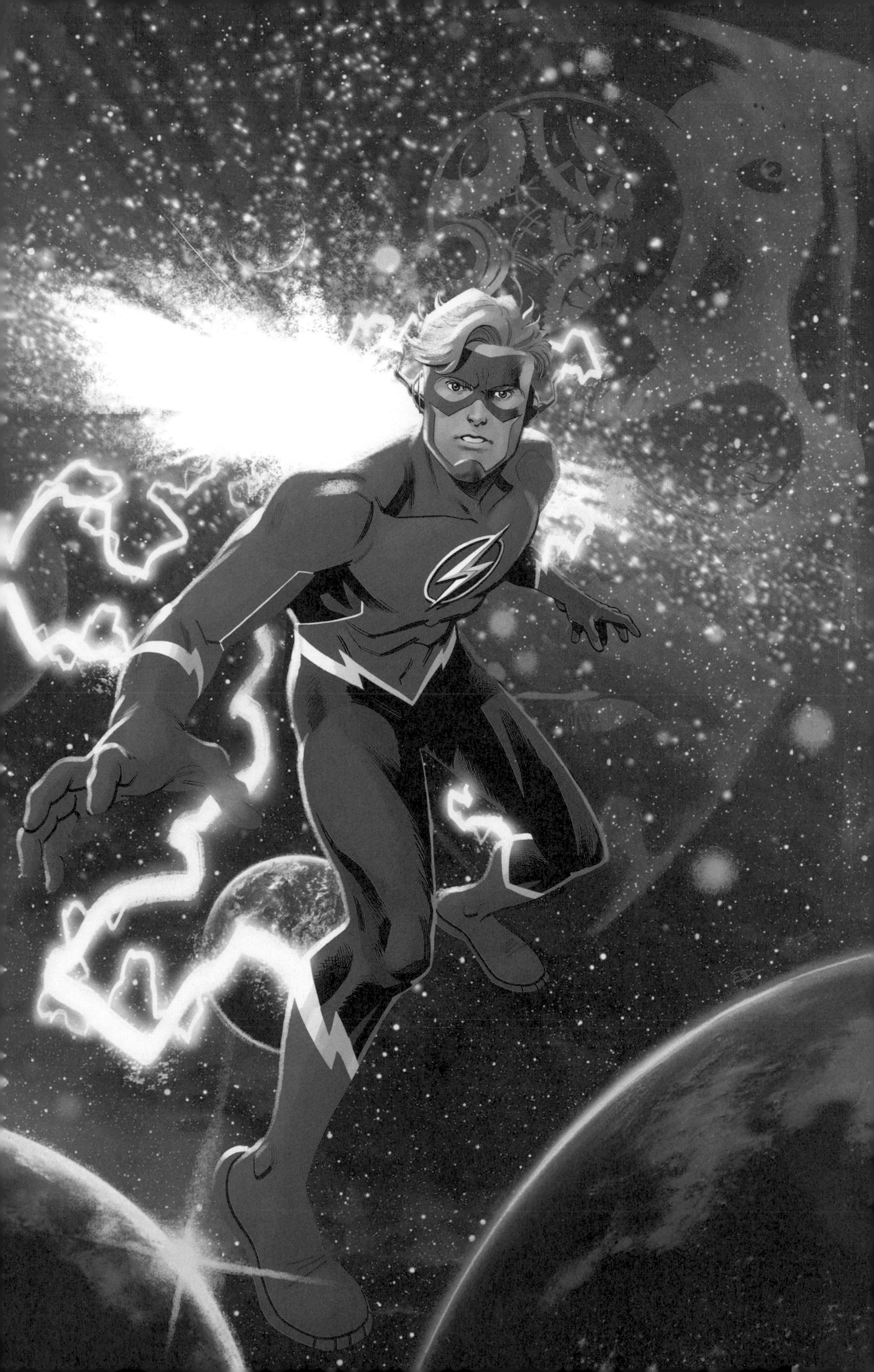

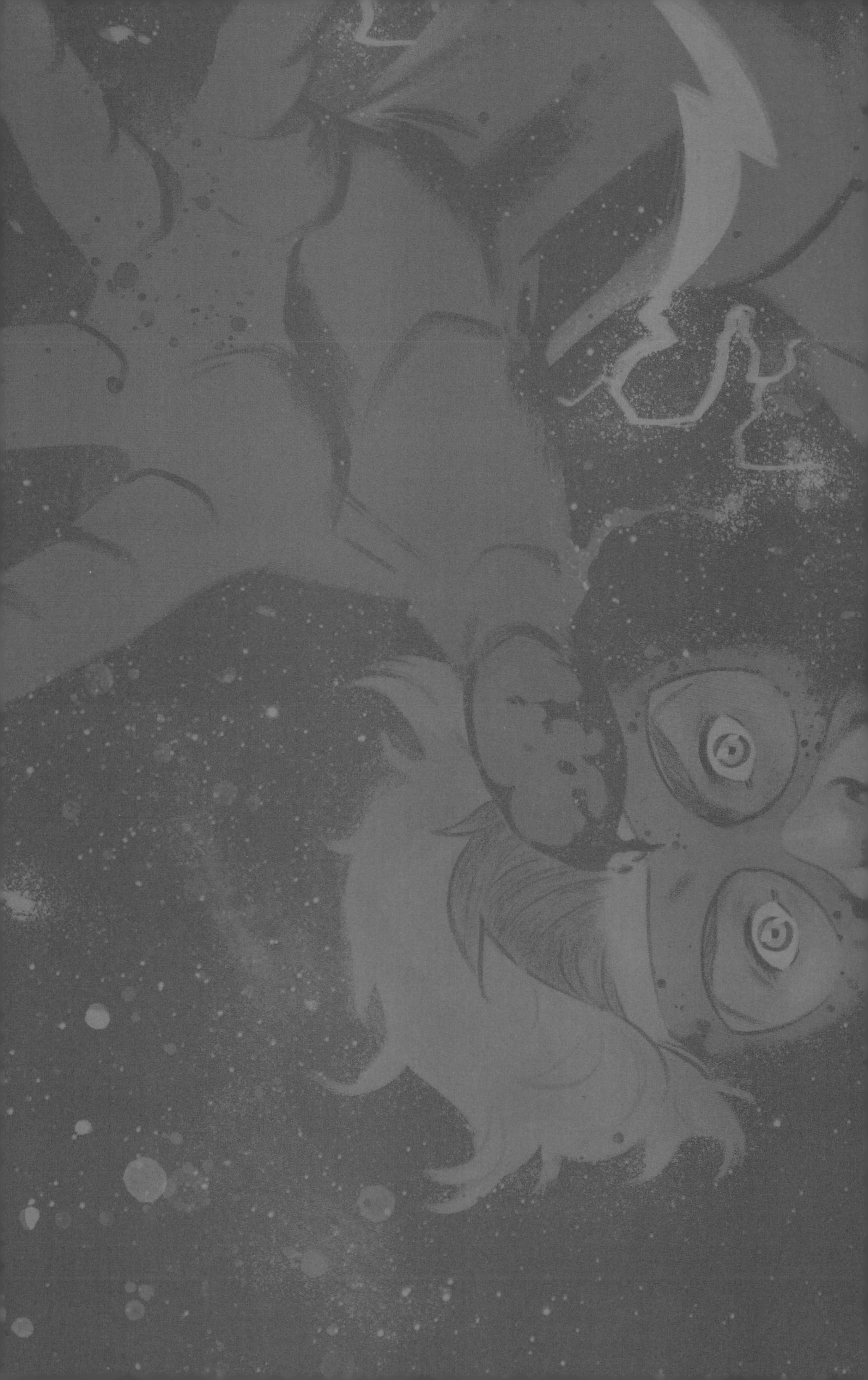

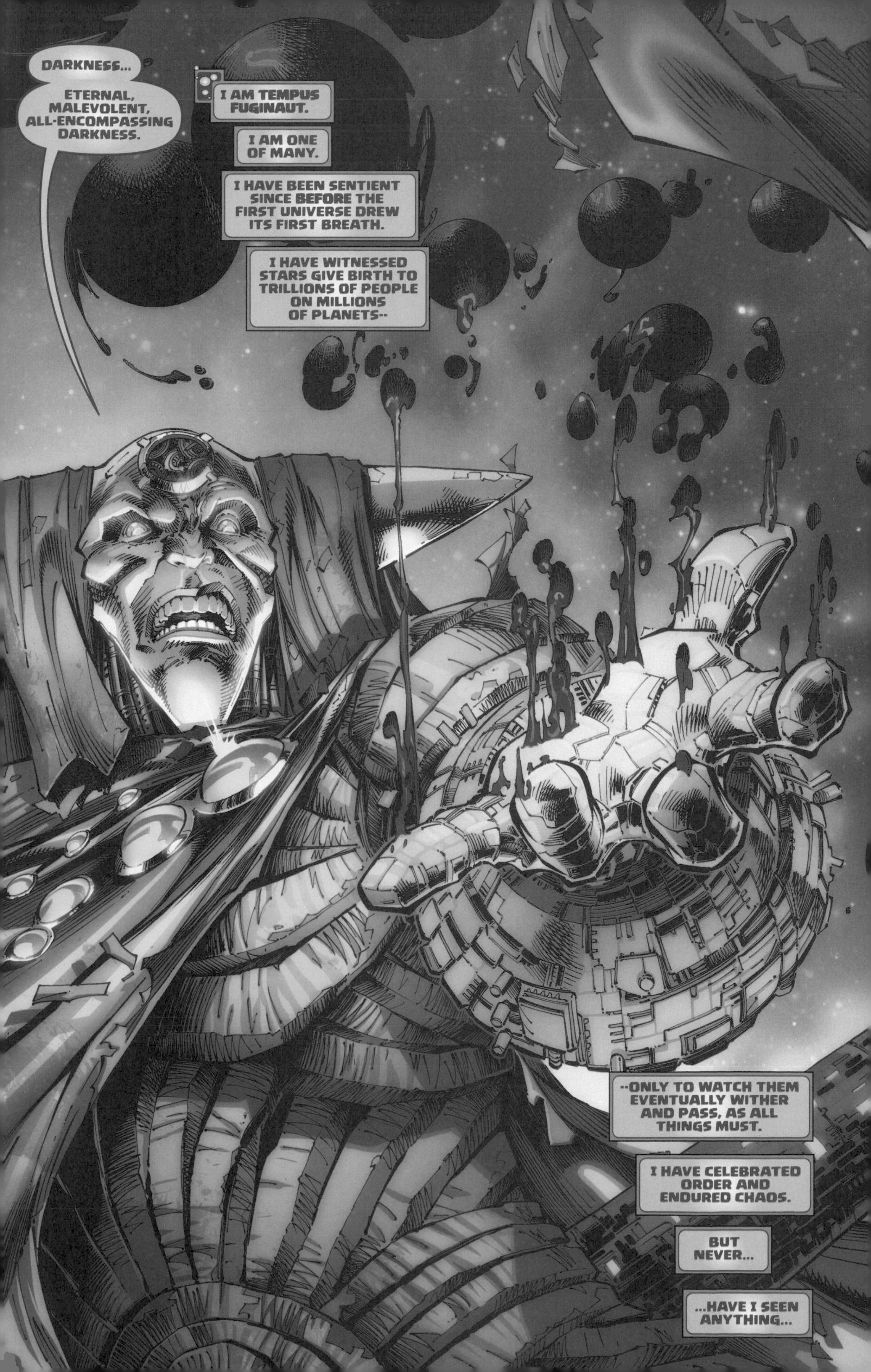
DARKNESS...
ETERNAL, MALEVOLENT, ALL-ENCOMPASSING DARKNESS.
I AM TEMPUS FUGINAUT.
I AM ONE OF MANY.
I HAVE BEEN SENTIENT SINCE BEFORE THE FIRST UNIVERSE DREW ITS FIRST BREATH.
I HAVE WITNESSED STARS GIVE BIRTH TO TRILLIONS OF PEOPLE ON MILLIONS OF PLANETS--
--ONLY TO WATCH THEM EVENTUALLY WITHER AND PASS, AS ALL THINGS MUST.
I HAVE CELEBRATED ORDER AND ENDURED CHAOS.
BUT NEVER...
...HAVE I SEEN ANYTHING...

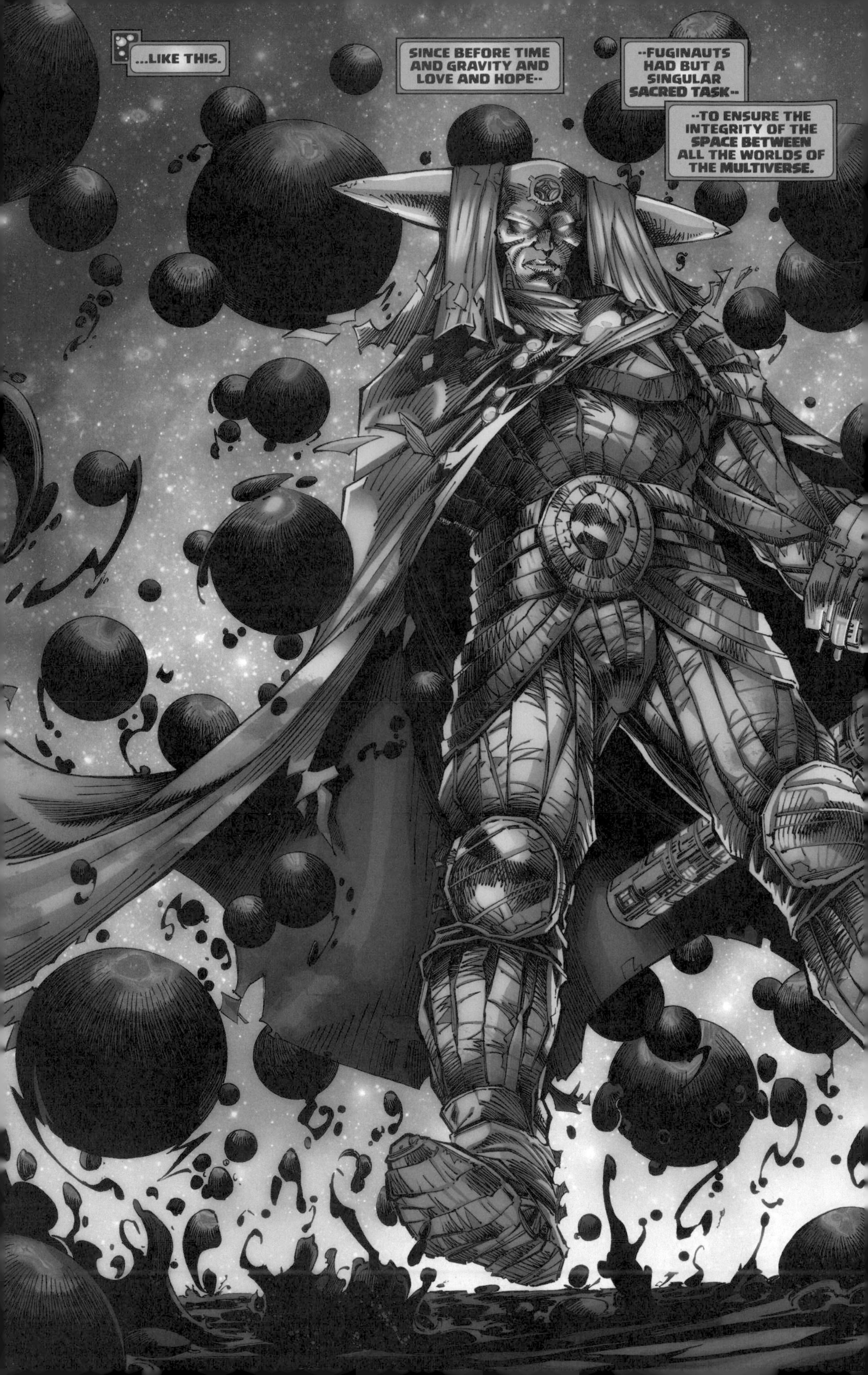
...LIKE THIS.
SINCE BEFORE TIME AND GRAVITY AND LOVE AND HOPE--
--FUGINAUTS HAD BUT A SINGULAR SACRED TASK--
--TO ENSURE THE INTEGRITY OF THE SPACE BETWEEN ALL THE WORLDS OF THE MULTIVERSE.

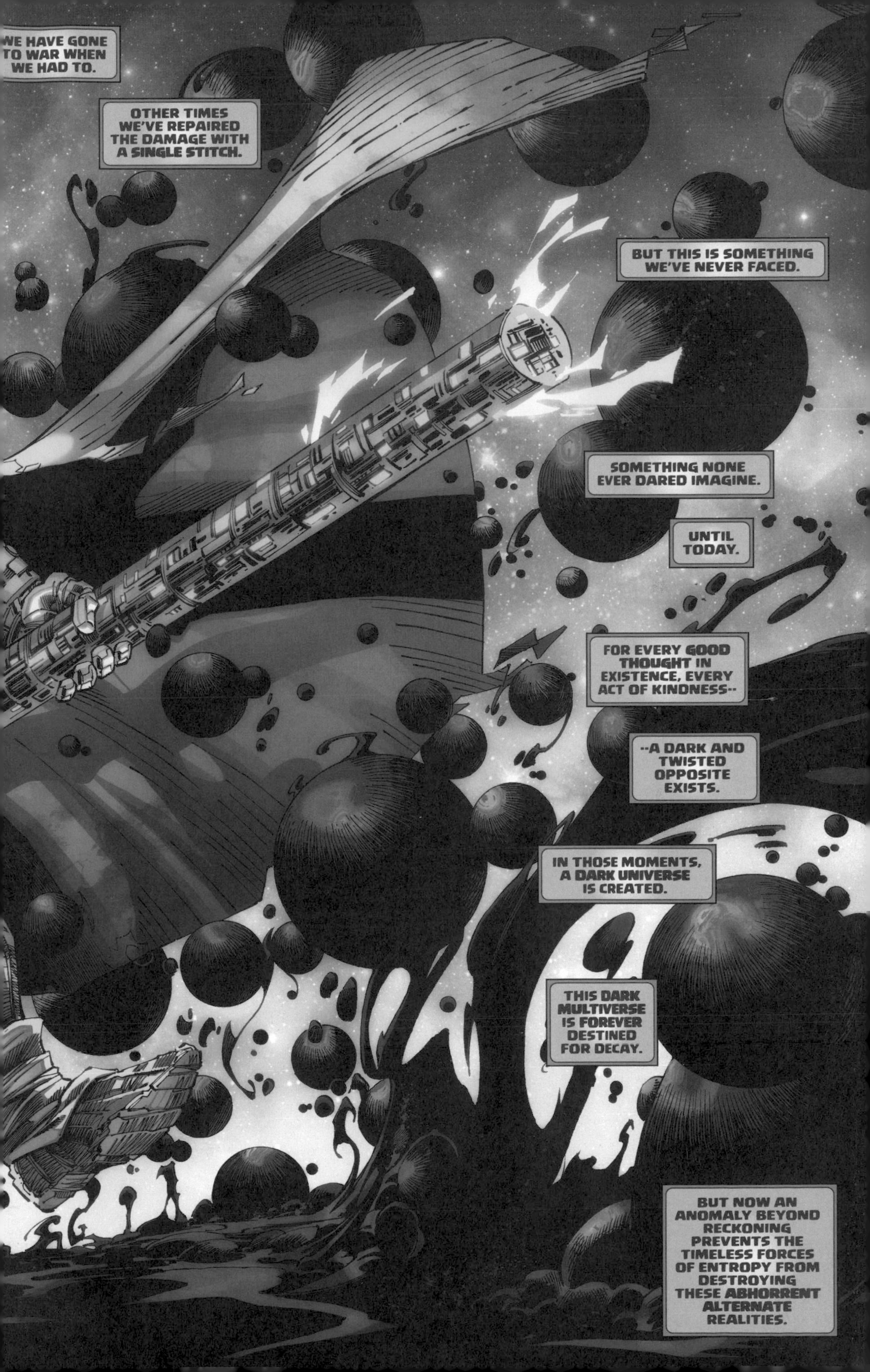
WE HAVE GONE TO WAR WHEN WE HAD TO.
OTHER TIMES WE'VE REPAIRED THE DAMAGE WITH A SINGLE STITCH.
BUT THIS IS SOMETHING WE'VE NEVER FACED.
SOMETHING NONE EVER DARED IMAGINE.
UNTIL TODAY.
FOR EVERY GOOD THOUGHT IN EXISTENCE, EVERY ACT OF KINDNESS--
--A DARK AND TWISTED OPPOSITE EXISTS.
IN THOSE MOMENTS, A DARK UNIVERSE IS CREATED.
THIS DARK MULTIVERSE IS FOREVER DESTINED FOR DECAY.
BUT NOW AN ANOMALY BEYOND RECKONING PREVENTS THE TIMELESS FORCES OF ENTROPY FROM DESTROYING THESE ABHORRENT ALTERNATE REALITIES.

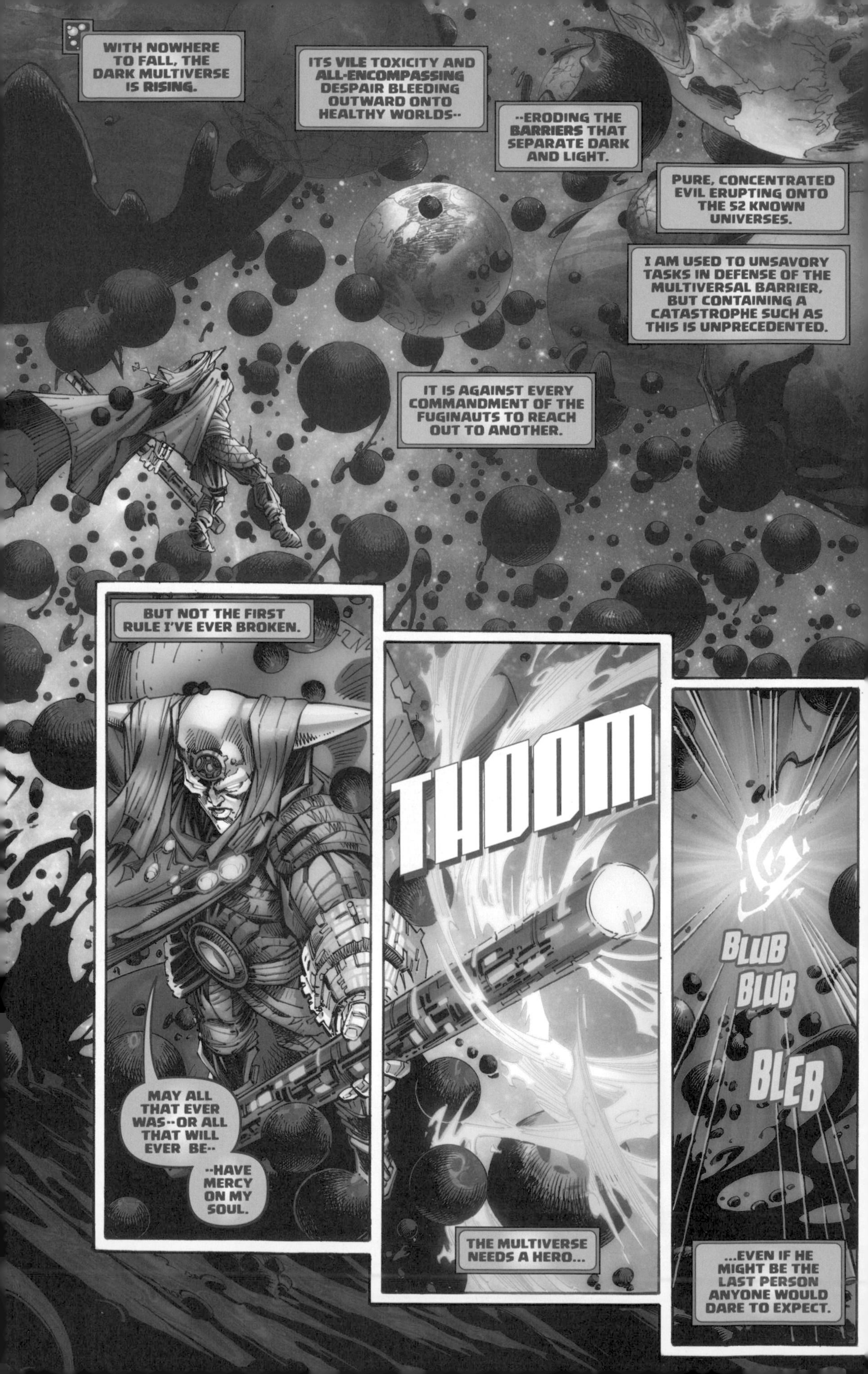
WITH NOWHERE TO FALL, THE DARK MULTIVERSE IS RISING.
ITS VILE TOXICITY AND ALL-ENCOMPASSING DESPAIR BLEEDING OUTWARD ONTO HEALTHY WORLDS--
--ERODING THE BARRIERS THAT SEPARATE DARK AND LIGHT.
PURE, CONCENTRATED EVIL ERUPTING ONTO THE 52 KNOWN UNIVERSES.
I AM USED TO UNSAVORY TASKS IN DEFENSE OF THE MULTIVERSAL BARRIER, BUT CONTAINING A CATASTROPHE SUCH AS THIS IS UNPRECEDENTED.
IT IS AGAINST EVERY COMMANDMENT OF THE FUGINAUTS TO REACH OUT TO ANOTHER.
BUT NOT THE FIRST RULE I'VE EVER BROKEN.
MAY ALL THAT EVER WAS--OR ALL THAT WILL EVER BE--
--HAVE MERCY ON MY SOUL.
THOOM
THE MULTIVERSE NEEDS A HERO...
BLUB
BLUB
BLEB
...EVEN IF HE MIGHT BE THE LAST PERSON ANYONE WOULD DARE TO EXPECT.

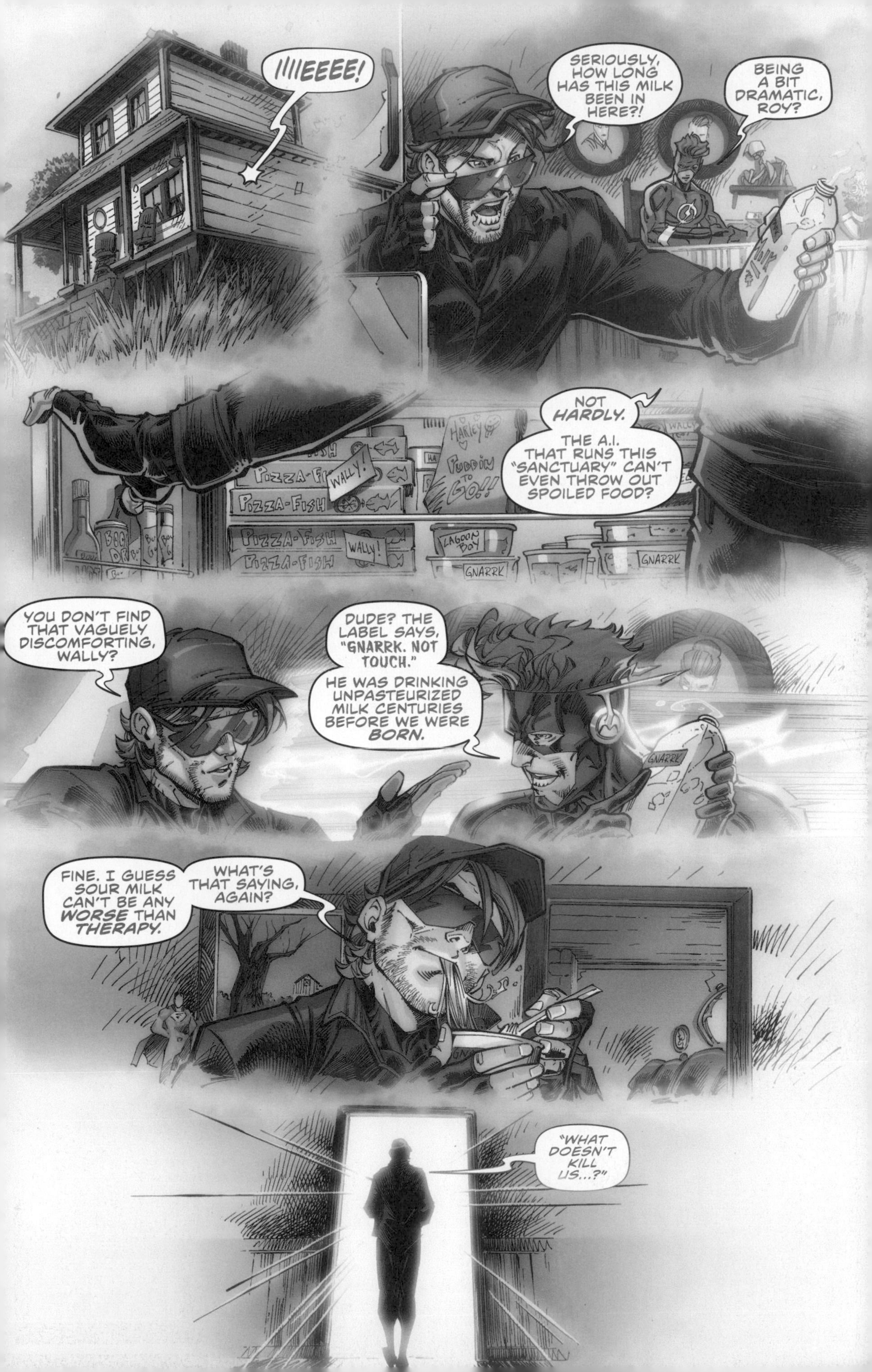
IIIIEEEE!
SERIOUSLY, HOW LONG HAS THIS MILK BEEN IN HERE?!
BEING A BIT DRAMATIC, ROY?
NOT HARDLY.
THE A.I. THAT RUNS THIS "SANCTUARY" CAN'T EVEN THROW OUT SPOILED FOOD?
WALLY
PIZZA-FISH
WALLY!
HARLEY
PUDDIN TO GO!!
LAGOON BOY
GNARRK
YOU DON'T FIND THAT VAGUELY DISCOMFORTING, WALLY?
DUDE? THE LABEL SAYS, "GNARRK. NOT TOUCH."
HE WAS DRINKING UNPASTEURIZED MILK CENTURIES BEFORE WE WERE BORN.
GNARRK
FINE. I GUESS SOUR MILK CAN'T BE ANY WORSE THAN THERAPY.
WHAT'S THAT SAYING, AGAIN?
"WHAT DOESN'T KILL US...?"

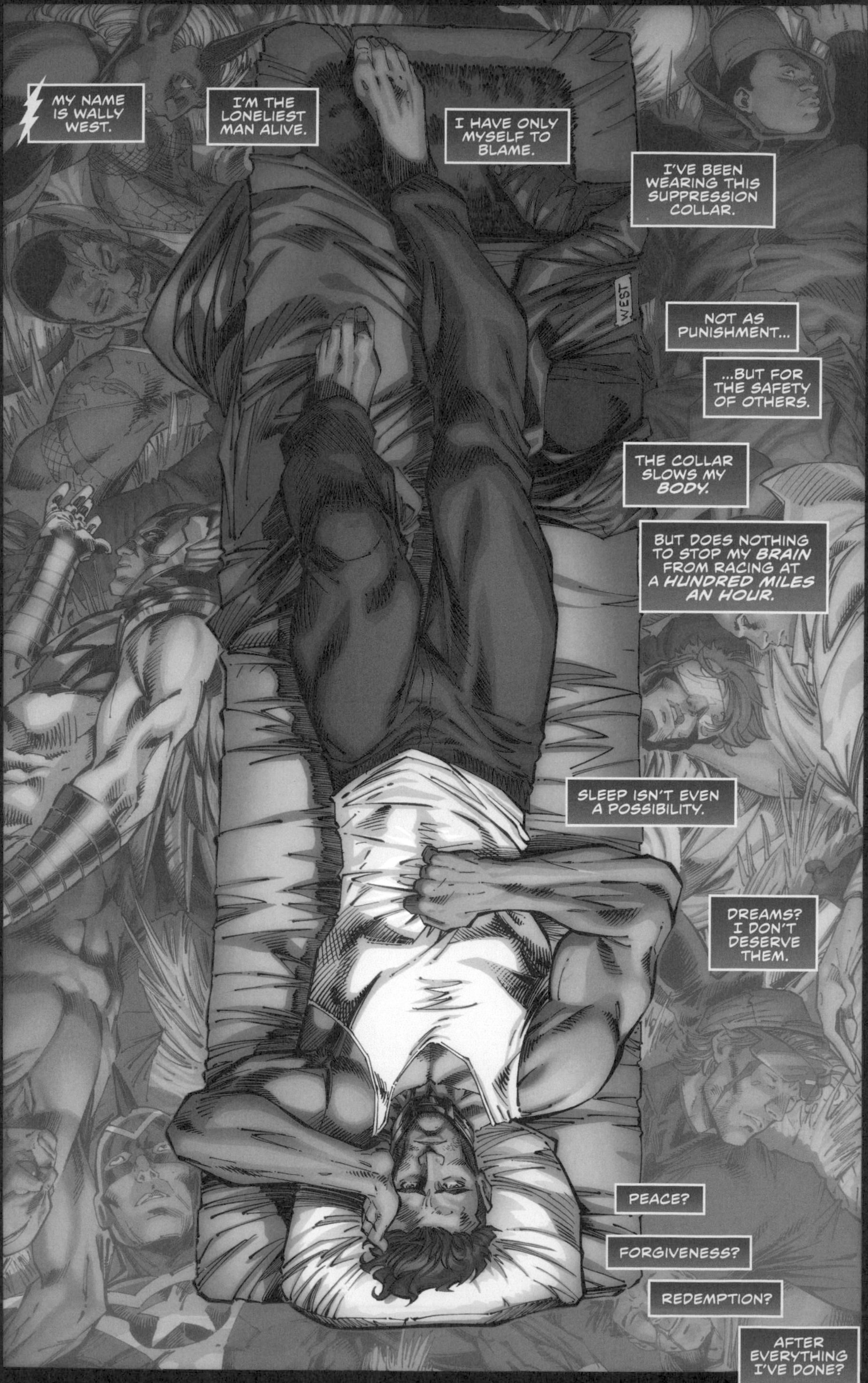
MY NAME IS WALLY WEST.
I'M THE LONELIEST MAN ALIVE.
I HAVE ONLY MYSELF TO BLAME.
I'VE BEEN WEARING THIS SUPPRESSION COLLAR.
WEST
NOT AS PUNISHMENT...
...BUT FOR THE SAFETY OF OTHERS.
THE COLLAR SLOWS MY *BODY.*
BUT DOES NOTHING TO STOP MY *BRAIN* FROM RACING AT A *HUNDRED MILES AN HOUR.*
SLEEP ISN'T EVEN A POSSIBILITY.
DREAMS? I DON'T DESERVE THEM.
PEACE?
FORGIVENESS?
REDEMPTION?
AFTER EVERYTHING I'VE DONE?

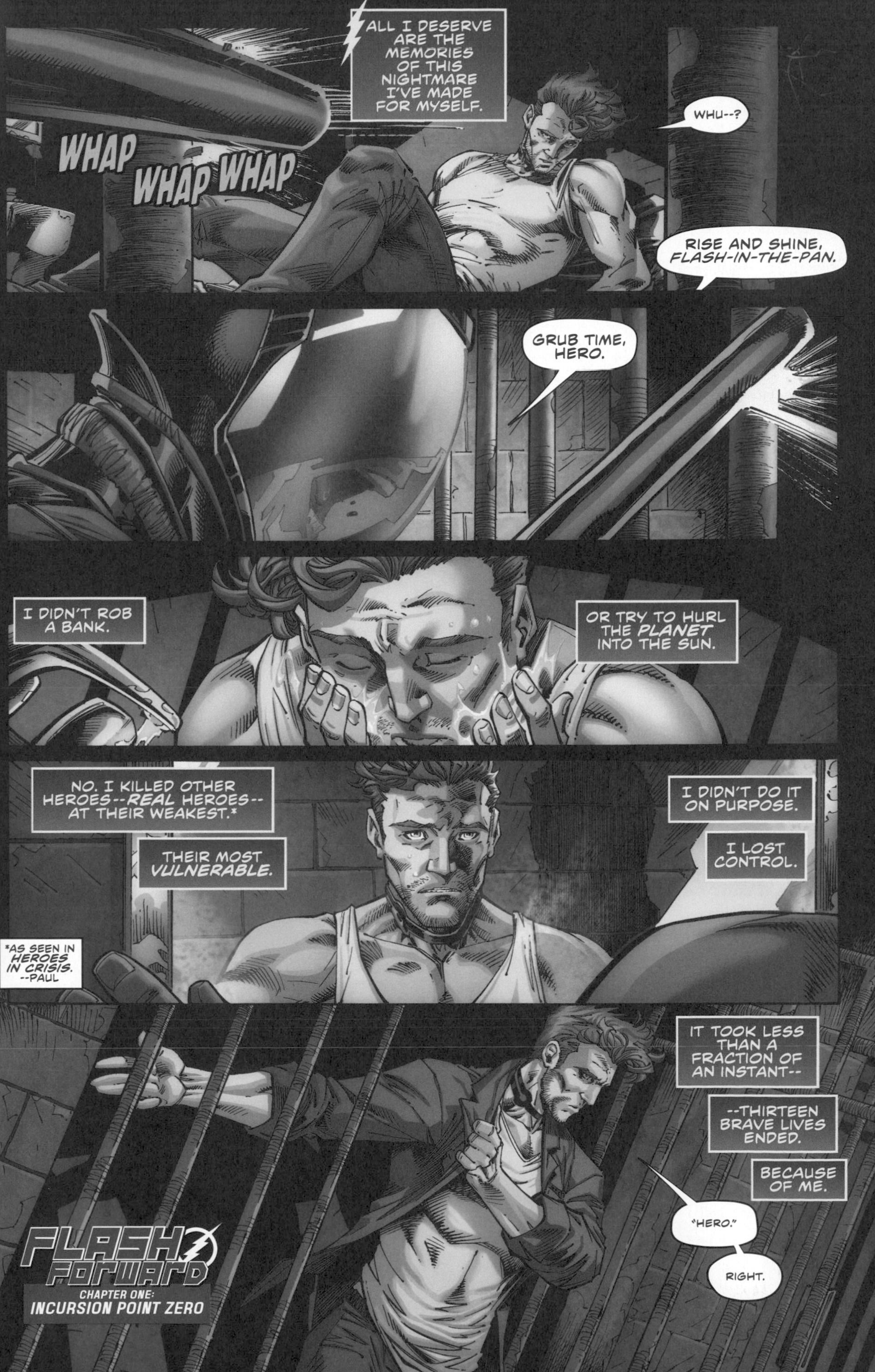

ALL I DESERVE ARE THE MEMORIES OF THIS NIGHTMARE I'VE MADE FOR MYSELF.
WHAP
WHAP WHAP
WHU--?
RISE AND SHINE, FLASH-IN-THE-PAN.
GRUB TIME, HERO.
I DIDN'T ROB A BANK.
OR TRY TO HURL THE PLANET INTO THE SUN.
NO. I KILLED OTHER HEROES--REAL HEROES--AT THEIR WEAKEST.*
THEIR MOST VULNERABLE.
I DIDN'T DO IT ON PURPOSE.
I LOST CONTROL.
*AS SEEN IN HEROES IN CRISIS. --PAUL
IT TOOK LESS THAN A FRACTION OF AN INSTANT--
--THIRTEEN BRAVE LIVES ENDED.
BECAUSE OF ME.
"HERO."
RIGHT.
FLASH FORWARD
CHAPTER ONE:
INCURSION POINT ZERO

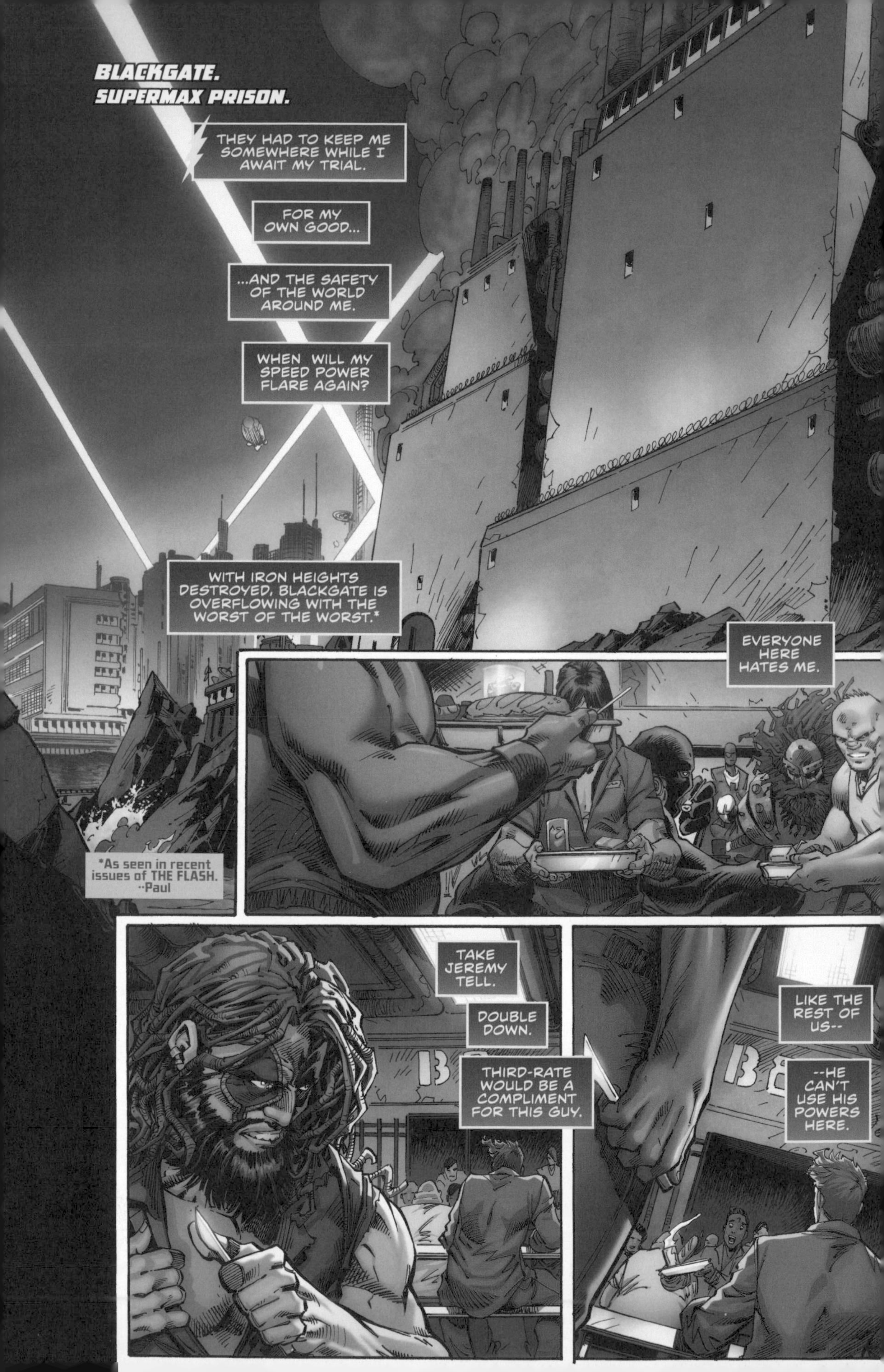
BLACKGATE.
SUPERMAX PRISON.
THEY HAD TO KEEP ME SOMEWHERE WHILE I AWAIT MY TRIAL.
FOR MY OWN GOOD...
...AND THE SAFETY OF THE WORLD AROUND ME.
WHEN WILL MY SPEED POWER FLARE AGAIN?
WITH IRON HEIGHTS DESTROYED, BLACKGATE IS OVERFLOWING WITH THE WORST OF THE WORST.*
*As seen in recent issues of THE FLASH. --Paul
EVERYONE HERE HATES ME.
TAKE JEREMY TELL.
DOUBLE DOWN.
THIRD-RATE WOULD BE A COMPLIMENT FOR THIS GUY.
LIKE THE REST OF US--
--HE CAN'T USE HIS POWERS HERE.

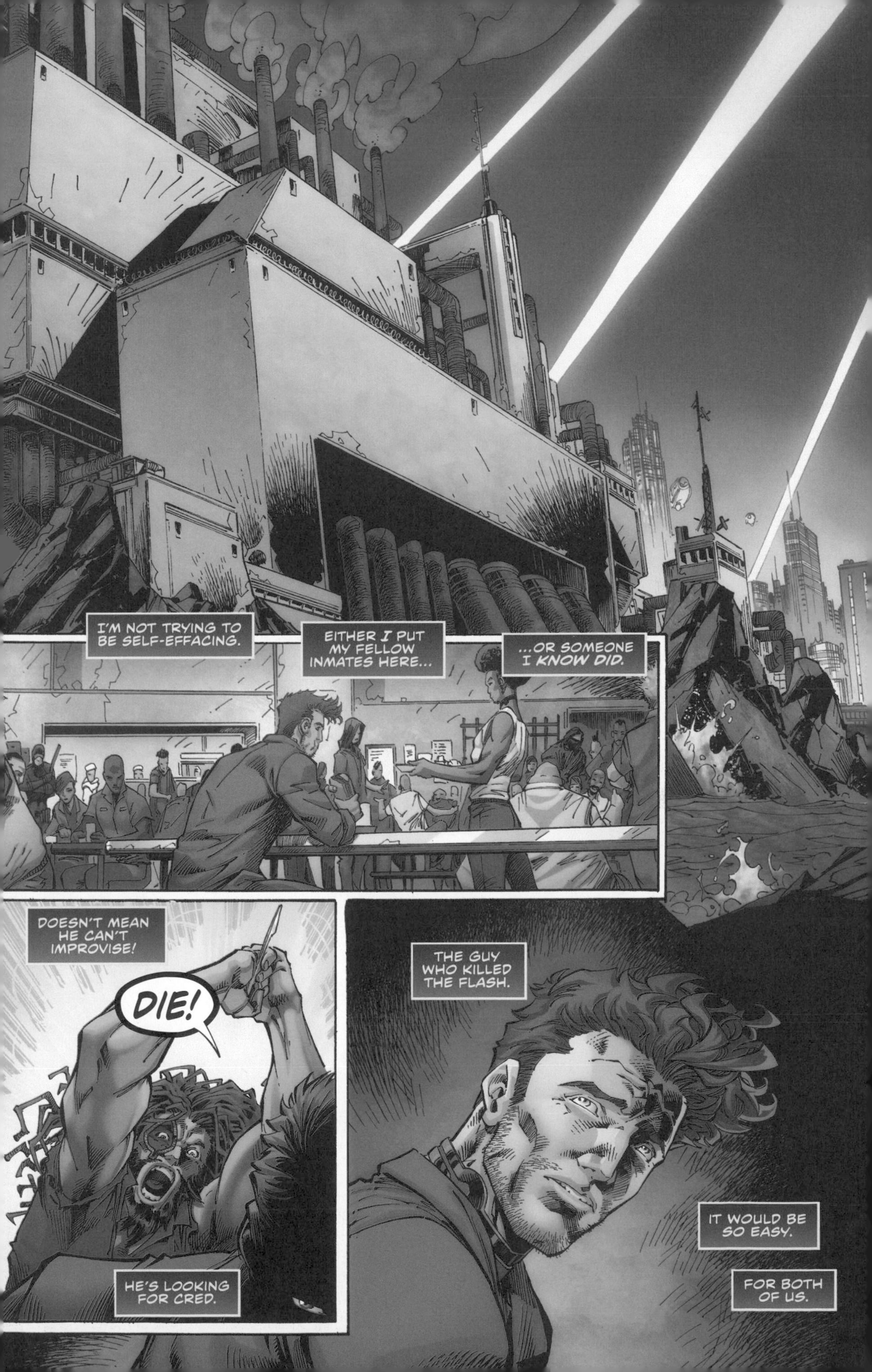
I'M NOT TRYING TO BE SELF-EFFACING.
EITHER *I* PUT MY FELLOW INMATES HERE...
...OR SOMEONE I *KNOW* DID.
DOESN'T MEAN HE CAN'T IMPROVISE!
DIE!
HE'S LOOKING FOR CRED.
THE GUY WHO KILLED THE FLASH.
IT WOULD BE SO EASY.
FOR BOTH OF US.

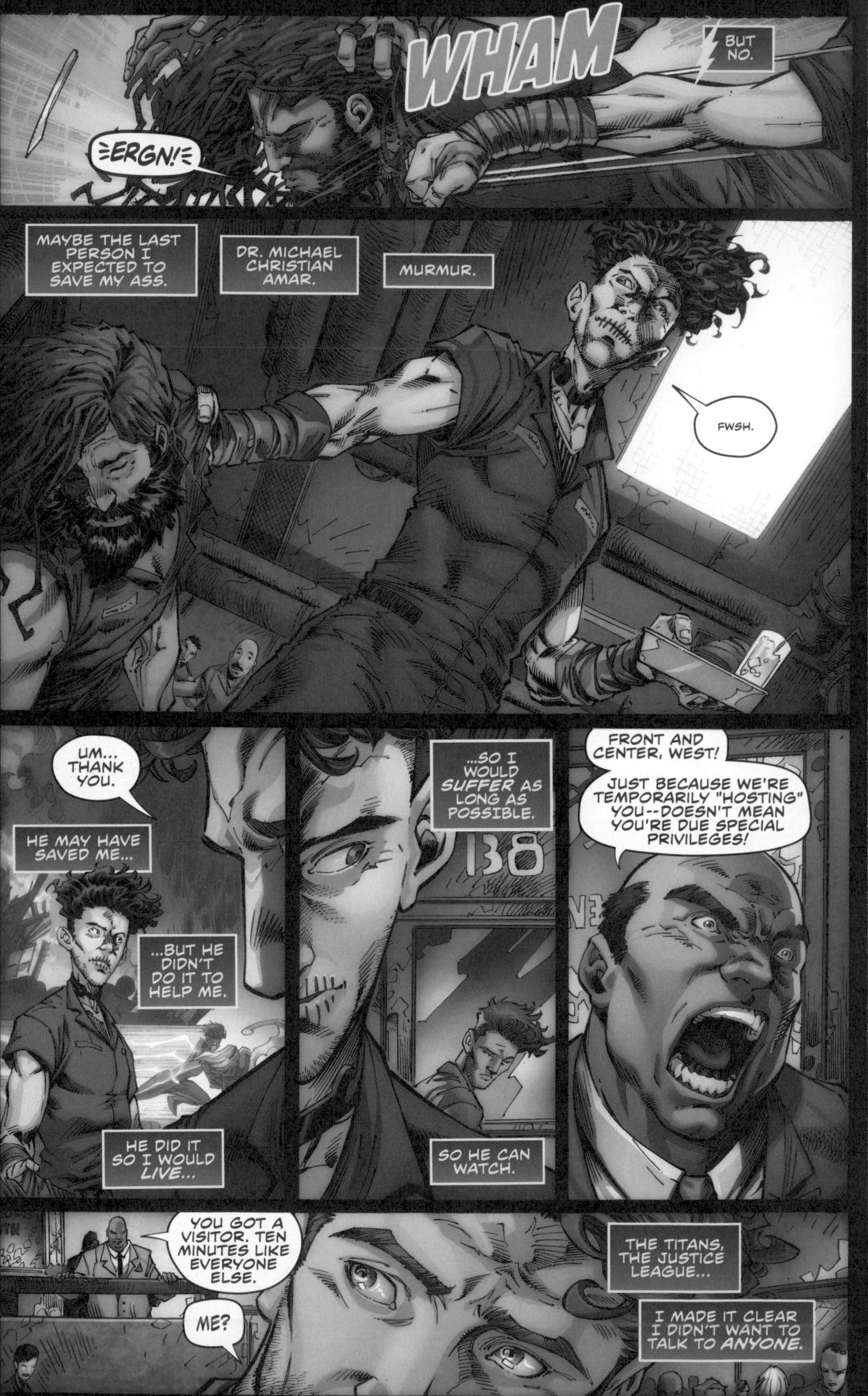
WHAM
BUT NO.
ERGN!
MAYBE THE LAST PERSON I EXPECTED TO SAVE MY ASS.
DR. MICHAEL CHRISTIAN AMAR.
MURMUR.
FWSH.
UM... THANK YOU.
HE MAY HAVE SAVED ME...
...BUT HE DIDN'T DO IT TO HELP ME.
HE DID IT SO I WOULD LIVE...
...SO I WOULD SUFFER AS LONG AS POSSIBLE.
138
SO HE CAN WATCH.
FRONT AND CENTER, WEST!
JUST BECAUSE WE'RE TEMPORARILY "HOSTING" YOU--DOESN'T MEAN YOU'RE DUE SPECIAL PRIVILEGES!
YOU GOT A VISITOR. TEN MINUTES LIKE EVERYONE ELSE.
ME?
THE TITANS, THE JUSTICE LEAGUE...
I MADE IT CLEAR I DIDN'T WANT TO TALK TO ANYONE.

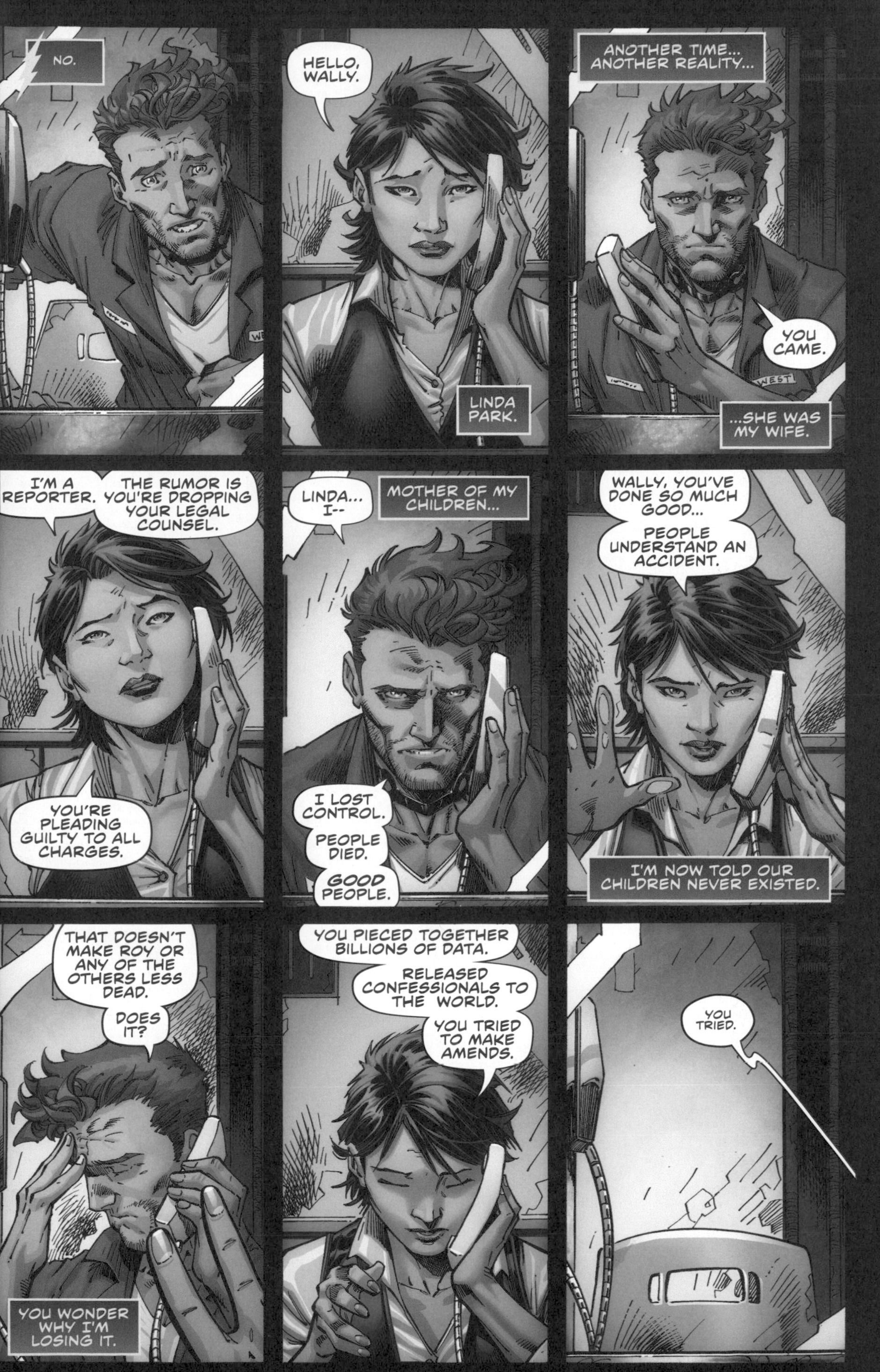
NO.
HELLO, WALLY.
LINDA PARK.
ANOTHER TIME... ANOTHER REALITY...
YOU CAME.
...SHE WAS MY WIFE.
I'M A REPORTER.
THE RUMOR IS YOU'RE DROPPING YOUR LEGAL COUNSEL.
YOU'RE PLEADING GUILTY TO ALL CHARGES.
LINDA... I--
MOTHER OF MY CHILDREN...
I LOST CONTROL.
PEOPLE DIED.
GOOD PEOPLE.
WALLY, YOU'VE DONE SO MUCH GOOD...
PEOPLE UNDERSTAND AN ACCIDENT.
I'M NOW TOLD OUR CHILDREN NEVER EXISTED.
THAT DOESN'T MAKE ROY OR ANY OF THE OTHERS LESS DEAD.
DOES IT?
YOU WONDER WHY I'M LOSING IT.
YOU PIECED TOGETHER BILLIONS OF DATA.
RELEASED CONFESSIONALS TO THE WORLD.
YOU TRIED TO MAKE AMENDS.
YOU TRIED.

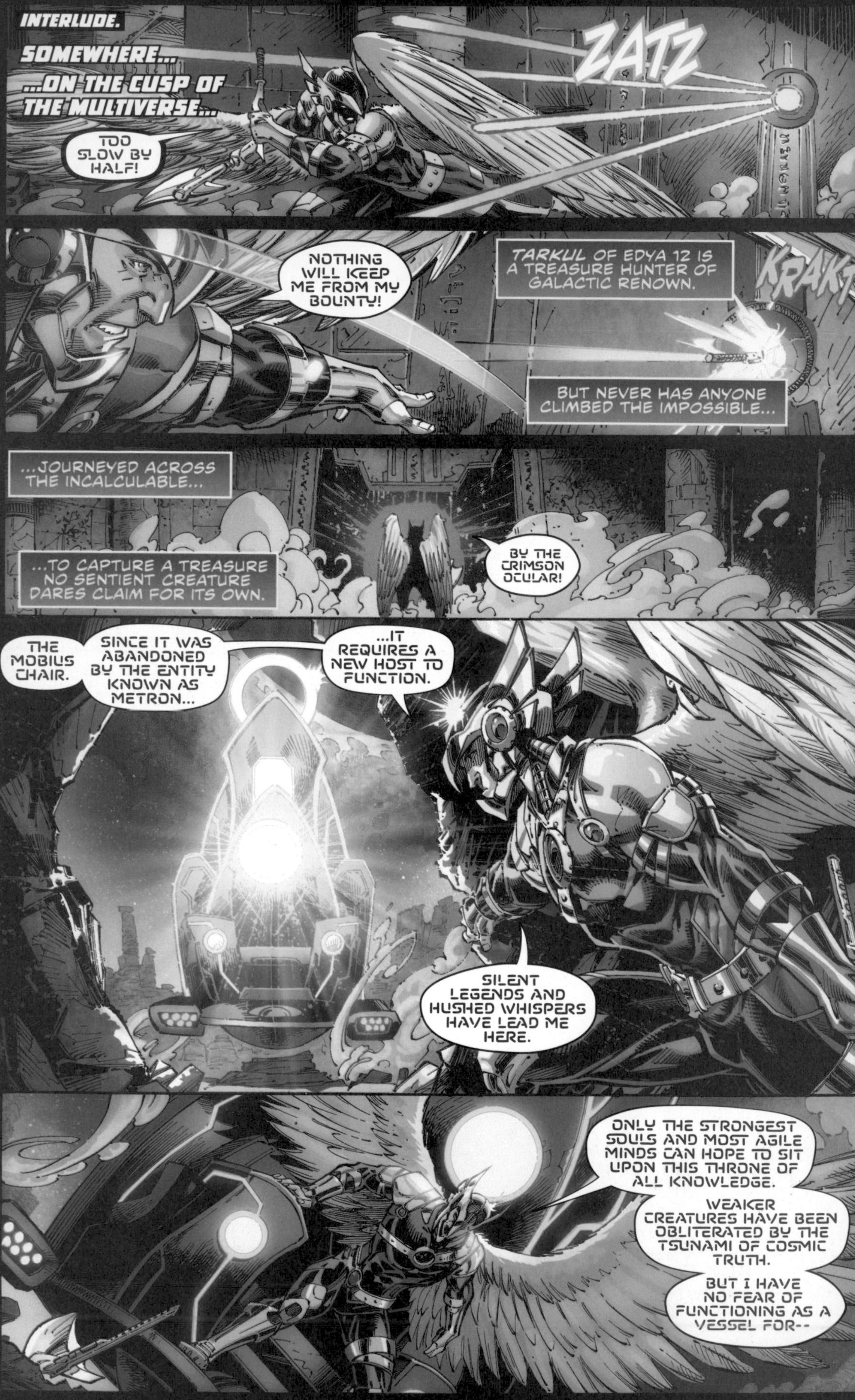
INTERLUDE.
SOMEWHERE...
...ON THE CUSP OF THE MULTIVERSE...
ZATZ
TOO SLOW BY HALF!
NOTHING WILL KEEP ME FROM MY BOUNTY!
TARKUL OF EDYA 12 IS A TREASURE HUNTER OF GALACTIC RENOWN.
KRAKT
BUT NEVER HAS ANYONE CLIMBED THE IMPOSSIBLE...
...JOURNEYED ACROSS THE INCALCULABLE...
...TO CAPTURE A TREASURE NO SENTIENT CREATURE DARES CLAIM FOR ITS OWN.
BY THE CRIMSON OCULAR!
THE MOBIUS CHAIR.
SINCE IT WAS ABANDONED BY THE ENTITY KNOWN AS METRON...
...IT REQUIRES A NEW HOST TO FUNCTION.
SILENT LEGENDS AND HUSHED WHISPERS HAVE LEAD ME HERE.
ONLY THE STRONGEST SOULS AND MOST AGILE MINDS CAN HOPE TO SIT UPON THIS THRONE OF ALL KNOWLEDGE.
WEAKER CREATURES HAVE BEEN OBLITERATED BY THE TSUNAMI OF COSMIC TRUTH.
BUT I HAVE NO FEAR OF FUNCTIONING AS A VESSEL FOR--

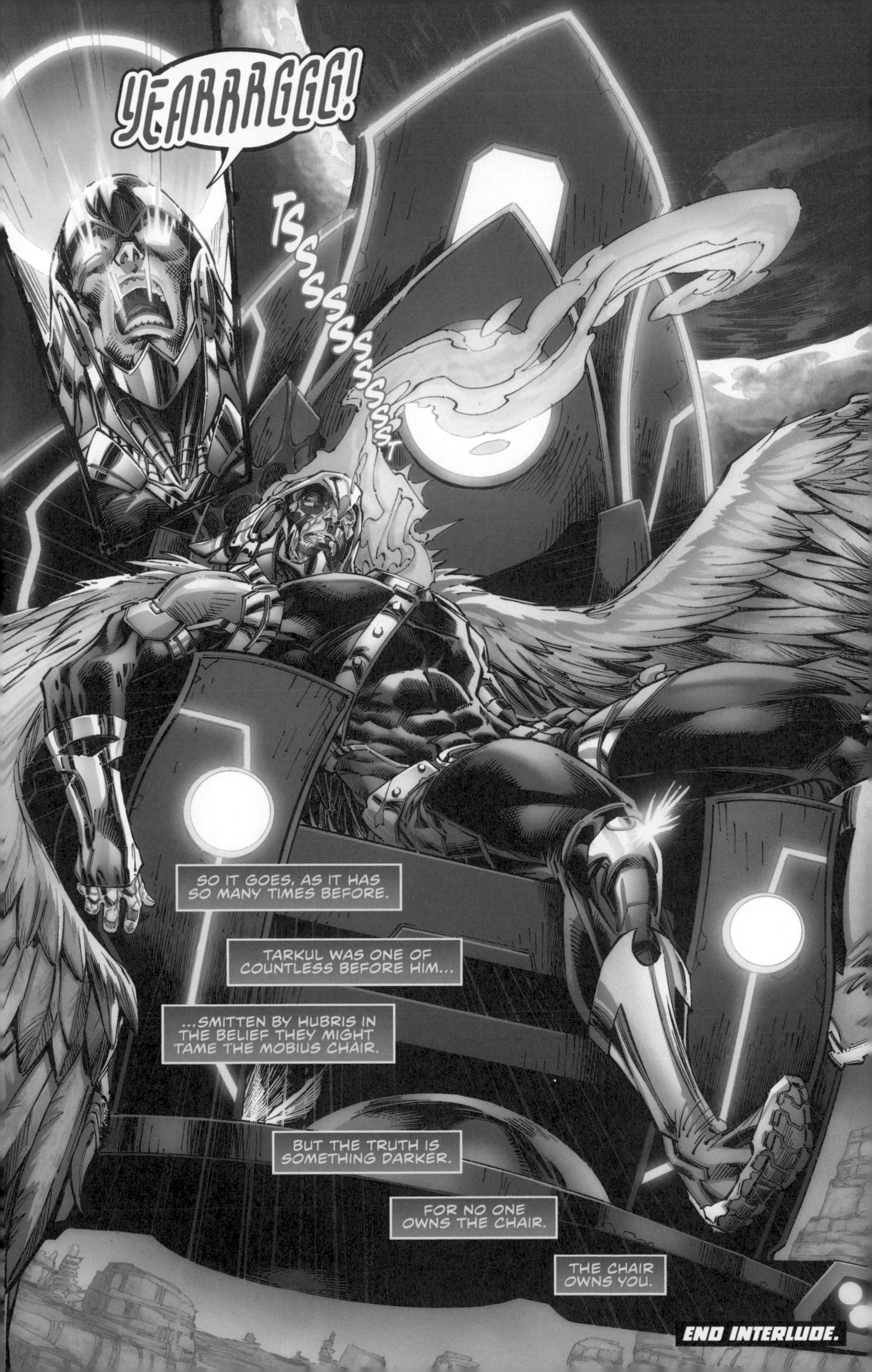
YEARRRGGG!
TSSSSSSSSSSST
SO IT GOES, AS IT HAS SO MANY TIMES BEFORE.
TARKUL WAS ONE OF COUNTLESS BEFORE HIM...
...SMITTEN BY HUBRIS IN THE BELIEF THEY MIGHT TAME THE MOBIUS CHAIR.
BUT THE TRUTH IS SOMETHING DARKER.
FOR NO ONE OWNS THE CHAIR.
THE CHAIR OWNS YOU.
END INTERLUDE.

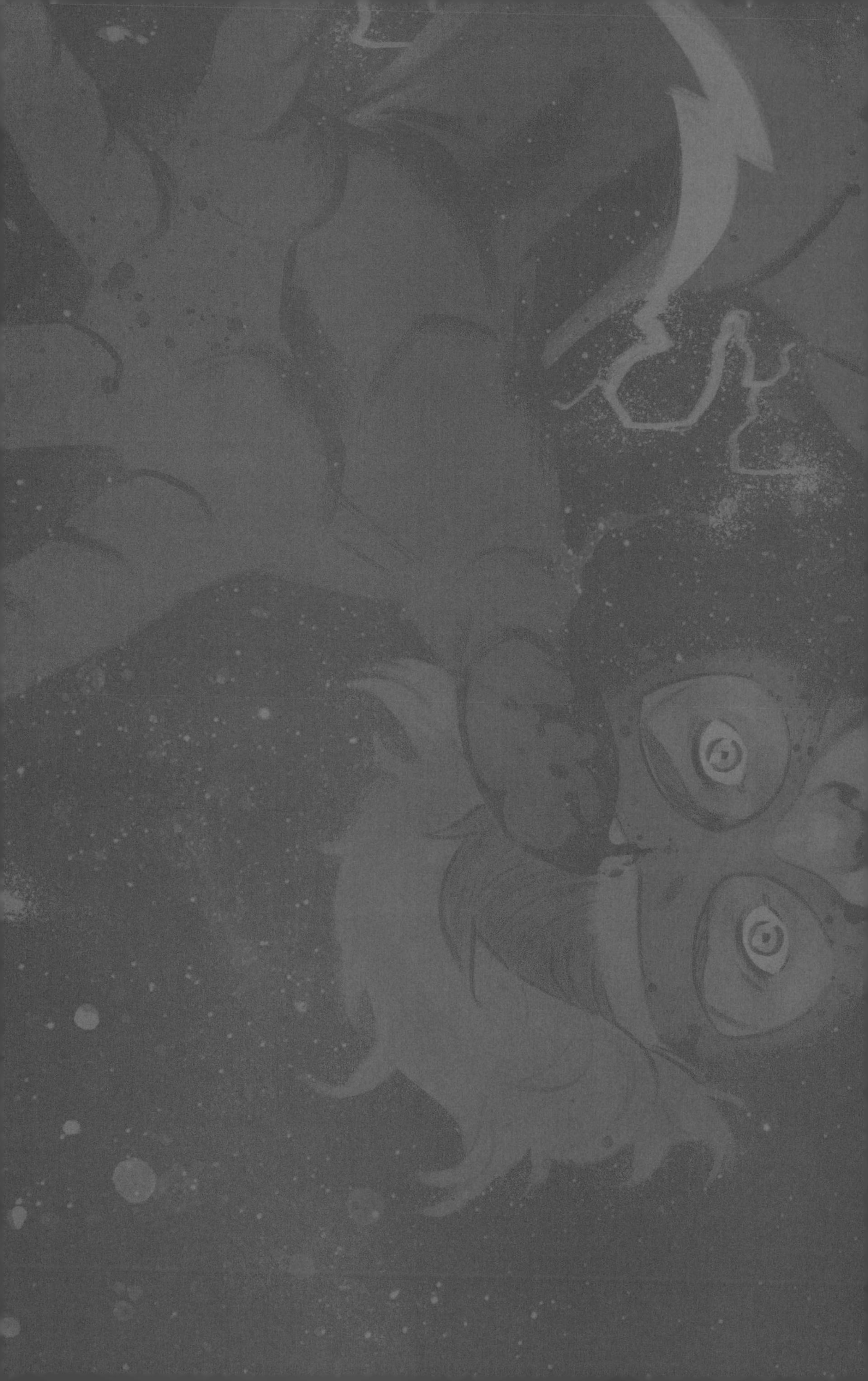

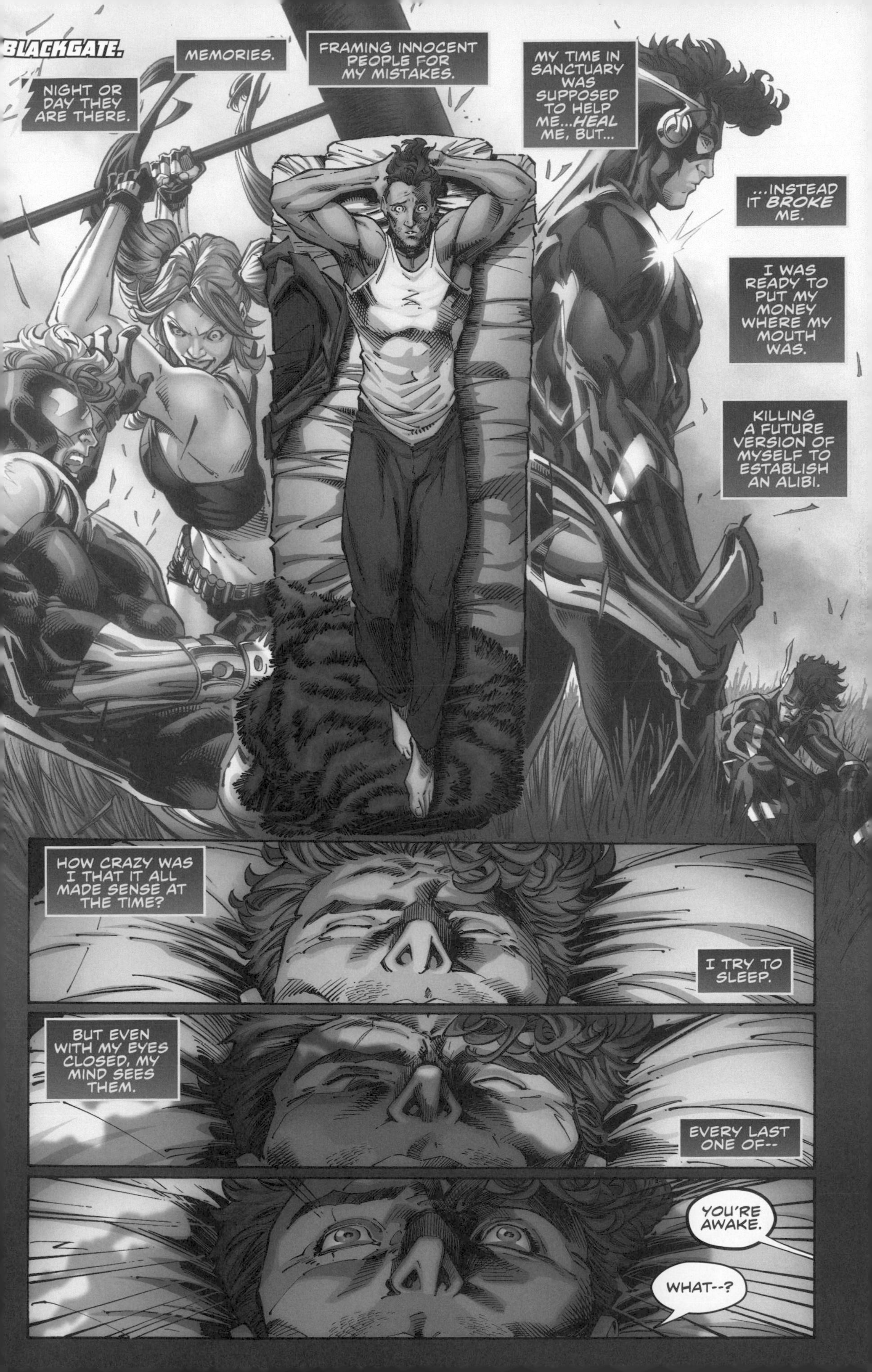
BLACKGATE.
NIGHT OR DAY THEY ARE THERE.
MEMORIES.
FRAMING INNOCENT PEOPLE FOR MY MISTAKES.
MY TIME IN SANCTUARY WAS SUPPOSED TO HELP ME...HEAL ME, BUT...
...INSTEAD IT BROKE ME.
I WAS READY TO PUT MY MONEY WHERE MY MOUTH WAS.
KILLING A FUTURE VERSION OF MYSELF TO ESTABLISH AN ALIBI.
HOW CRAZY WAS I THAT IT ALL MADE SENSE AT THE TIME?
I TRY TO SLEEP.
BUT EVEN WITH MY EYES CLOSED, MY MIND SEES THEM.
EVERY LAST ONE OF--
YOU'RE AWAKE.
WHAT--?

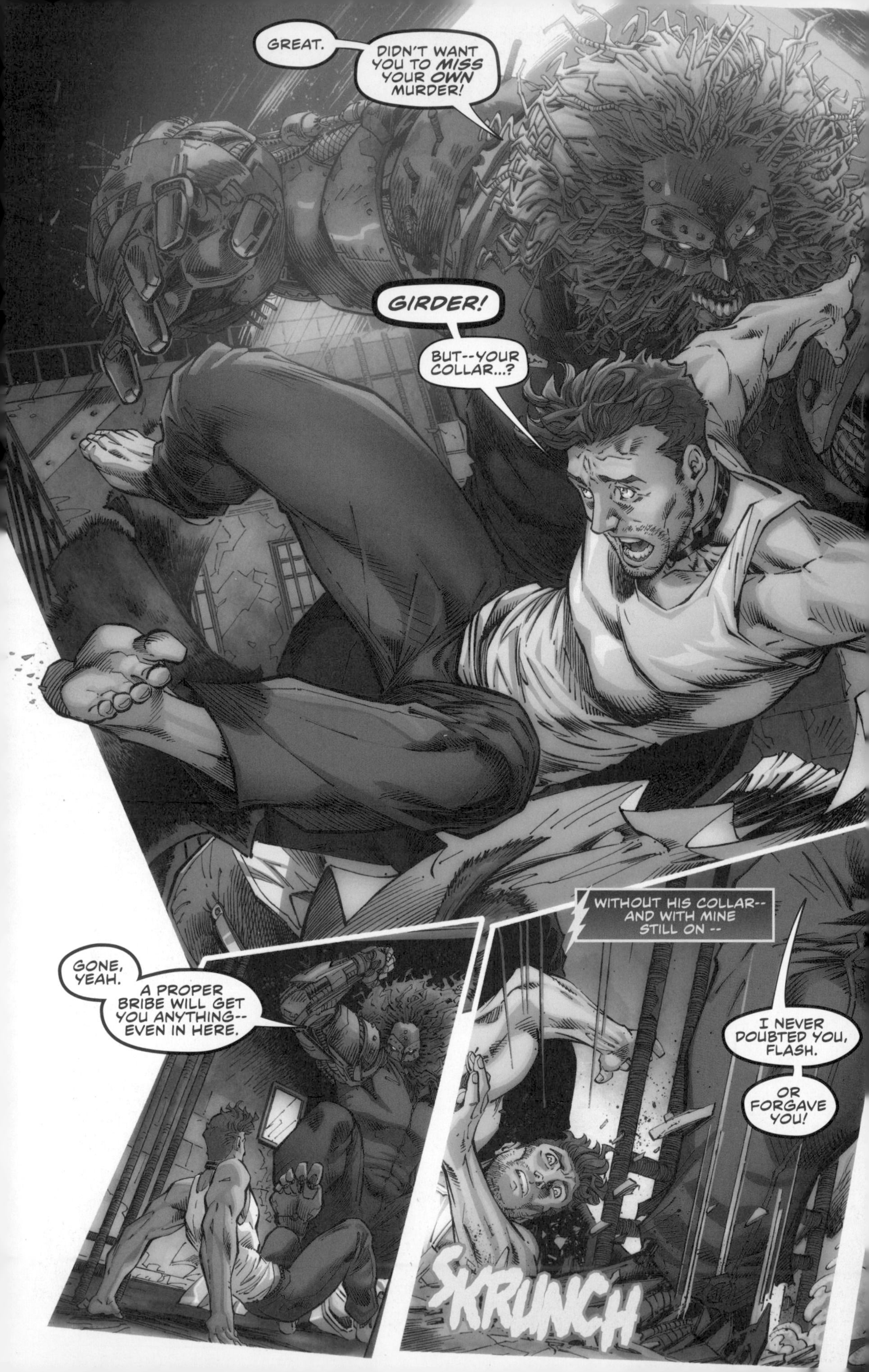
GREAT.
DIDN'T WANT YOU TO MISS YOUR OWN MURDER!
GIRDER!
BUT--YOUR COLLAR...?
GONE, YEAH.
A PROPER BRIBE WILL GET YOU ANYTHING-- EVEN IN HERE.
WITHOUT HIS COLLAR-- AND WITH MINE STILL ON --
I NEVER DOUBTED YOU, FLASH.
OR FORGAVE YOU!
SKRUNCH

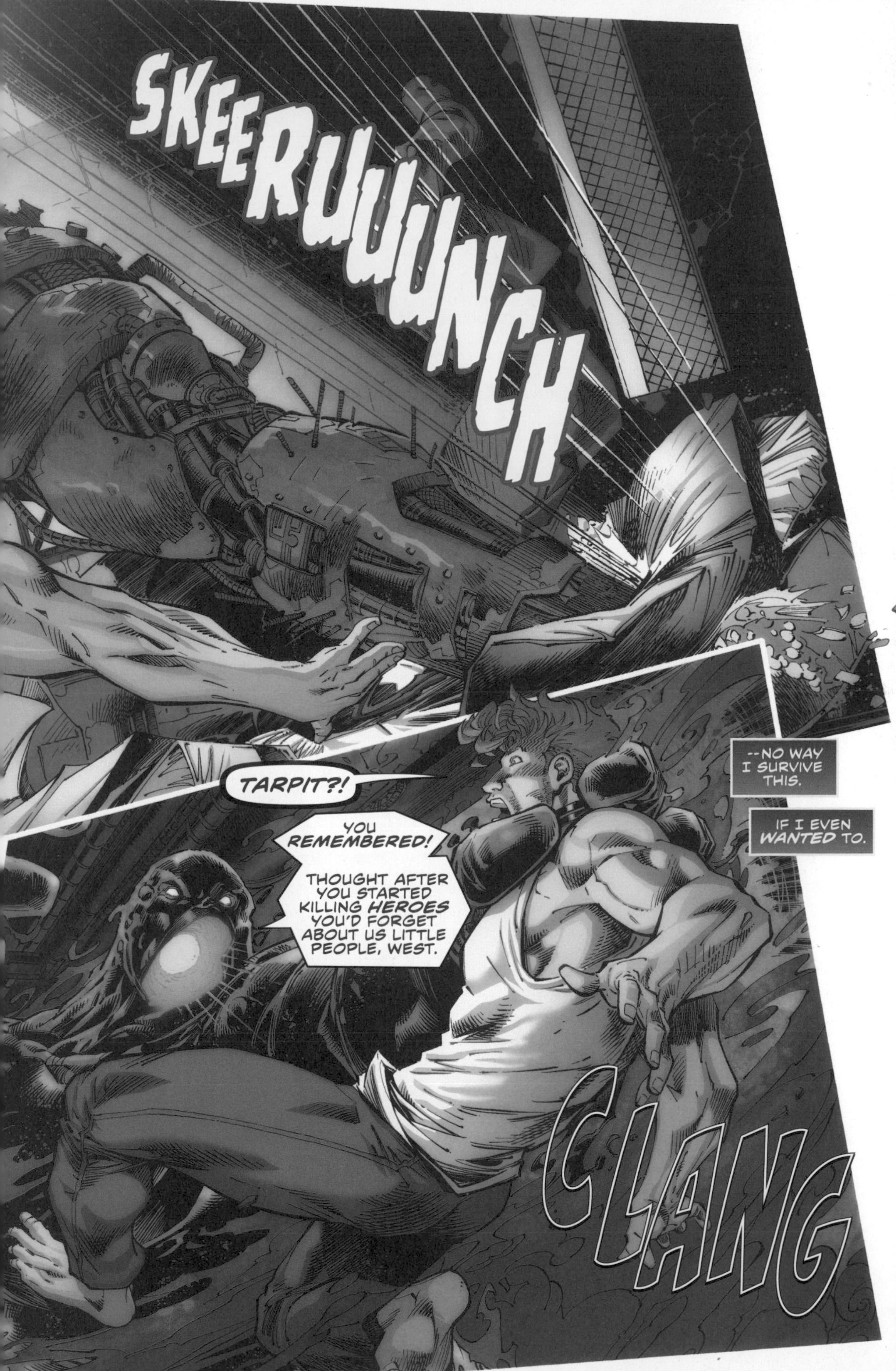
SKEERUUUUNCH
TARPIT?!
--NO WAY I SURVIVE THIS.
IF I EVEN WANTED TO.
YOU REMEMBERED!
THOUGHT AFTER YOU STARTED KILLING HEROES YOU'D FORGET ABOUT US LITTLE PEOPLE, WEST.
CLANG

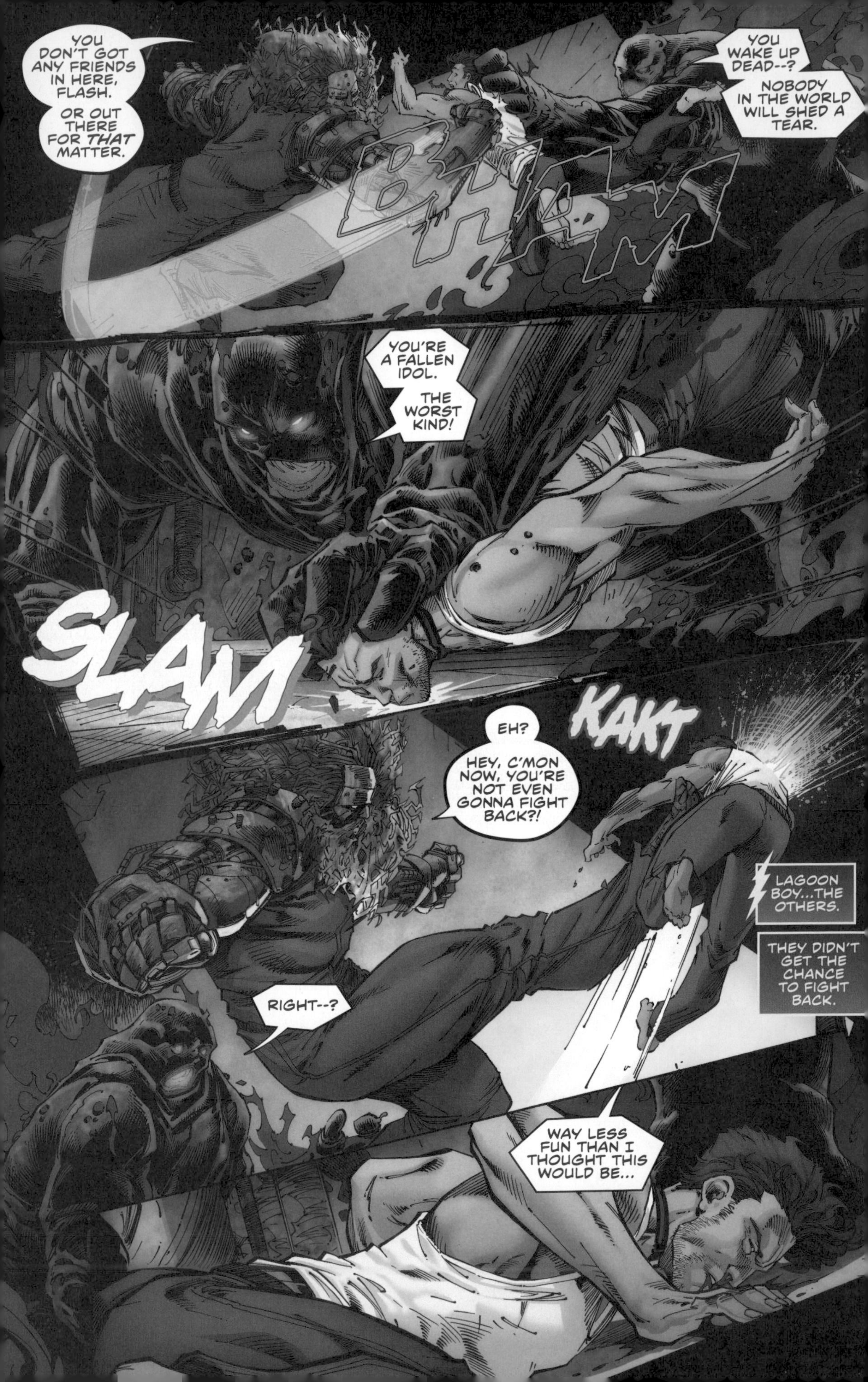
YOU DON'T GOT ANY FRIENDS IN HERE, FLASH.
OR OUT THERE FOR *THAT* MATTER.
YOU WAKE UP DEAD--?
NOBODY IN THE WORLD WILL SHED A TEAR.
BLAM
YOU'RE A FALLEN IDOL.
THE WORST KIND!
SLAM
KAKT
EH?
HEY, C'MON NOW, YOU'RE NOT EVEN GONNA FIGHT BACK?!
LAGOON BOY...THE OTHERS.
THEY DIDN'T GET THE CHANCE TO FIGHT BACK.
RIGHT--?
WAY LESS FUN THAN I THOUGHT THIS WOULD BE...

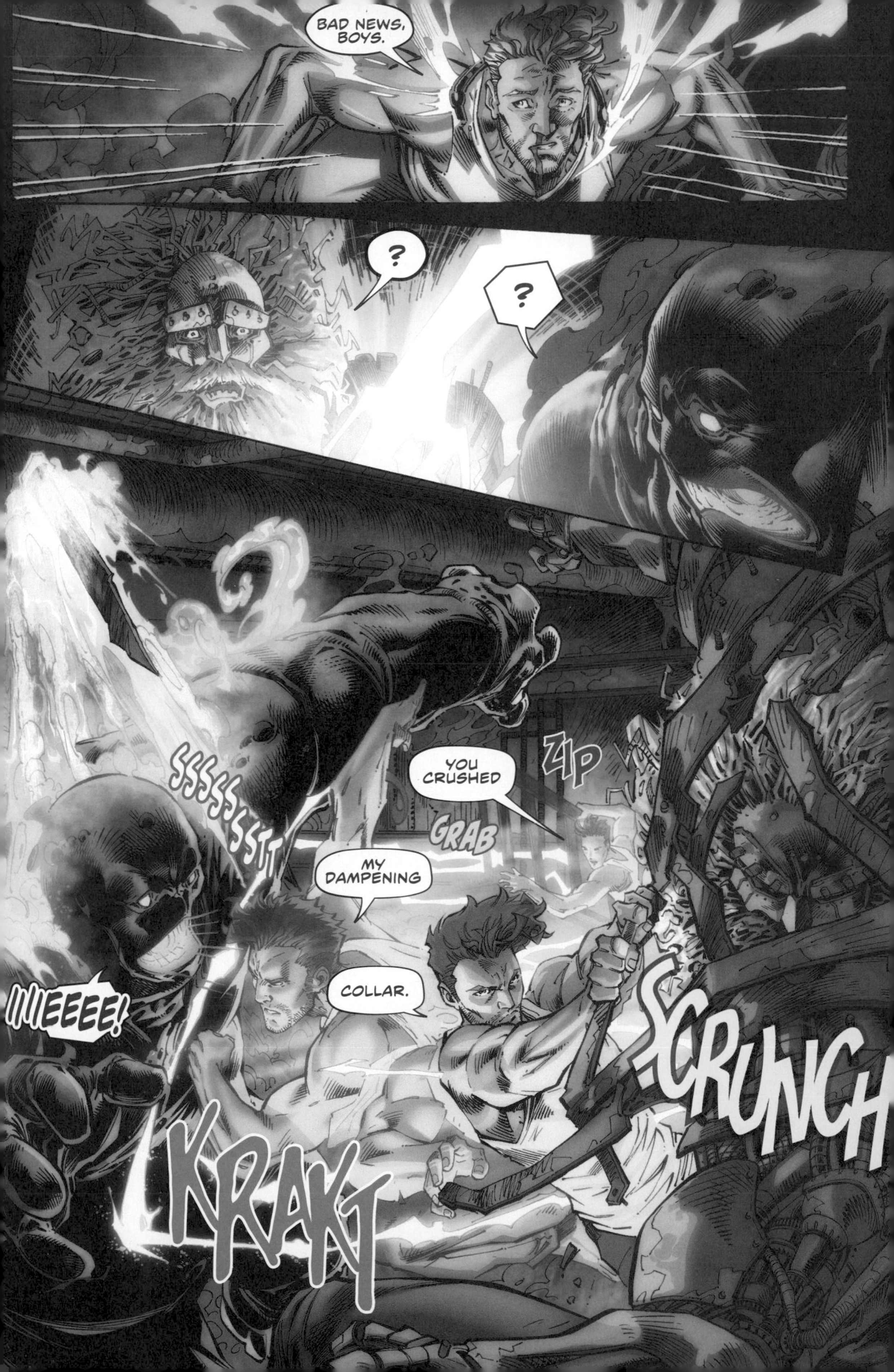
BAD NEWS, BOYS.
?
?
SSSSSSSTT
ZIP
YOU CRUSHED
GRAB
MY DAMPENING
COLLAR.
IIIIEEEEE!
SCRUNCH
KRAKT

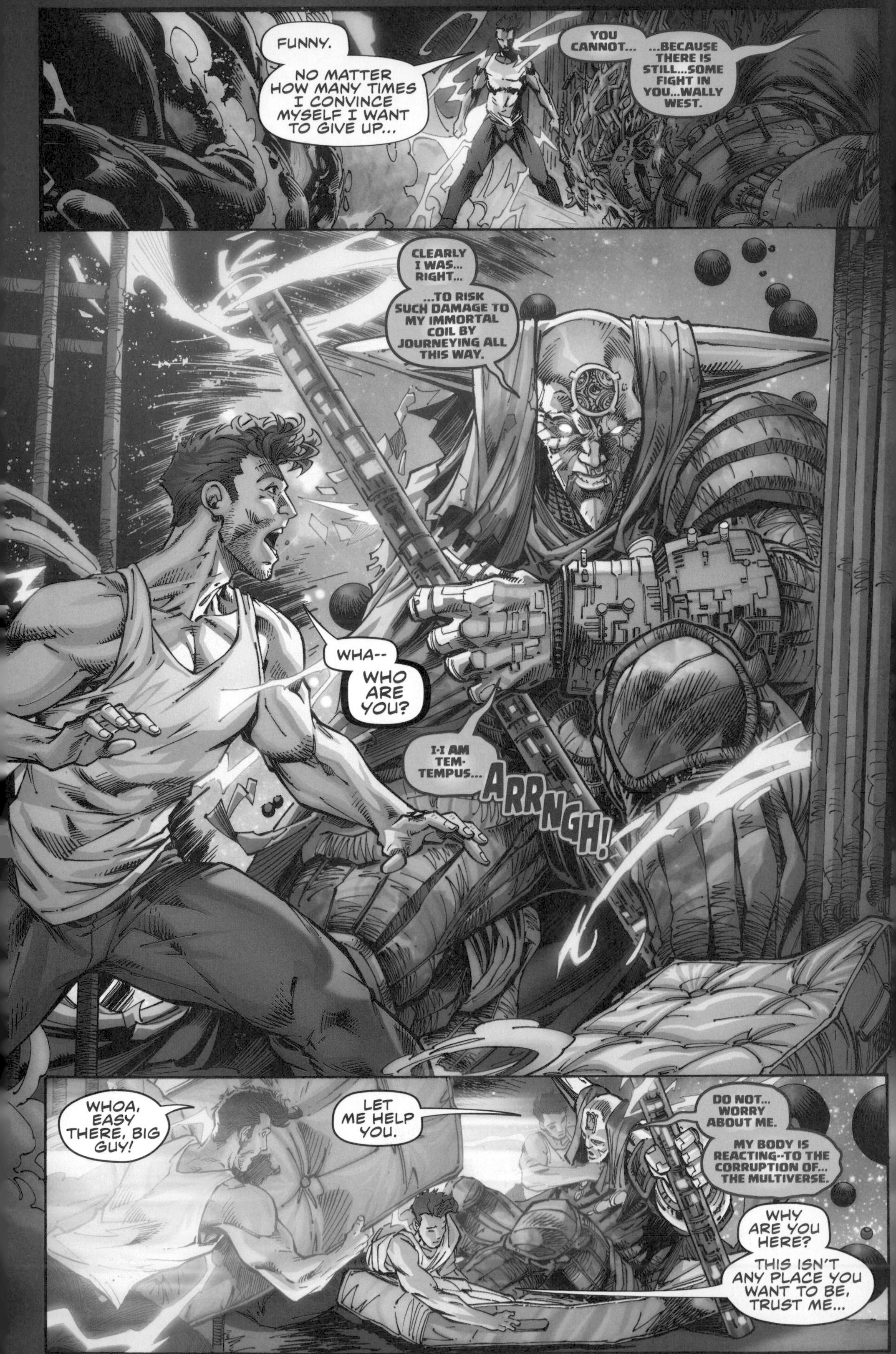
FUNNY.
NO MATTER HOW MANY TIMES I CONVINCE MYSELF I WANT TO GIVE UP...
YOU CANNOT...
...BECAUSE THERE IS STILL...SOME FIGHT IN YOU...WALLY WEST.
CLEARLY I WAS... RIGHT...
...TO RISK SUCH DAMAGE TO MY IMMORTAL COIL BY JOURNEYING ALL THIS WAY.
WHA--
WHO ARE YOU?
I-I AM TEM-TEMPUS...
ARRNGH!
WHOA, EASY THERE, BIG GUY!
LET ME HELP YOU.
DO NOT... WORRY ABOUT ME.
MY BODY IS REACTING--TO THE CORRUPTION OF... THE MULTIVERSE.
WHY ARE YOU HERE?
THIS ISN'T ANY PLACE YOU WANT TO BE, TRUST ME...

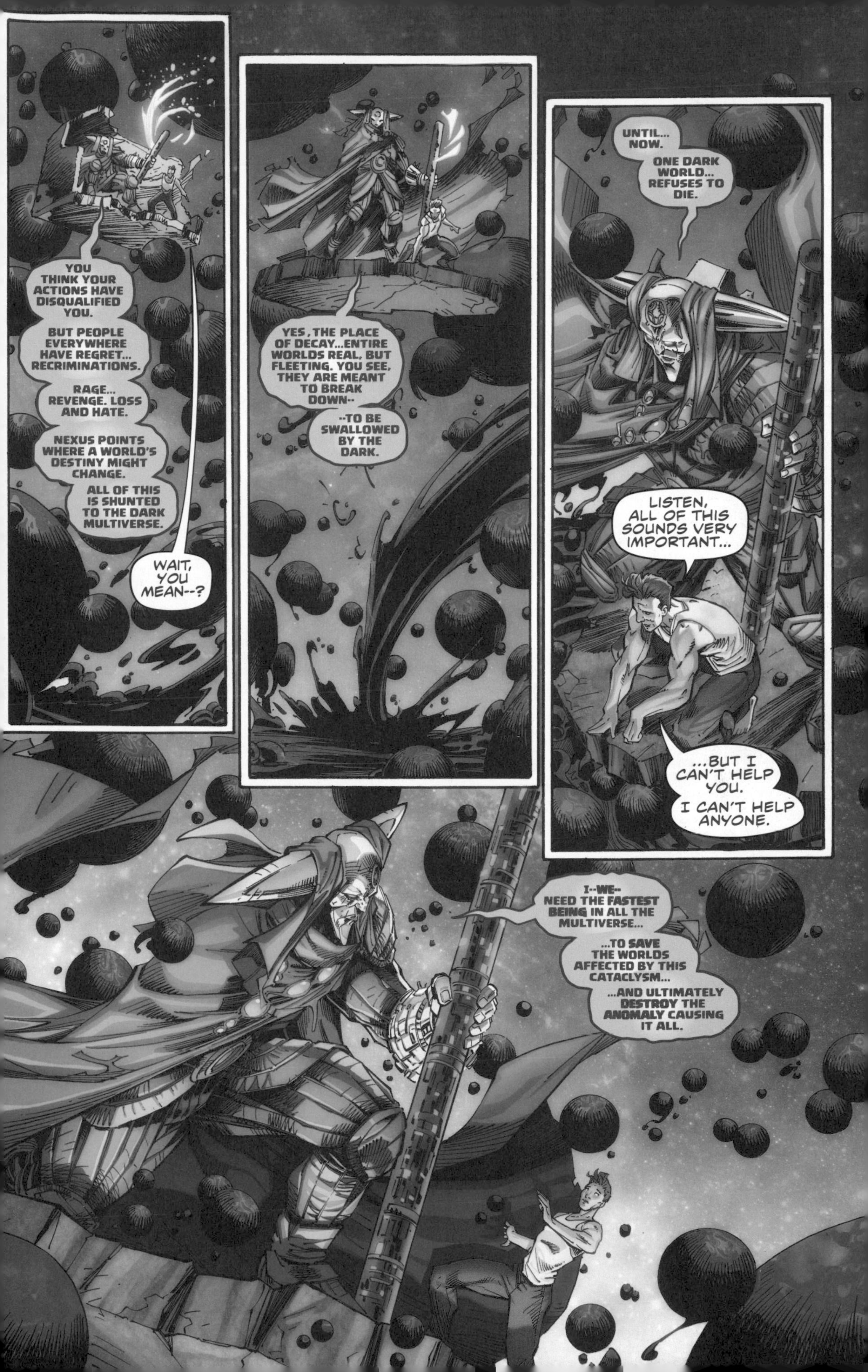
YOU THINK YOUR ACTIONS HAVE DISQUALIFIED YOU.
BUT PEOPLE EVERYWHERE HAVE REGRET... RECRIMINATIONS.
RAGE... REVENGE. LOSS AND HATE.
NEXUS POINTS WHERE A WORLD'S DESTINY MIGHT CHANGE.
ALL OF THIS IS SHUNTED TO THE DARK MULTIVERSE.
WAIT, YOU MEAN--?
YES, THE PLACE OF DECAY...ENTIRE WORLDS REAL, BUT FLEETING. YOU SEE, THEY ARE MEANT TO BREAK DOWN--
--TO BE SWALLOWED BY THE DARK.
UNTIL... NOW.
ONE DARK WORLD... REFUSES TO DIE.
LISTEN, ALL OF THIS SOUNDS VERY IMPORTANT...
...BUT I CAN'T HELP YOU.
I CAN'T HELP ANYONE.
I--WE-- NEED THE FASTEST BEING IN ALL THE MULTIVERSE...
...TO SAVE THE WORLDS AFFECTED BY THIS CATACLYSM...
...AND ULTIMATELY DESTROY THE ANOMALY CAUSING IT ALL.

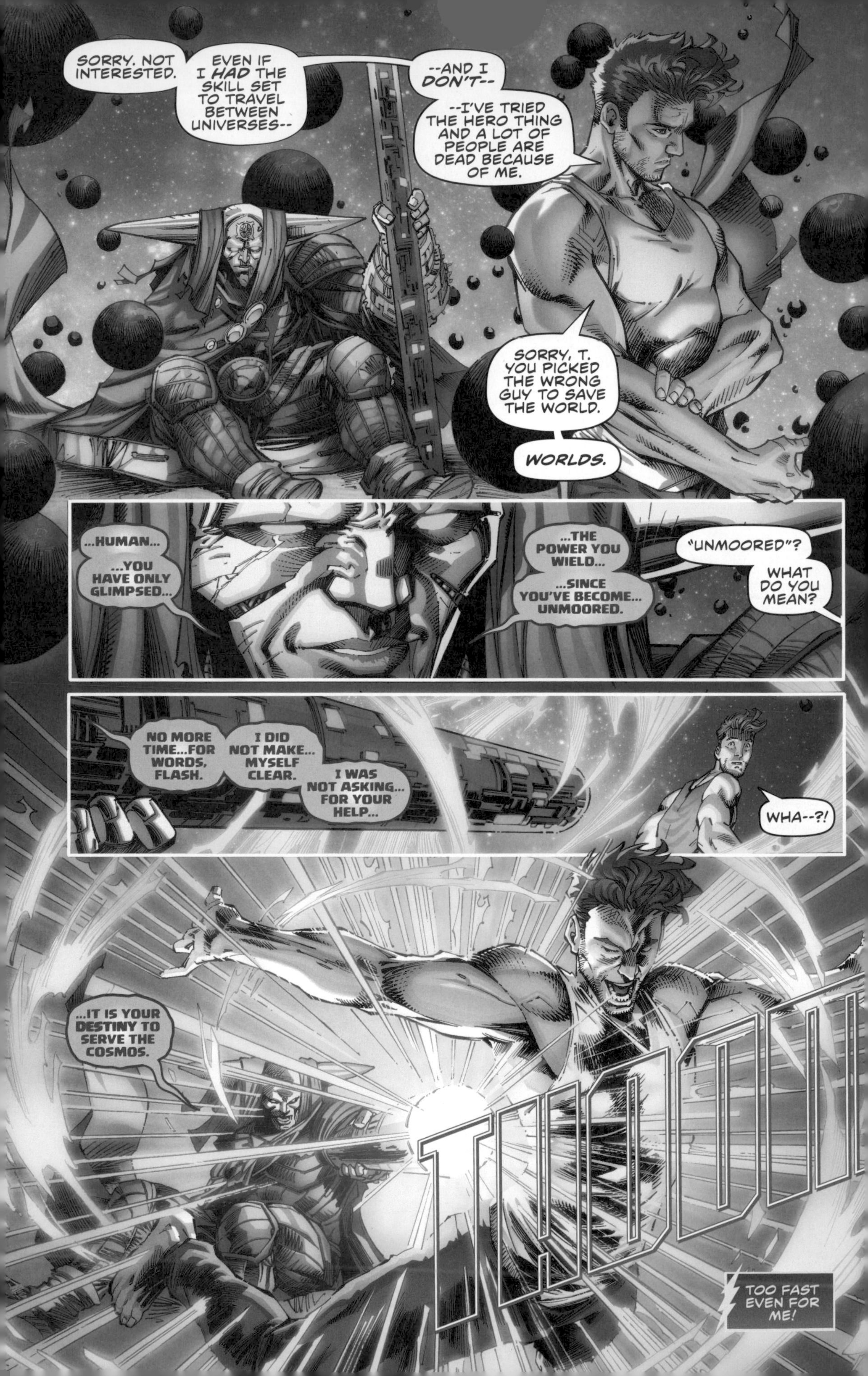
SORRY. NOT INTERESTED.
EVEN IF I HAD THE SKILL SET TO TRAVEL BETWEEN UNIVERSES--
--AND I DON'T--
--I'VE TRIED THE HERO THING AND A LOT OF PEOPLE ARE DEAD BECAUSE OF ME.
SORRY, T. YOU PICKED THE WRONG GUY TO SAVE THE WORLD.
WORLDS.
...HUMAN...
...YOU HAVE ONLY GLIMPSED...
...THE POWER YOU WIELD...
...SINCE YOU'VE BECOME... UNMOORED.
"UNMOORED"?
WHAT DO YOU MEAN?
NO MORE TIME...FOR WORDS, FLASH.
I DID NOT MAKE... MYSELF CLEAR.
I WAS NOT ASKING... FOR YOUR HELP...
WHA--?!
...IT IS YOUR DESTINY TO SERVE THE COSMOS.
TOO FAST EVEN FOR ME!

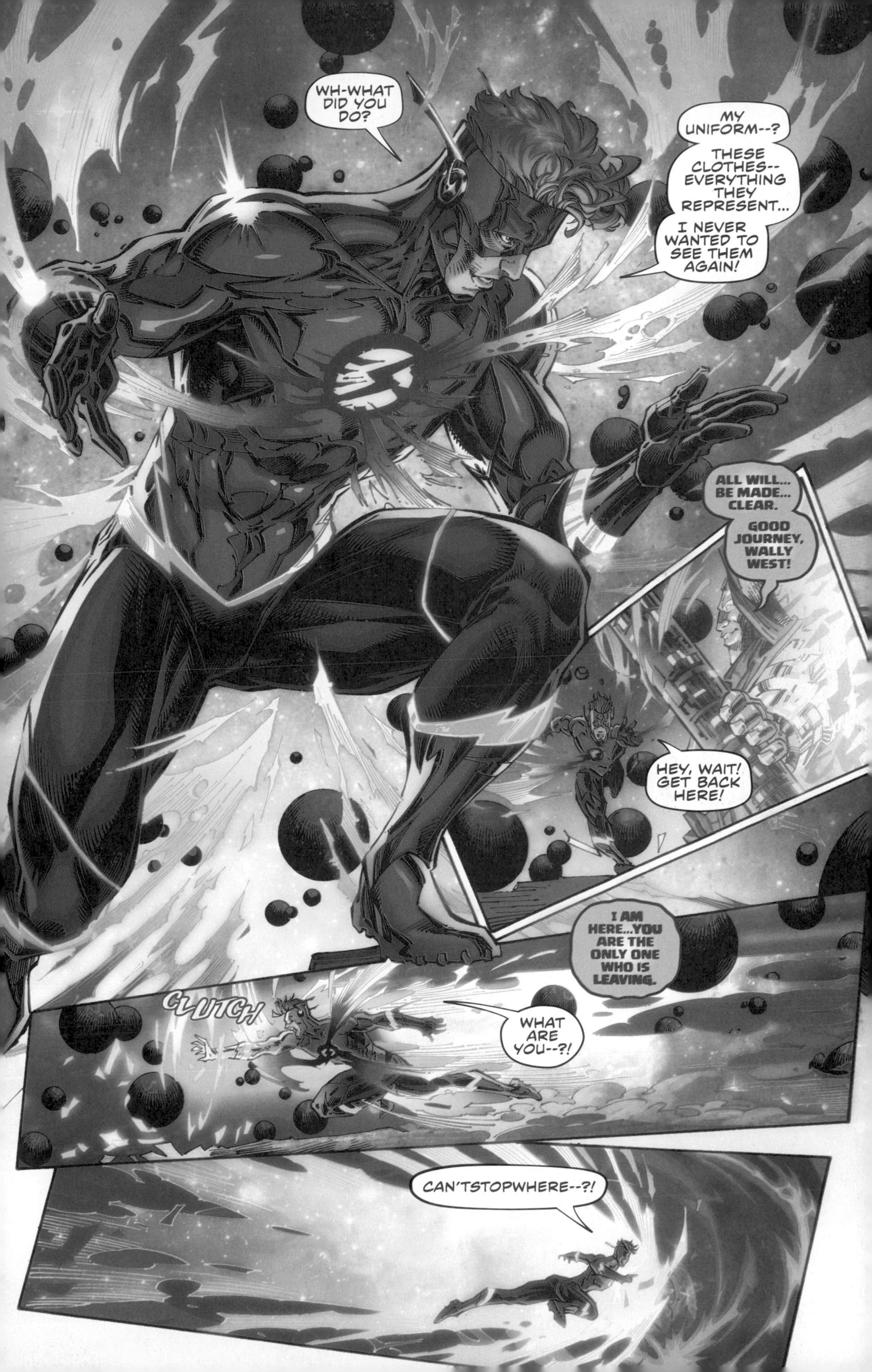
WH-WHAT DID YOU DO?
MY UNIFORM--?
THESE CLOTHES--EVERYTHING THEY REPRESENT...
I NEVER WANTED TO SEE THEM AGAIN!
ALL WILL... BE MADE... CLEAR.
GOOD JOURNEY, WALLY WEST!
HEY, WAIT! GET BACK HERE!
I AM HERE...YOU ARE THE ONLY ONE WHO IS LEAVING.
CLUTCH
WHAT ARE YOU--?!
CAN'TSTOPWHERE--?!

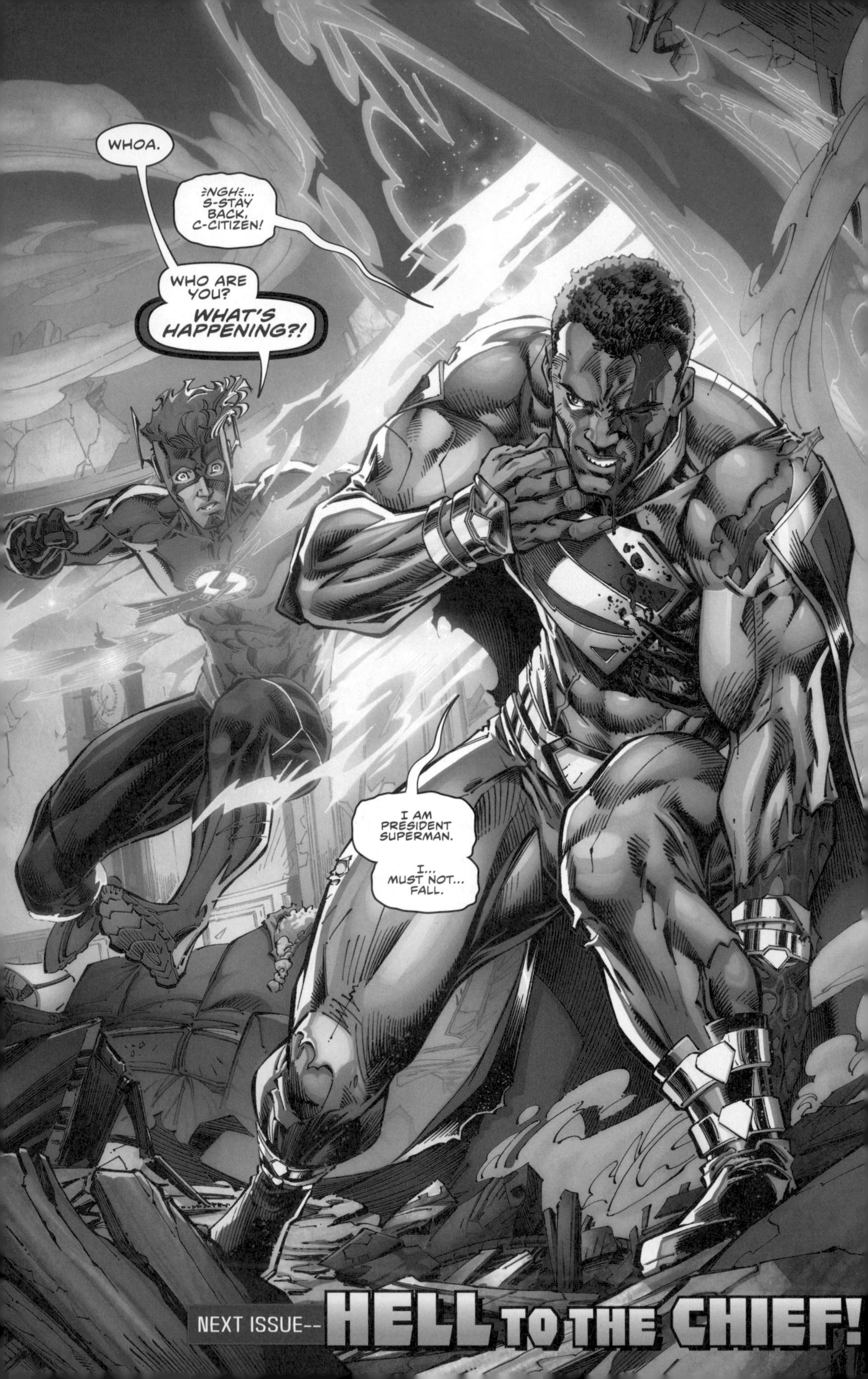
WHOA.
NGH... S-STAY BACK, C-CITIZEN!
WHO ARE YOU? WHAT'S HAPPENING?!
I AM PRESIDENT SUPERMAN.
I... MUST NOT... FALL.
NEXT ISSUE-- HELL TO THE CHIEF!

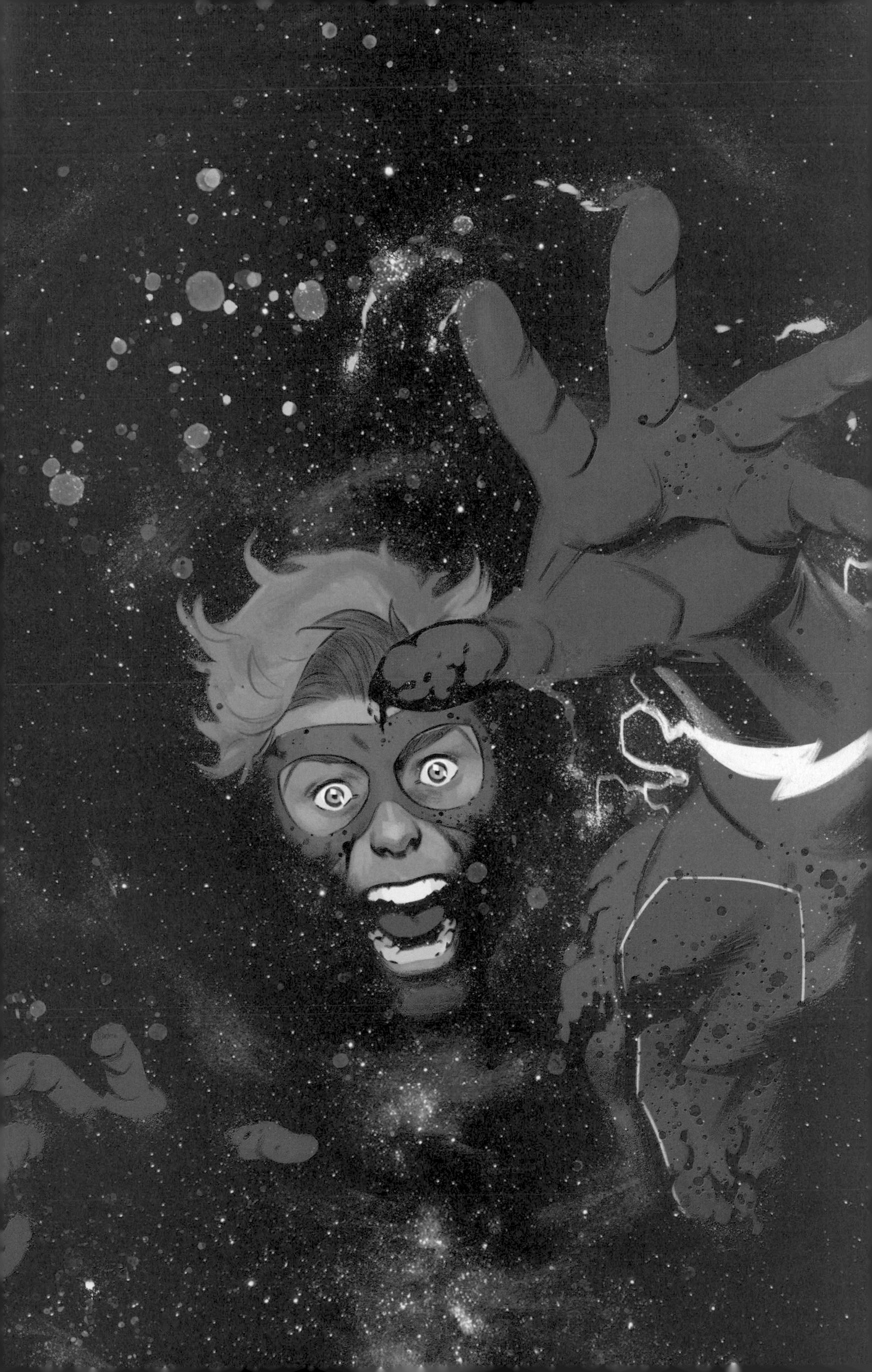

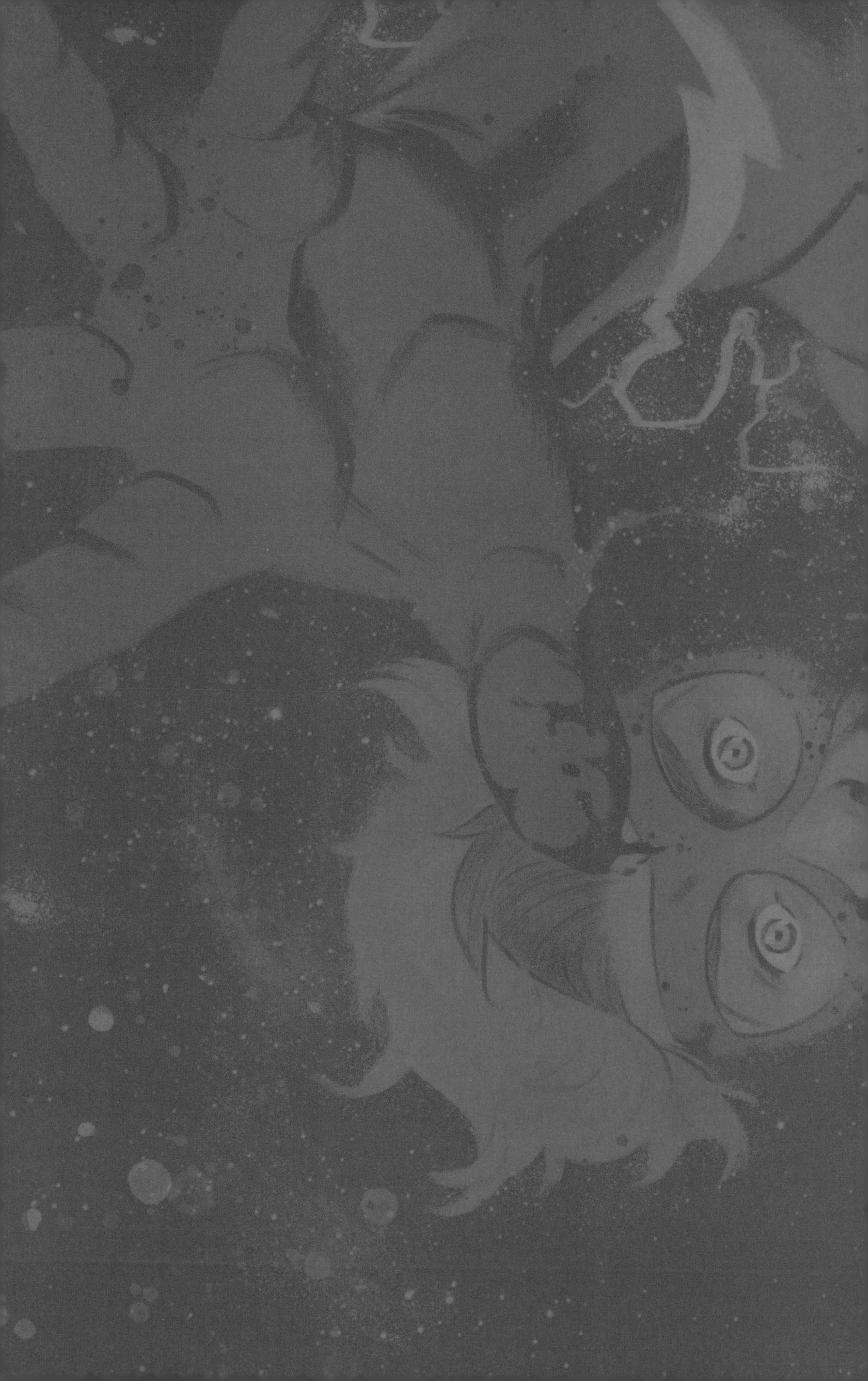

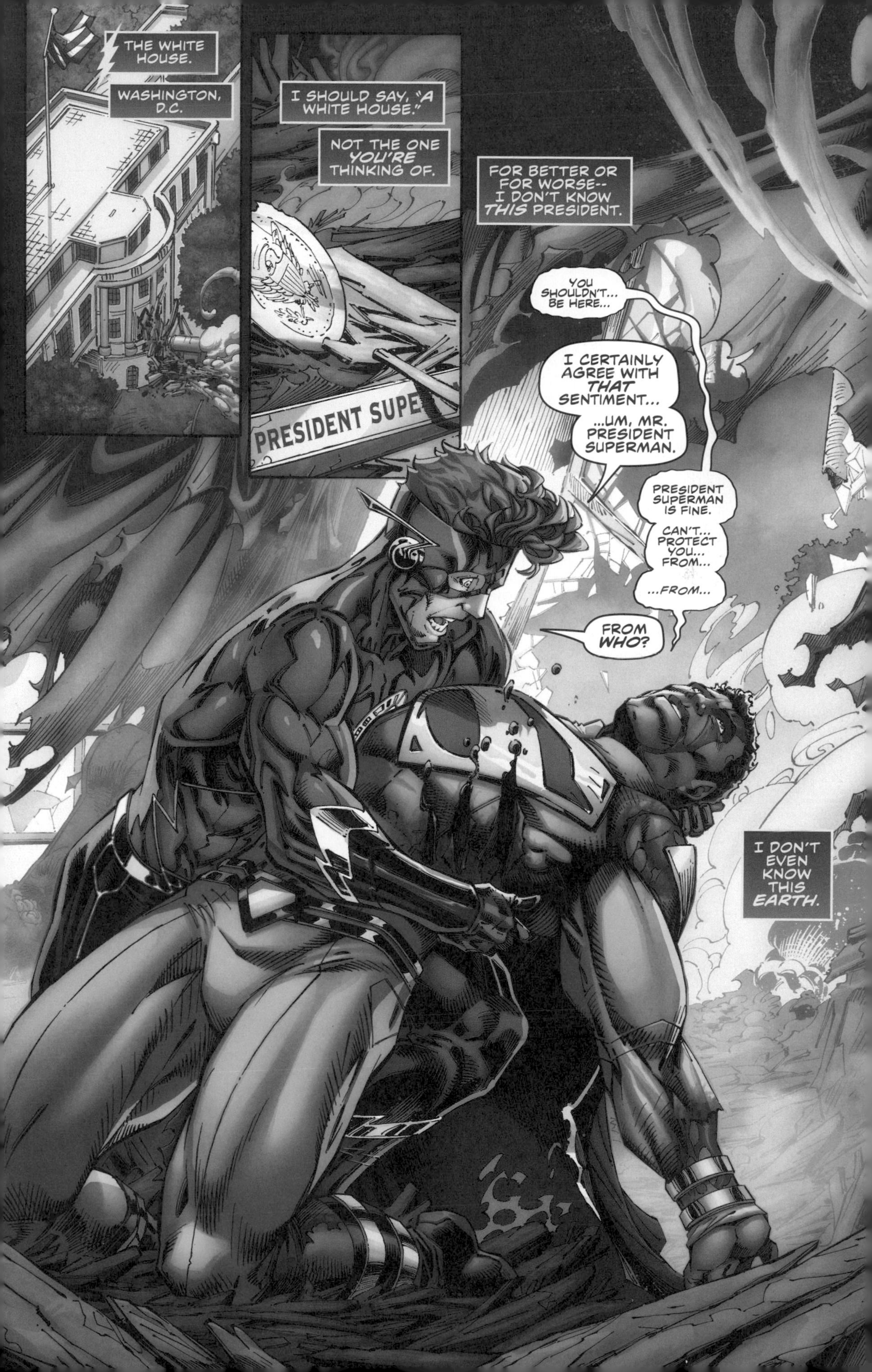
THE WHITE HOUSE.
WASHINGTON, D.C.
I SHOULD SAY, "A WHITE HOUSE."
NOT THE ONE *YOU'RE* THINKING OF.
PRESIDENT SUPE
FOR BETTER OR FOR WORSE-- I DON'T KNOW *THIS* PRESIDENT.
YOU SHOULDN'T... BE HERE...
I CERTAINLY AGREE WITH *THAT* SENTIMENT...
...UM, MR. PRESIDENT SUPERMAN.
PRESIDENT SUPERMAN IS FINE.
CAN'T... PROTECT YOU... FROM...
...FROM...
FROM *WHO?*
I DON'T EVEN KNOW THIS *EARTH*.

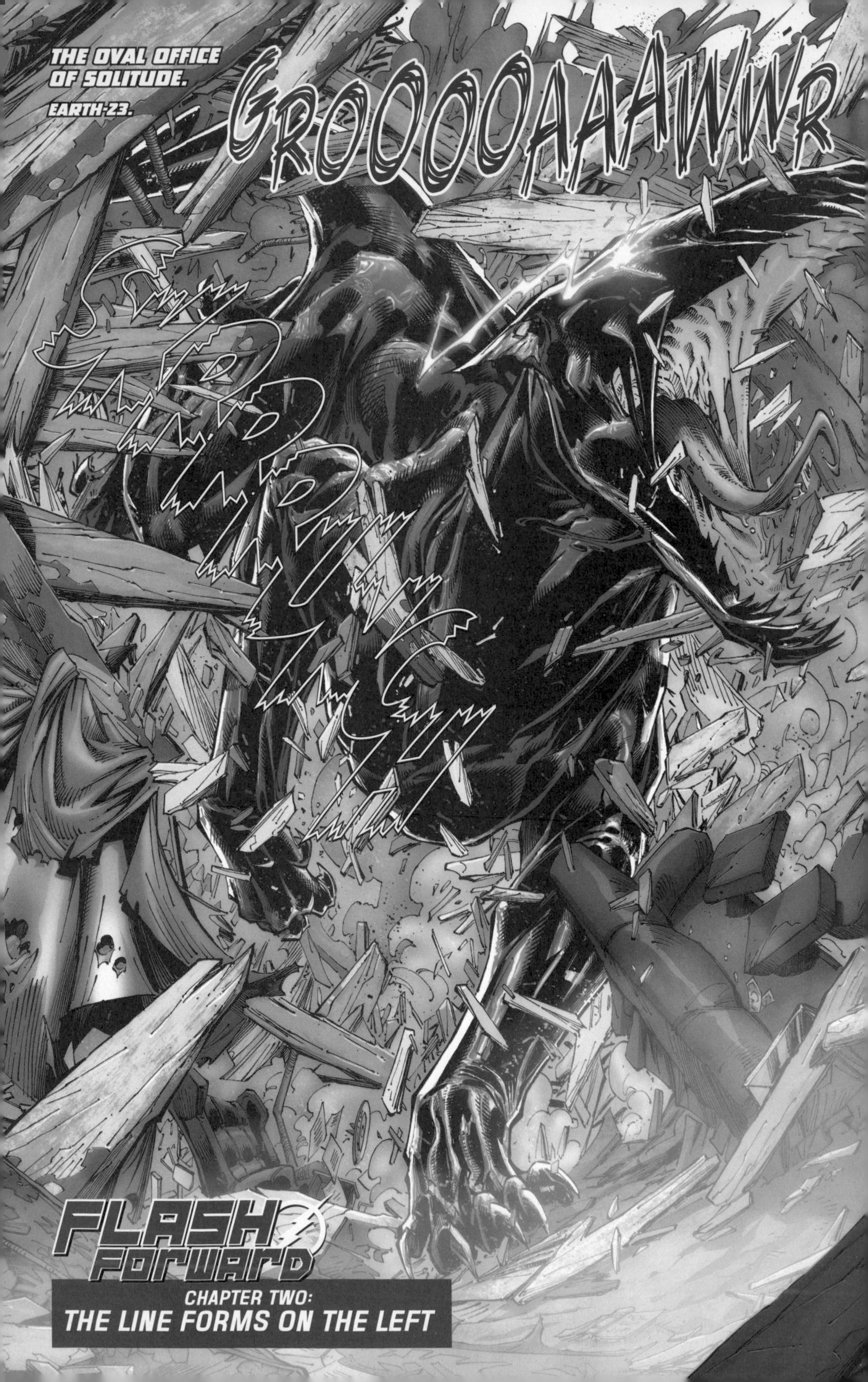
THE OVAL OFFICE OF SOLITUDE.
EARTH-23.
GROOOOAAAWWR
FLASH FORWARD
CHAPTER TWO:
THE LINE FORMS ON THE LEFT

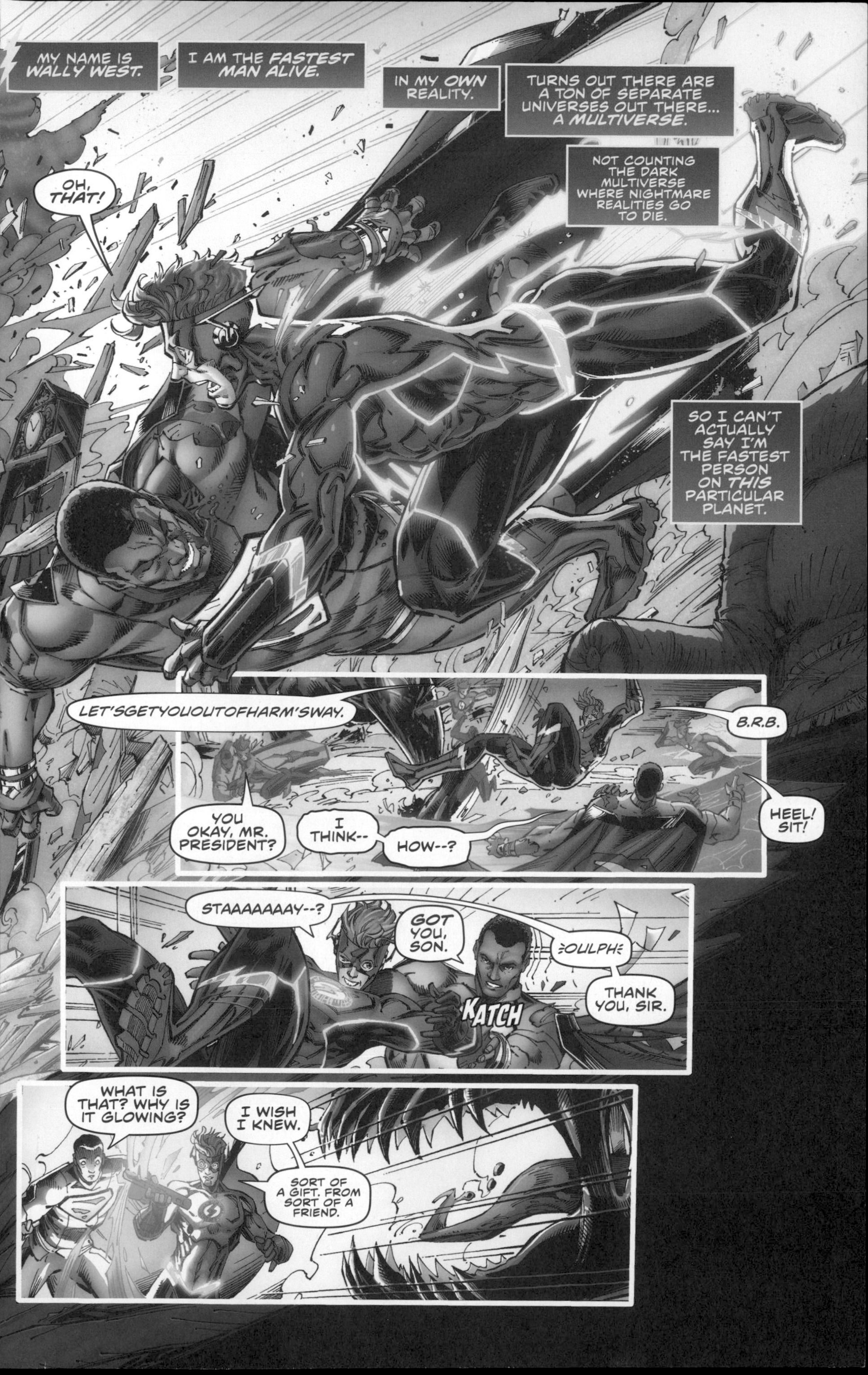
MY NAME IS WALLY WEST.
I AM THE FASTEST MAN ALIVE.
IN MY OWN REALITY.
TURNS OUT THERE ARE A TON OF SEPARATE UNIVERSES OUT THERE... A MULTIVERSE.
NOT COUNTING THE DARK MULTIVERSE WHERE NIGHTMARE REALITIES GO TO DIE.
OH, THAT!
SO I CAN'T ACTUALLY SAY I'M THE FASTEST PERSON ON THIS PARTICULAR PLANET.
LET'SGETYOUOUTOFHARM'SWAY.
B.R.B.
YOU OKAY, MR. PRESIDENT?
I THINK--
HOW--?
HEEL! SIT!
STAAAAAAAY--?
GOT YOU, SON.
OULPH
THANK YOU, SIR.
KATCH
WHAT IS THAT? WHY IS IT GLOWING?
I WISH I KNEW.
SORT OF A GIFT. FROM SORT OF A FRIEND.

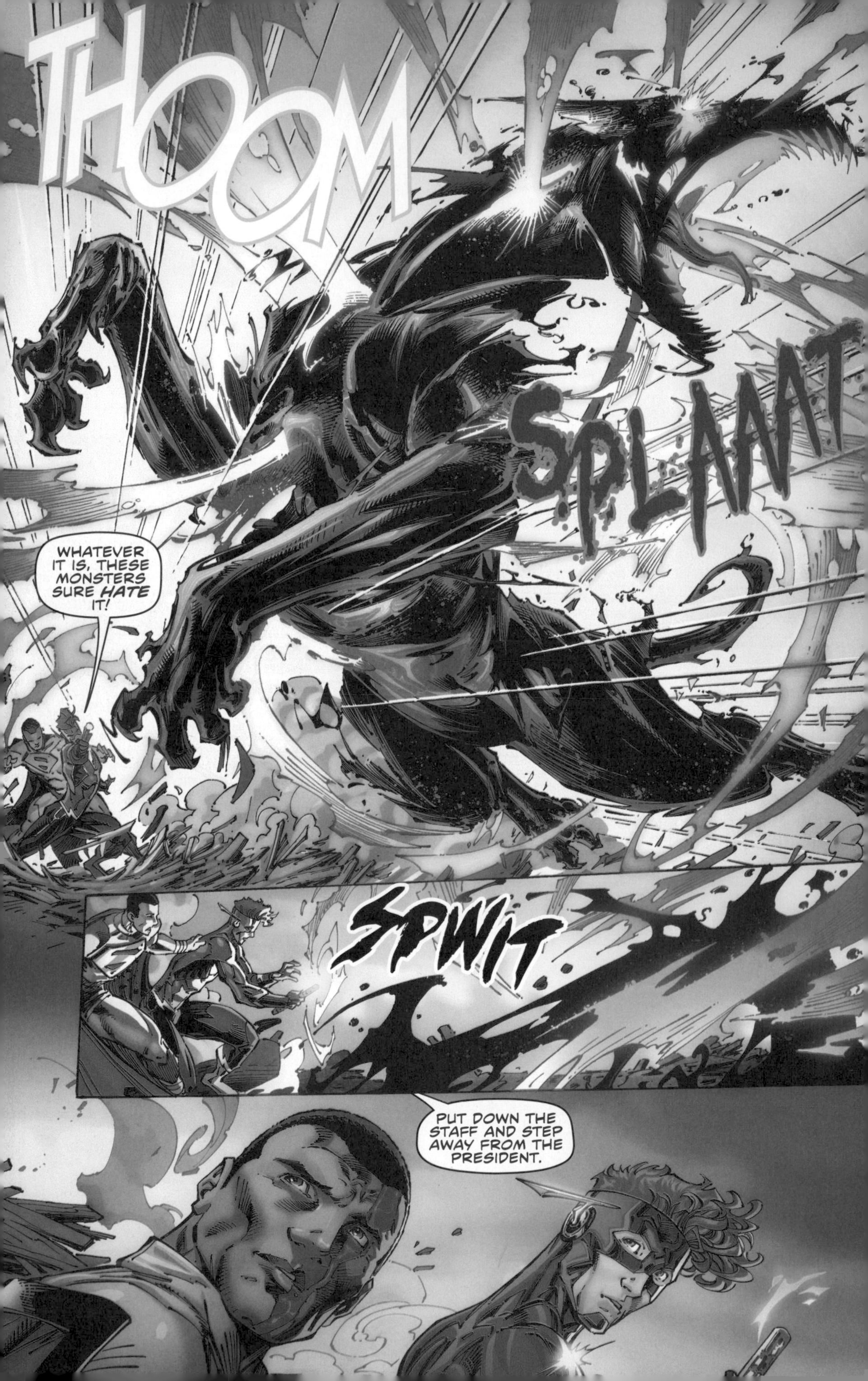
THOOM
SPLAAAT
WHATEVER IT IS, THESE MONSTERS SURE HATE IT!
SPWIT
PUT DOWN THE STAFF AND STEP AWAY FROM THE PRESIDENT.

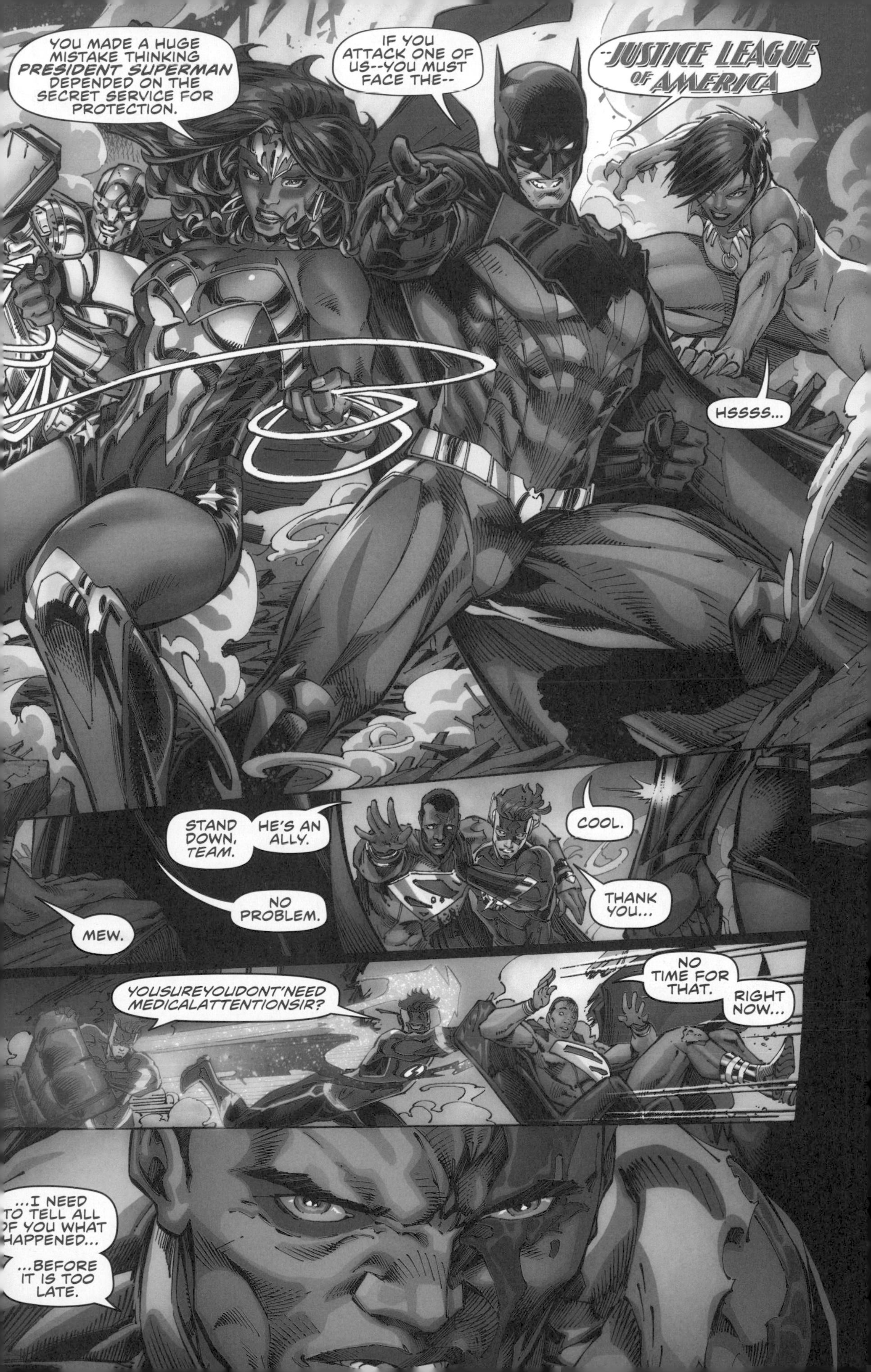
YOU MADE A HUGE MISTAKE THINKING PRESIDENT SUPERMAN DEPENDED ON THE SECRET SERVICE FOR PROTECTION.
IF YOU ATTACK ONE OF US--YOU MUST FACE THE--
--JUSTICE LEAGUE OF AMERICA
HSSSS...
STAND DOWN, TEAM.
HE'S AN ALLY.
COOL.
NO PROBLEM.
THANK YOU...
MEW.
YOUSUREYOUDONT'NEED MEDICALATTENTIONSIR?
NO TIME FOR THAT.
RIGHT NOW...
...I NEED TO TELL ALL OF YOU WHAT HAPPENED...
...BEFORE IT IS TOO LATE.

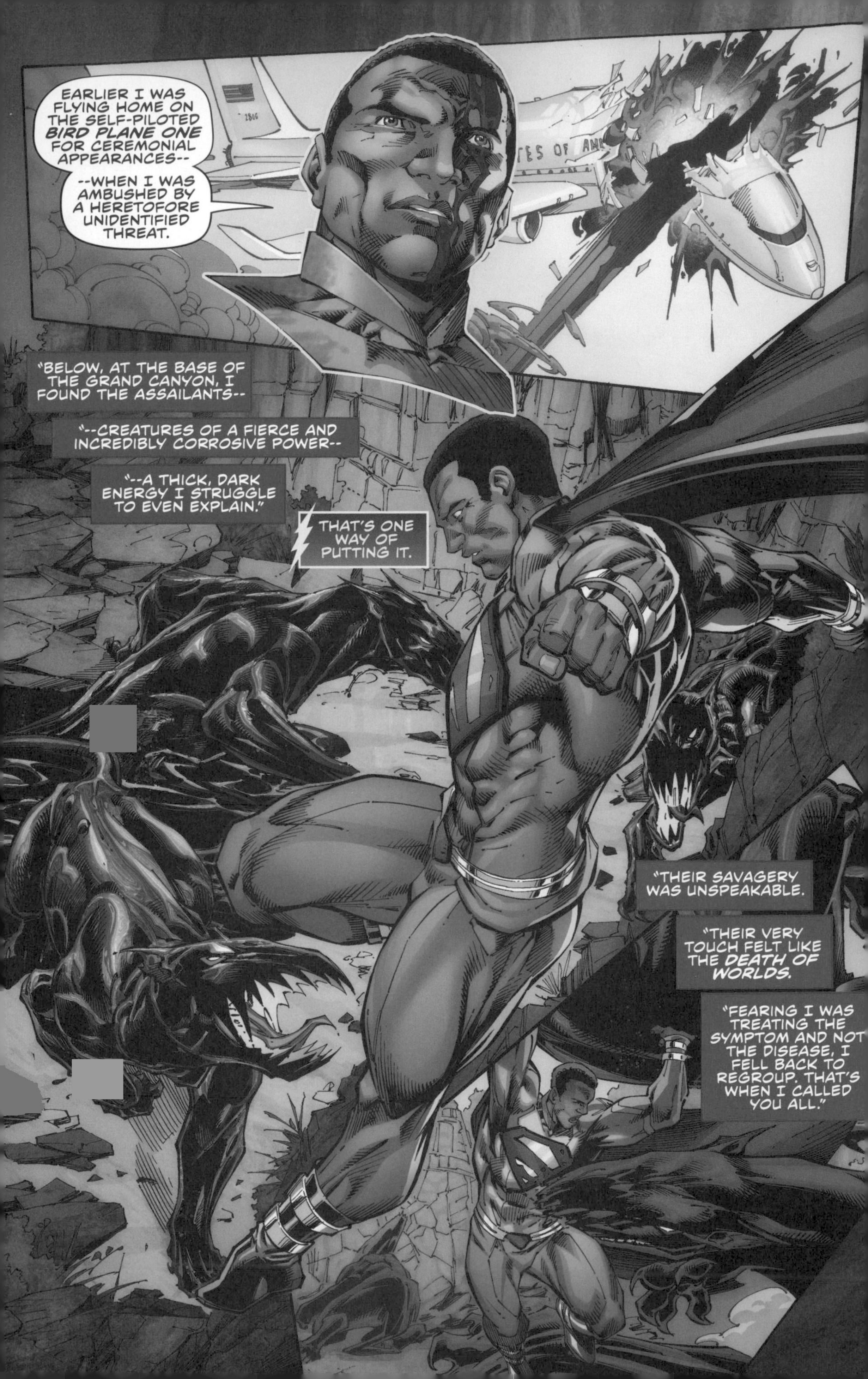
EARLIER I WAS FLYING HOME ON THE SELF-PILOTED BIRD PLANE ONE FOR CEREMONIAL APPEARANCES--
--WHEN I WAS AMBUSHED BY A HERETOFORE UNIDENTIFIED THREAT.
"BELOW, AT THE BASE OF THE GRAND CANYON, I FOUND THE ASSAILANTS--
"--CREATURES OF A FIERCE AND INCREDIBLY CORROSIVE POWER--
"--A THICK, DARK ENERGY I STRUGGLE TO EVEN EXPLAIN."
THAT'S ONE WAY OF PUTTING IT.
"THEIR SAVAGERY WAS UNSPEAKABLE.
"THEIR VERY TOUCH FELT LIKE THE DEATH OF WORLDS.
"FEARING I WAS TREATING THE SYMPTOM AND NOT THE DISEASE, I FELL BACK TO REGROUP. THAT'S WHEN I CALLED YOU ALL."

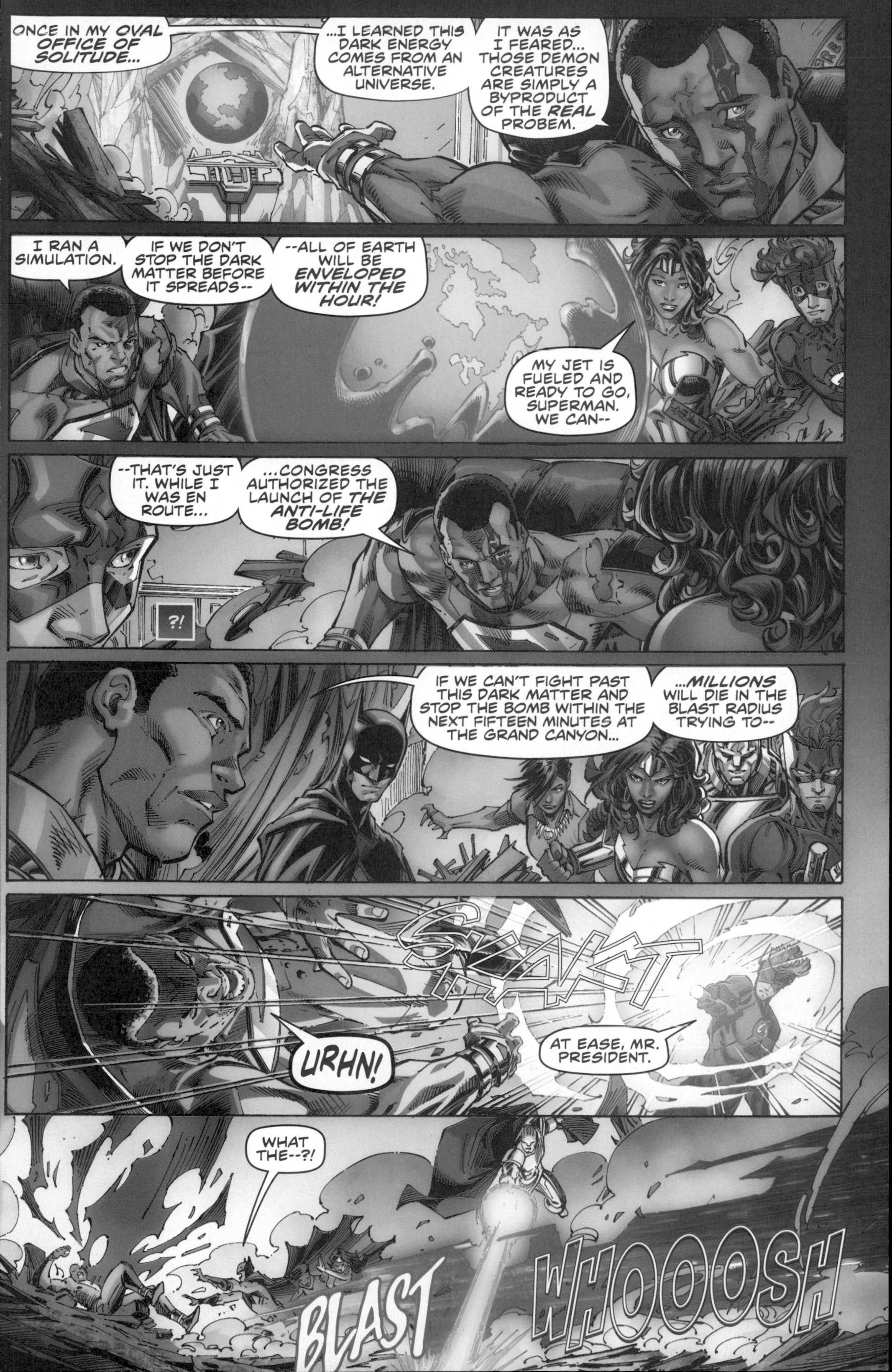
ONCE IN MY OVAL OFFICE OF SOLITUDE...
...I LEARNED THIS DARK ENERGY COMES FROM AN ALTERNATIVE UNIVERSE.
IT WAS AS I FEARED... THOSE DEMON CREATURES ARE SIMPLY A BYPRODUCT OF THE REAL PROBEM.
I RAN A SIMULATION.
IF WE DON'T STOP THE DARK MATTER BEFORE IT SPREADS--
--ALL OF EARTH WILL BE ENVELOPED WITHIN THE HOUR!
MY JET IS FUELED AND READY TO GO, SUPERMAN. WE CAN--
--THAT'S JUST IT. WHILE I WAS EN ROUTE...
...CONGRESS AUTHORIZED THE LAUNCH OF THE ANTI-LIFE BOMB!
?!
IF WE CAN'T FIGHT PAST THIS DARK MATTER AND STOP THE BOMB WITHIN THE NEXT FIFTEEN MINUTES AT THE GRAND CANYON...
...MILLIONS WILL DIE IN THE BLAST RADIUS TRYING TO--
SKAKT
URHN!
AT EASE, MR. PRESIDENT.
WHAT THE--?!
BLAST
WHOOOSH

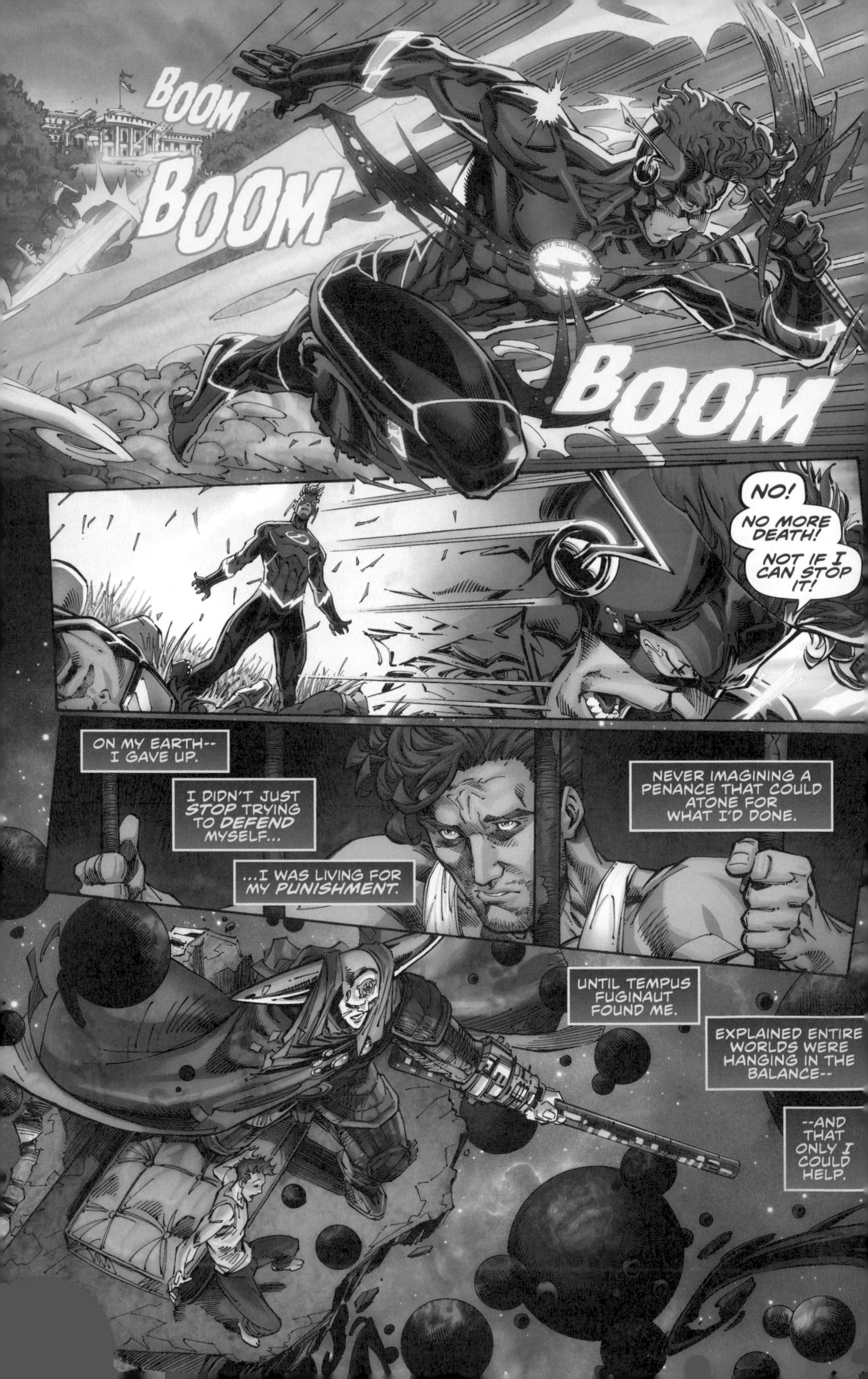
BOOM
BOOM
BOOM
NO!
NO MORE DEATH!
NOT IF I CAN STOP IT!
ON MY EARTH-- I GAVE UP.
I DIDN'T JUST STOP TRYING TO DEFEND MYSELF...
...I WAS LIVING FOR MY PUNISHMENT.
NEVER IMAGINING A PENANCE THAT COULD ATONE FOR WHAT I'D DONE.
UNTIL TEMPUS FUGINAUT FOUND ME.
EXPLAINED ENTIRE WORLDS WERE HANGING IN THE BALANCE--
--AND THAT ONLY I COULD HELP.

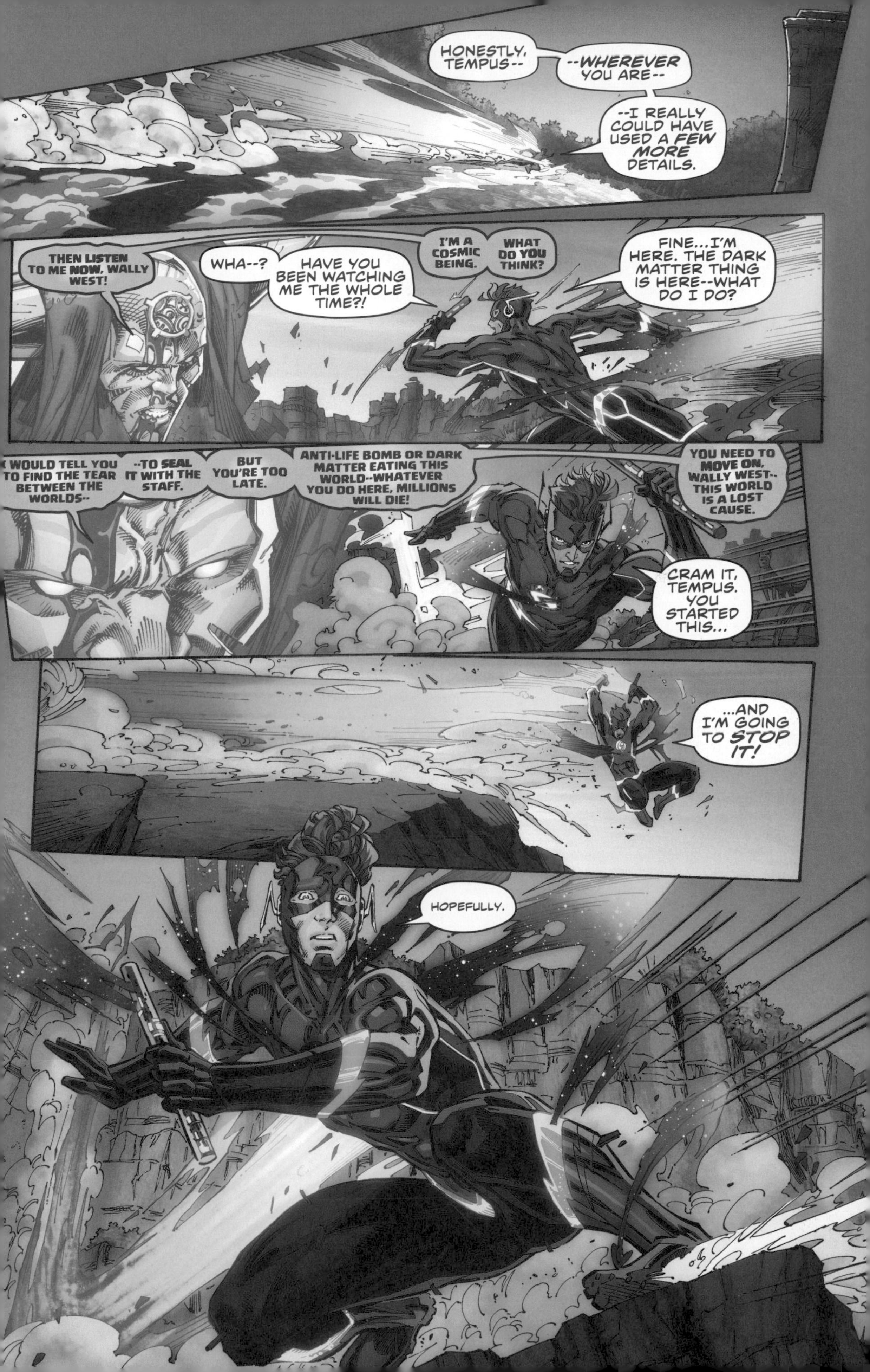
HONESTLY, TEMPUS--
--*WHEREVER* YOU ARE--
--I REALLY COULD HAVE USED A *FEW MORE* DETAILS.
THEN LISTEN TO ME NOW, WALLY WEST!
WHA--?
HAVE YOU BEEN WATCHING ME THE WHOLE TIME?!
I'M A COSMIC BEING.
WHAT DO YOU THINK?
FINE...I'M HERE. THE DARK MATTER THING IS HERE--WHAT DO I DO?
I WOULD TELL YOU TO FIND THE TEAR BETWEEN THE WORLDS--
--TO SEAL IT WITH THE STAFF.
BUT YOU'RE TOO LATE.
ANTI-LIFE BOMB OR DARK MATTER EATING THIS WORLD--WHATEVER YOU DO HERE, MILLIONS WILL DIE!
YOU NEED TO MOVE ON, WALLY WEST-- THIS WORLD IS A LOST CAUSE.
CRAM IT, TEMPUS. YOU STARTED THIS...
...AND I'M GOING TO *STOP IT!*
HOPEFULLY.

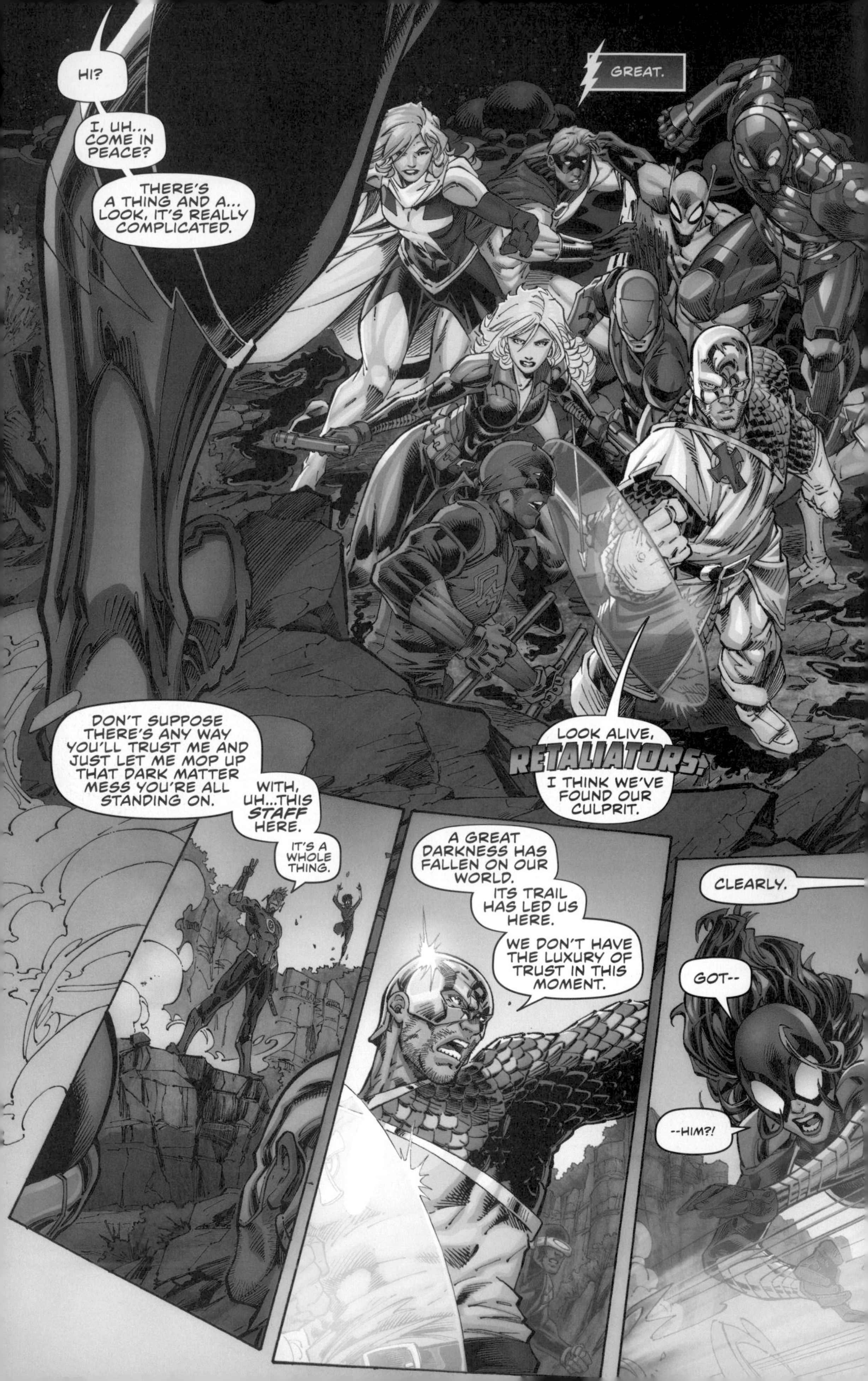
HI?
I, UH... COME IN PEACE?
THERE'S A THING AND A... LOOK, IT'S REALLY COMPLICATED.
GREAT.
DON'T SUPPOSE THERE'S ANY WAY YOU'LL TRUST ME AND JUST LET ME MOP UP THAT DARK MATTER MESS YOU'RE ALL STANDING ON.
WITH, UH...THIS STAFF HERE.
IT'S A WHOLE THING.
LOOK ALIVE, RETALIATORS!
I THINK WE'VE FOUND OUR CULPRIT.
A GREAT DARKNESS HAS FALLEN ON OUR WORLD.
ITS TRAIL HAS LED US HERE.
WE DON'T HAVE THE LUXURY OF TRUST IN THIS MOMENT.
CLEARLY.
GOT--
--HIM?!

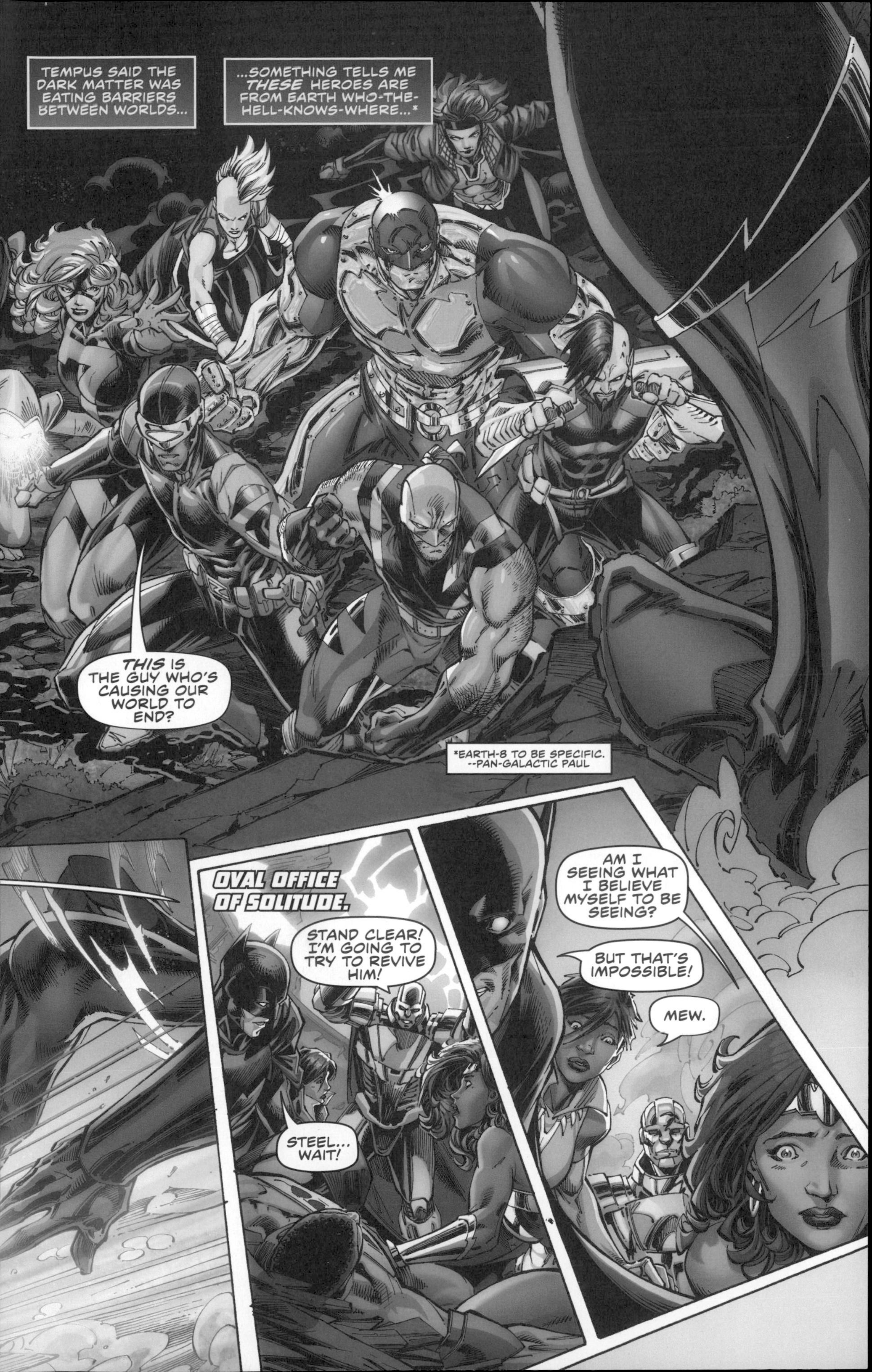

TEMPUS SAID THE DARK MATTER WAS EATING BARRIERS BETWEEN WORLDS...
...SOMETHING TELLS ME *THESE* HEROES ARE FROM EARTH WHO-THE-HELL-KNOWS-WHERE...*
THIS IS THE GUY WHO'S CAUSING OUR WORLD TO END?
*EARTH-8 TO BE SPECIFIC. --PAN-GALACTIC PAUL
OVAL OFFICE OF SOLITUDE.
STAND CLEAR! I'M GOING TO TRY TO REVIVE HIM!
STEEL... WAIT!
AM I SEEING WHAT I BELIEVE MYSELF TO BE SEEING?
BUT THAT'S IMPOSSIBLE!
MEW.

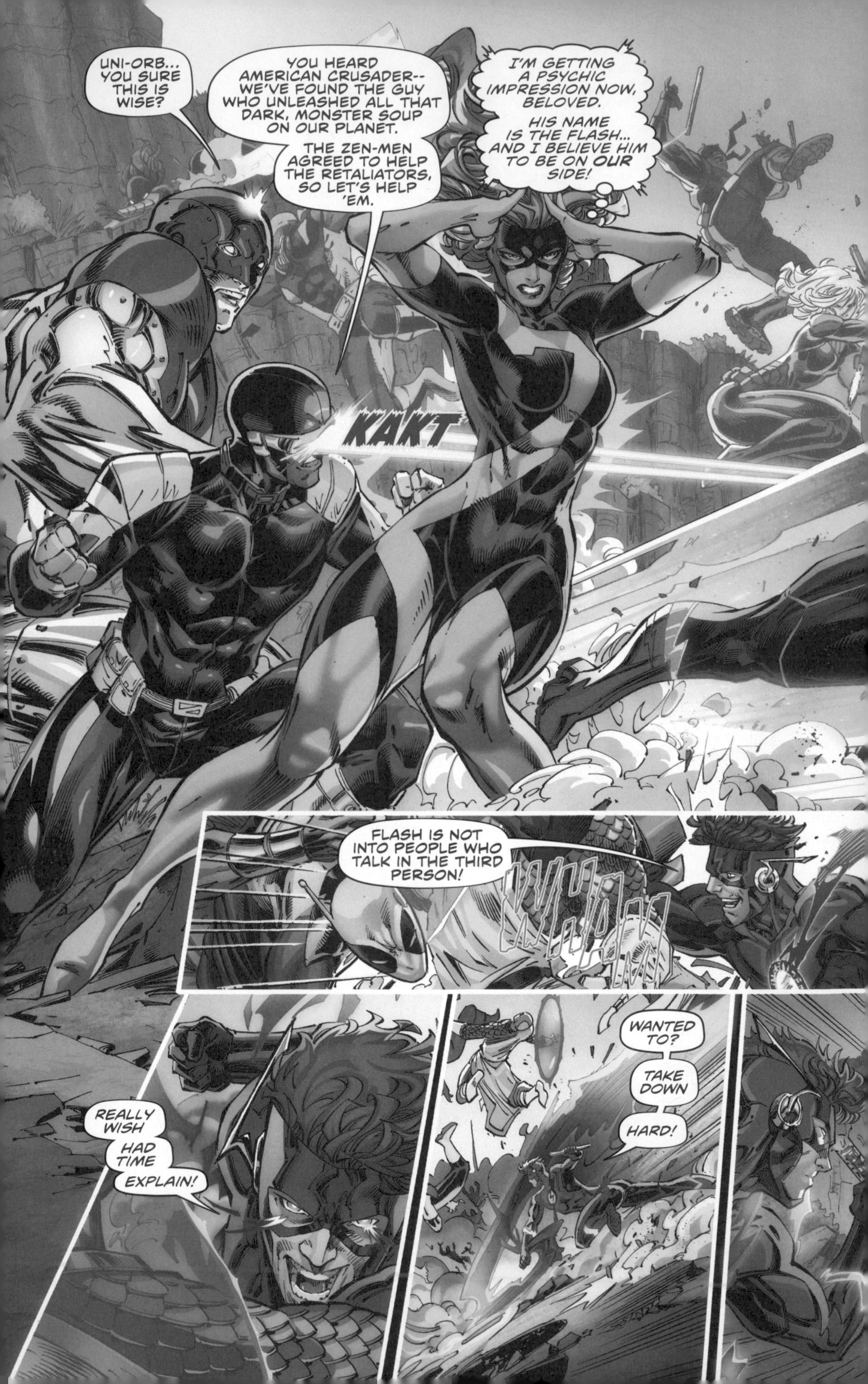
UNI-ORB... YOU SURE THIS IS WISE?
YOU HEARD AMERICAN CRUSADER-- WE'VE FOUND THE GUY WHO UNLEASHED ALL THAT DARK, MONSTER SOUP ON OUR PLANET.
THE ZEN-MEN AGREED TO HELP THE RETALIATORS, SO LET'S HELP 'EM.
I'M GETTING A PSYCHIC IMPRESSION NOW, BELOVED.
HIS NAME IS THE FLASH... AND I BELIEVE HIM TO BE ON **OUR** SIDE!
KAKT
FLASH IS NOT INTO PEOPLE WHO TALK IN THE THIRD PERSON!
WHAM
REALLY WISH
HAD TIME
EXPLAIN!
WANTED TO?
TAKE DOWN
HARD!

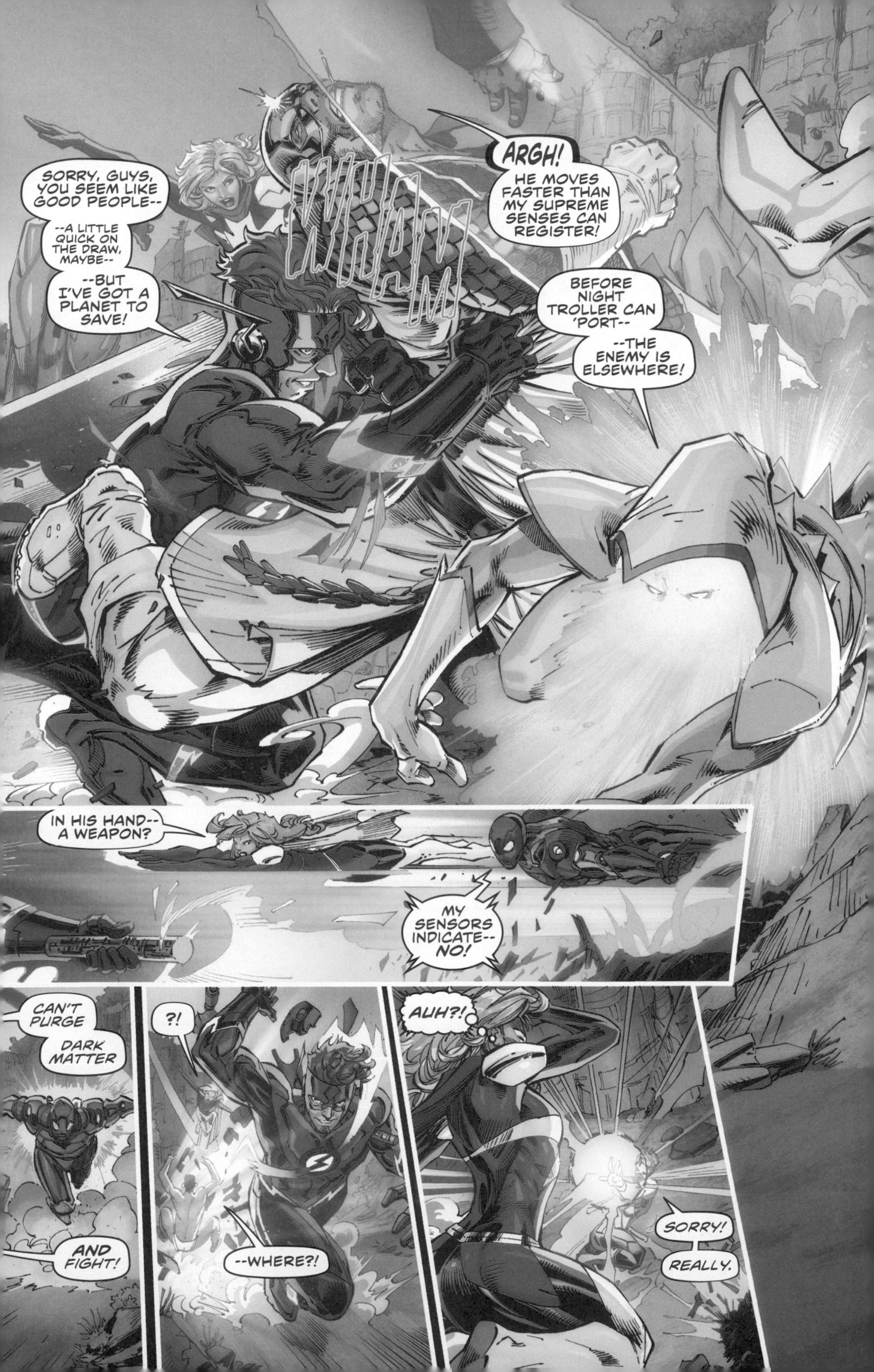
SORRY, GUYS, YOU SEEM LIKE GOOD PEOPLE--
--A LITTLE QUICK ON THE DRAW, MAYBE--
--BUT I'VE GOT A PLANET TO SAVE!
WHAM
ARGH!
HE MOVES FASTER THAN MY SUPREME SENSES CAN REGISTER!
BEFORE NIGHT TROLLER CAN 'PORT--
--THE ENEMY IS ELSEWHERE!
IN HIS HAND-- A WEAPON?
MY SENSORS INDICATE-- NO!
CAN'T PURGE
DARK MATTER
AND FIGHT!
?!
--WHERE?!
AUH?!
SORRY!
REALLY.

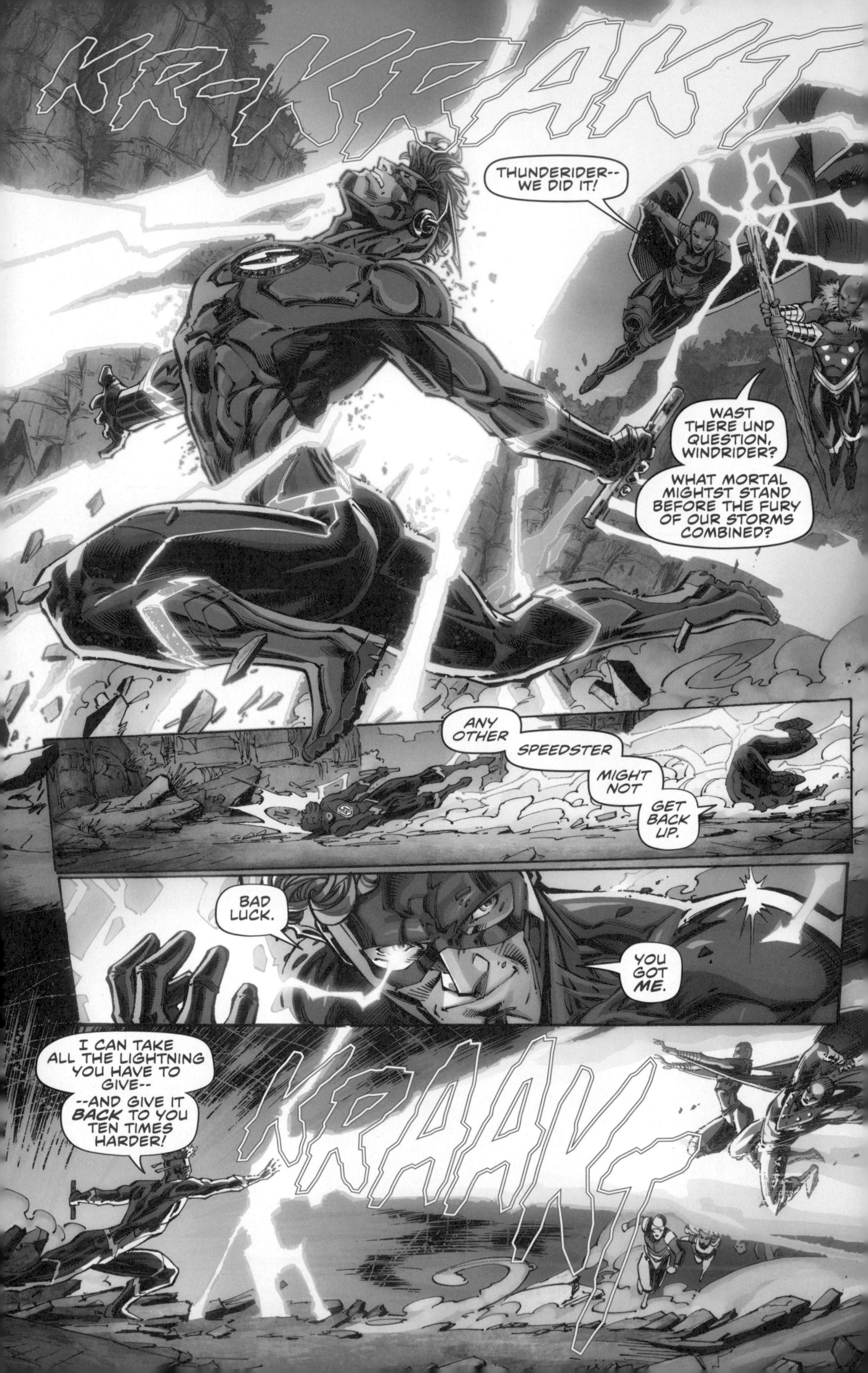
KR-KRRAKT
THUNDERIDER-- WE DID IT!
WAST THERE UND QUESTION, WINDRIDER?
WHAT MORTAL MIGHTST STAND BEFORE THE FURY OF OUR STORMS COMBINED?
ANY OTHER
SPEEDSTER
MIGHT NOT
GET BACK UP.
BAD LUCK.
YOU GOT ME.
I CAN TAKE ALL THE LIGHTNING YOU HAVE TO GIVE--
--AND GIVE IT BACK TO YOU TEN TIMES HARDER!
KRAAKT

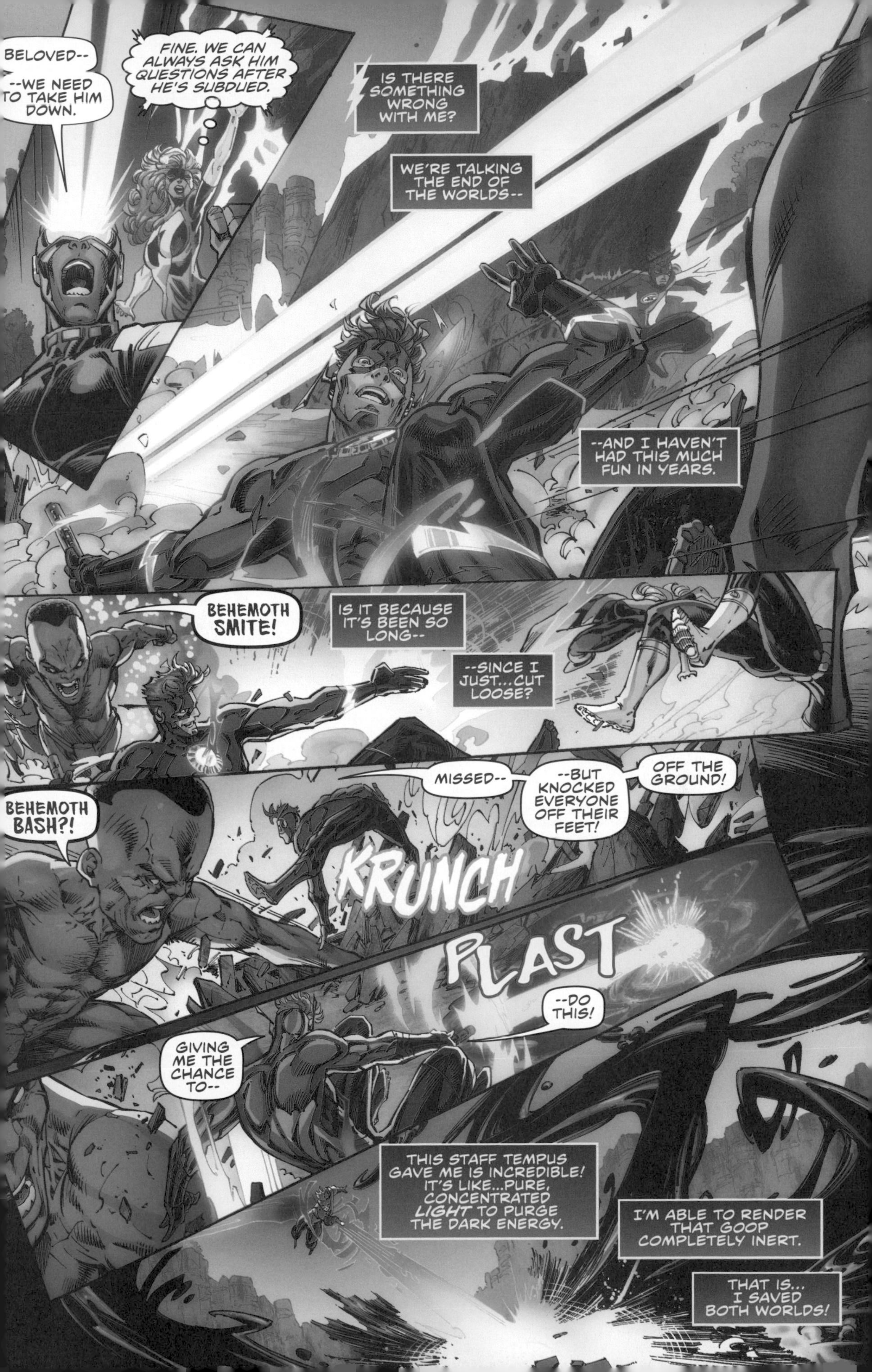
BELOVED--
--WE NEED TO TAKE HIM DOWN.
FINE. WE CAN ALWAYS ASK HIM QUESTIONS AFTER HE'S SUBDUED.
IS THERE SOMETHING WRONG WITH ME?
WE'RE TALKING THE END OF THE WORLDS--
--AND I HAVEN'T HAD THIS MUCH FUN IN YEARS.
BEHEMOTH SMITE!
IS IT BECAUSE IT'S BEEN SO LONG--
--SINCE I JUST...CUT LOOSE?
BEHEMOTH BASH?!
MISSED--
--BUT KNOCKED EVERYONE OFF THEIR FEET!
OFF THE GROUND!
KRUNCH
PLAST
GIVING ME THE CHANCE TO--
--DO THIS!
THIS STAFF TEMPUS GAVE ME IS INCREDIBLE! IT'S LIKE...PURE, CONCENTRATED LIGHT TO PURGE THE DARK ENERGY.
I'M ABLE TO RENDER THAT GOOP COMPLETELY INERT.
THAT IS... I SAVED BOTH WORLDS!

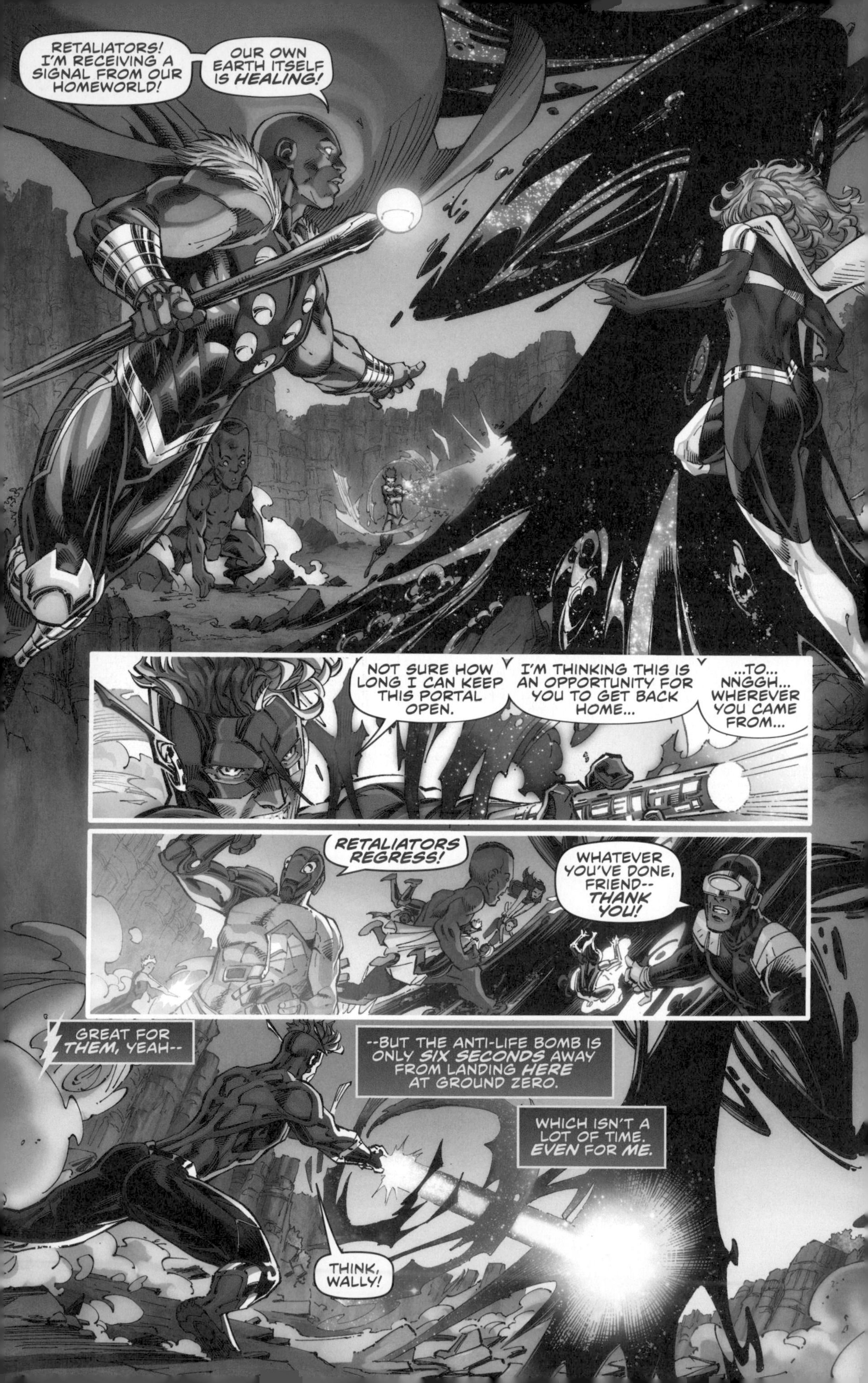
RETALIATORS! I'M RECEIVING A SIGNAL FROM OUR HOMEWORLD!
OUR OWN EARTH ITSELF IS HEALING!
NOT SURE HOW LONG I CAN KEEP THIS PORTAL OPEN.
I'M THINKING THIS IS AN OPPORTUNITY FOR YOU TO GET BACK HOME...
...TO... NNGGH... WHEREVER YOU CAME FROM...
RETALIATORS REGRESS!
WHATEVER YOU'VE DONE, FRIEND-- THANK YOU!
GREAT FOR THEM, YEAH--
--BUT THE ANTI-LIFE BOMB IS ONLY SIX SECONDS AWAY FROM LANDING HERE AT GROUND ZERO.
WHICH ISN'T A LOT OF TIME. EVEN FOR ME.
THINK, WALLY!

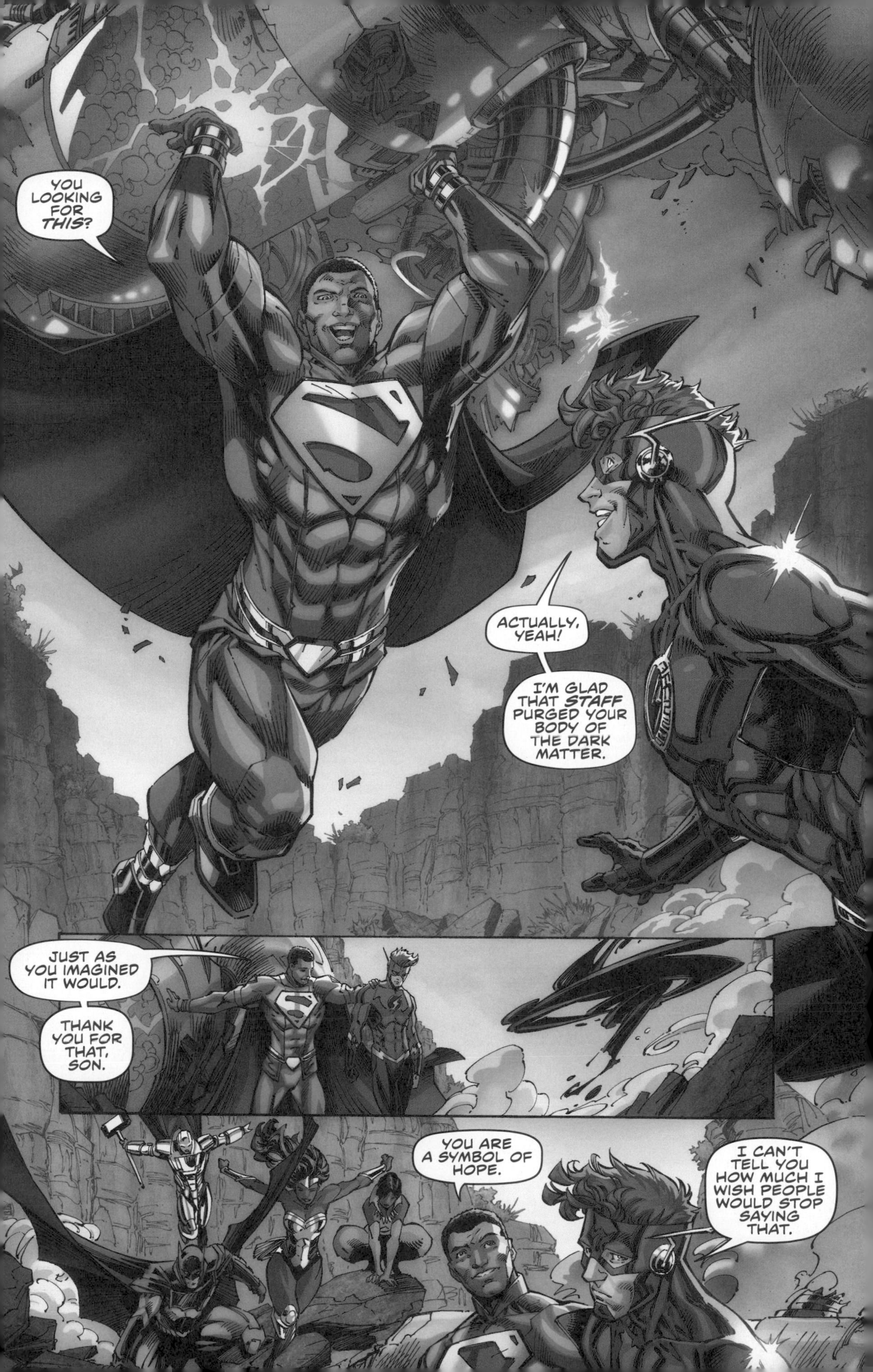
YOU LOOKING FOR THIS?
ACTUALLY, YEAH!
I'M GLAD THAT STAFF PURGED YOUR BODY OF THE DARK MATTER.
JUST AS YOU IMAGINED IT WOULD.
THANK YOU FOR THAT, SON.
YOU ARE A SYMBOL OF HOPE.
I CAN'T TELL YOU HOW MUCH I WISH PEOPLE WOULD STOP SAYING THAT.

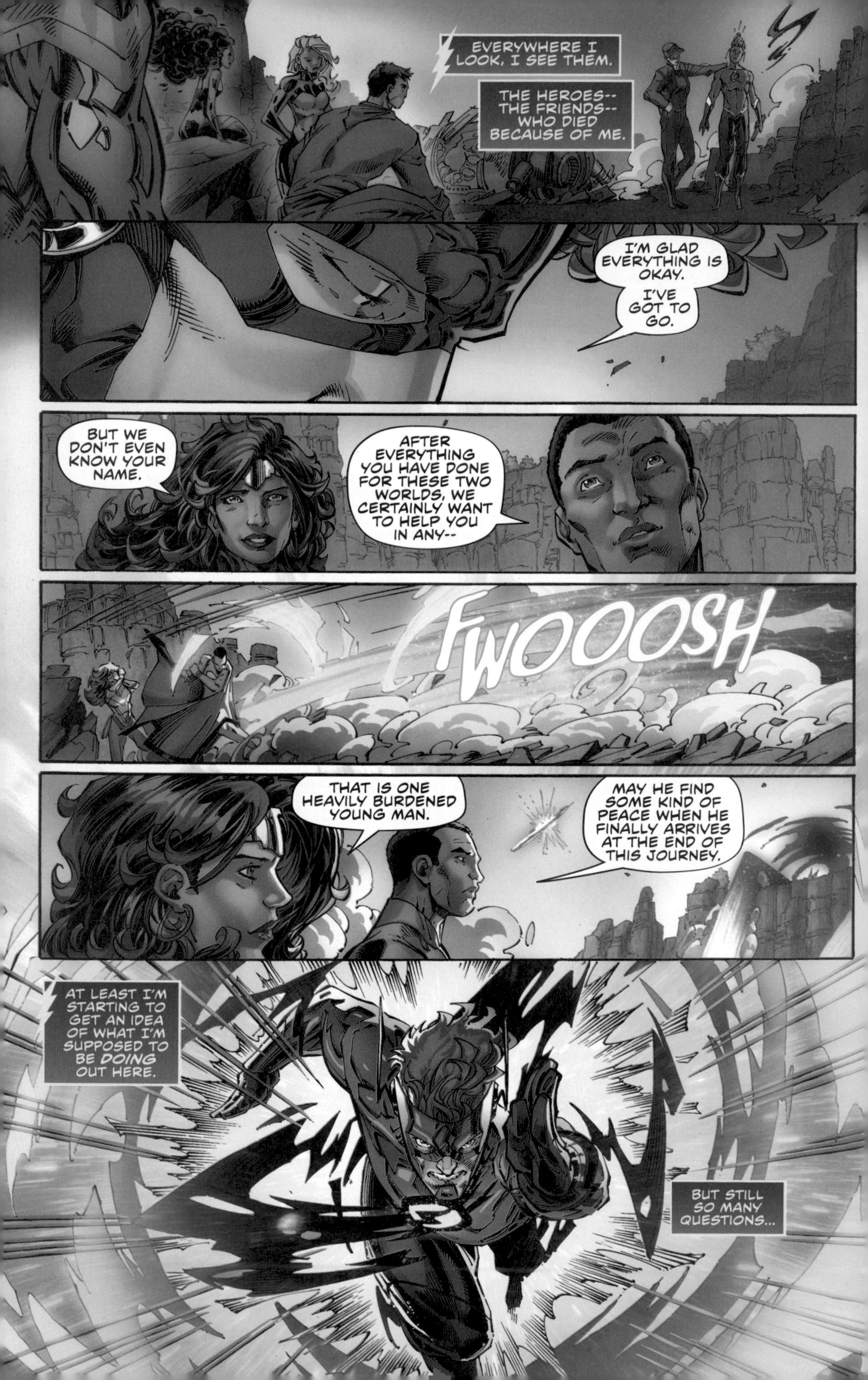
EVERYWHERE I LOOK, I SEE THEM.
THE HEROES-- THE FRIENDS-- WHO DIED BECAUSE OF ME.
I'M GLAD EVERYTHING IS OKAY.
I'VE GOT TO GO.
BUT WE DON'T EVEN KNOW YOUR NAME.
AFTER EVERYTHING YOU HAVE DONE FOR THESE TWO WORLDS, WE CERTAINLY WANT TO HELP YOU IN ANY--
FWOOOSH
THAT IS ONE HEAVILY BURDENED YOUNG MAN.
MAY HE FIND SOME KIND OF PEACE WHEN HE FINALLY ARRIVES AT THE END OF THIS JOURNEY.
AT LEAST I'M STARTING TO GET AN IDEA OF WHAT I'M SUPPOSED TO BE DOING OUT HERE.
BUT STILL SO MANY QUESTIONS...

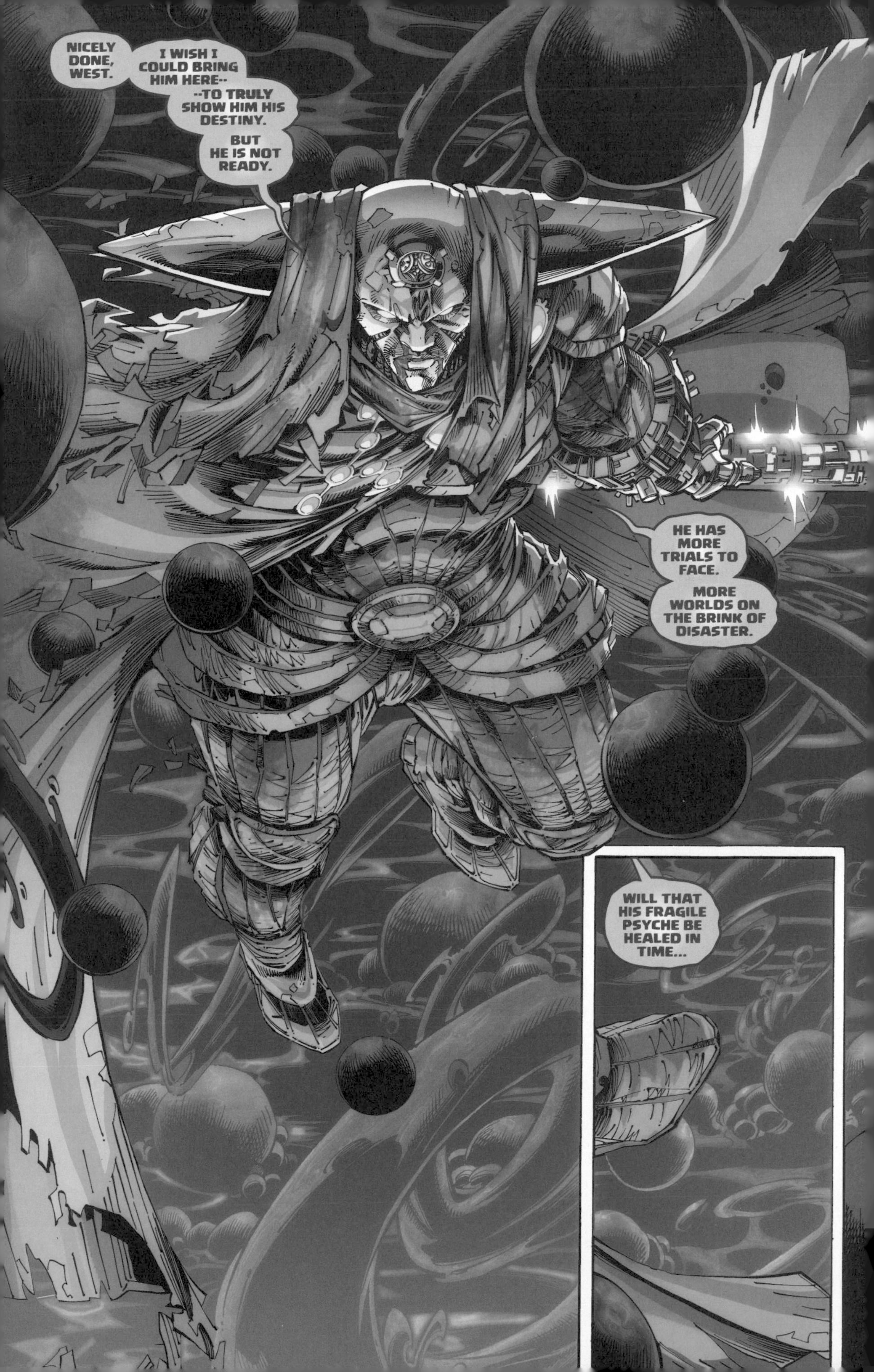
NICELY DONE, WEST.
I WISH I COULD BRING HIM HERE--
--TO TRULY SHOW HIM HIS DESTINY.
BUT HE IS NOT READY.
HE HAS MORE TRIALS TO FACE.
MORE WORLDS ON THE BRINK OF DISASTER.
WILL THAT HIS FRAGILE PSYCHE BE HEALED IN TIME...

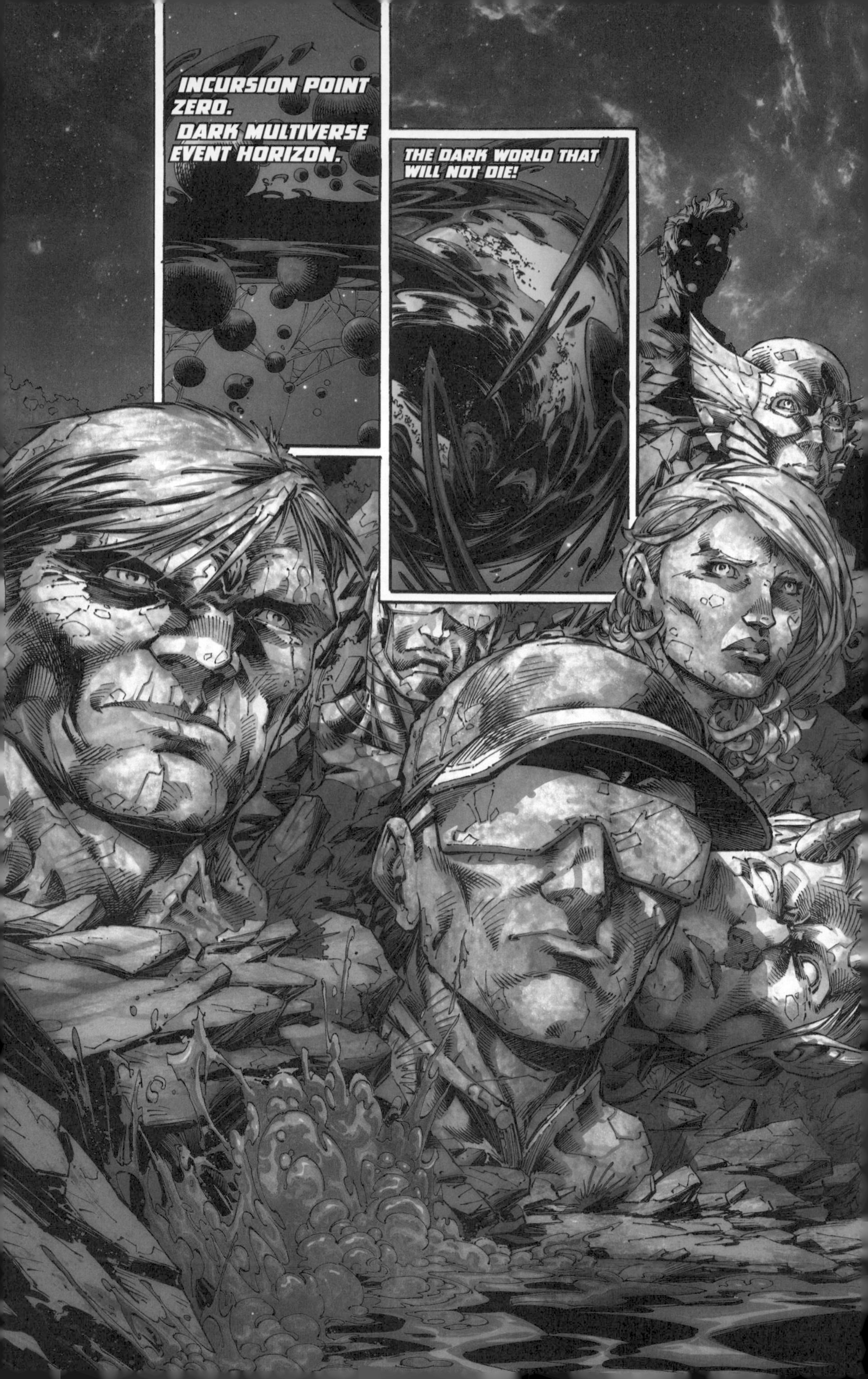
INCURSION POINT ZERO.
DARK MULTIVERSE EVENT HORIZON.
THE DARK WORLD THAT WILL NOT DIE!

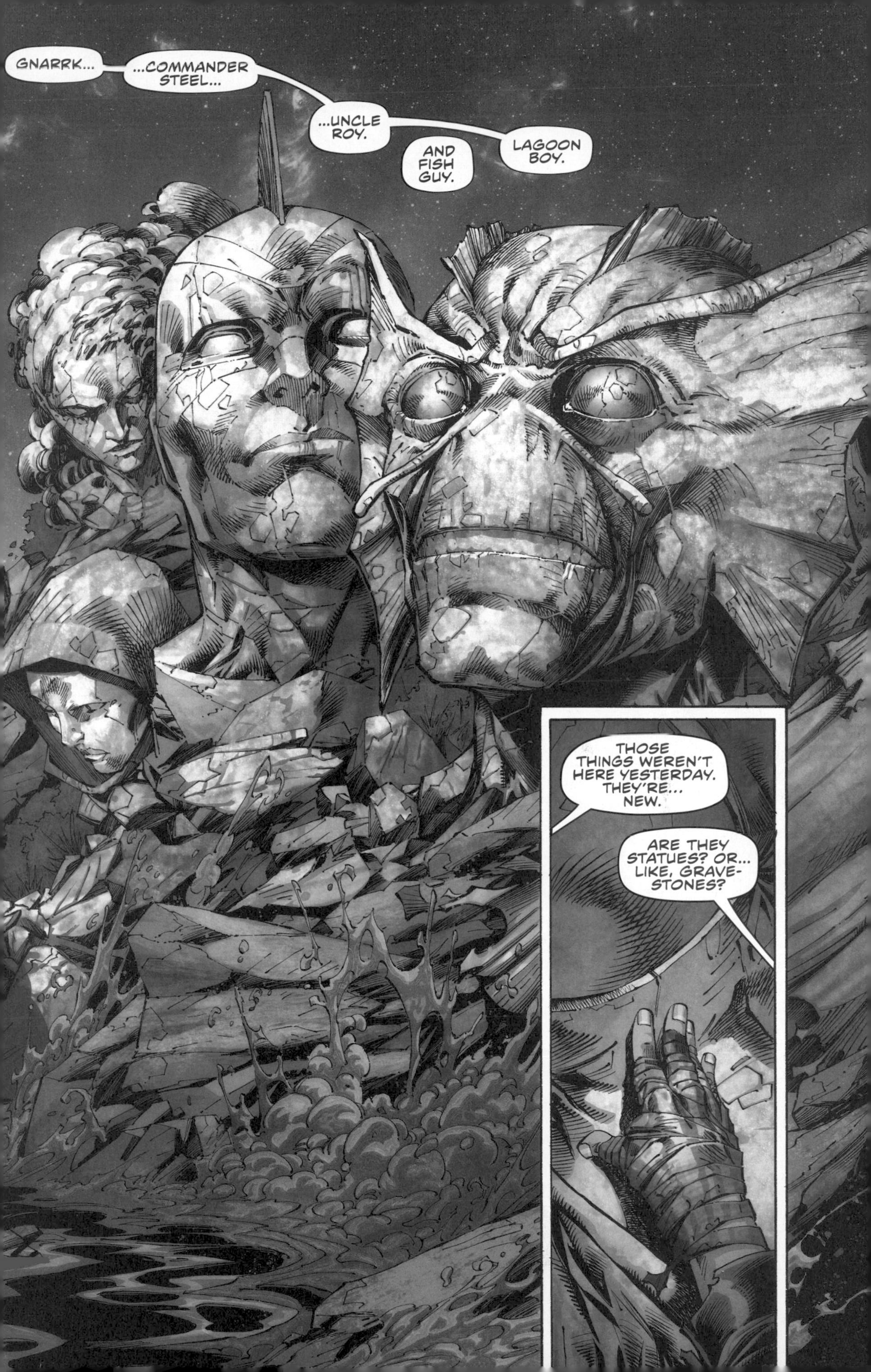
GNARRK...
...COMMANDER STEEL...
...UNCLE ROY.
LAGOON BOY.
AND FISH GUY.
THOSE THINGS WEREN'T HERE YESTERDAY. THEY'RE... NEW.
ARE THEY STATUES? OR... LIKE, GRAVE-STONES?

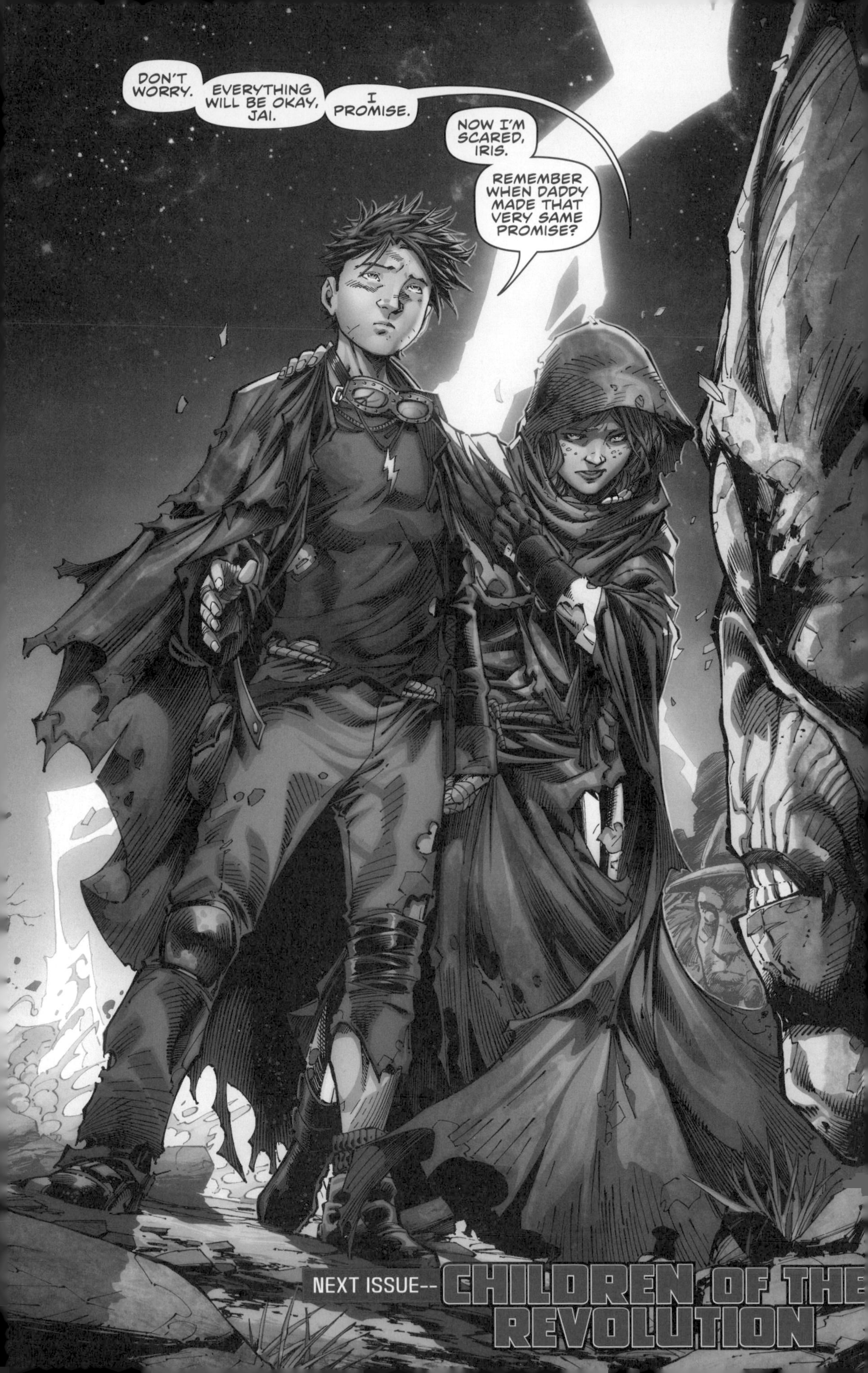
DON'T WORRY.
EVERYTHING WILL BE OKAY, JAI.
I PROMISE.
NOW I'M SCARED, IRIS.
REMEMBER WHEN DADDY MADE THAT VERY SAME PROMISE?
NEXT ISSUE--
CHILDREN OF THE REVOLUTION

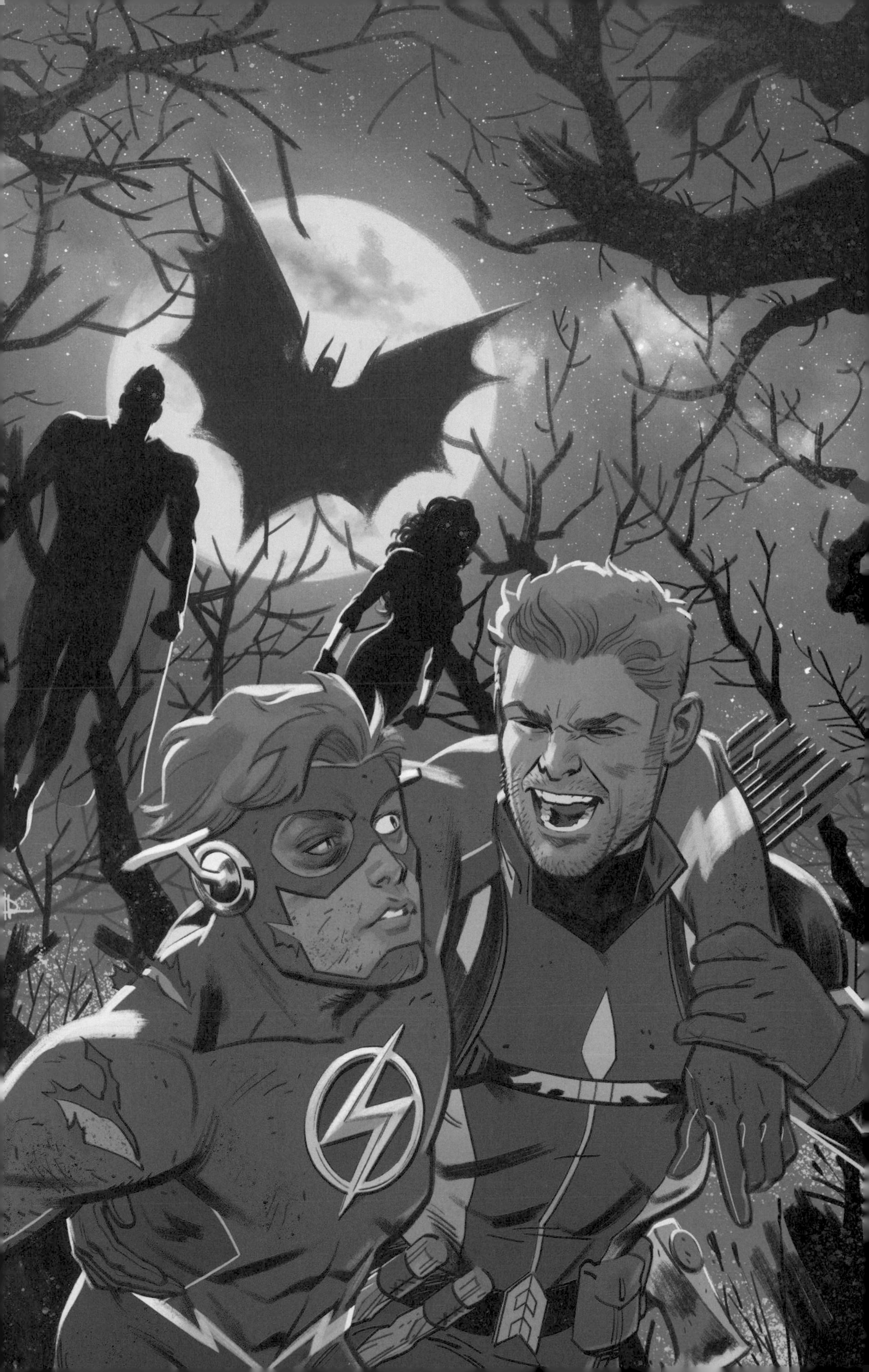

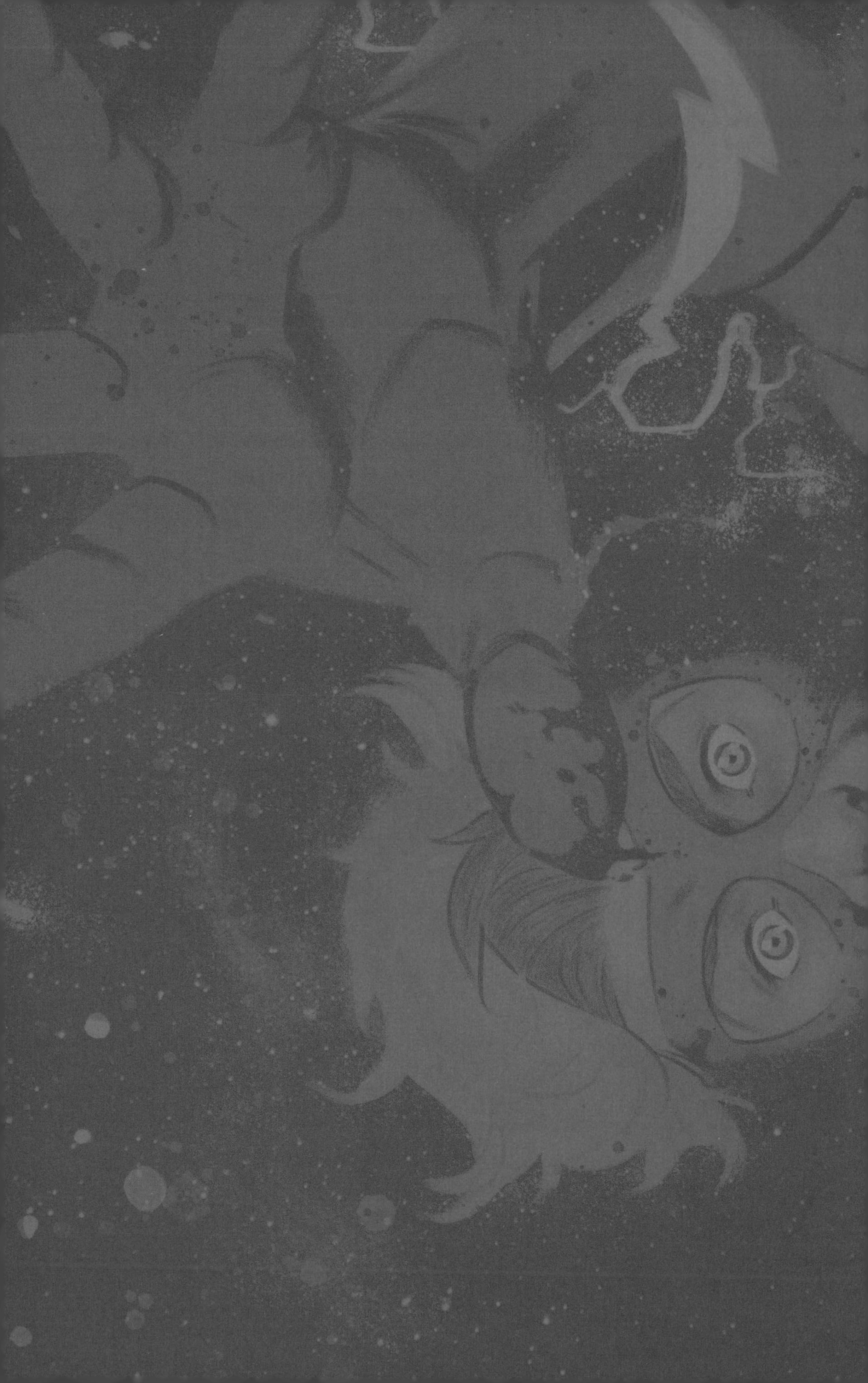

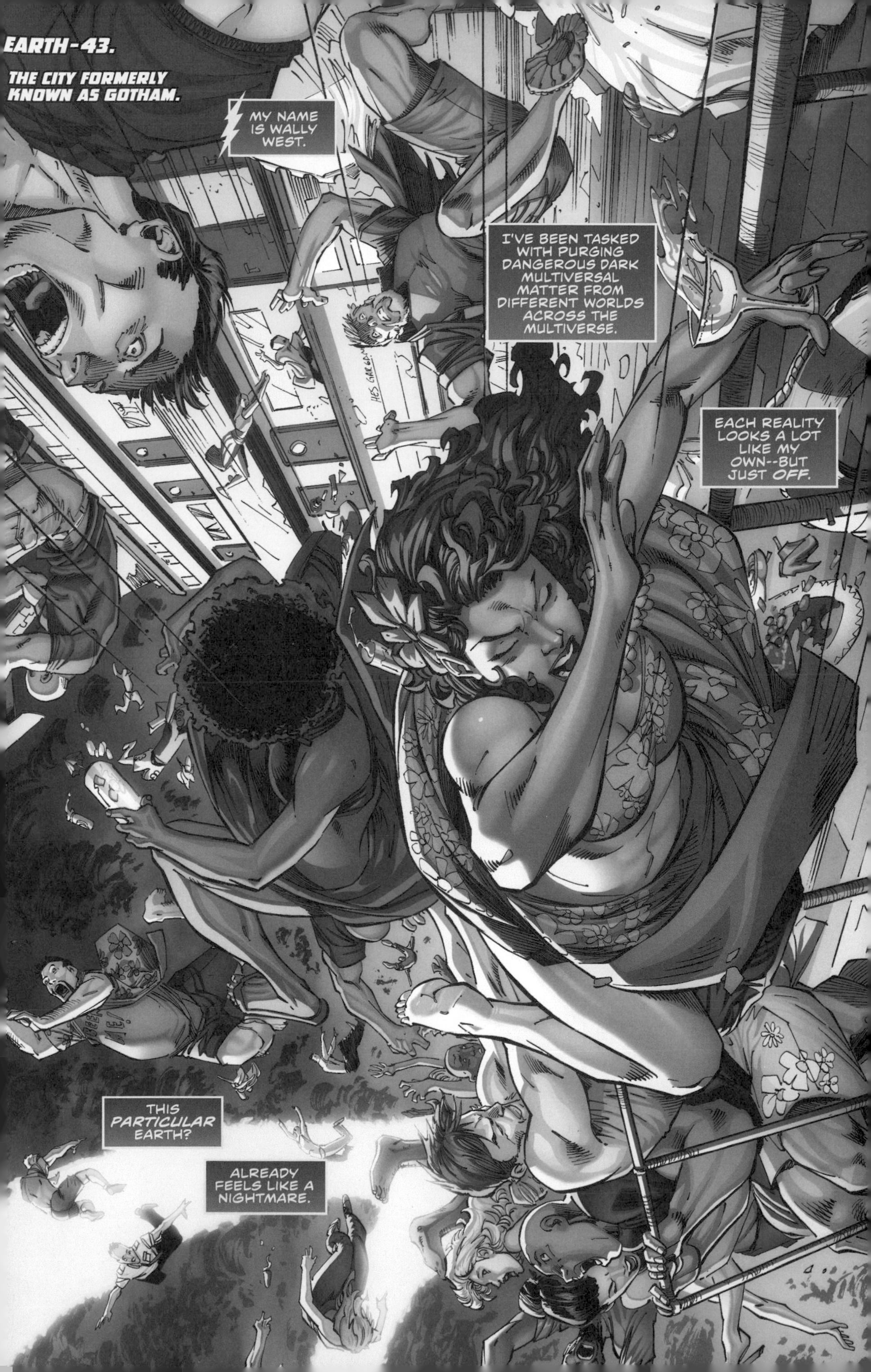
EARTH-43.
THE CITY FORMERLY KNOWN AS GOTHAM.
MY NAME IS WALLY WEST.
I'VE BEEN TASKED WITH PURGING DANGEROUS DARK MULTIVERSAL MATTER FROM DIFFERENT WORLDS ACROSS THE MULTIVERSE.
EACH REALITY LOOKS A LOT LIKE MY OWN--BUT JUST OFF.
THIS PARTICULAR EARTH?
ALREADY FEELS LIKE A NIGHTMARE.

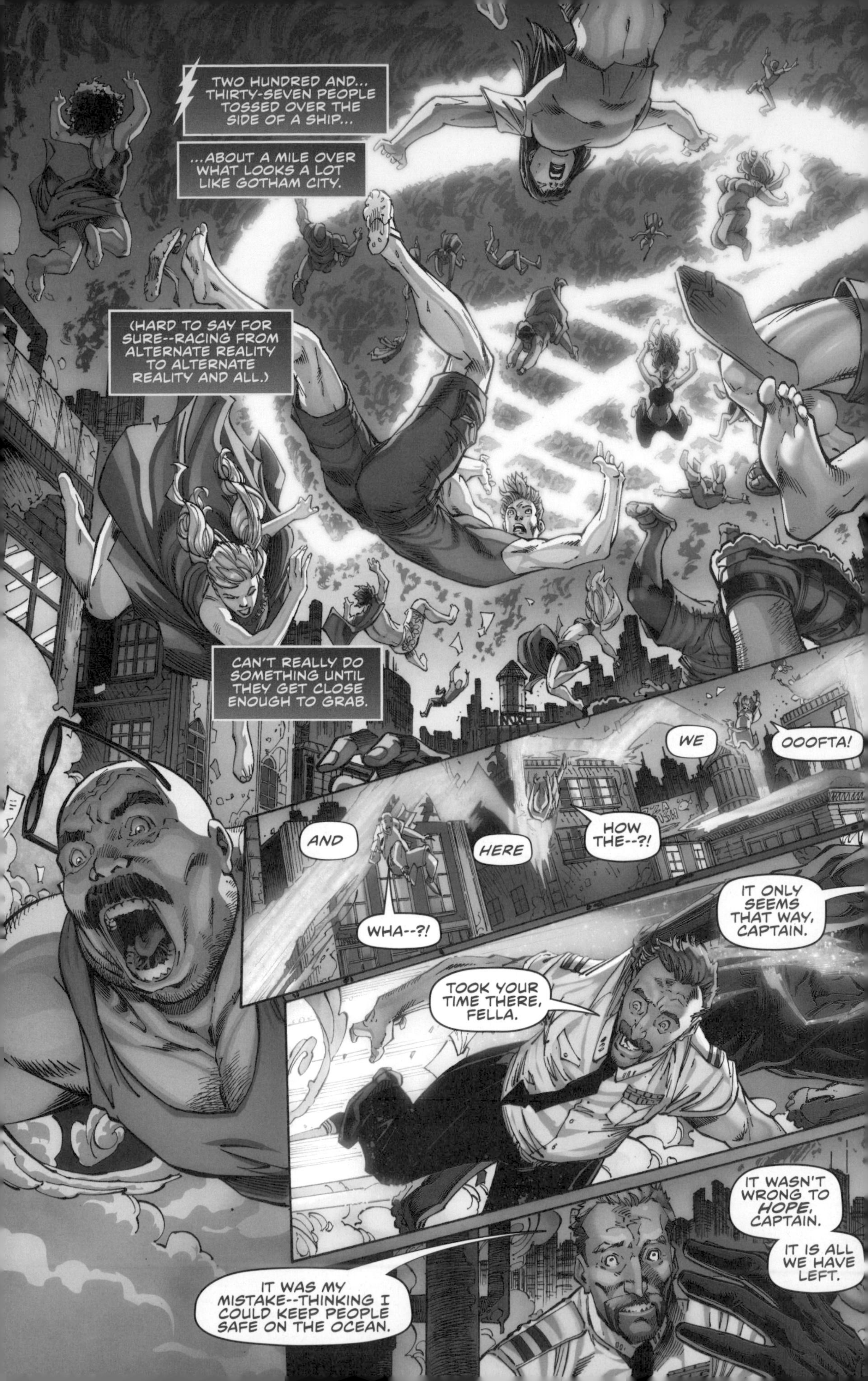
TWO HUNDRED AND... THIRTY-SEVEN PEOPLE TOSSED OVER THE SIDE OF A SHIP...
...ABOUT A MILE OVER WHAT LOOKS A LOT LIKE GOTHAM CITY.
(HARD TO SAY FOR SURE--RACING FROM ALTERNATE REALITY TO ALTERNATE REALITY AND ALL.)
CAN'T REALLY DO SOMETHING UNTIL THEY GET CLOSE ENOUGH TO GRAB.
AND
HERE
WE
HOW THE--?!
OOOFTA!
WHA--?!
IT ONLY SEEMS THAT WAY, CAPTAIN.
TOOK YOUR TIME THERE, FELLA.
IT WAS MY MISTAKE--THINKING I COULD KEEP PEOPLE SAFE ON THE OCEAN.
IT WASN'T WRONG TO *HOPE*, CAPTAIN.
IT IS ALL WE HAVE LEFT.

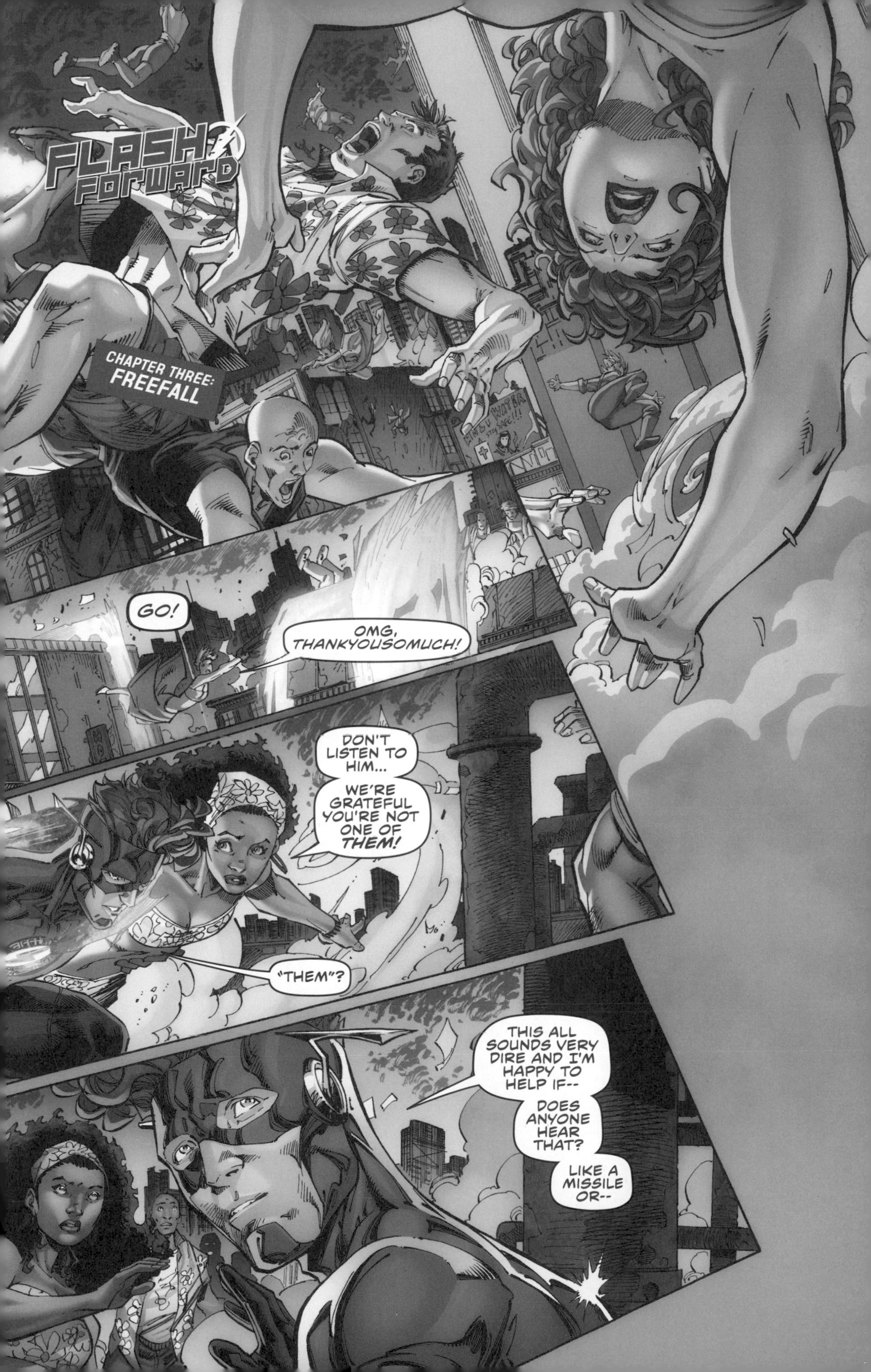
FLASH FORWARD
CHAPTER THREE: FREEFALL
GO!
OMG, THANKYOUSOMUCH!
DON'T LISTEN TO HIM...
WE'RE GRATEFUL YOU'RE NOT ONE OF THEM!
"THEM"?
THIS ALL SOUNDS VERY DIRE AND I'M HAPPY TO HELP IF--
DOES ANYONE HEAR THAT?
LIKE A MISSILE OR--

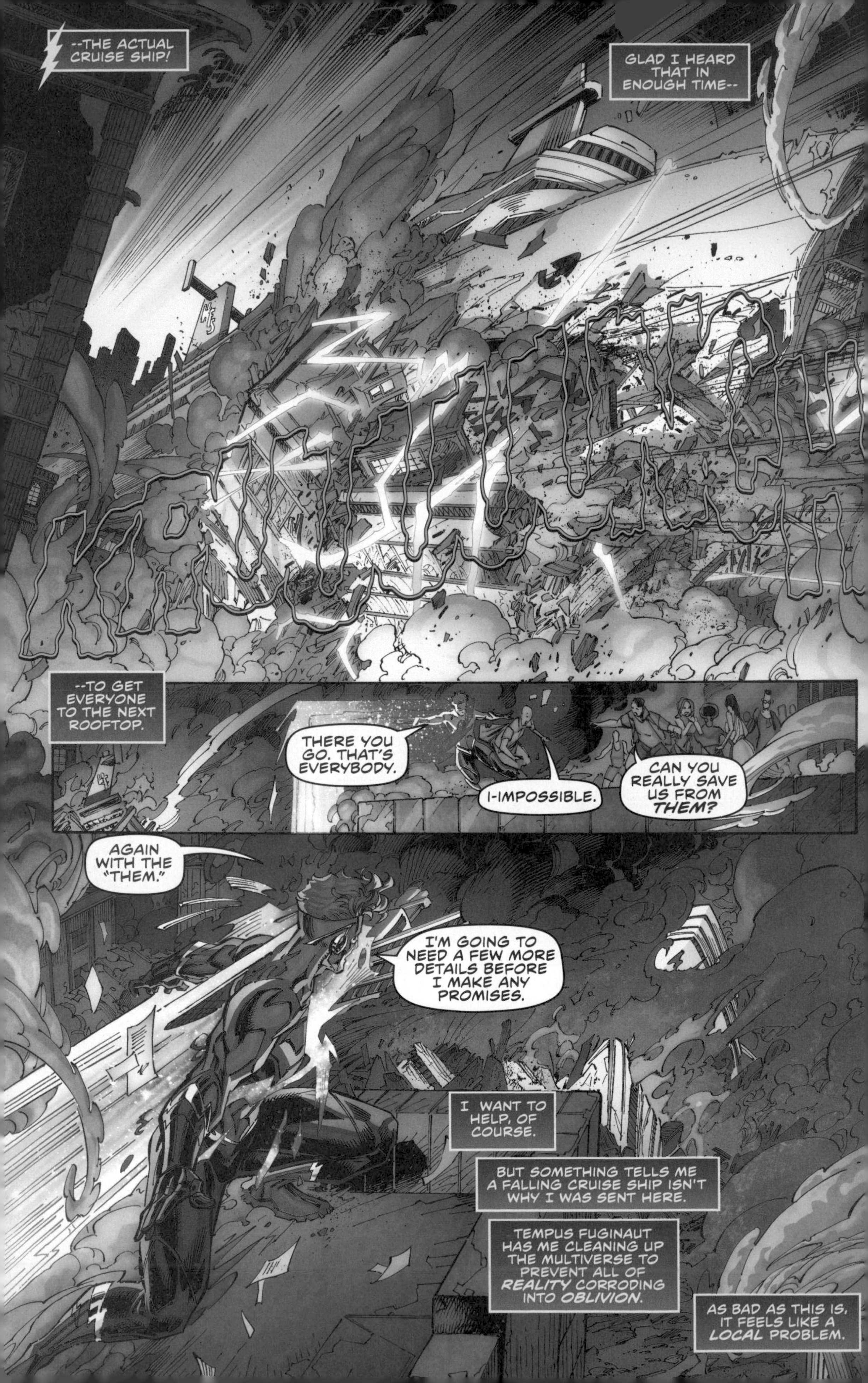
--THE ACTUAL CRUISE SHIP!
GLAD I HEARD THAT IN ENOUGH TIME--
--TO GET EVERYONE TO THE NEXT ROOFTOP.
THERE YOU GO. THAT'S EVERYBODY.
I-IMPOSSIBLE.
CAN YOU REALLY SAVE US FROM *THEM?*
AGAIN WITH THE "THEM."
I'M GOING TO NEED A FEW MORE DETAILS BEFORE I MAKE ANY PROMISES.
I WANT TO HELP, OF COURSE.
BUT SOMETHING TELLS ME A FALLING CRUISE SHIP ISN'T WHY I WAS SENT HERE.
TEMPUS FUGINAUT HAS ME CLEANING UP THE MULTIVERSE TO PREVENT ALL OF *REALITY* CORRODING INTO *OBLIVION*.
AS BAD AS THIS IS, IT FEELS LIKE A *LOCAL* PROBLEM.

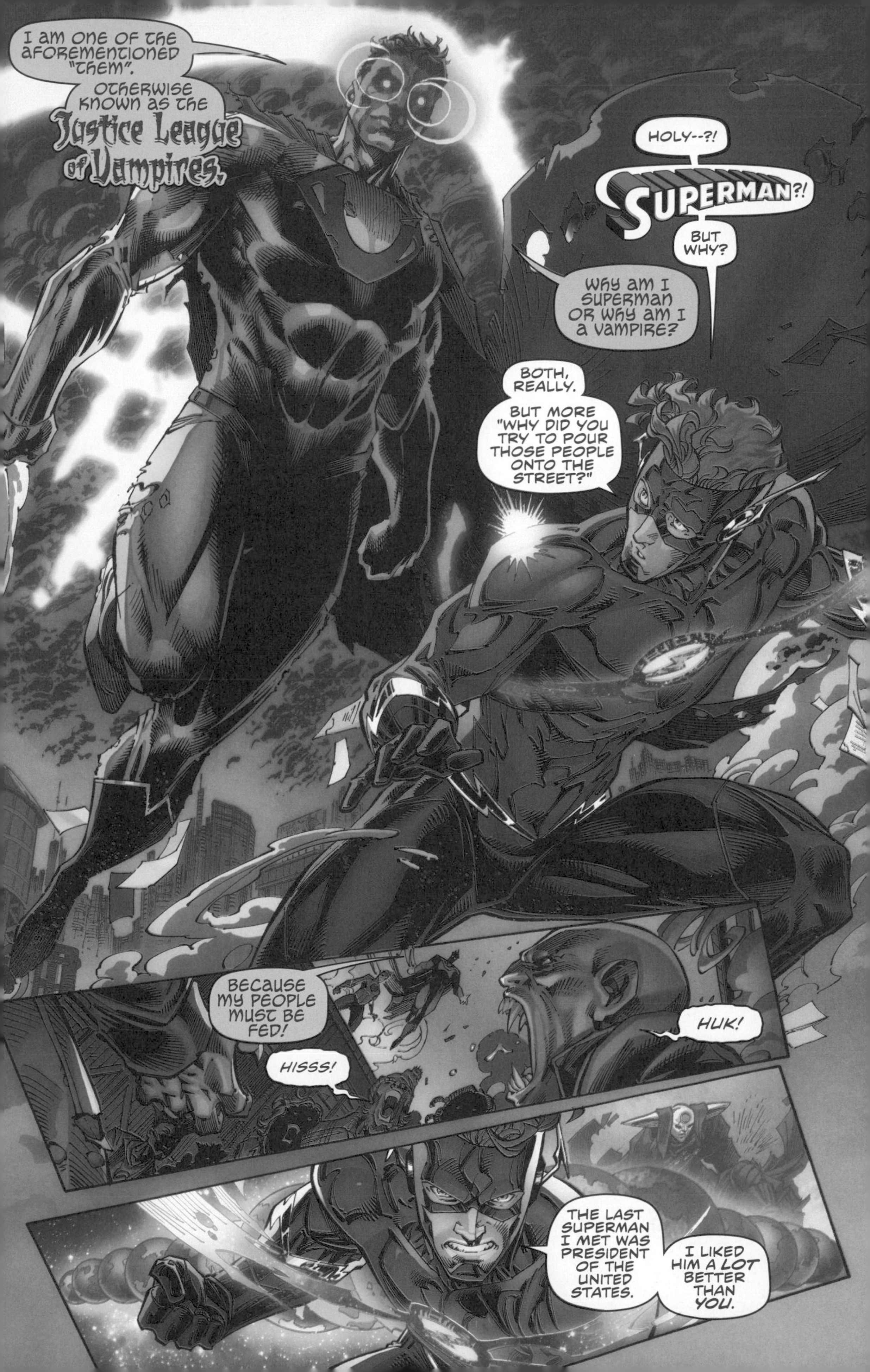
I AM ONE OF THE AFOREMENTIONED "THEM".
OTHERWISE KNOWN AS THE
Justice League of Vampires.
HOLY--?!
SUPERMAN?!
BUT WHY?
WHY AM I SUPERMAN OR WHY AM I A VAMPIRE?
BOTH, REALLY.
BUT MORE "WHY DID YOU TRY TO POUR THOSE PEOPLE ONTO THE STREET?"
BECAUSE MY PEOPLE MUST BE FED!
HISSS!
HUK!
THE LAST SUPERMAN I MET WAS PRESIDENT OF THE UNITED STATES.
I LIKED HIM A LOT BETTER THAN YOU.

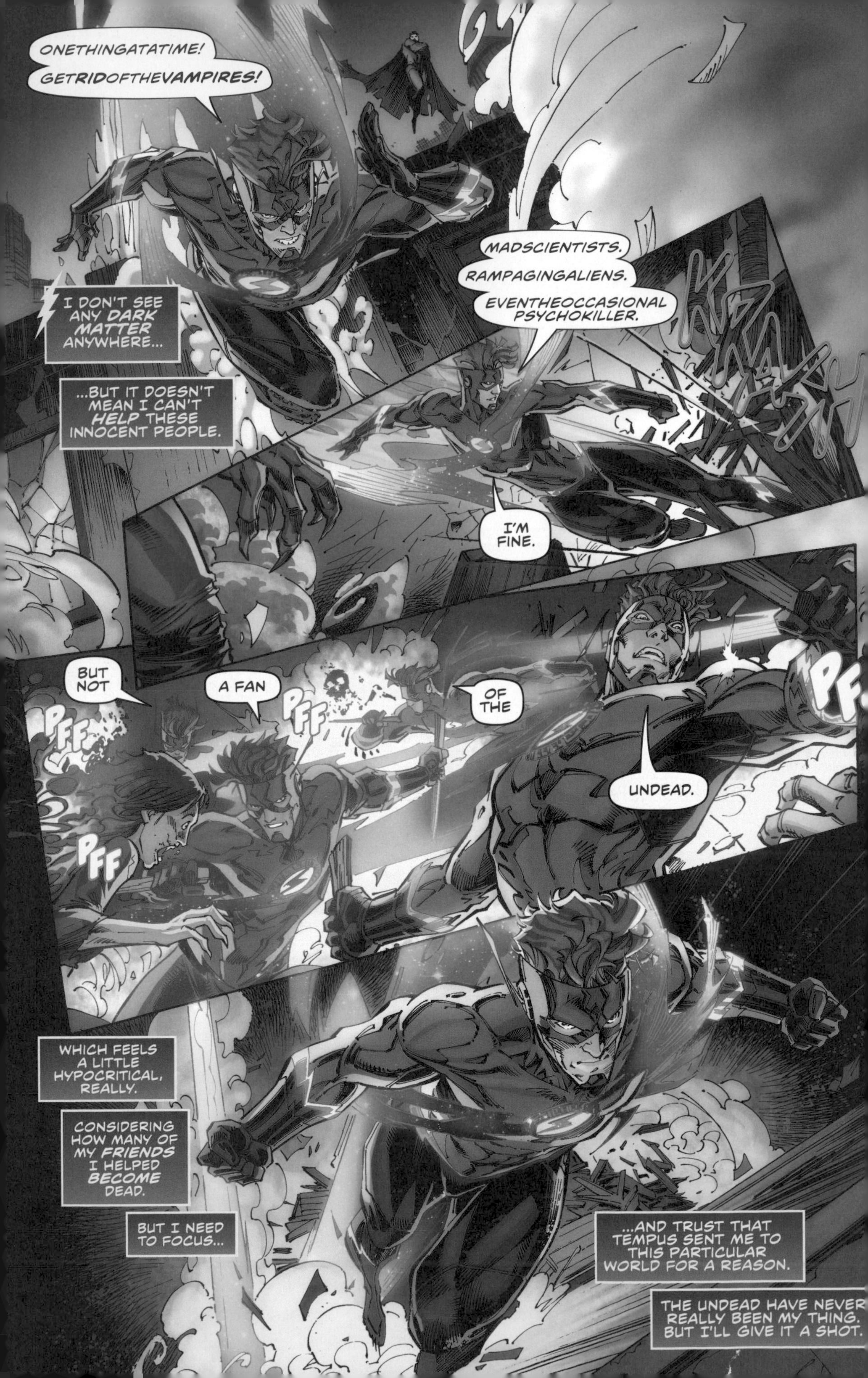

ONETHINGATATIME!
GETRIDOFTHEVAMPIRES!
I DON'T SEE ANY *DARK MATTER* ANYWHERE...
...BUT IT DOESN'T MEAN I CAN'T *HELP* THESE INNOCENT PEOPLE.
MADSCIENTISTS.
RAMPAGINGALIENS.
EVENTHEOCCASIONAL PSYCHOKILLER.
I'M FINE.
BUT NOT
A FAN
OF THE
UNDEAD.
PFF
PFF
PFF
PF
WHICH FEELS A LITTLE HYPOCRITICAL, REALLY.
CONSIDERING HOW MANY OF MY *FRIENDS* I HELPED *BECOME* DEAD.
BUT I NEED TO FOCUS...
...AND TRUST THAT TEMPUS SENT ME TO THIS PARTICULAR WORLD FOR A REASON.
THE UNDEAD HAVE NEVER REALLY BEEN MY THING. BUT I'LL GIVE IT A SHOT.

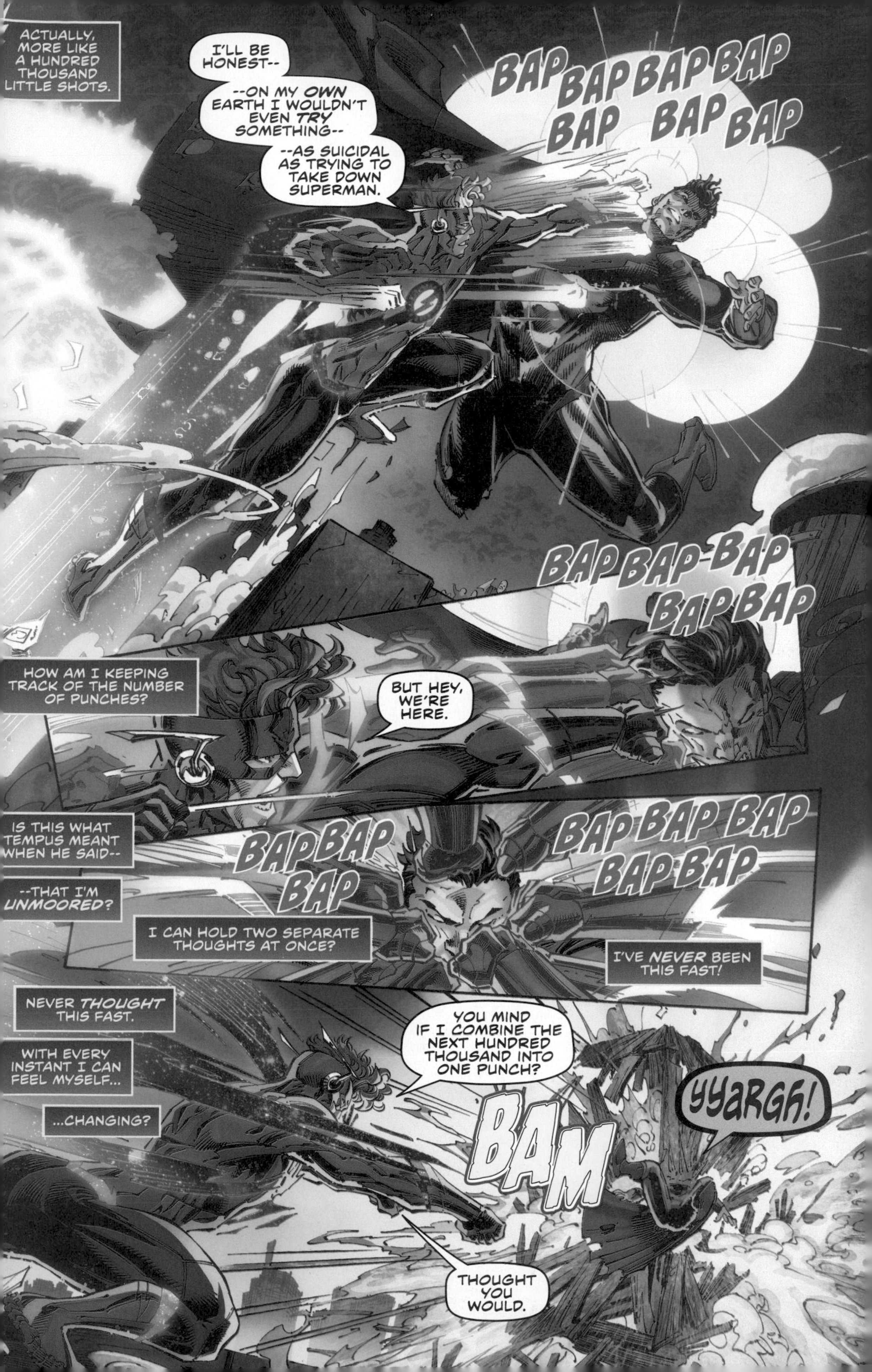
ACTUALLY, MORE LIKE A HUNDRED THOUSAND LITTLE SHOTS.
I'LL BE HONEST--
--ON MY *OWN* EARTH I WOULDN'T EVEN *TRY* SOMETHING--
--AS SUICIDAL AS TRYING TO TAKE DOWN SUPERMAN.
BAP BAP BAP BAP BAP BAP BAP BAP
BAP BAP-BAP BAP BAP
HOW AM I KEEPING TRACK OF THE NUMBER OF PUNCHES?
BUT HEY, WE'RE HERE.
IS THIS WHAT TEMPUS MEANT WHEN HE SAID--
--THAT I'M *UNMOORED*?
BAP BAP BAP
BAP BAP BAP BAP BAP
I CAN HOLD TWO SEPARATE THOUGHTS AT ONCE?
I'VE *NEVER* BEEN THIS FAST!
NEVER *THOUGHT* THIS FAST.
WITH EVERY INSTANT I CAN FEEL MYSELF...
...CHANGING?
YOU MIND IF I COMBINE THE NEXT HUNDRED THOUSAND INTO ONE PUNCH?
BAM
YYARGH!
THOUGHT YOU WOULD.

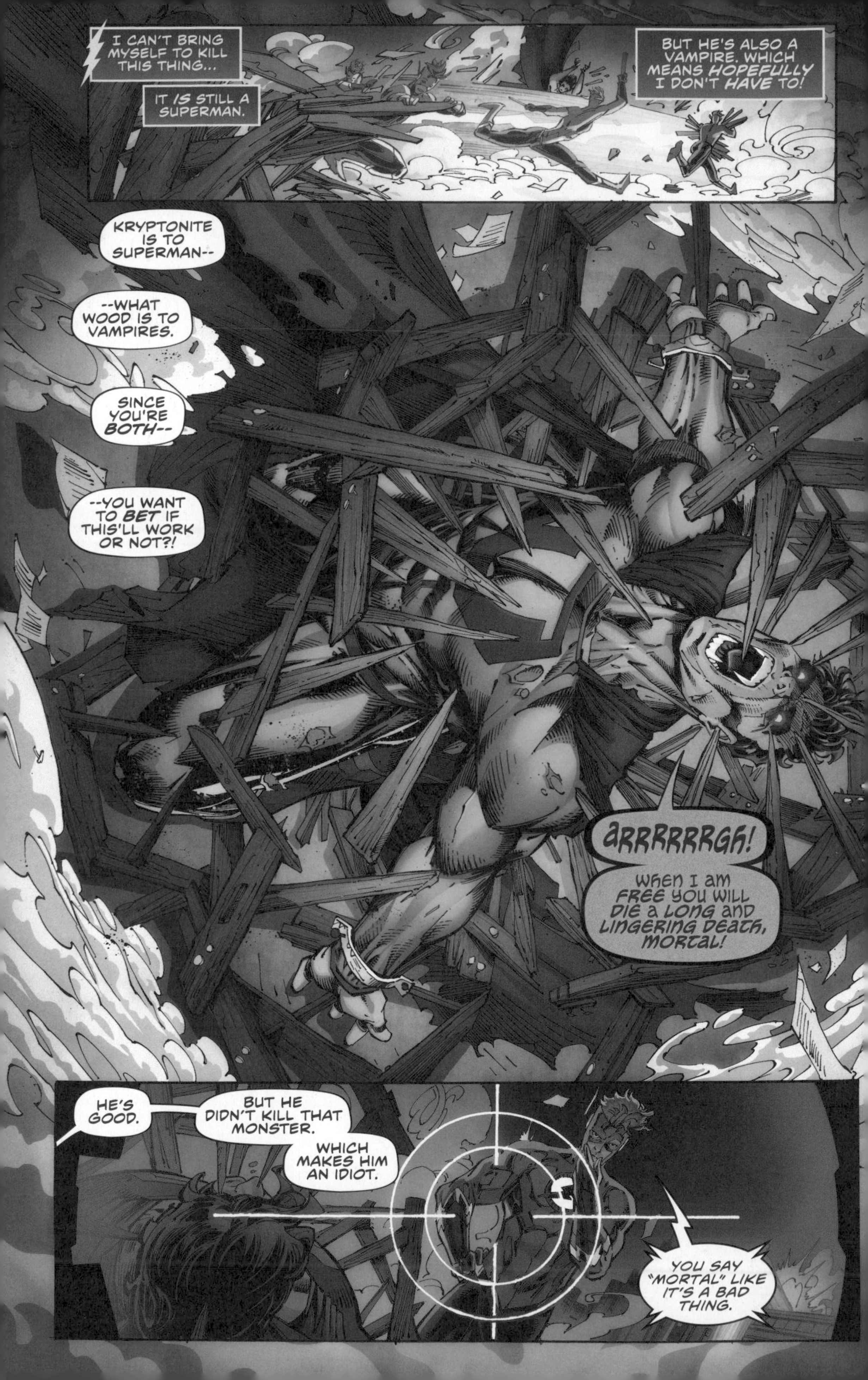
I CAN'T BRING MYSELF TO KILL THIS THING...
IT IS STILL A SUPERMAN.
BUT HE'S ALSO A VAMPIRE. WHICH MEANS HOPEFULLY I DON'T HAVE TO!
KRYPTONITE IS TO SUPERMAN--
--WHAT WOOD IS TO VAMPIRES.
SINCE YOU'RE BOTH--
--YOU WANT TO BET IF THIS'LL WORK OR NOT?!
ARRRRRRGH!
WHEN I AM FREE YOU WILL DIE A LONG AND LINGERING DEATH, MORTAL!
HE'S GOOD.
BUT HE DIDN'T KILL THAT MONSTER.
WHICH MAKES HIM AN IDIOT.
YOU SAY "MORTAL" LIKE IT'S A BAD THING.

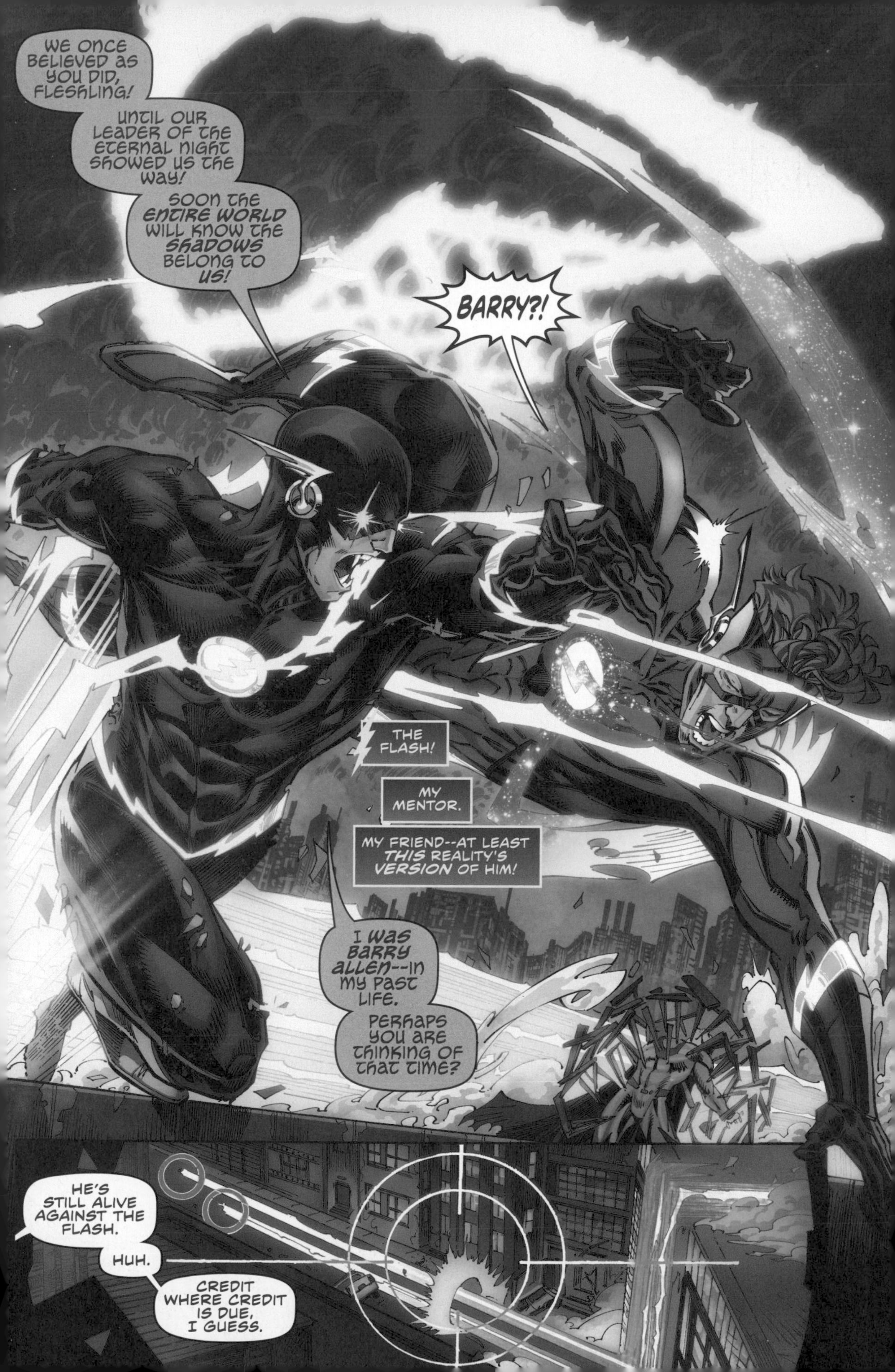

WE ONCE BELIEVED AS YOU DID, FLESHLING!
UNTIL OUR LEADER OF THE ETERNAL NIGHT SHOWED US THE WAY!
SOON THE *ENTIRE WORLD* WILL KNOW THE *SHADOWS* BELONG TO *US!*
BARRY?!
THE FLASH!
MY MENTOR.
MY FRIEND--AT LEAST *THIS* REALITY'S *VERSION* OF HIM!
I *WAS* BARRY ALLEN--IN MY PAST LIFE.
PERHAPS YOU ARE THINKING OF THAT TIME?
HE'S STILL ALIVE AGAINST THE FLASH.
HUH.
CREDIT WHERE CREDIT IS DUE, I GUESS.

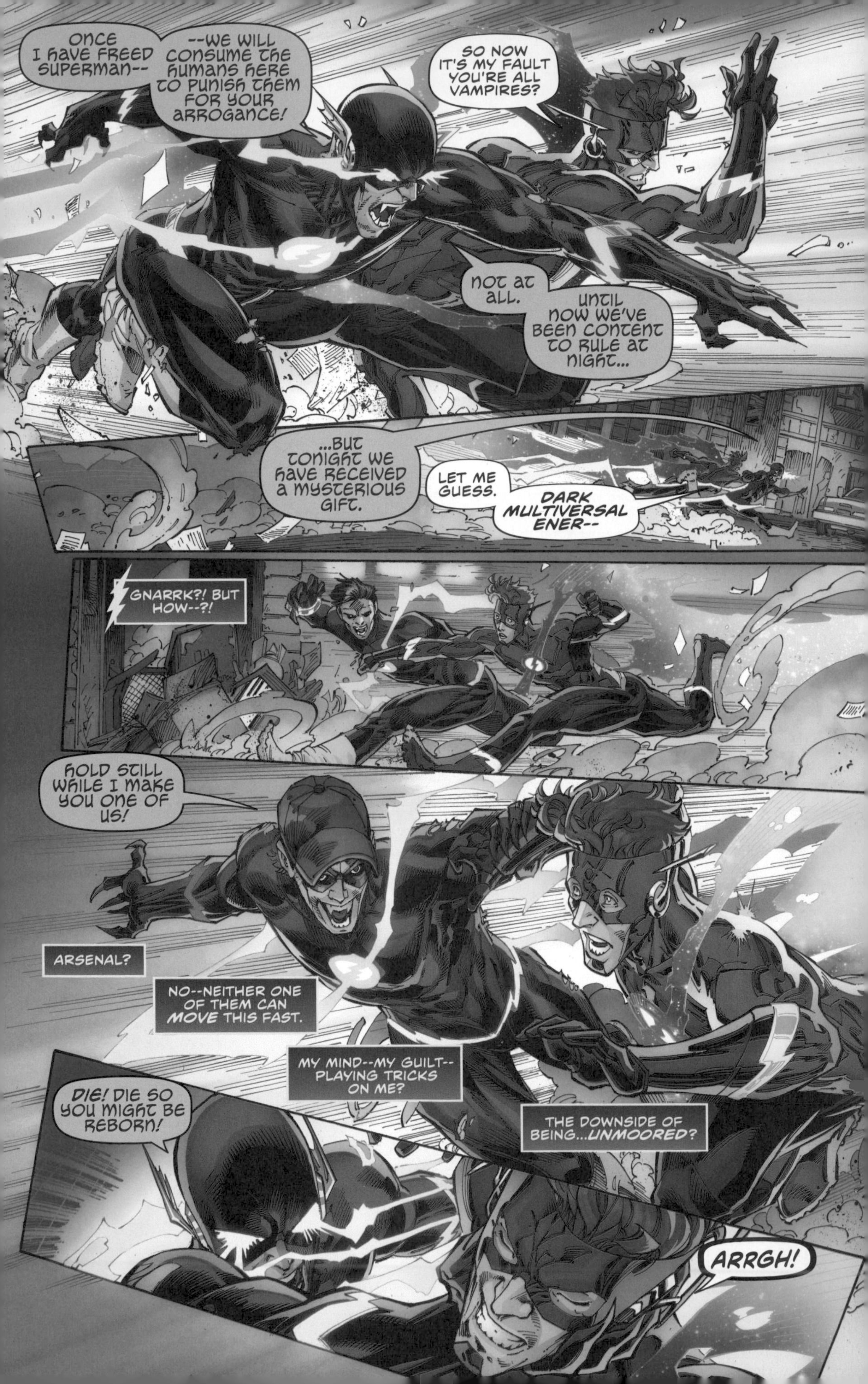
ONCE I HAVE FREED SUPERMAN--
--WE WILL CONSUME THE HUMANS HERE TO PUNISH THEM FOR YOUR ARROGANCE!
SO NOW IT'S MY FAULT YOU'RE ALL VAMPIRES?
NOT AT ALL.
UNTIL NOW WE'VE BEEN CONTENT TO RULE AT NIGHT...
...BUT TONIGHT WE HAVE RECEIVED A MYSTERIOUS GIFT.
LET ME GUESS.
DARK MULTIVERSAL ENER--
GNARRK?! BUT HOW--?!
HOLD STILL WHILE I MAKE YOU ONE OF US!
ARSENAL?
NO--NEITHER ONE OF THEM CAN MOVE THIS FAST.
MY MIND--MY GUILT--PLAYING TRICKS ON ME?
DIE! DIE SO YOU MIGHT BE REBORN!
THE DOWNSIDE OF BEING...UNMOORED?
ARRGH!

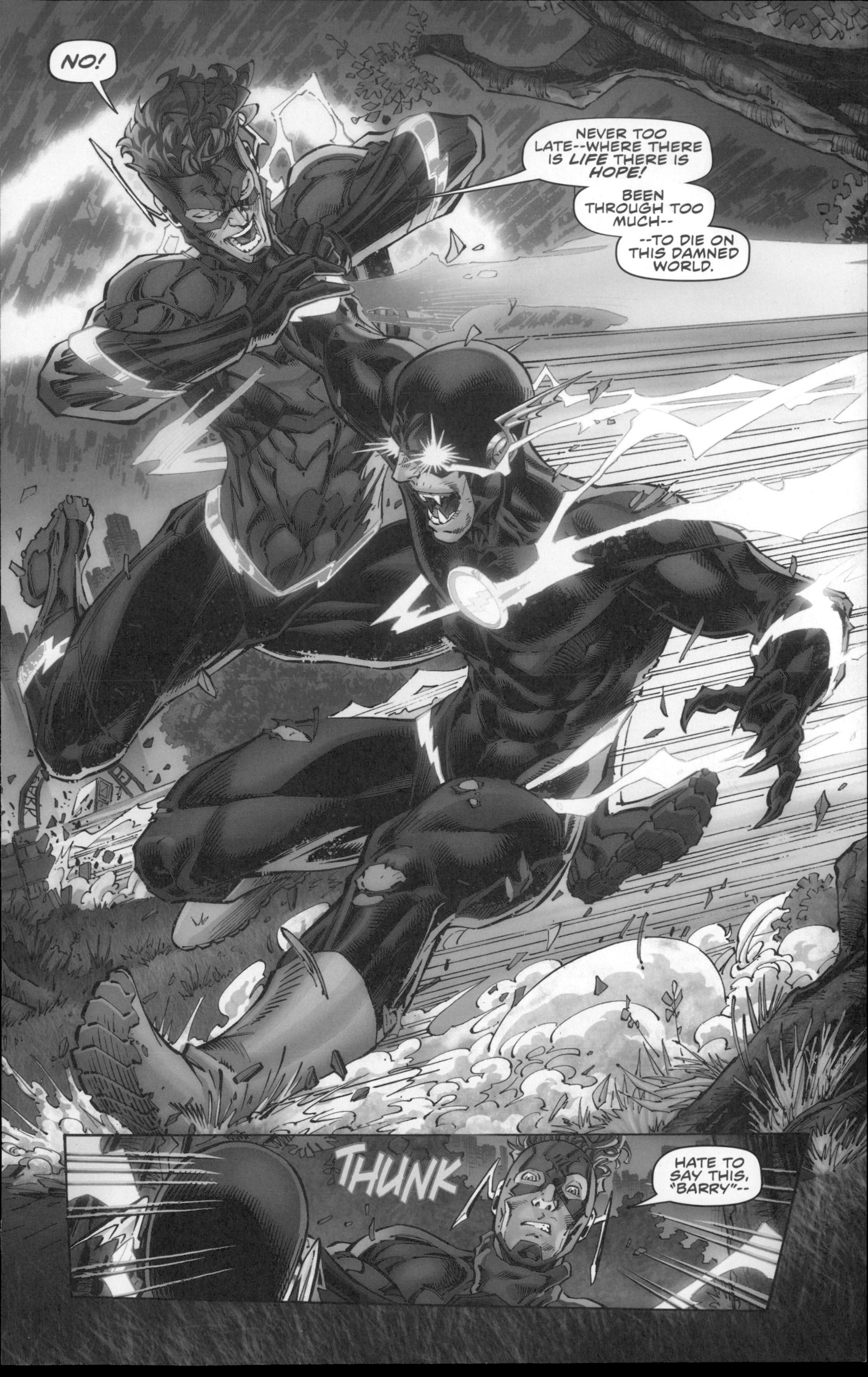
NO!
NEVER TOO LATE--WHERE THERE IS *LIFE* THERE IS *HOPE!*
BEEN THROUGH TOO MUCH--
--TO DIE ON THIS DAMNED WORLD.
THUNK
HATE TO SAY THIS, "BARRY"--

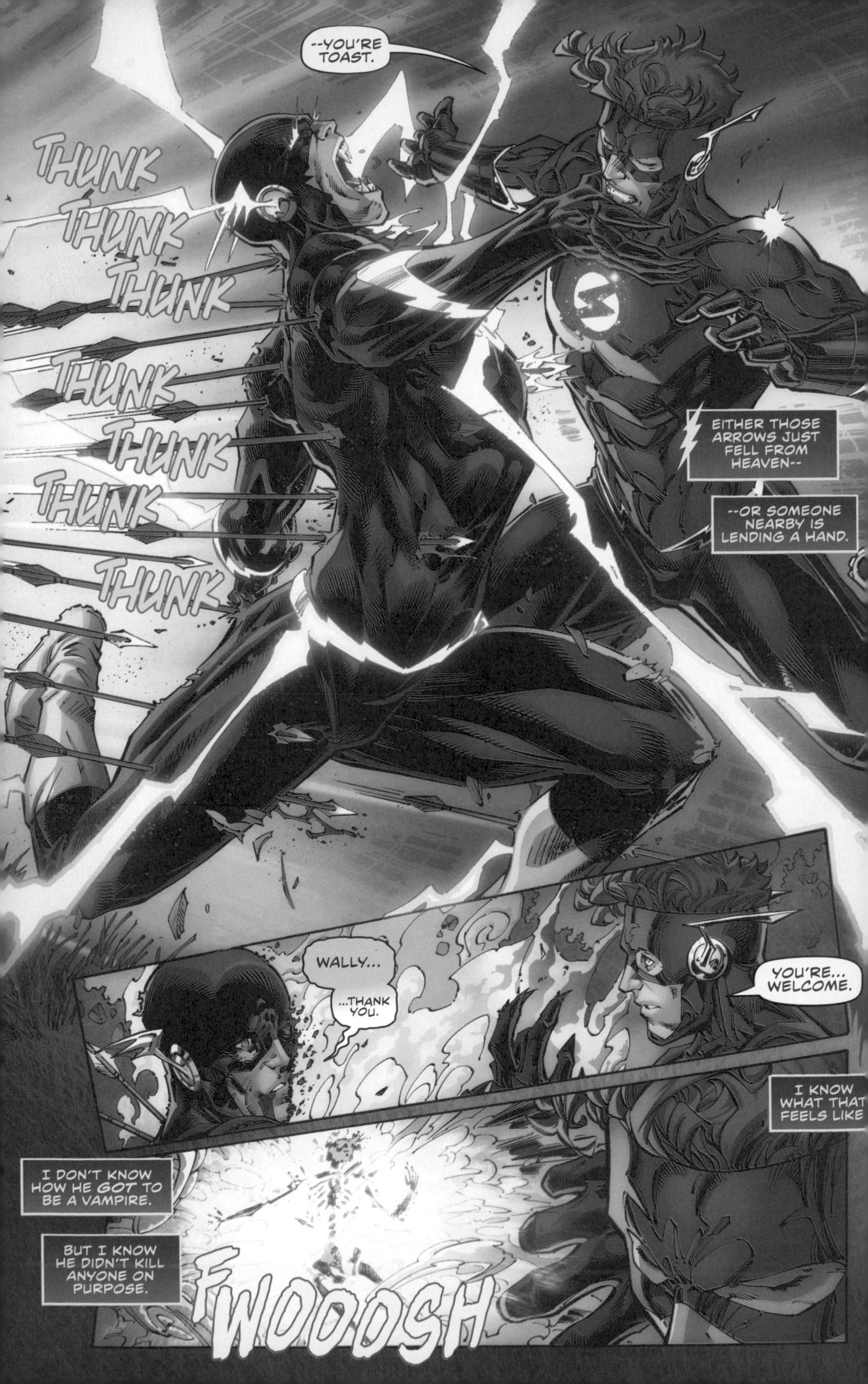
--YOU'RE TOAST.
THUNK
THUNK
THUNK
THUNK
THUNK
THUNK
THUNK
EITHER THOSE ARROWS JUST FELL FROM HEAVEN--
--OR SOMEONE NEARBY IS LENDING A HAND.
WALLY...
...THANK YOU.
YOU'RE... WELCOME.
I KNOW WHAT THAT FEELS LIKE
I DON'T KNOW HOW HE GOT TO BE A VAMPIRE.
BUT I KNOW HE DIDN'T KILL ANYONE ON PURPOSE.
FWOOOSH

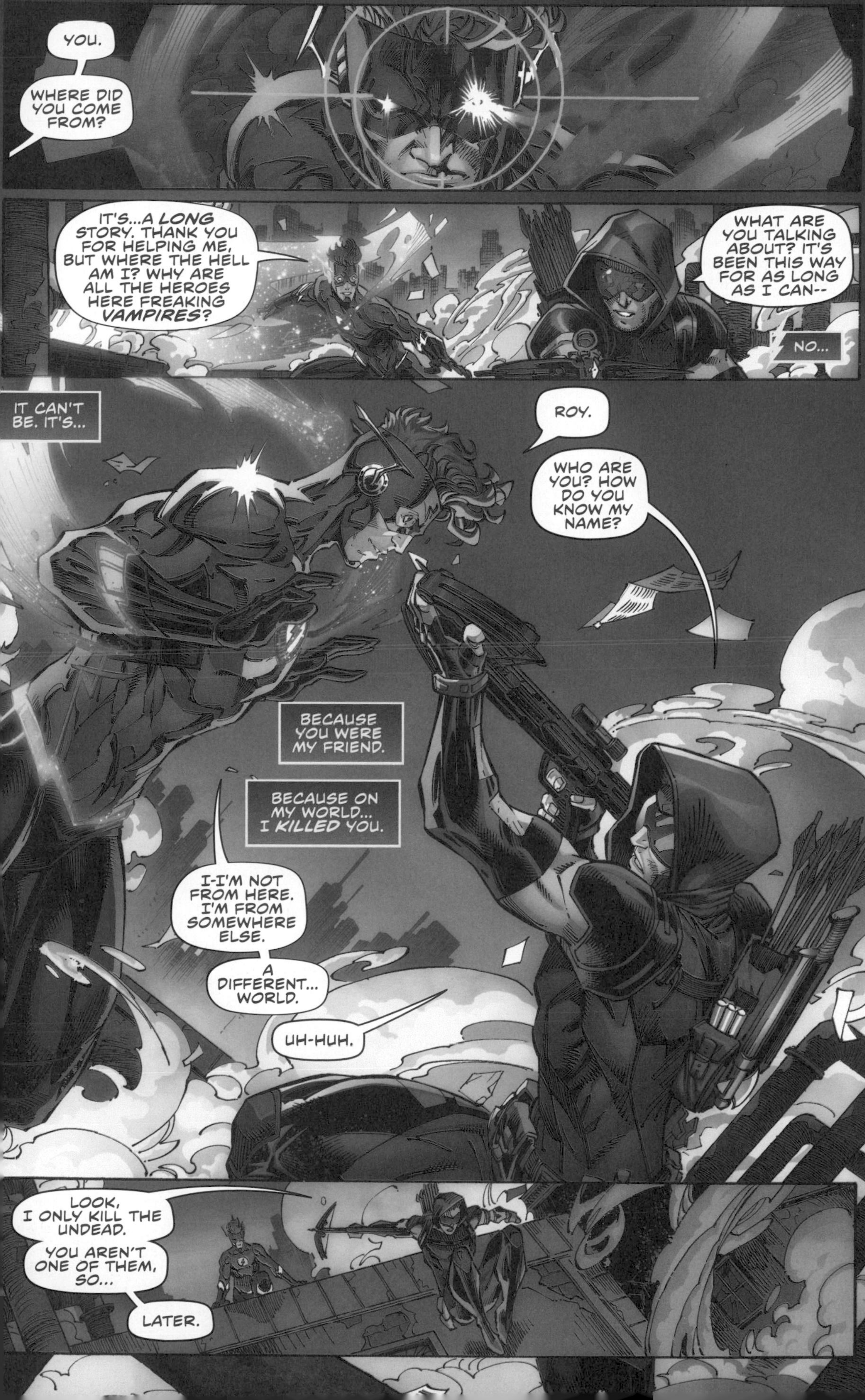
YOU.
WHERE DID YOU COME FROM?
IT'S...A LONG STORY. THANK YOU FOR HELPING ME, BUT WHERE THE HELL AM I? WHY ARE ALL THE HEROES HERE FREAKING VAMPIRES?
WHAT ARE YOU TALKING ABOUT? IT'S BEEN THIS WAY FOR AS LONG AS I CAN--
NO...
IT CAN'T BE. IT'S...
ROY.
WHO ARE YOU? HOW DO YOU KNOW MY NAME?
BECAUSE YOU WERE MY FRIEND.
BECAUSE ON MY WORLD... I KILLED YOU.
I-I'M NOT FROM HERE. I'M FROM SOMEWHERE ELSE.
A DIFFERENT... WORLD.
UH-HUH.
LOOK, I ONLY KILL THE UNDEAD.
YOU AREN'T ONE OF THEM, SO...
LATER.

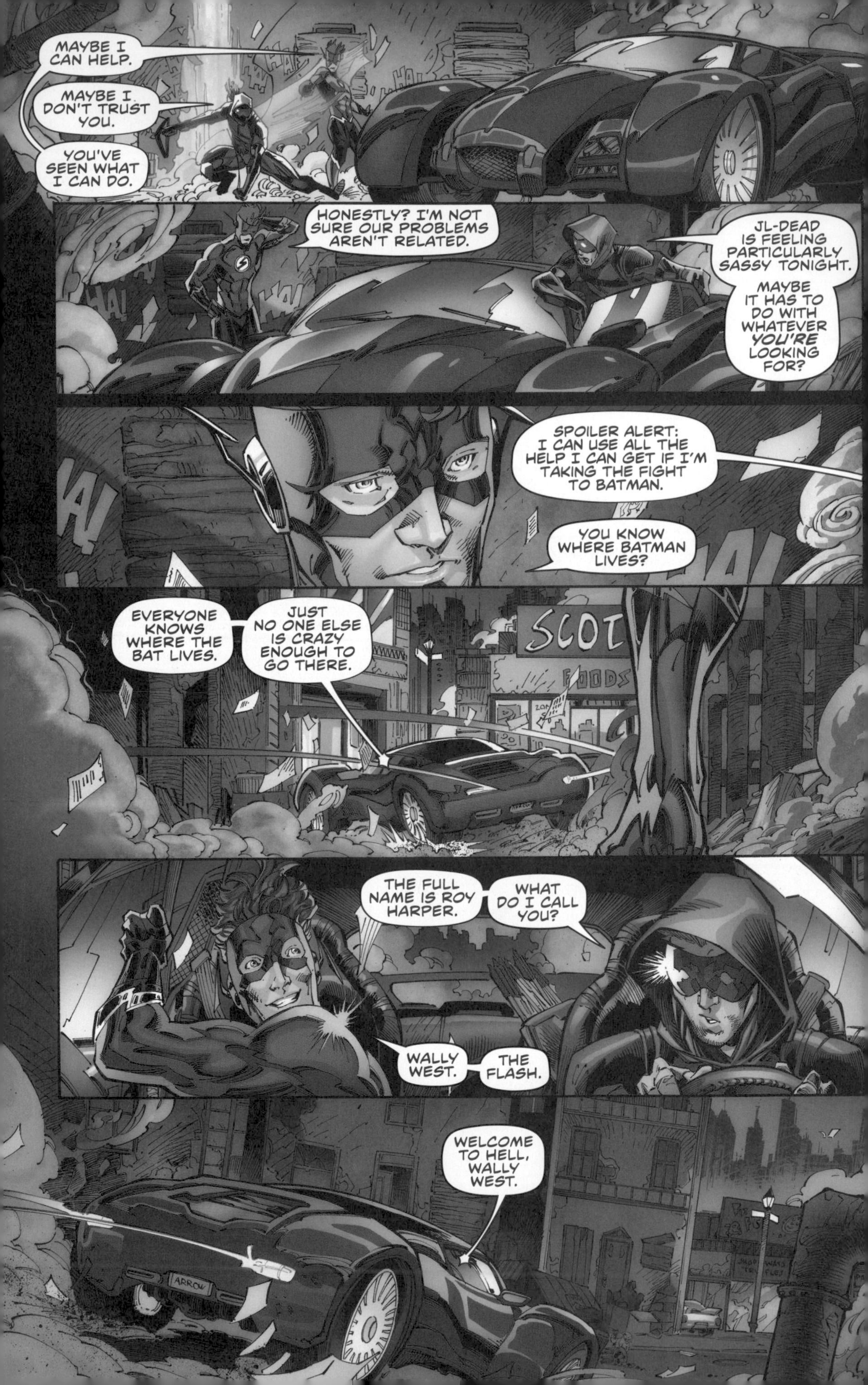
MAYBE I CAN HELP.
MAYBE I DON'T TRUST YOU.
YOU'VE SEEN WHAT I CAN DO.
HONESTLY? I'M NOT SURE OUR PROBLEMS AREN'T RELATED.
JL-DEAD IS FEELING PARTICULARLY SASSY TONIGHT.
MAYBE IT HAS TO DO WITH WHATEVER *YOU'RE* LOOKING FOR?
SPOILER ALERT: I CAN USE ALL THE HELP I CAN GET IF I'M TAKING THE FIGHT TO BATMAN.
YOU KNOW WHERE BATMAN LIVES?
EVERYONE KNOWS WHERE THE BAT LIVES.
JUST NO ONE ELSE IS CRAZY ENOUGH TO GO THERE.
SCOT
FOODS
THE FULL NAME IS ROY HARPER.
WHAT DO I CALL YOU?
WALLY WEST.
THE FLASH.
WELCOME TO HELL, WALLY WEST.
ARROW

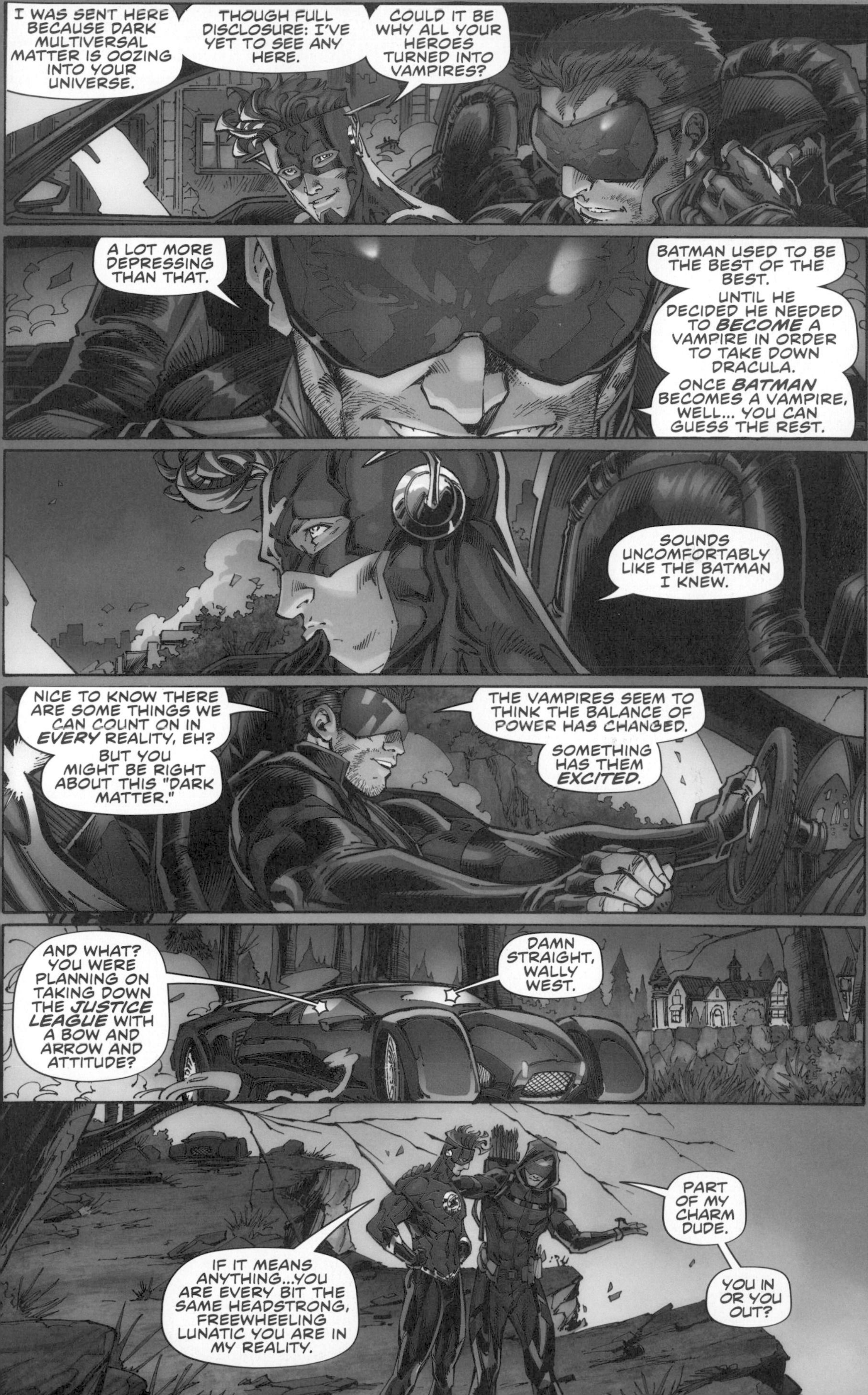
I WAS SENT HERE BECAUSE DARK MULTIVERSAL MATTER IS OOZING INTO YOUR UNIVERSE.
THOUGH FULL DISCLOSURE: I'VE YET TO SEE ANY HERE.
COULD IT BE WHY ALL YOUR HEROES TURNED INTO VAMPIRES?
A LOT MORE DEPRESSING THAN THAT.
BATMAN USED TO BE THE BEST OF THE BEST.
UNTIL HE DECIDED HE NEEDED TO BECOME A VAMPIRE IN ORDER TO TAKE DOWN DRACULA.
ONCE BATMAN BECOMES A VAMPIRE, WELL... YOU CAN GUESS THE REST.
SOUNDS UNCOMFORTABLY LIKE THE BATMAN I KNEW.
NICE TO KNOW THERE ARE SOME THINGS WE CAN COUNT ON IN EVERY REALITY, EH?
BUT YOU MIGHT BE RIGHT ABOUT THIS "DARK MATTER."
THE VAMPIRES SEEM TO THINK THE BALANCE OF POWER HAS CHANGED.
SOMETHING HAS THEM EXCITED.
AND WHAT? YOU WERE PLANNING ON TAKING DOWN THE JUSTICE LEAGUE WITH A BOW AND ARROW AND ATTITUDE?
DAMN STRAIGHT, WALLY WEST.
PART OF MY CHARM DUDE.
YOU IN OR YOU OUT?
IF IT MEANS ANYTHING...YOU ARE EVERY BIT THE SAME HEADSTRONG, FREEWHEELING LUNATIC YOU ARE IN MY REALITY.

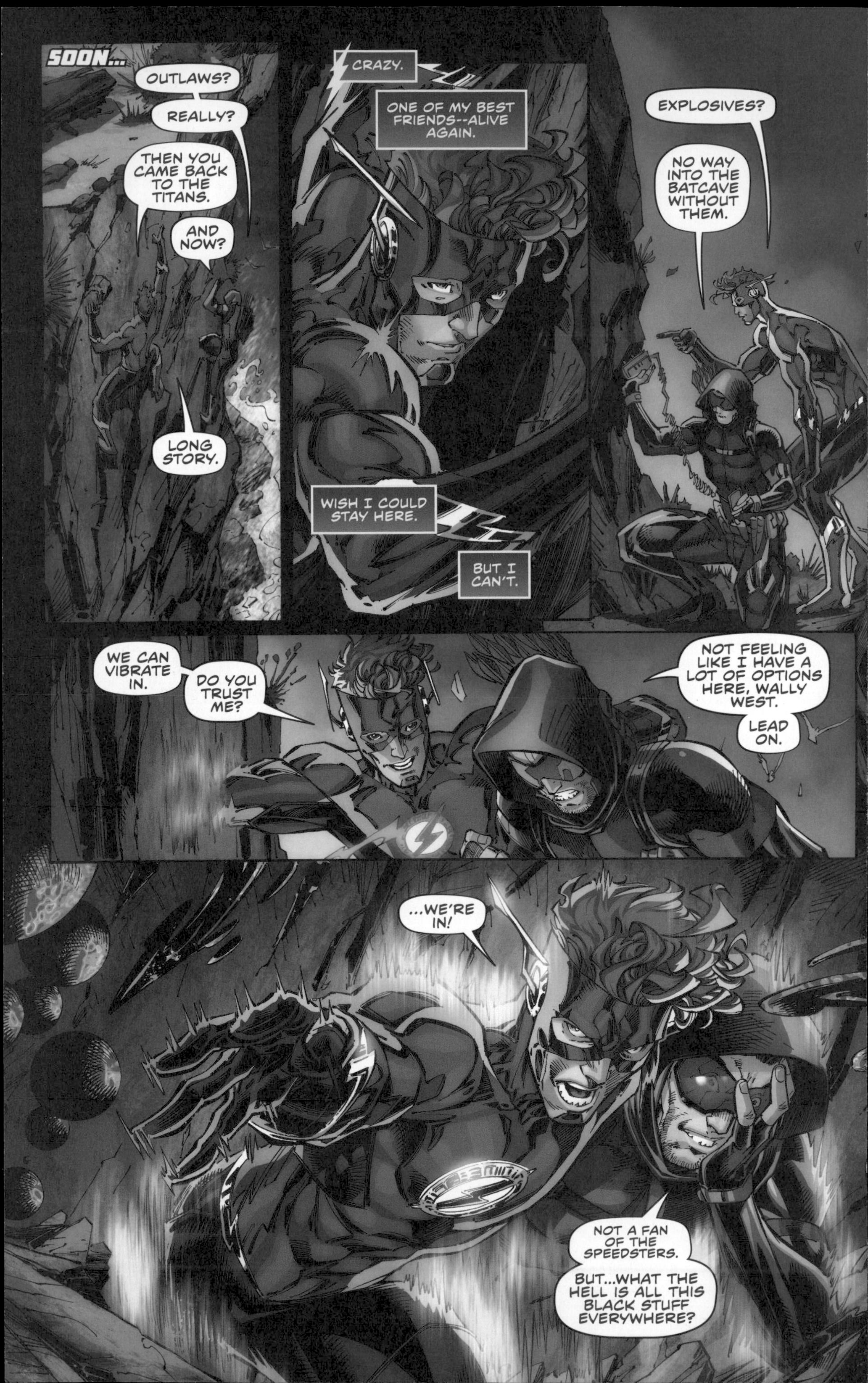
SOON...
OUTLAWS?
REALLY?
THEN YOU CAME BACK TO THE TITANS.
AND NOW?
LONG STORY.
CRAZY.
ONE OF MY BEST FRIENDS--ALIVE AGAIN.
WISH I COULD STAY HERE.
BUT I CAN'T.
EXPLOSIVES?
NO WAY INTO THE BATCAVE WITHOUT THEM.
WE CAN VIBRATE IN.
DO YOU TRUST ME?
NOT FEELING LIKE I HAVE A LOT OF OPTIONS HERE, WALLY WEST.
LEAD ON.
...WE'RE IN!
NOT A FAN OF THE SPEEDSTERS.
BUT...WHAT THE HELL IS ALL THIS BLACK STUFF EVERYWHERE?

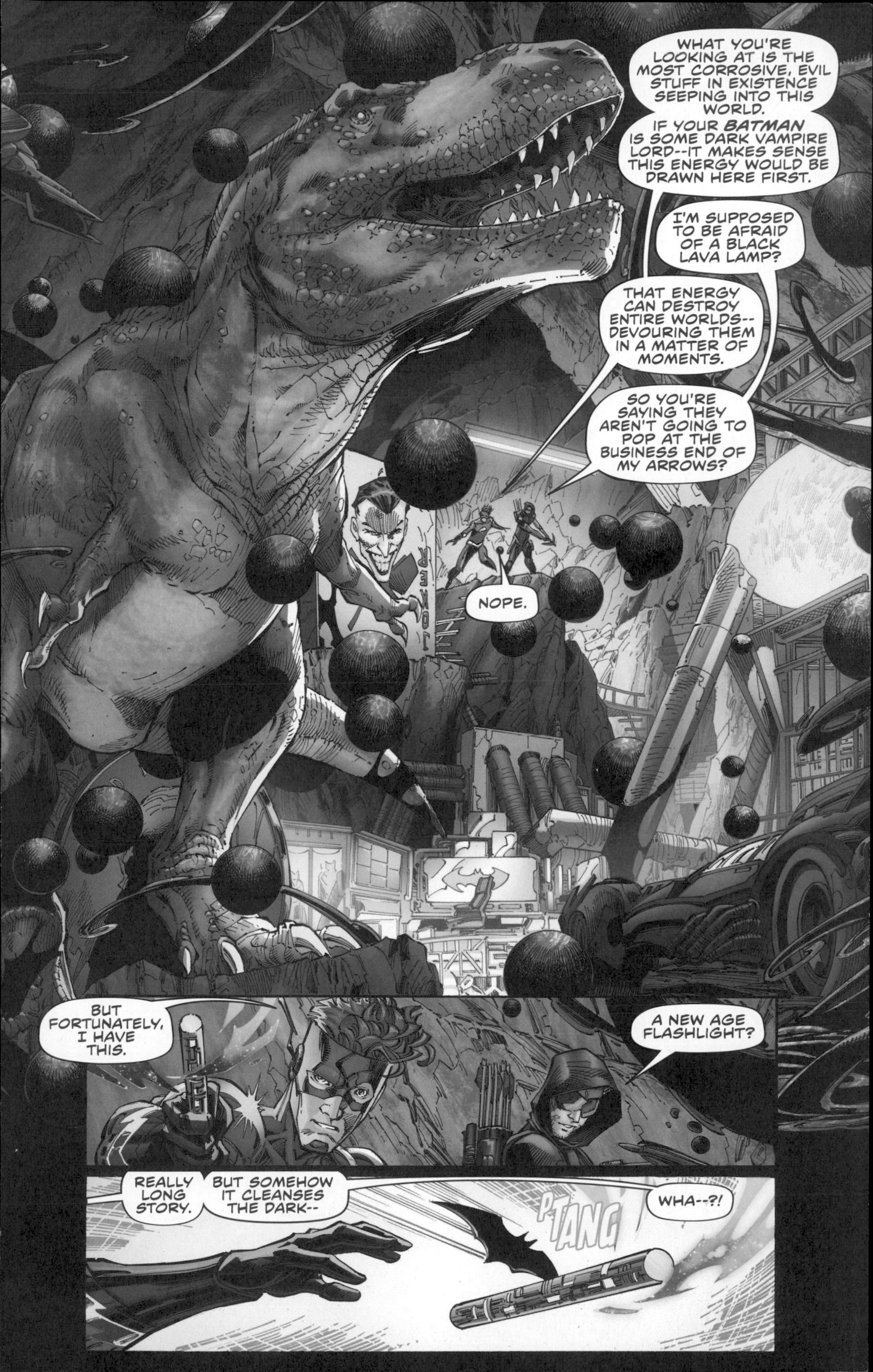
WHAT YOU'RE LOOKING AT IS THE MOST CORROSIVE, EVIL STUFF IN EXISTENCE SEEPING INTO THIS WORLD.
IF YOUR BATMAN IS SOME DARK VAMPIRE LORD--IT MAKES SENSE THIS ENERGY WOULD BE DRAWN HERE FIRST.
I'M SUPPOSED TO BE AFRAID OF A BLACK LAVA LAMP?
THAT ENERGY CAN DESTROY ENTIRE WORLDS--DEVOURING THEM IN A MATTER OF MOMENTS.
SO YOU'RE SAYING THEY AREN'T GOING TO POP AT THE BUSINESS END OF MY ARROWS?
NOPE.
BUT FORTUNATELY, I HAVE THIS.
A NEW AGE FLASHLIGHT?
REALLY LONG STORY.
BUT SOMEHOW IT CLEANSES THE DARK--
PTANG
WHA--?!

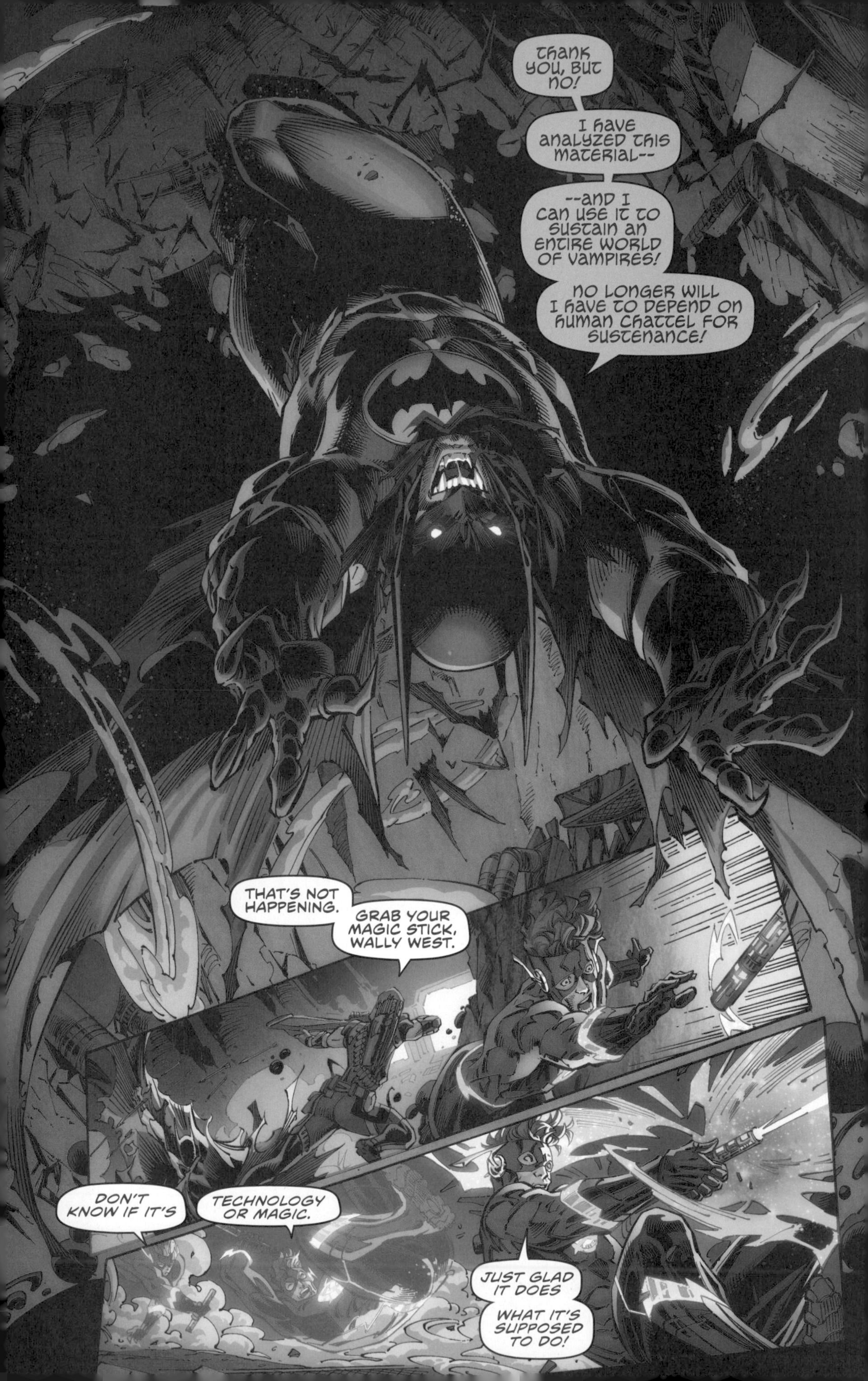
THANK YOU, BUT NO!
I HAVE ANALYZED THIS MATERIAL--
--AND I CAN USE IT TO SUSTAIN AN ENTIRE WORLD OF VAMPIRES!
NO LONGER WILL I HAVE TO DEPEND ON HUMAN CHATTEL FOR SUSTENANCE!
THAT'S NOT HAPPENING.
GRAB YOUR MAGIC STICK, WALLY WEST.
DON'T KNOW IF IT'S
TECHNOLOGY OR MAGIC.
JUST GLAD IT DOES
WHAT IT'S SUPPOSED TO DO!

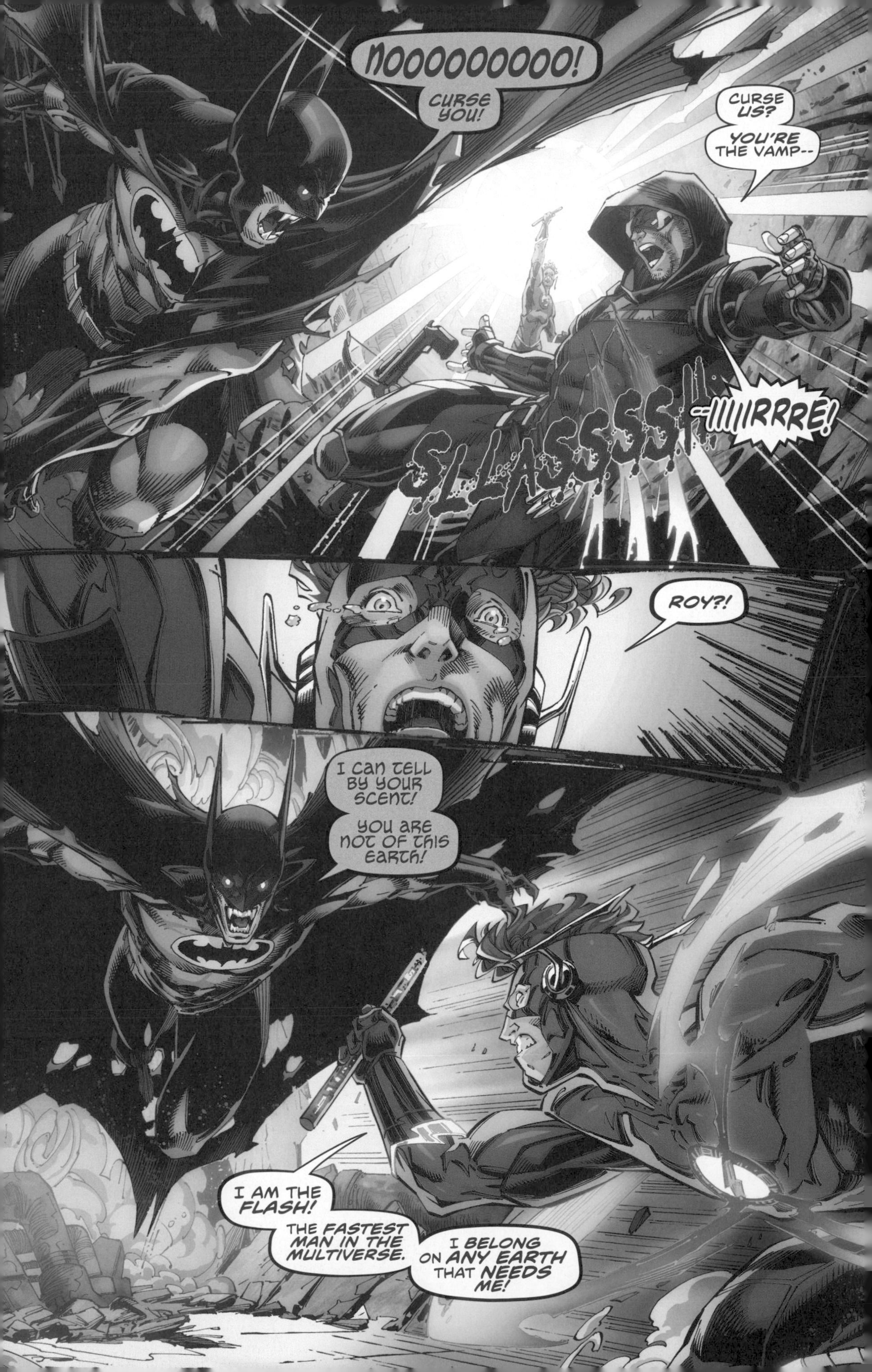
NOOOOOOOOO!
CURSE YOU!
CURSE US?
YOU'RE THE VAMP--
SLLASSSSSH-IIIIIIRRRE!
ROY?!
I CAN TELL BY YOUR SCENT!
YOU ARE NOT OF THIS EARTH!
I AM THE FLASH!
THE FASTEST MAN IN THE MULTIVERSE.
I BELONG ON ANY EARTH THAT NEEDS ME!

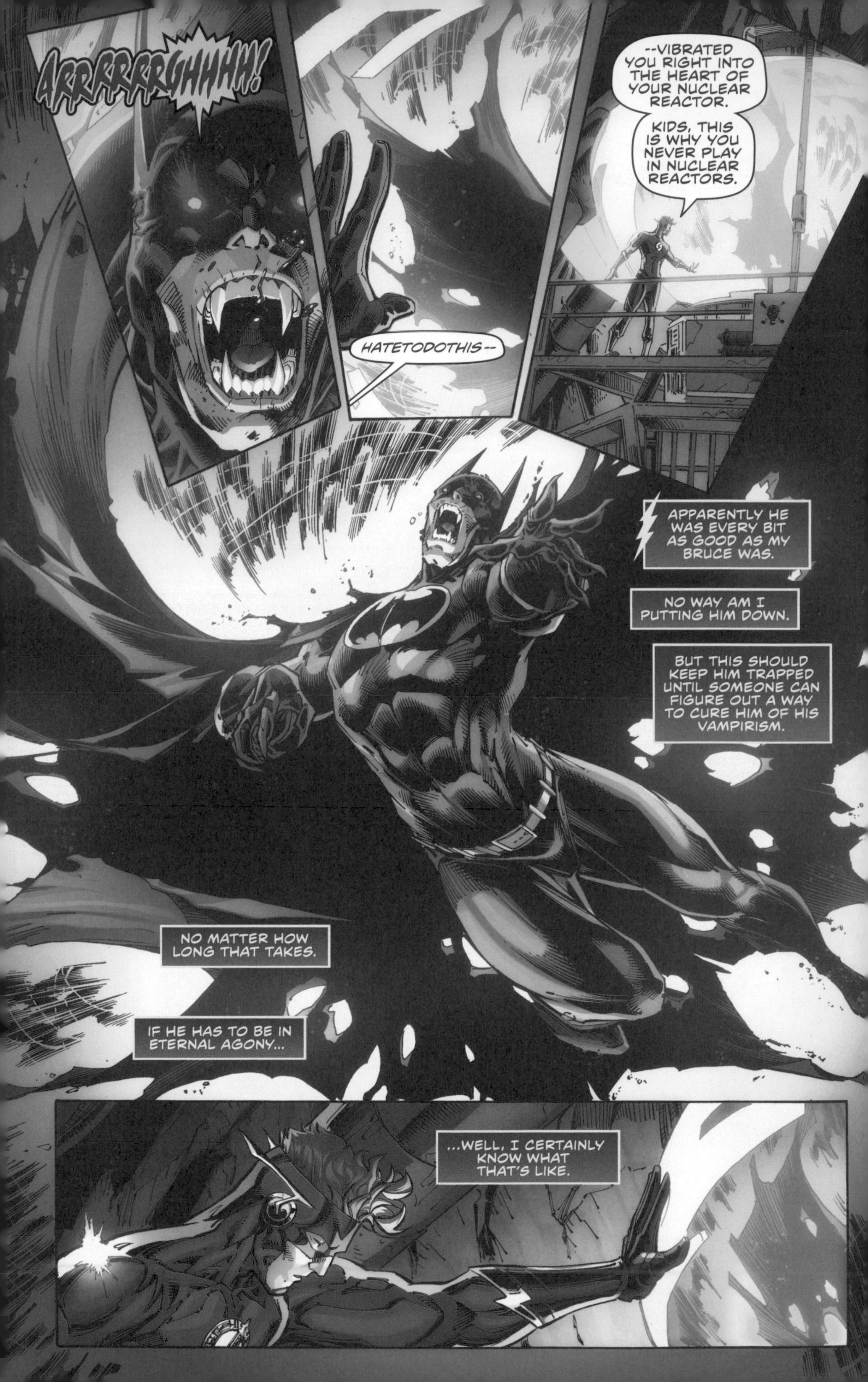
ARRRRRRGHHHH!
HATETODOTHIS--
--VIBRATED YOU RIGHT INTO THE HEART OF YOUR NUCLEAR REACTOR.
KIDS, THIS IS WHY YOU NEVER PLAY IN NUCLEAR REACTORS.
APPARENTLY HE WAS EVERY BIT AS GOOD AS MY BRUCE WAS.
NO WAY AM I PUTTING HIM DOWN.
BUT THIS SHOULD KEEP HIM TRAPPED UNTIL SOMEONE CAN FIGURE OUT A WAY TO CURE HIM OF HIS VAMPIRISM.
NO MATTER HOW LONG THAT TAKES.
IF HE HAS TO BE IN ETERNAL AGONY...
...WELL, I CERTAINLY KNOW WHAT THAT'S LIKE.

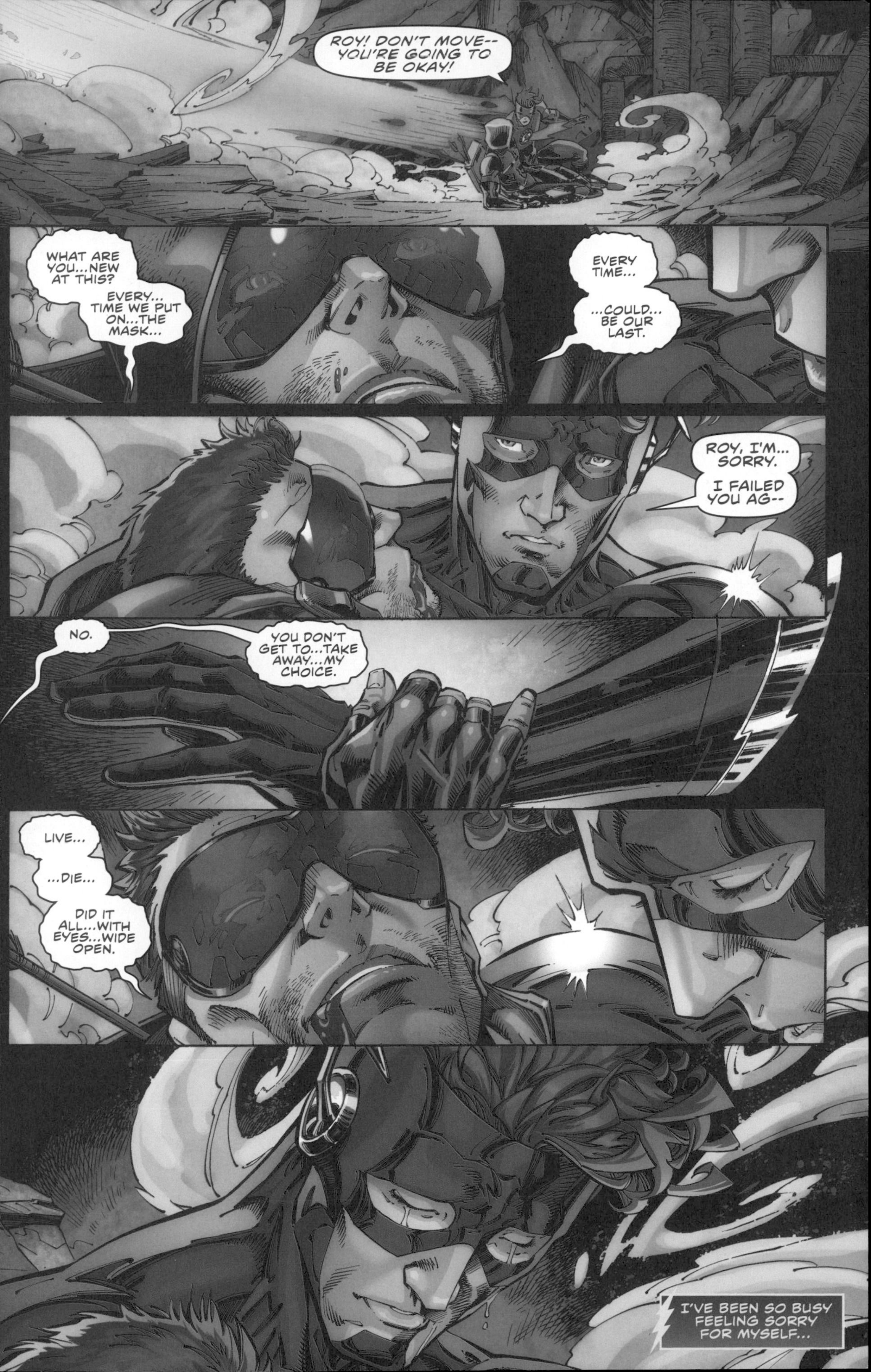

ROY! DON'T MOVE-- YOU'RE GOING TO BE OKAY!
WHAT ARE YOU...NEW AT THIS?
EVERY... TIME WE PUT ON...THE MASK...
EVERY TIME...
...COULD... BE OUR LAST.
ROY, I'M... SORRY.
I FAILED YOU AG--
NO.
YOU DON'T GET TO...TAKE AWAY...MY CHOICE.
LIVE...
...DIE...
DID IT ALL...WITH EYES...WIDE OPEN.
I'VE BEEN SO BUSY FEELING SORRY FOR MYSELF...

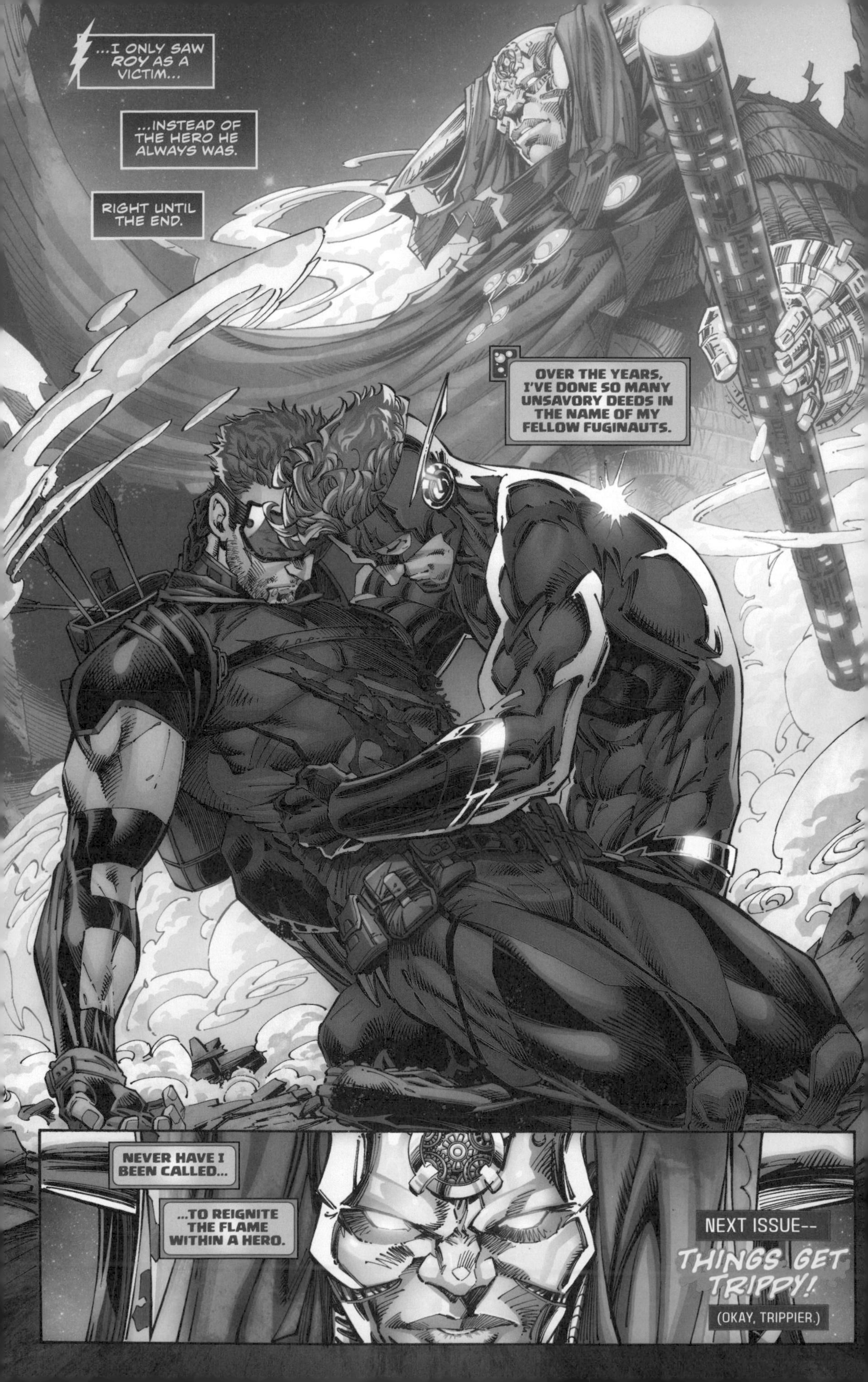

...I ONLY SAW ROY AS A VICTIM...
...INSTEAD OF THE HERO HE ALWAYS WAS.
RIGHT UNTIL THE END.
OVER THE YEARS, I'VE DONE SO MANY UNSAVORY DEEDS IN THE NAME OF MY FELLOW FUGINAUTS.
NEVER HAVE I BEEN CALLED...
...TO REIGNITE THE FLAME WITHIN A HERO.
NEXT ISSUE--
THINGS GET TRIPPY!
(OKAY, TRIPPIER.)

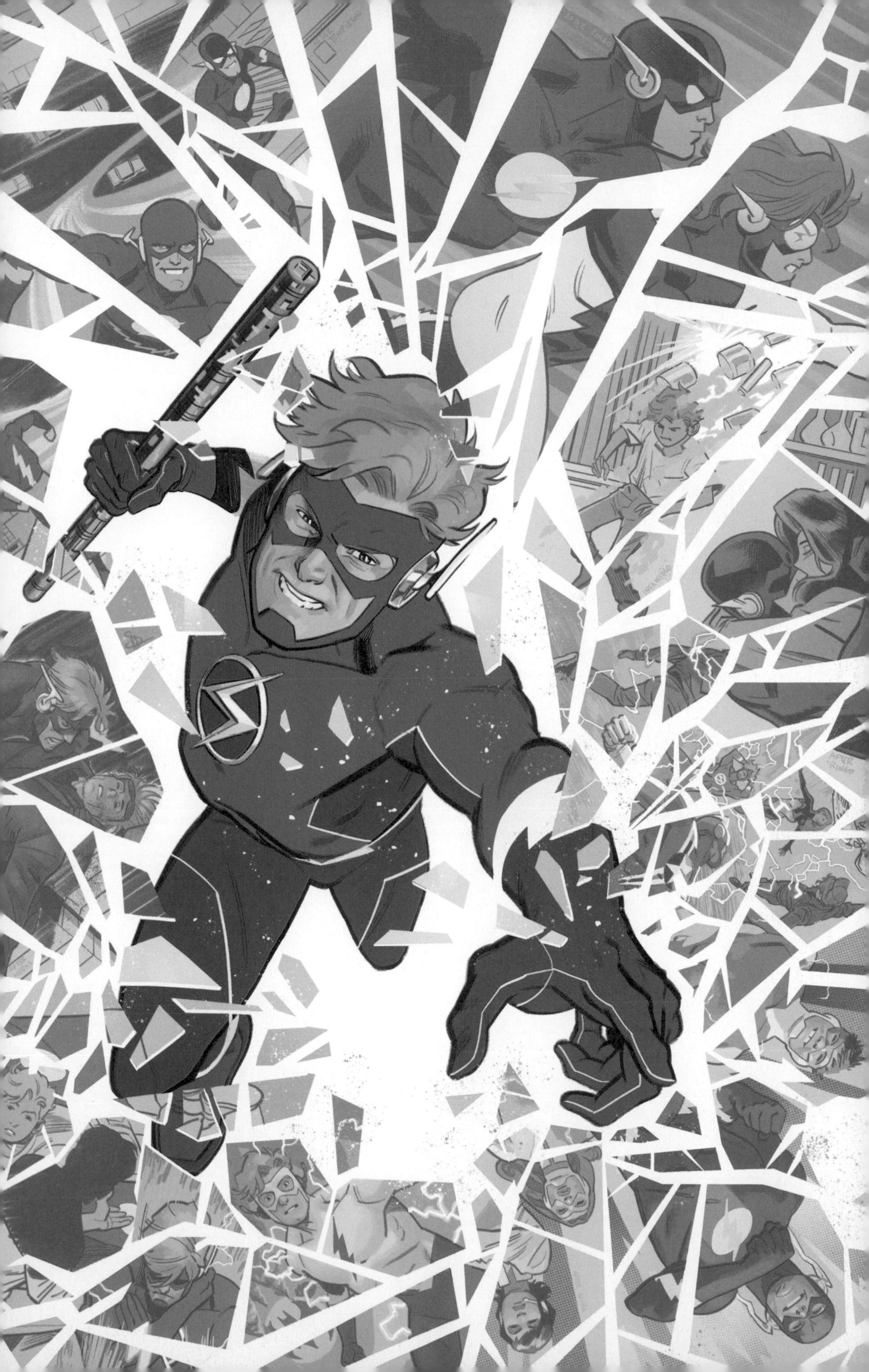

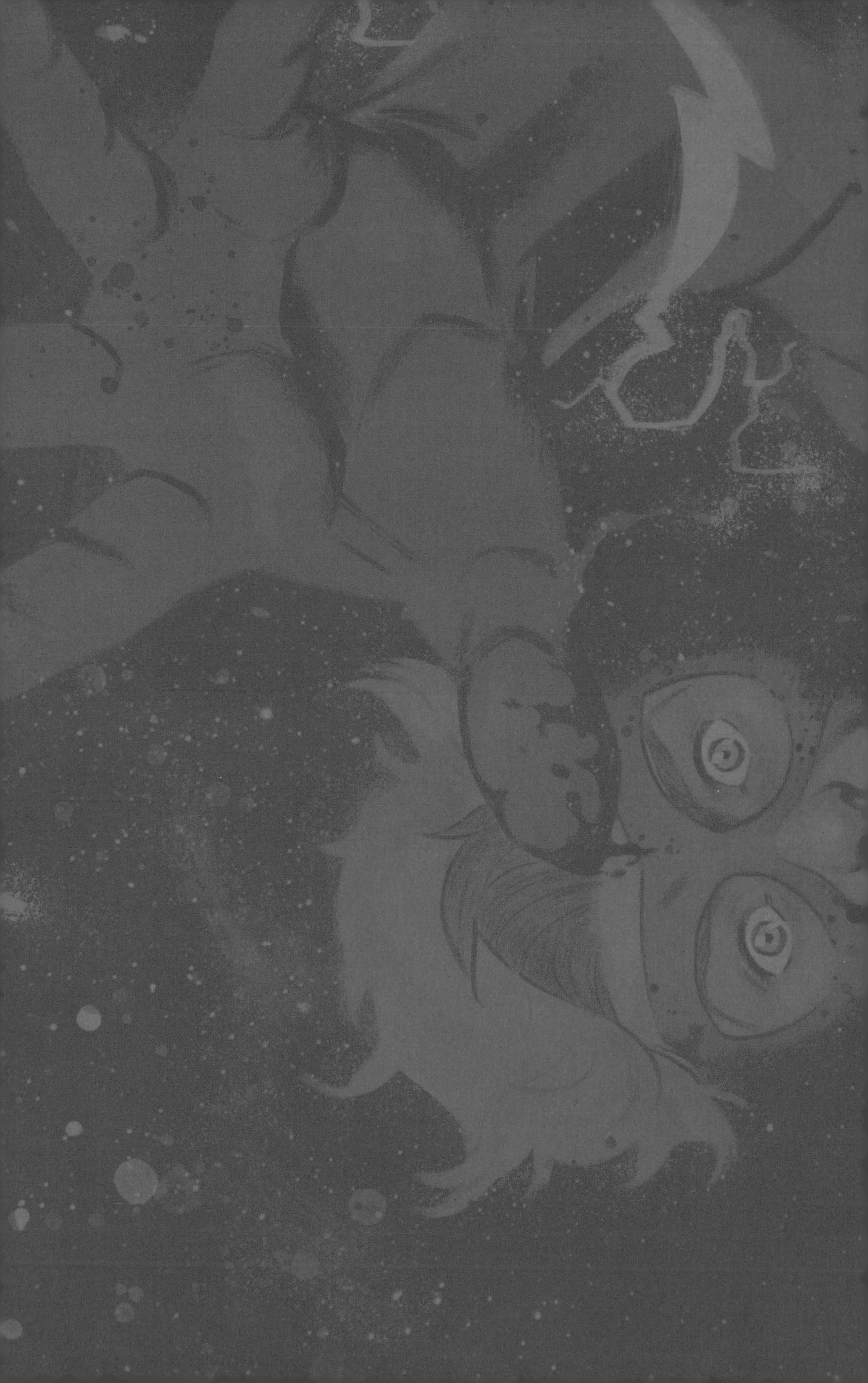

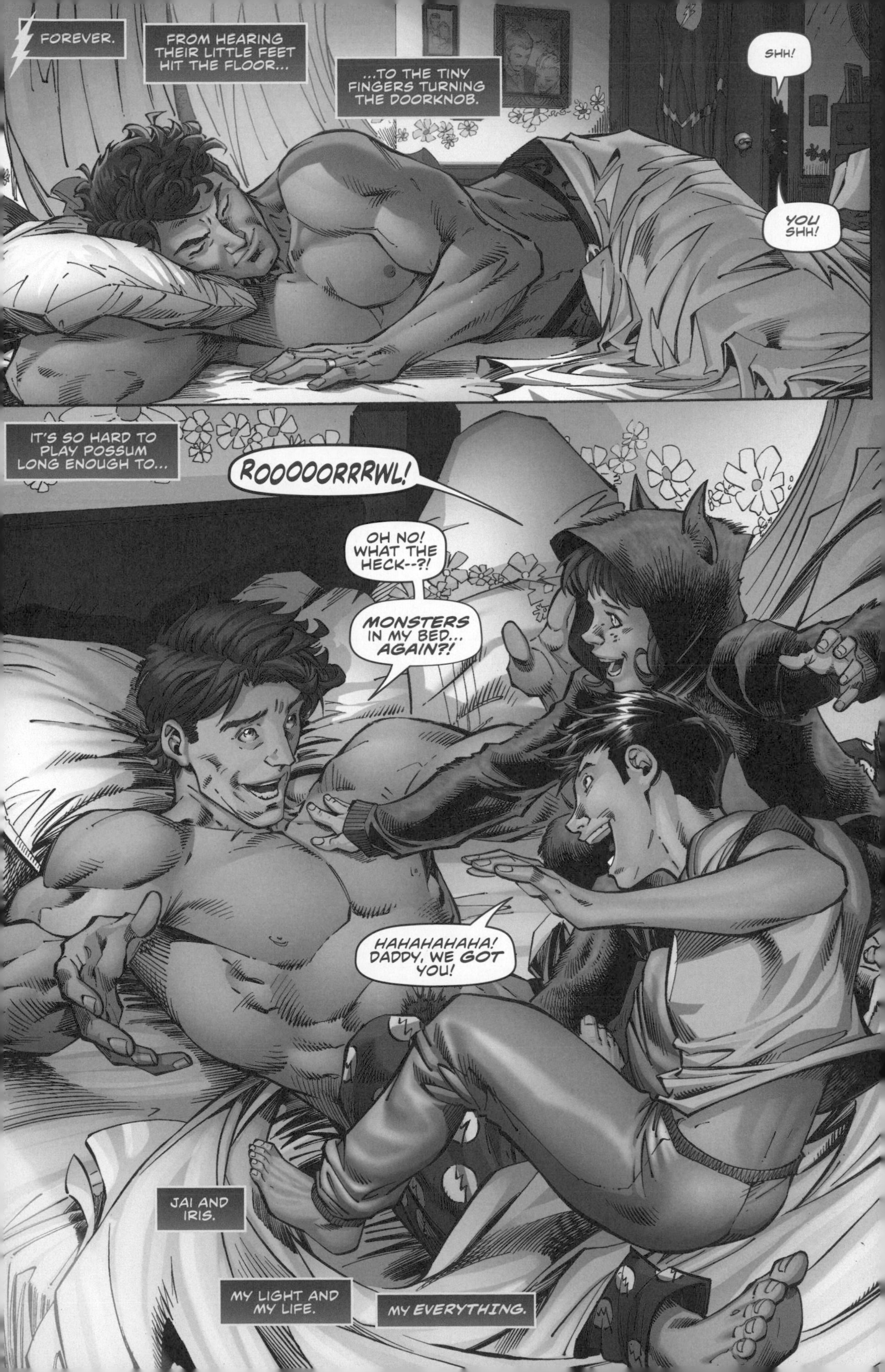
FOREVER.
FROM HEARING THEIR LITTLE FEET HIT THE FLOOR...
...TO THE TINY FINGERS TURNING THE DOORKNOB.
SHH!
YOU SHH!
IT'S SO HARD TO PLAY POSSUM LONG ENOUGH TO...
ROOOOORRRWL!
OH NO! WHAT THE HECK--?!
MONSTERS IN MY BED... AGAIN?!
HAHAHAHAHA! DADDY, WE GOT YOU!
JAI AND IRIS.
MY LIGHT AND MY LIFE.
MY EVERYTHING.

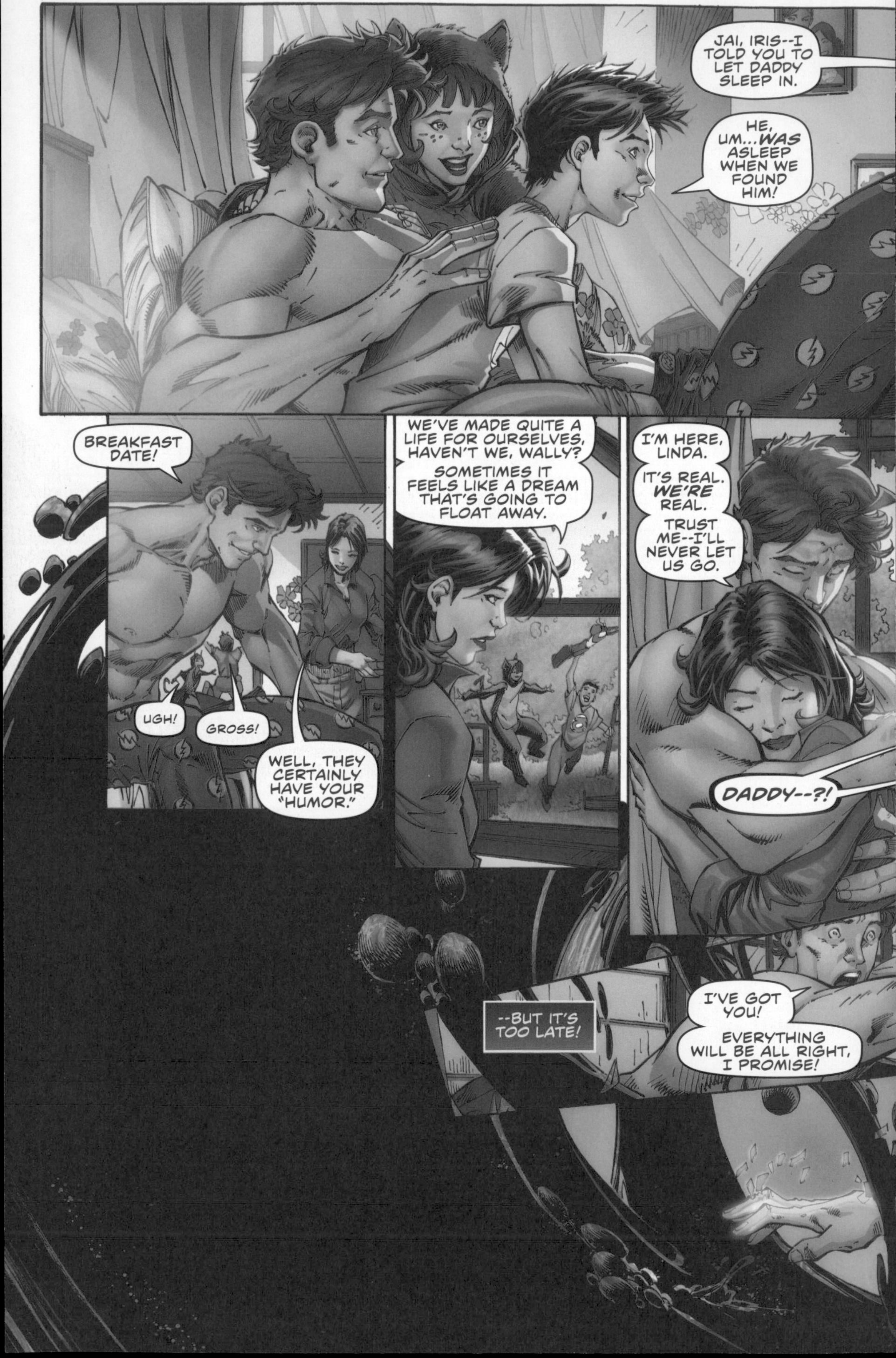

JAI, IRIS--I TOLD YOU TO LET DADDY SLEEP IN.
HE, UM...WAS ASLEEP WHEN WE FOUND HIM!
BREAKFAST DATE!
UGH!
GROSS!
WELL, THEY CERTAINLY HAVE YOUR "HUMOR."
WE'VE MADE QUITE A LIFE FOR OURSELVES, HAVEN'T WE, WALLY?
SOMETIMES IT FEELS LIKE A DREAM THAT'S GOING TO FLOAT AWAY.
I'M HERE, LINDA.
IT'S REAL. WE'RE REAL.
TRUST ME--I'LL NEVER LET US GO.
DADDY--?!
--BUT IT'S TOO LATE!
I'VE GOT YOU!
EVERYTHING WILL BE ALL RIGHT, I PROMISE!

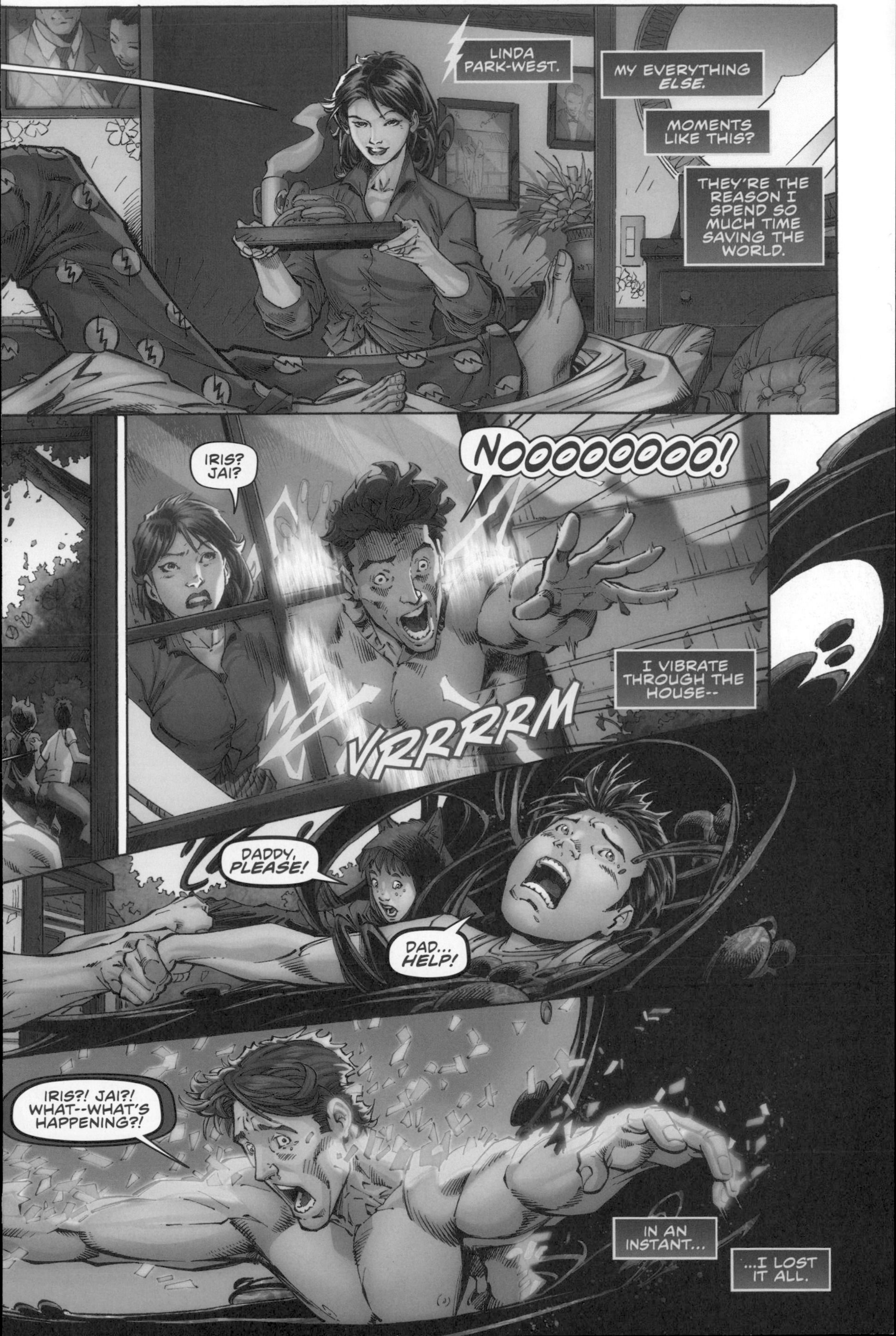
LINDA PARK-WEST.
MY EVERYTHING *ELSE.*
MOMENTS LIKE THIS?
THEY'RE THE REASON I SPEND SO MUCH TIME SAVING THE WORLD.
IRIS? JAI?
NOOOOOOOO!
I VIBRATE THROUGH THE HOUSE--
VRRRRM
DADDY, PLEASE!
DAD... HELP!
IRIS?! JAI?! WHAT--WHAT'S HAPPENING?!
IN AN INSTANT...
...I LOST IT ALL.

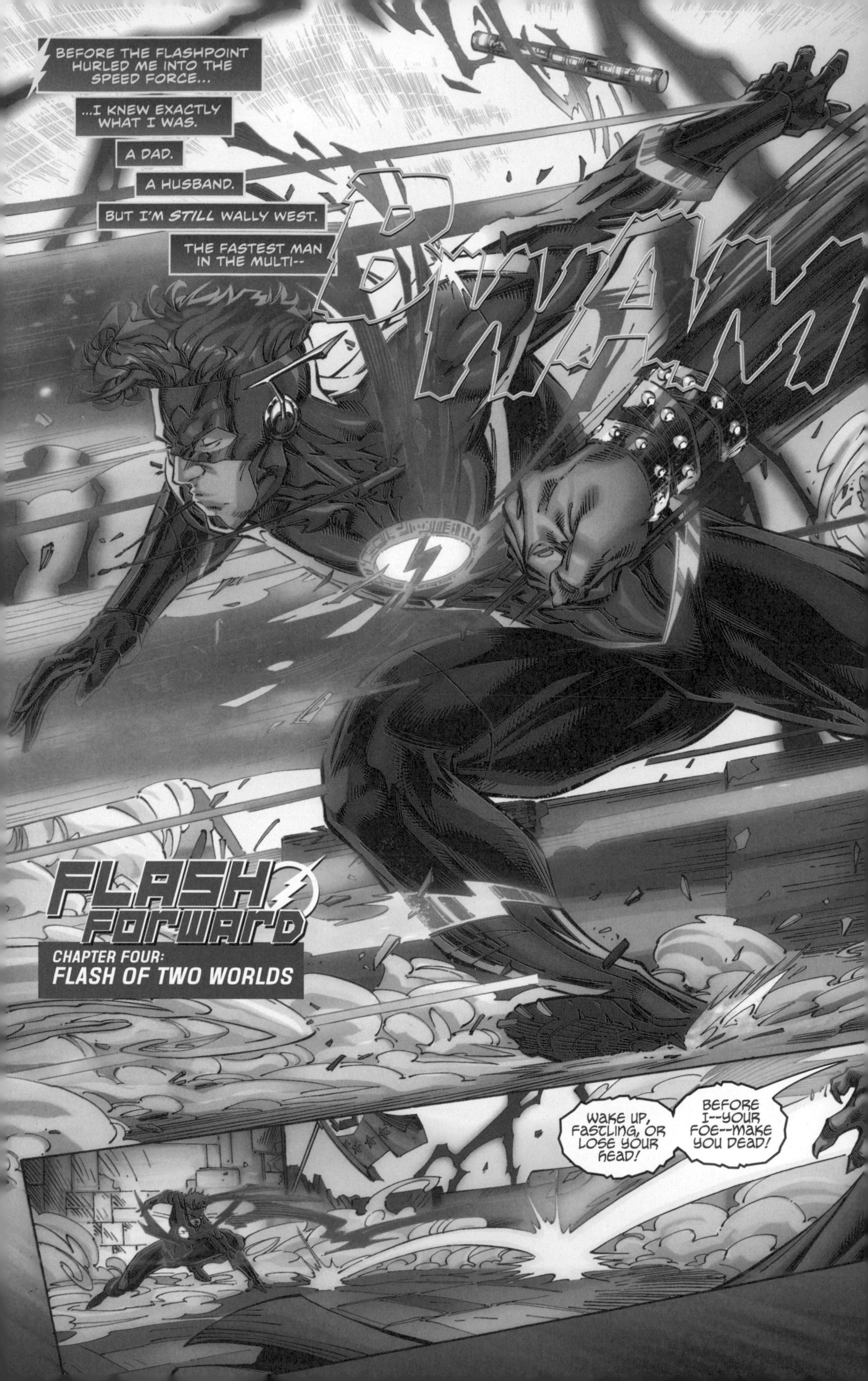
BEFORE THE FLASHPOINT HURLED ME INTO THE SPEED FORCE...
...I KNEW EXACTLY WHAT I WAS.
A DAD.
A HUSBAND.
BUT I'M STILL WALLY WEST.
THE FASTEST MAN IN THE MULTI--
FLASH FORWARD
CHAPTER FOUR:
FLASH OF TWO WORLDS
WAKE UP, FASTLING, OR LOSE YOUR HEAD!
BEFORE I--YOUR FOE--MAKE YOU DEAD!

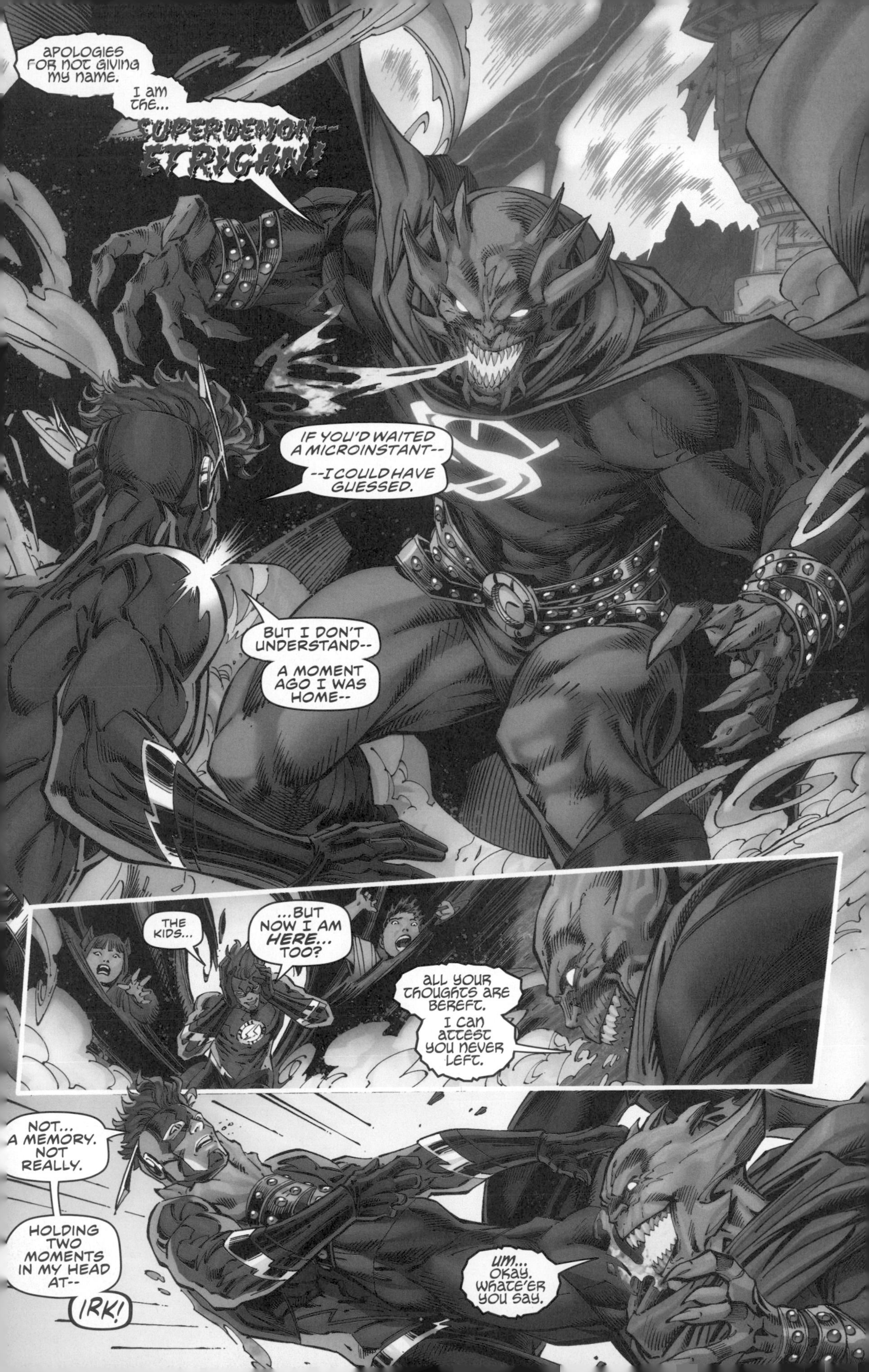
APOLOGIES FOR NOT GIVING MY NAME.
I AM THE...
SUPERDEMON--ETRIGAN!
IF YOU'D WAITED A MICROINSTANT--
--I COULD HAVE GUESSED.
BUT I DON'T UNDERSTAND--
A MOMENT AGO I WAS HOME--
THE KIDS...
...BUT NOW I AM HERE... TOO?
ALL YOUR THOUGHTS ARE BEREFT.
I CAN ATTEST YOU NEVER LEFT.
NOT... A MEMORY. NOT REALLY.
HOLDING TWO MOMENTS IN MY HEAD AT--
IRK!
UM... OKAY. WHATE'ER YOU SAY.

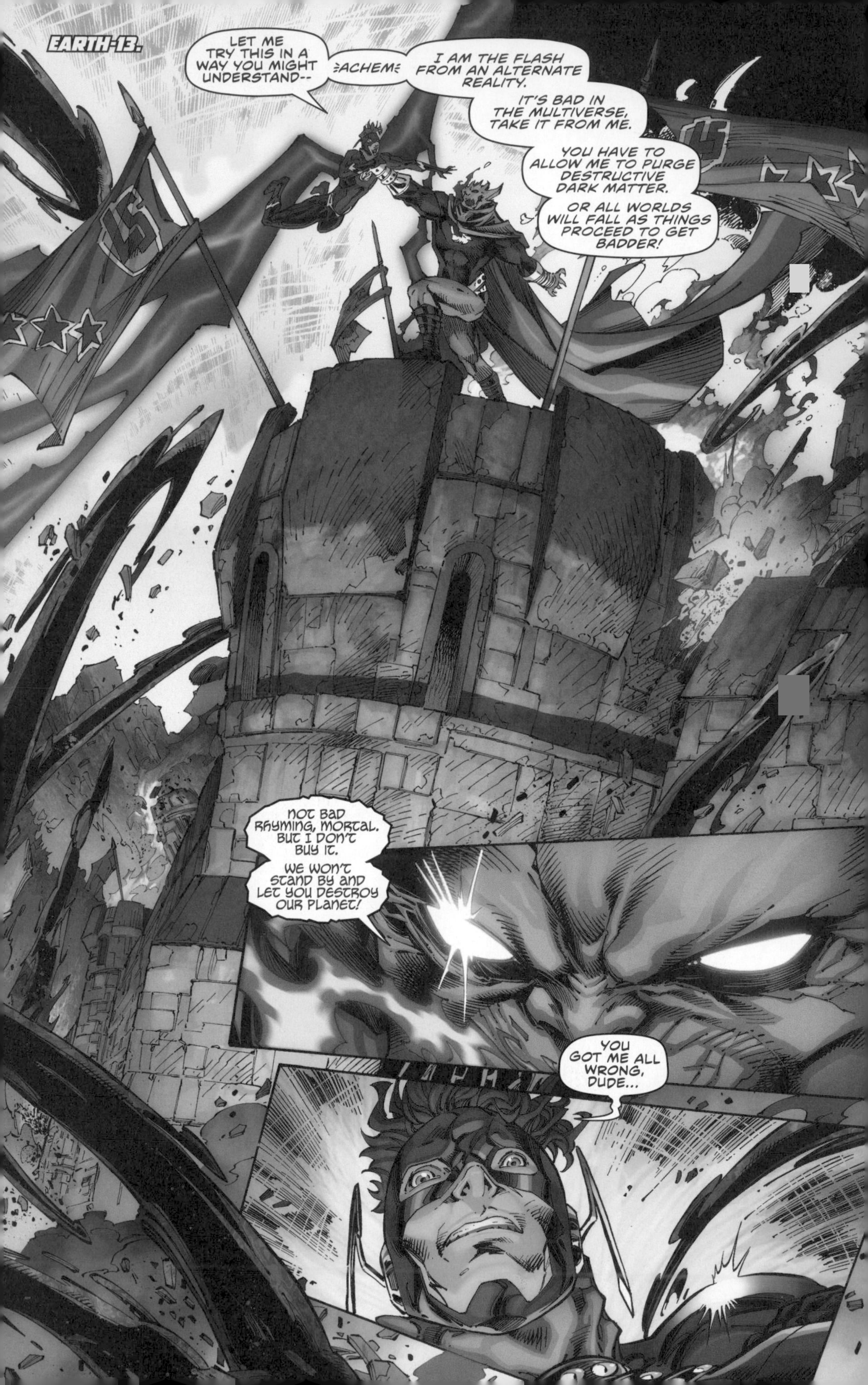
EARTH-13.
LET ME TRY THIS IN A WAY YOU MIGHT UNDERSTAND--
ACHEM
I AM THE FLASH FROM AN ALTERNATE REALITY.
IT'S BAD IN THE MULTIVERSE, TAKE IT FROM ME.
YOU HAVE TO ALLOW ME TO PURGE DESTRUCTIVE DARK MATTER.
OR ALL WORLDS WILL FALL AS THINGS PROCEED TO GET BADDER!
NOT BAD RHYMING, MORTAL. BUT I DON'T BUY IT.
WE WON'T STAND BY AND LET YOU DESTROY OUR PLANET!
YOU GOT ME ALL WRONG, DUDE...

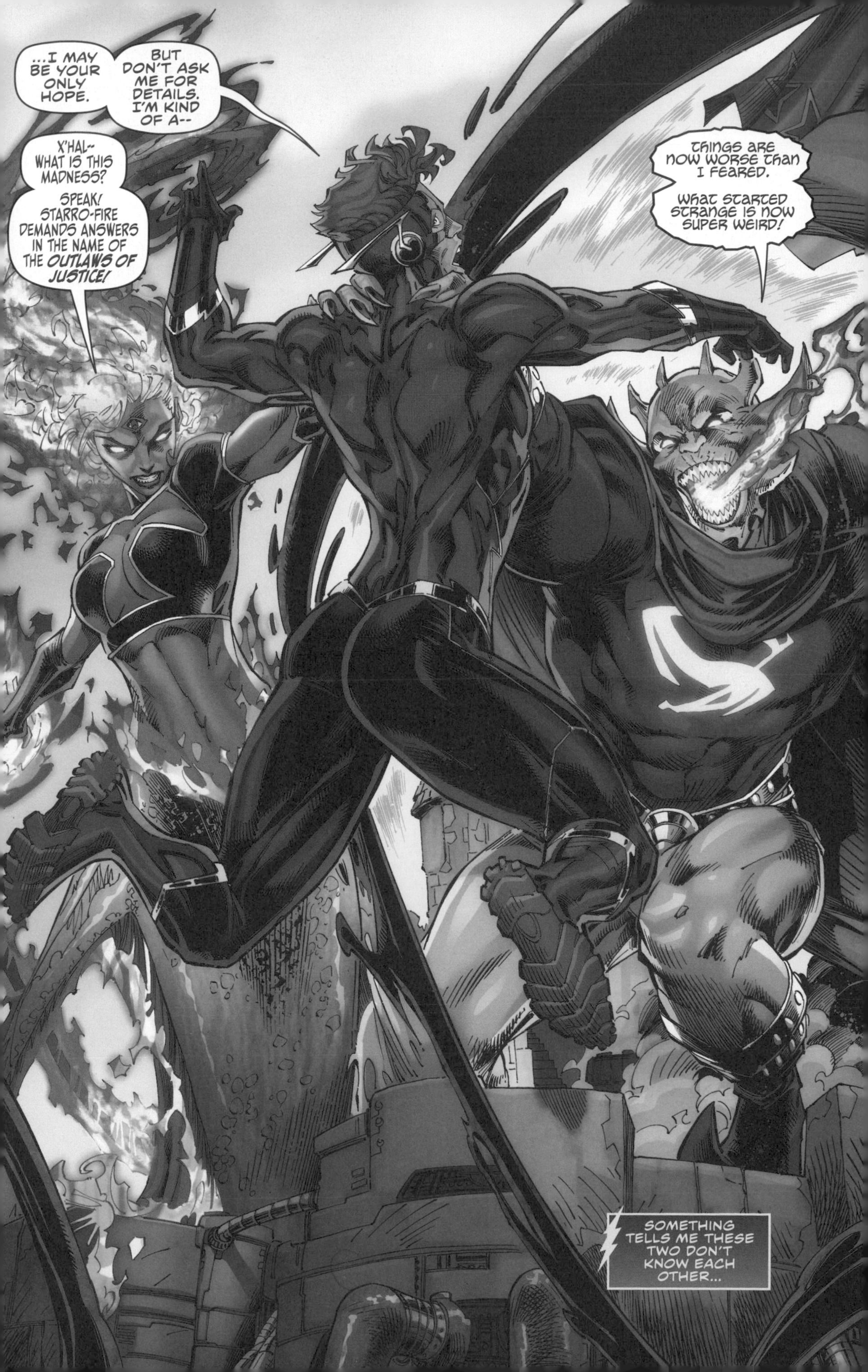
...I MAY BE YOUR ONLY HOPE.
BUT DON'T ASK ME FOR DETAILS. I'M KIND OF A--
X'HAL-- WHAT IS THIS MADNESS?
SPEAK! STARRO-FIRE DEMANDS ANSWERS IN THE NAME OF THE *OUTLAWS OF JUSTICE!*
THINGS ARE NOW WORSE THAN I FEARED.
WHAT STARTED STRANGE IS NOW SUPER WEIRD!
SOMETHING TELLS ME THESE TWO DON'T KNOW EACH OTHER...

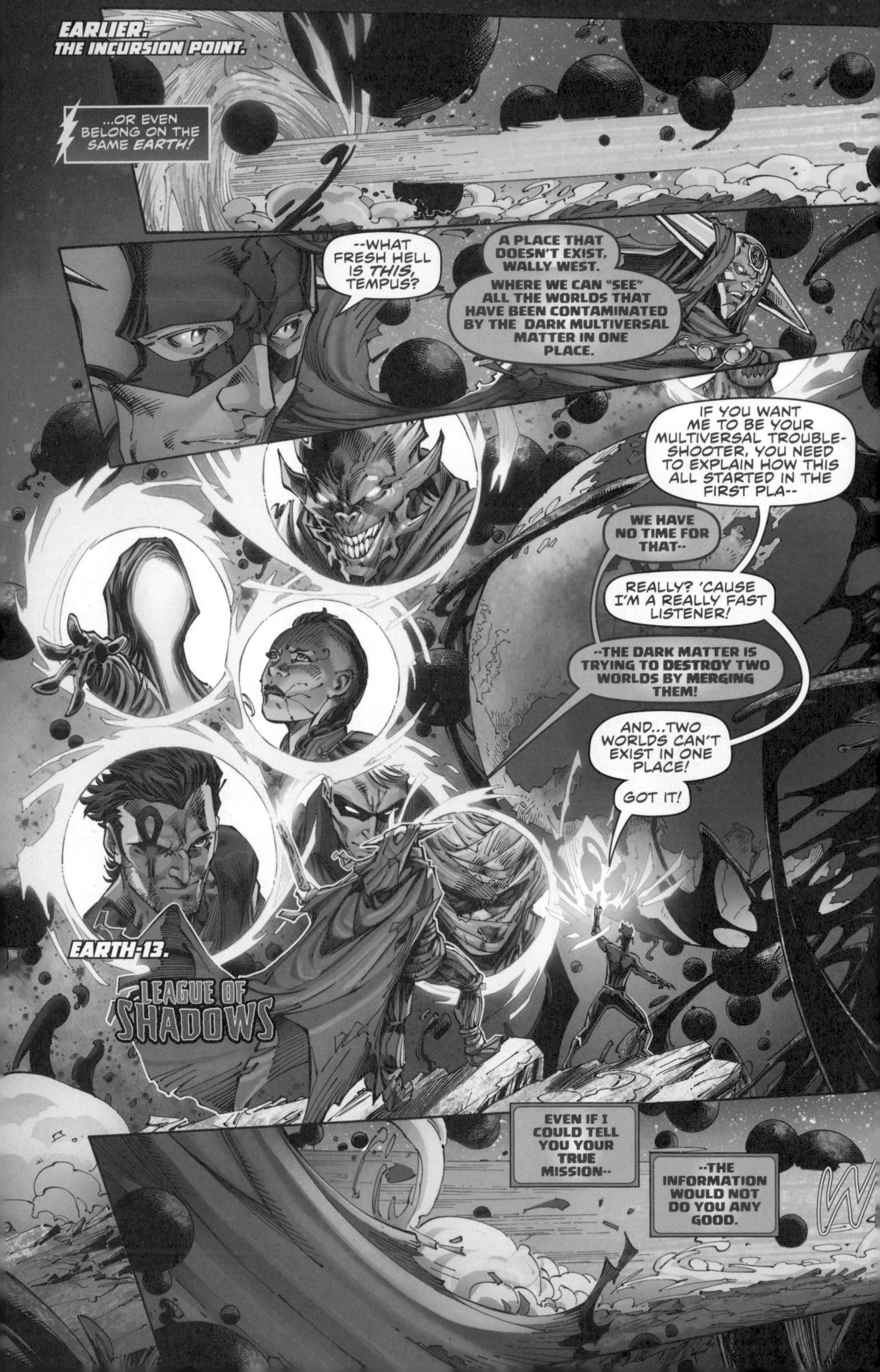
EARLIER. THE INCURSION POINT.
...OR EVEN BELONG ON THE SAME EARTH!
--WHAT FRESH HELL IS THIS, TEMPUS?
A PLACE THAT DOESN'T EXIST, WALLY WEST.
WHERE WE CAN "SEE" ALL THE WORLDS THAT HAVE BEEN CONTAMINATED BY THE DARK MULTIVERSAL MATTER IN ONE PLACE.
IF YOU WANT ME TO BE YOUR MULTIVERSAL TROUBLE-SHOOTER, YOU NEED TO EXPLAIN HOW THIS ALL STARTED IN THE FIRST PLA--
WE HAVE NO TIME FOR THAT--
REALLY? 'CAUSE I'M A REALLY FAST LISTENER!
--THE DARK MATTER IS TRYING TO DESTROY TWO WORLDS BY MERGING THEM!
AND...TWO WORLDS CAN'T EXIST IN ONE PLACE!
GOT IT!
EARTH-13.
LEAGUE OF SHADOWS
EVEN IF I COULD TELL YOU YOUR TRUE MISSION--
--THE INFORMATION WOULD NOT DO YOU ANY GOOD.

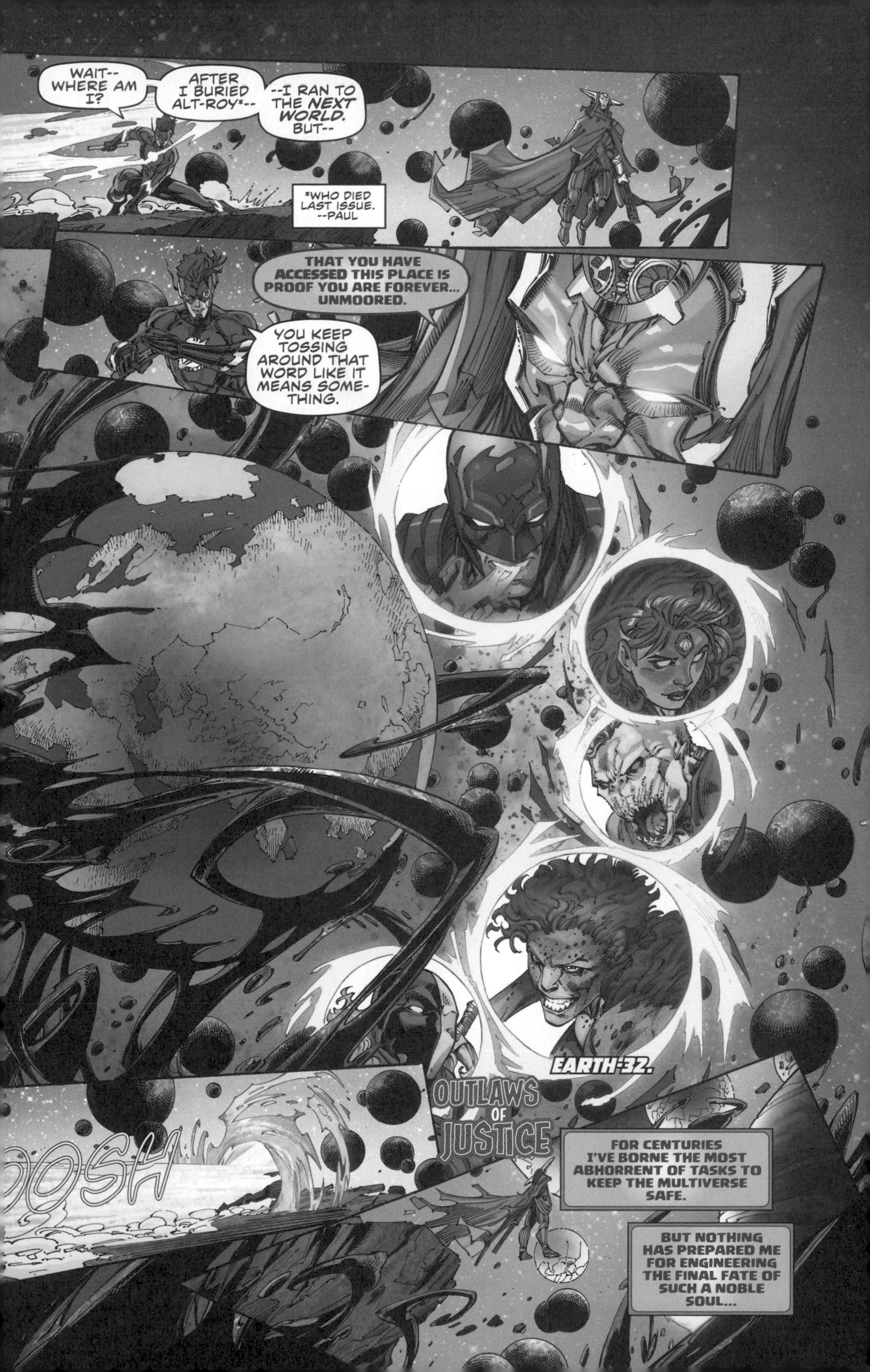
WAIT-- WHERE AM I?
AFTER I BURIED ALT-ROY*--
--I RAN TO THE NEXT WORLD. BUT--
*WHO DIED LAST ISSUE. --PAUL
THAT YOU HAVE ACCESSED THIS PLACE IS PROOF YOU ARE FOREVER... UNMOORED.
YOU KEEP TOSSING AROUND THAT WORD LIKE IT MEANS SOME-THING.
EARTH-32.
OUTLAWS OF JUSTICE
OOSH
FOR CENTURIES I'VE BORNE THE MOST ABHORRENT OF TASKS TO KEEP THE MULTIVERSE SAFE.
BUT NOTHING HAS PREPARED ME FOR ENGINEERING THE FINAL FATE OF SUCH A NOBLE SOUL...

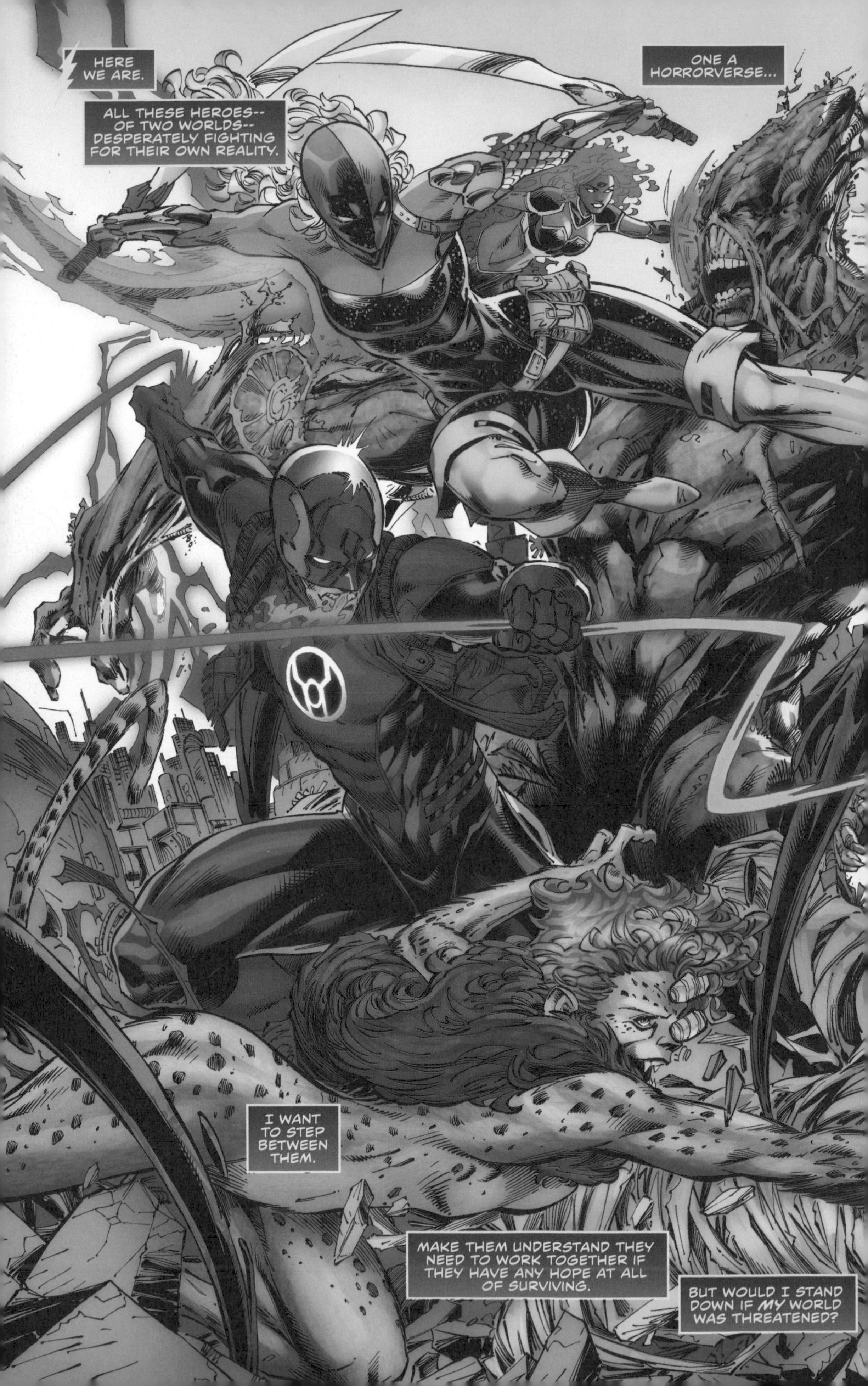
HERE WE ARE.
ALL THESE HEROES-- OF TWO WORLDS-- DESPERATELY FIGHTING FOR THEIR OWN REALITY.
ONE A HORRORVERSE...
I WANT TO STEP BETWEEN THEM.
MAKE THEM UNDERSTAND THEY NEED TO WORK TOGETHER IF THEY HAVE ANY HOPE AT ALL OF SURVIVING.
BUT WOULD I STAND DOWN IF MY WORLD WAS THREATENED?

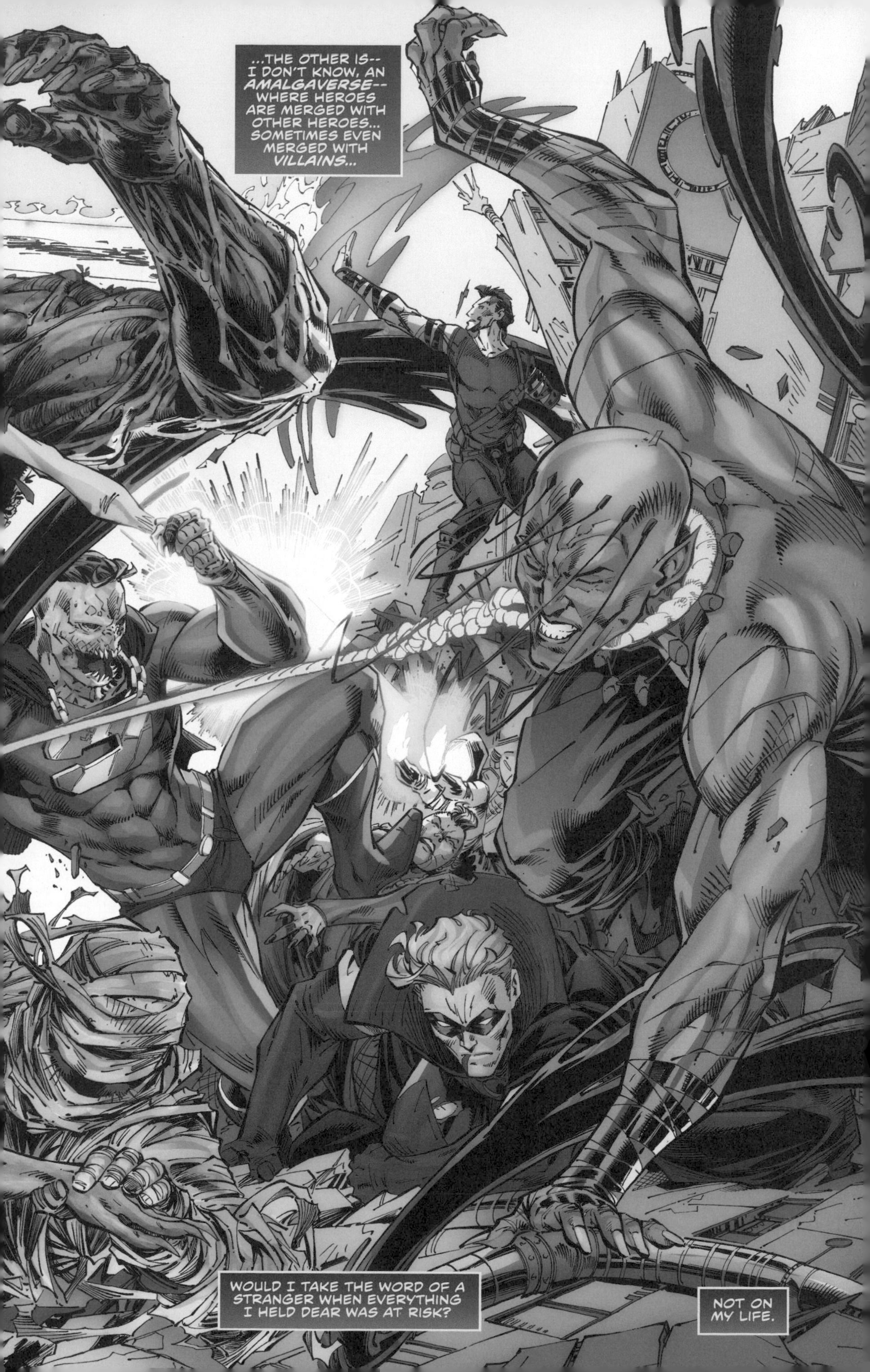
...THE OTHER IS-- I DON'T KNOW, AN *AMALGAVERSE*-- WHERE HEROES ARE MERGED WITH OTHER HEROES... SOMETIMES EVEN MERGED WITH *VILLAINS*...
WOULD I TAKE THE WORD OF A STRANGER WHEN EVERYTHING I HELD DEAR WAS AT RISK?
NOT ON MY LIFE.

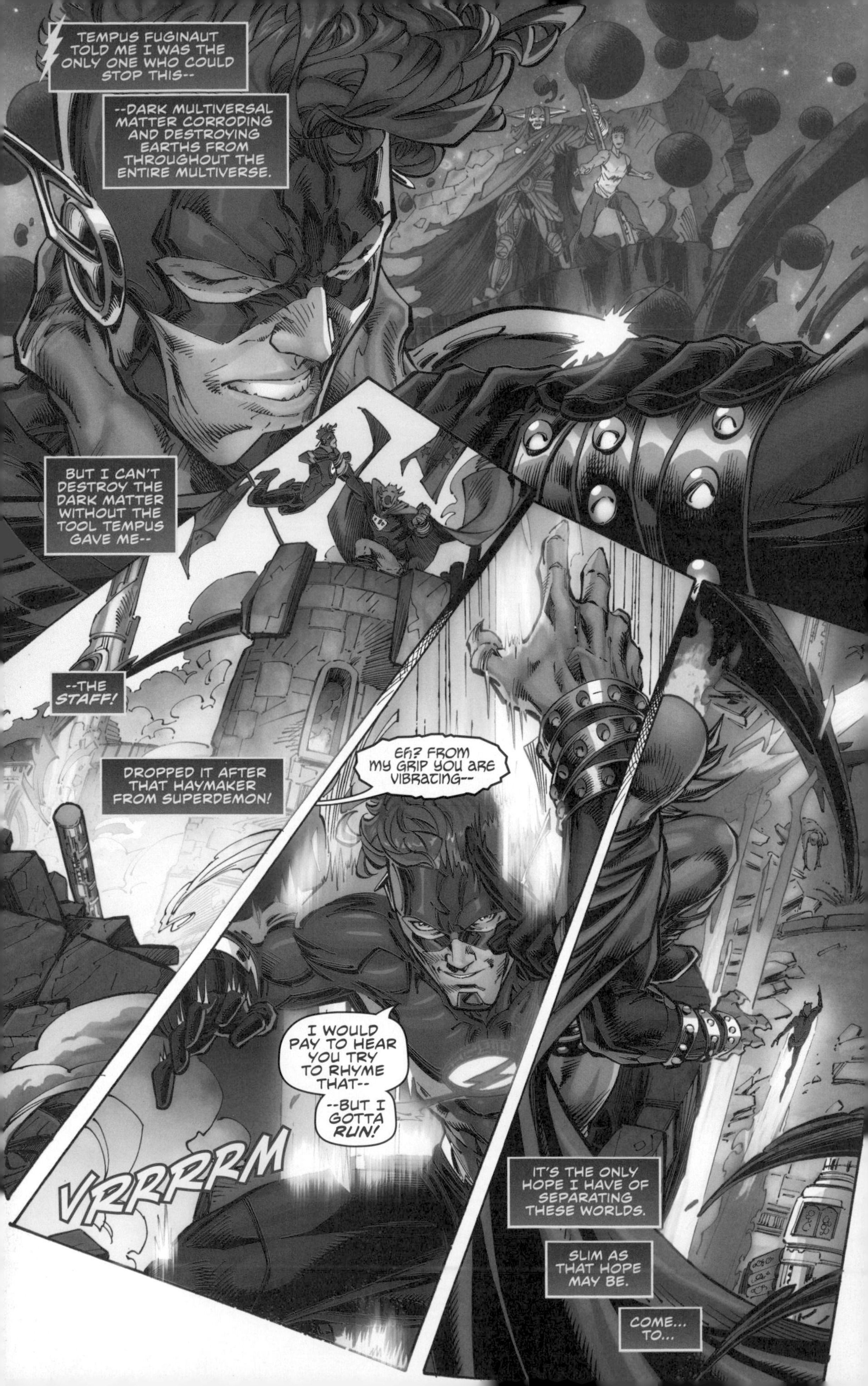
TEMPUS FUGINAUT TOLD ME I WAS THE ONLY ONE WHO COULD STOP THIS--
--DARK MULTIVERSAL MATTER CORRODING AND DESTROYING EARTHS FROM THROUGHOUT THE ENTIRE MULTIVERSE.
BUT I CAN'T DESTROY THE DARK MATTER WITHOUT THE TOOL TEMPUS GAVE ME--
--THE STAFF!
DROPPED IT AFTER THAT HAYMAKER FROM SUPERDEMON!
EH? FROM MY GRIP YOU ARE VIBRATING--
I WOULD PAY TO HEAR YOU TRY TO RHYME THAT--
--BUT I GOTTA RUN!
VRRRRRM
IT'S THE ONLY HOPE I HAVE OF SEPARATING THESE WORLDS.
SLIM AS THAT HOPE MAY BE.
COME... TO...

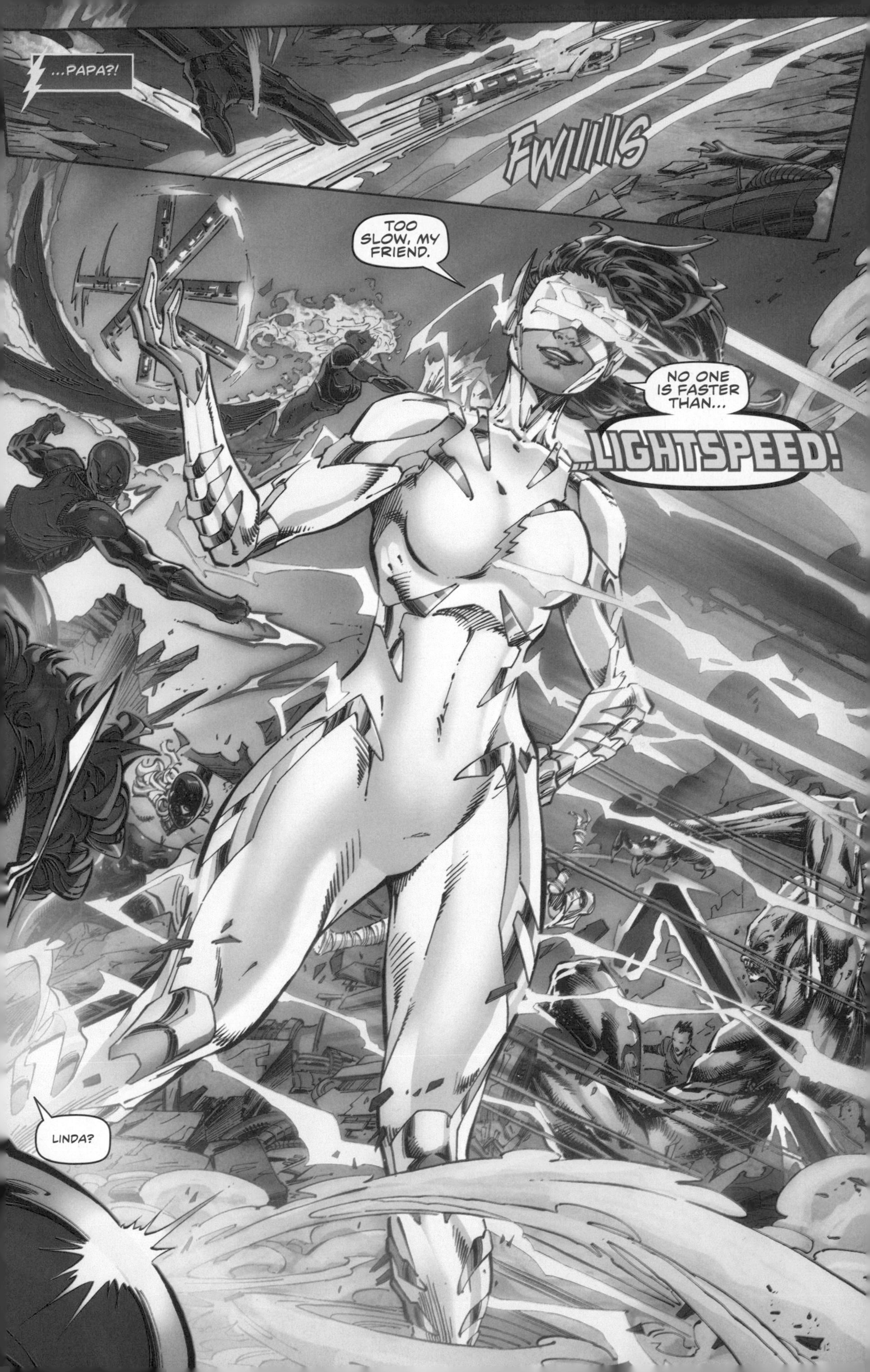
...PAPA?!
FWIIIIS
TOO SLOW, MY FRIEND.
NO ONE IS FASTER THAN...
...LIGHTSPEED!
LINDA?

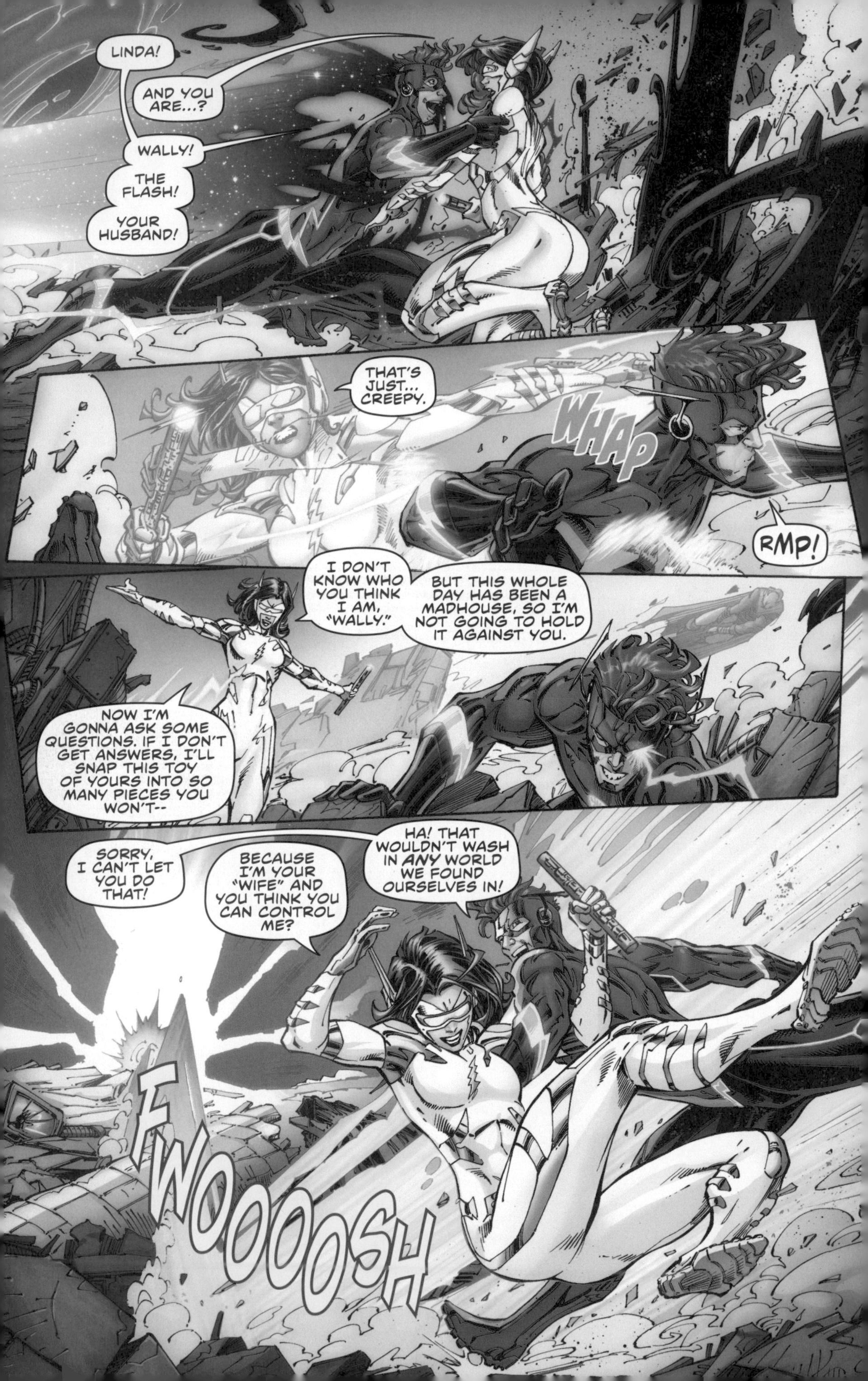
LINDA!
AND YOU ARE...?
WALLY!
THE FLASH!
YOUR HUSBAND!
THAT'S JUST... CREEPY.
WHAP
RMP!
I DON'T KNOW WHO YOU THINK I AM, "WALLY."
BUT THIS WHOLE DAY HAS BEEN A MADHOUSE, SO I'M NOT GOING TO HOLD IT AGAINST YOU.
NOW I'M GONNA ASK SOME QUESTIONS. IF I DON'T GET ANSWERS, I'LL SNAP THIS TOY OF YOURS INTO SO MANY PIECES YOU WON'T--
SORRY, I CAN'T LET YOU DO THAT!
BECAUSE I'M YOUR "WIFE" AND YOU THINK YOU CAN CONTROL ME?
HA! THAT WOULDN'T WASH IN *ANY* WORLD WE FOUND OURSELVES IN!
FWOOOOSH

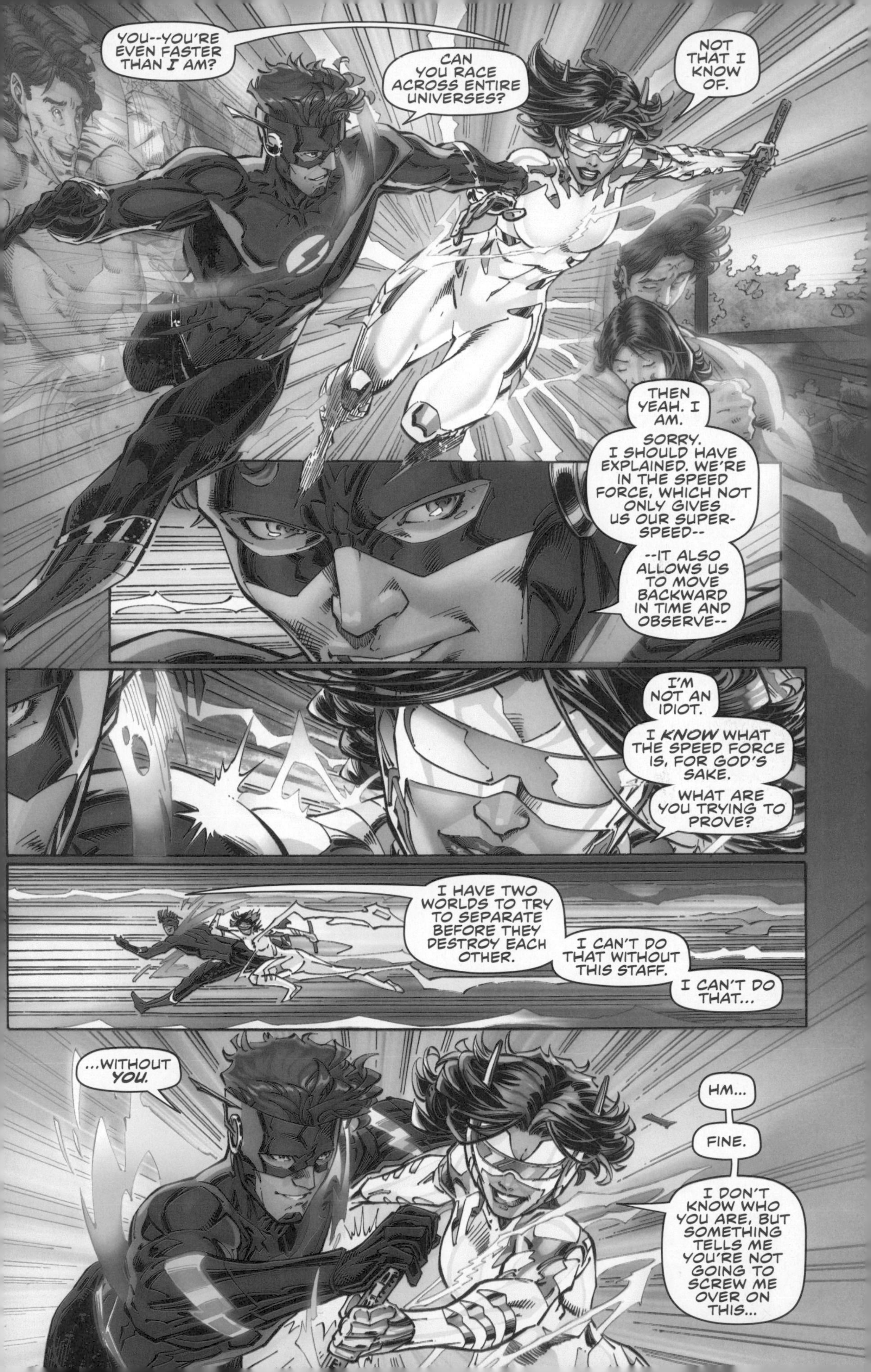
YOU--YOU'RE EVEN FASTER THAN I AM?
CAN YOU RACE ACROSS ENTIRE UNIVERSES?
NOT THAT I KNOW OF.
THEN YEAH. I AM.
SORRY. I SHOULD HAVE EXPLAINED. WE'RE IN THE SPEED FORCE, WHICH NOT ONLY GIVES US OUR SUPER-SPEED--
--IT ALSO ALLOWS US TO MOVE BACKWARD IN TIME AND OBSERVE--
I'M NOT AN IDIOT.
I KNOW WHAT THE SPEED FORCE IS, FOR GOD'S SAKE.
WHAT ARE YOU TRYING TO PROVE?
I HAVE TWO WORLDS TO TRY TO SEPARATE BEFORE THEY DESTROY EACH OTHER.
I CAN'T DO THAT WITHOUT THIS STAFF.
I CAN'T DO THAT...
...WITHOUT YOU.
HM...
FINE.
I DON'T KNOW WHO YOU ARE, BUT SOMETHING TELLS ME YOU'RE NOT GOING TO SCREW ME OVER ON THIS...

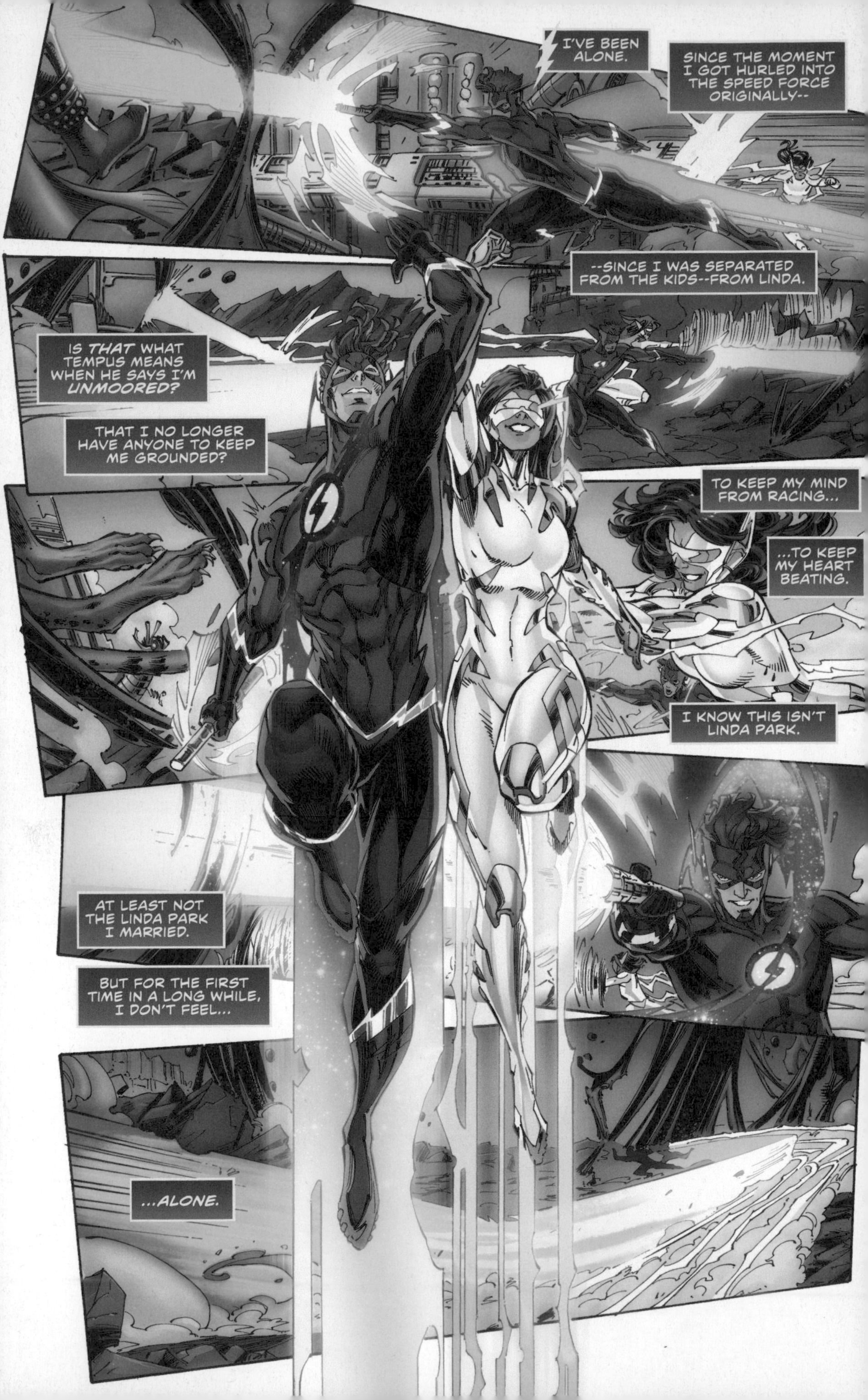
I'VE BEEN ALONE.
SINCE THE MOMENT I GOT HURLED INTO THE SPEED FORCE ORIGINALLY--
--SINCE I WAS SEPARATED FROM THE KIDS--FROM LINDA.
IS *THAT* WHAT TEMPUS MEANS WHEN HE SAYS I'M *UNMOORED*?
THAT I NO LONGER HAVE ANYONE TO KEEP ME GROUNDED?
TO KEEP MY MIND FROM RACING...
...TO KEEP MY HEART BEATING.
I KNOW THIS ISN'T LINDA PARK.
AT LEAST NOT THE LINDA PARK I MARRIED.
BUT FOR THE FIRST TIME IN A LONG WHILE, I DON'T FEEL...
...ALONE.

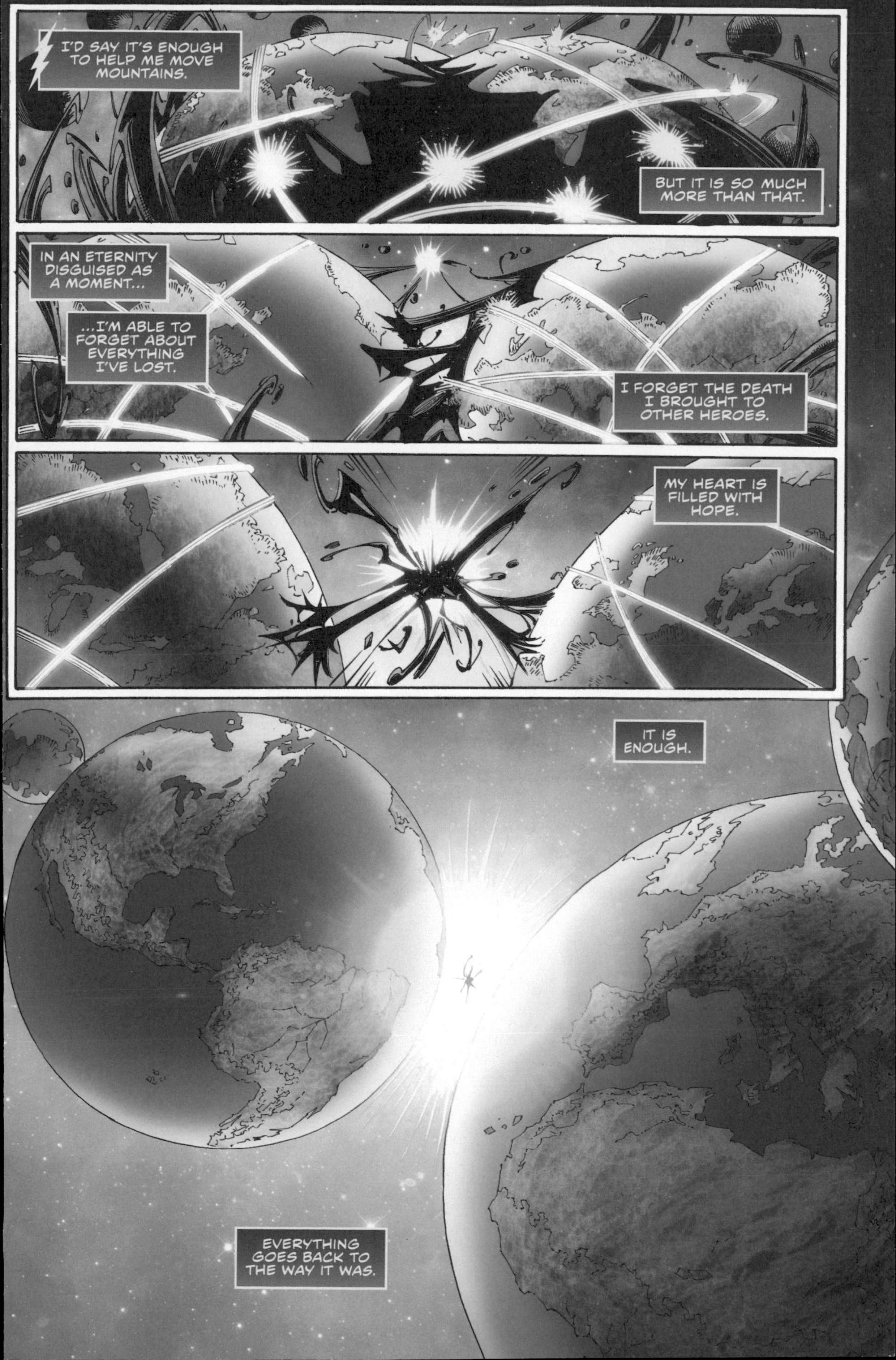
I'D SAY IT'S ENOUGH TO HELP ME MOVE MOUNTAINS.
BUT IT IS SO MUCH MORE THAN THAT.
IN AN ETERNITY DISGUISED AS A MOMENT...
...I'M ABLE TO FORGET ABOUT EVERYTHING I'VE LOST.
I FORGET THE DEATH I BROUGHT TO OTHER HEROES.
MY HEART IS FILLED WITH HOPE.
IT IS ENOUGH.
EVERYTHING GOES BACK TO THE WAY IT WAS.

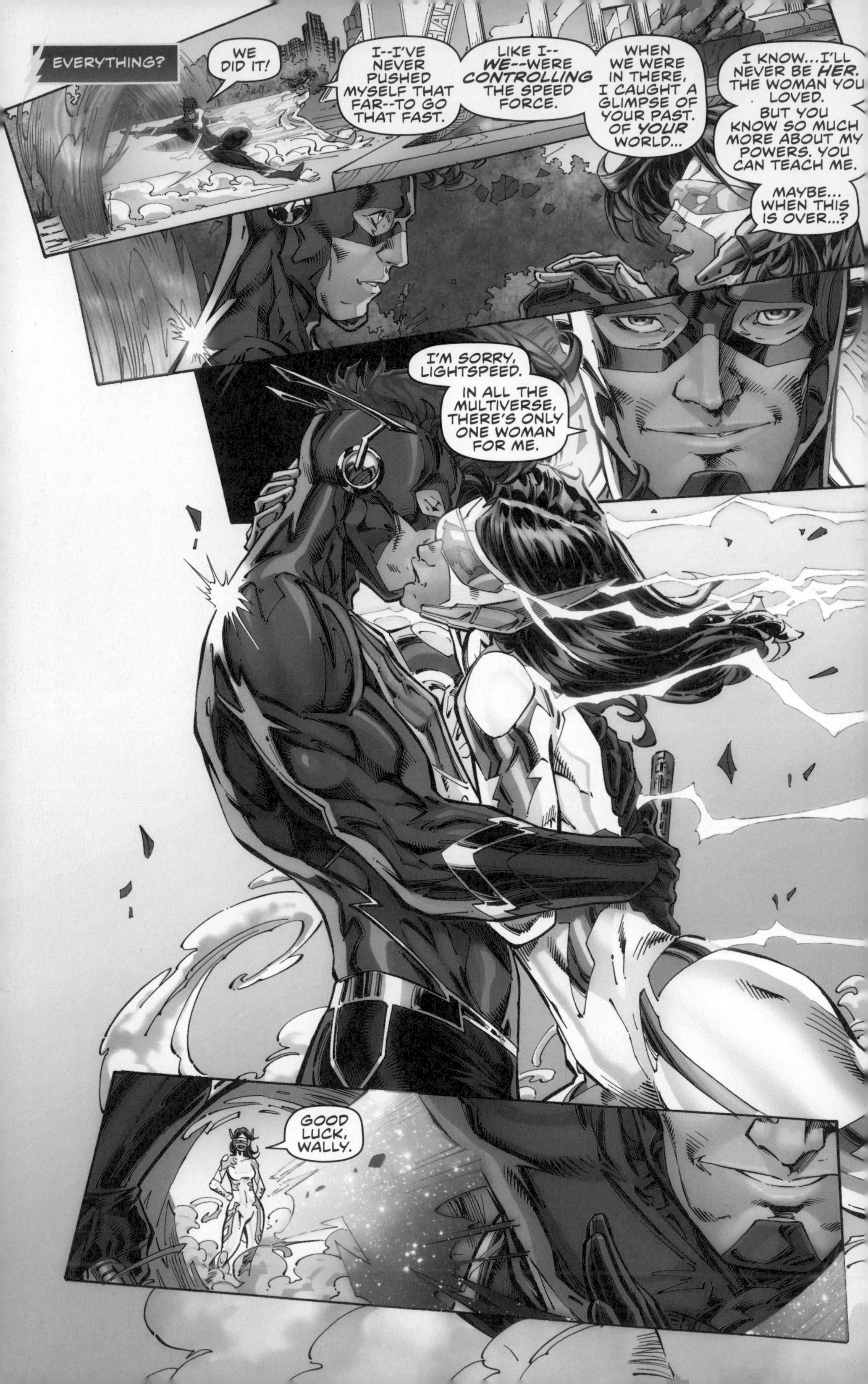
EVERYTHING?
WE DID IT!
I--I'VE NEVER PUSHED MYSELF THAT FAR--TO GO THAT FAST.
LIKE I--WE--WERE CONTROLLING THE SPEED FORCE.
WHEN WE WERE IN THERE, I CAUGHT A GLIMPSE OF YOUR PAST. OF YOUR WORLD...
I KNOW...I'LL NEVER BE HER. THE WOMAN YOU LOVED.
BUT YOU KNOW SO MUCH MORE ABOUT MY POWERS. YOU CAN TEACH ME.
MAYBE... WHEN THIS IS OVER...?
I'M SORRY, LIGHTSPEED.
IN ALL THE MULTIVERSE, THERE'S ONLY ONE WOMAN FOR ME.
GOOD LUCK, WALLY.

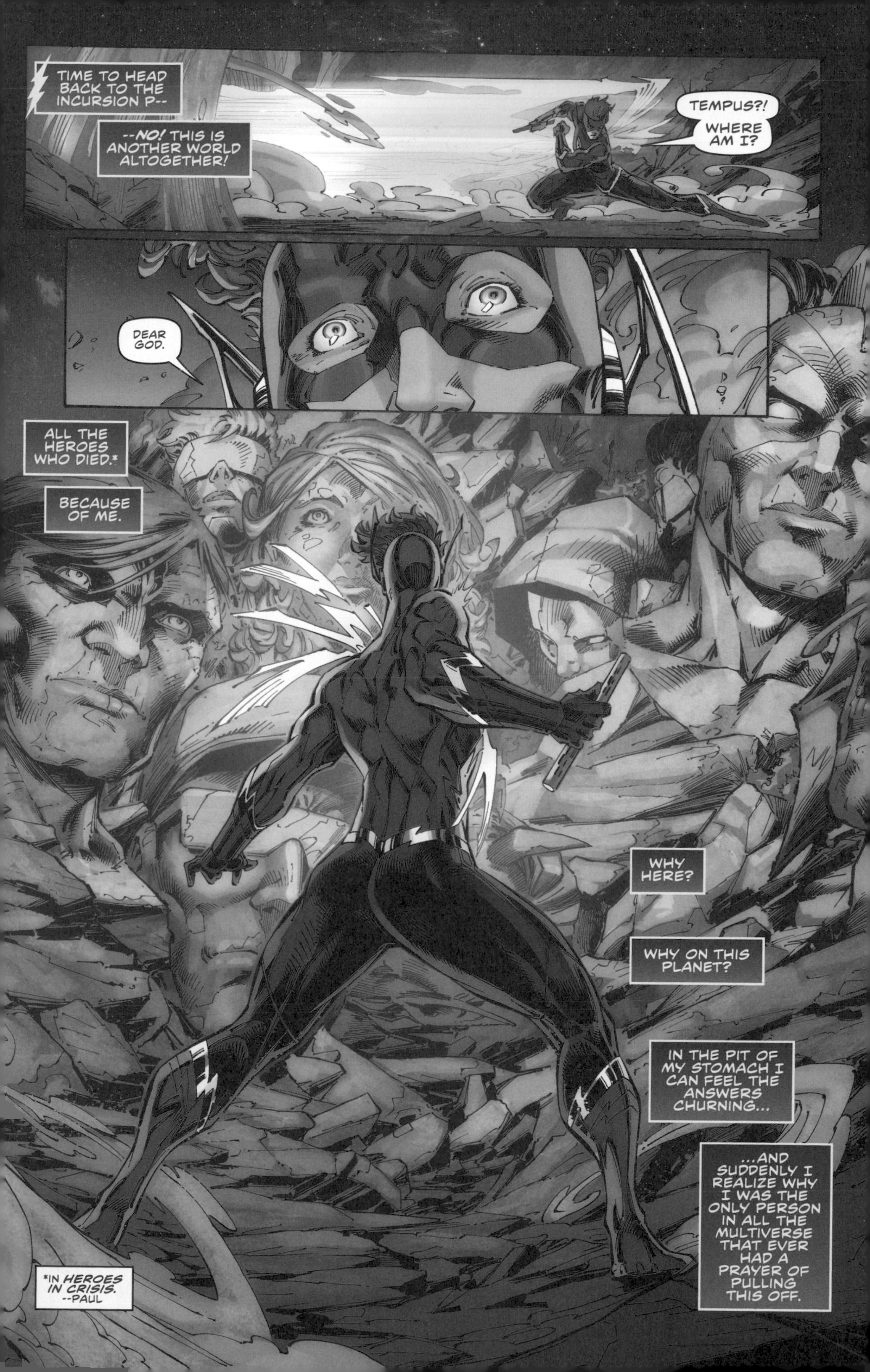
TIME TO HEAD BACK TO THE INCURSION P--
--NO! THIS IS ANOTHER WORLD ALTOGETHER!
TEMPUS?! WHERE AM I?
DEAR GOD.
ALL THE HEROES WHO DIED.*
BECAUSE OF ME.
WHY HERE?
WHY ON THIS PLANET?
IN THE PIT OF MY STOMACH I CAN FEEL THE ANSWERS CHURNING...
...AND SUDDENLY I REALIZE WHY I WAS THE ONLY PERSON IN ALL THE MULTIVERSE THAT EVER HAD A PRAYER OF PULLING THIS OFF.
*IN HEROES IN CRISIS. --PAUL

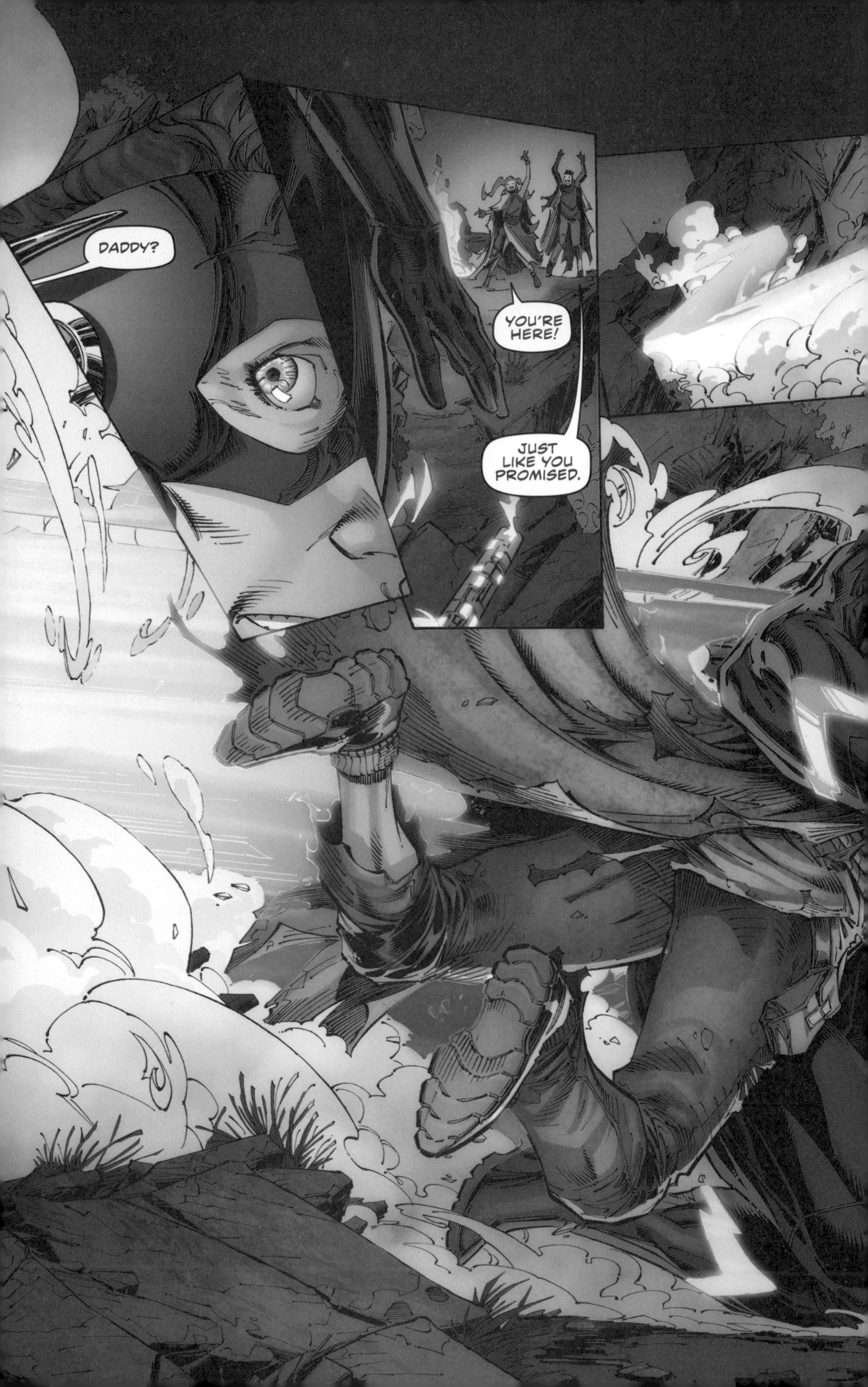
DADDY?
YOU'RE HERE!
JUST LIKE YOU PROMISED.

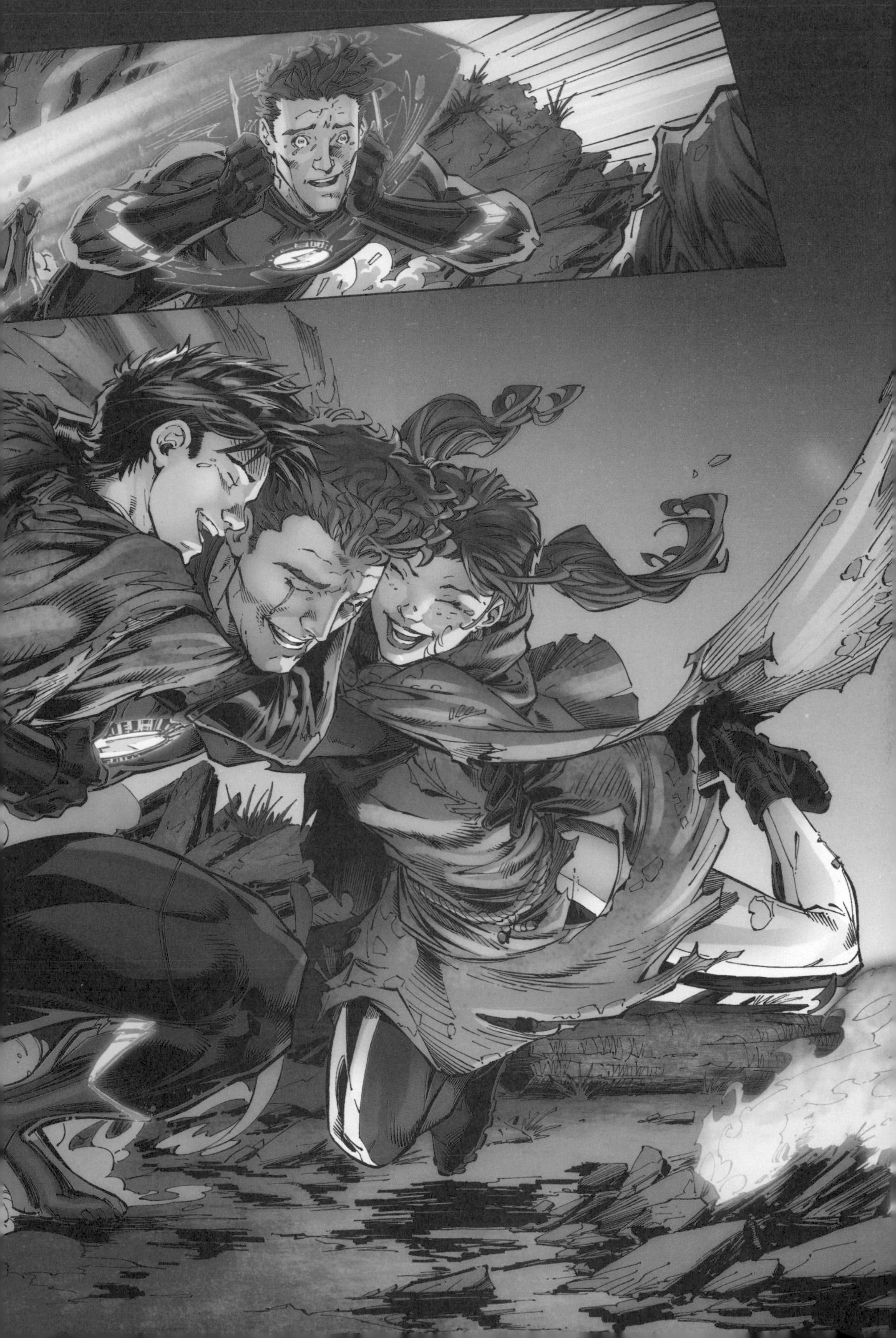

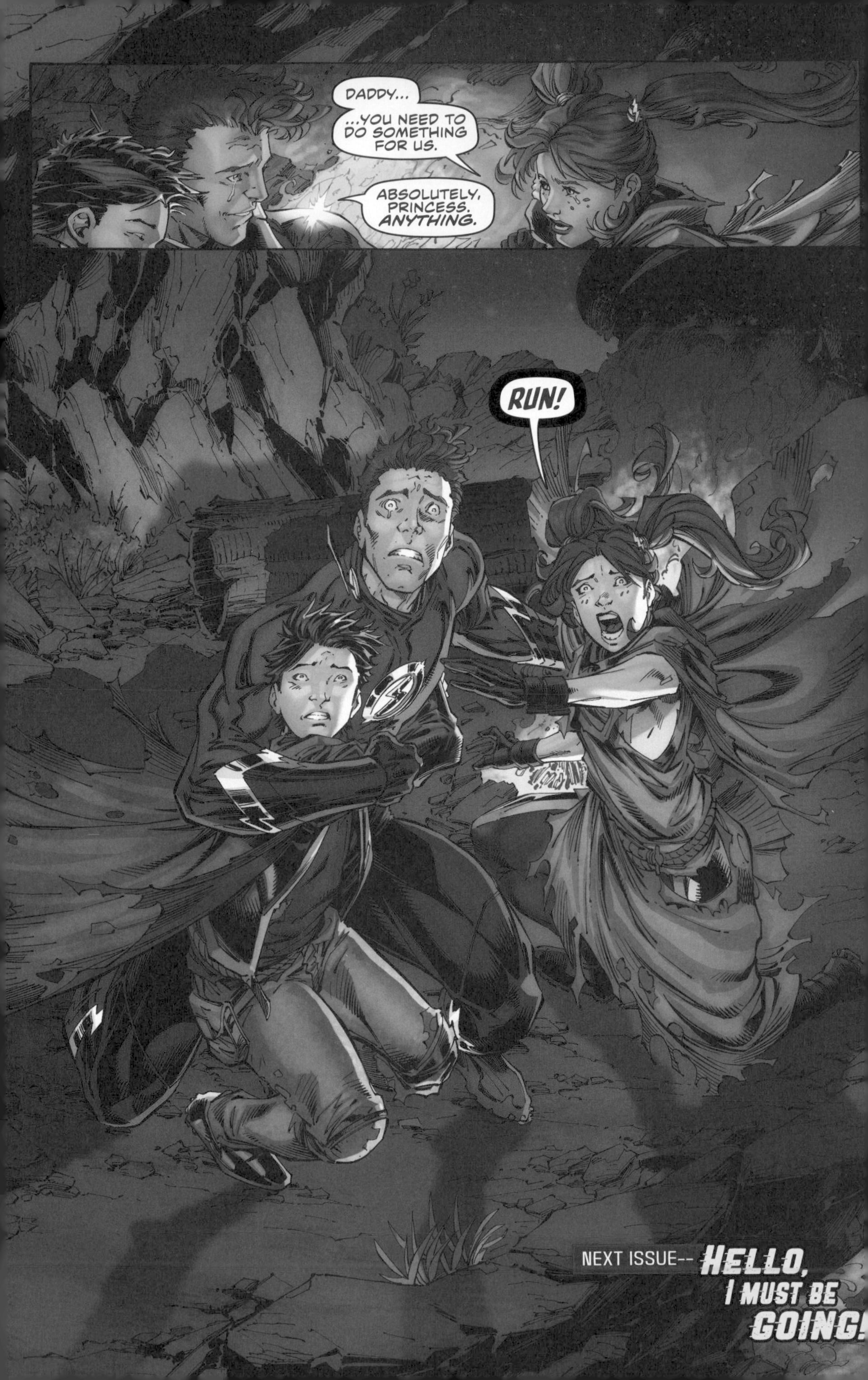

DADDY...
...YOU NEED TO DO SOMETHING FOR US.
ABSOLUTELY, PRINCESS. ANYTHING.
RUN!
NEXT ISSUE-- HELLO, I MUST BE GOING!

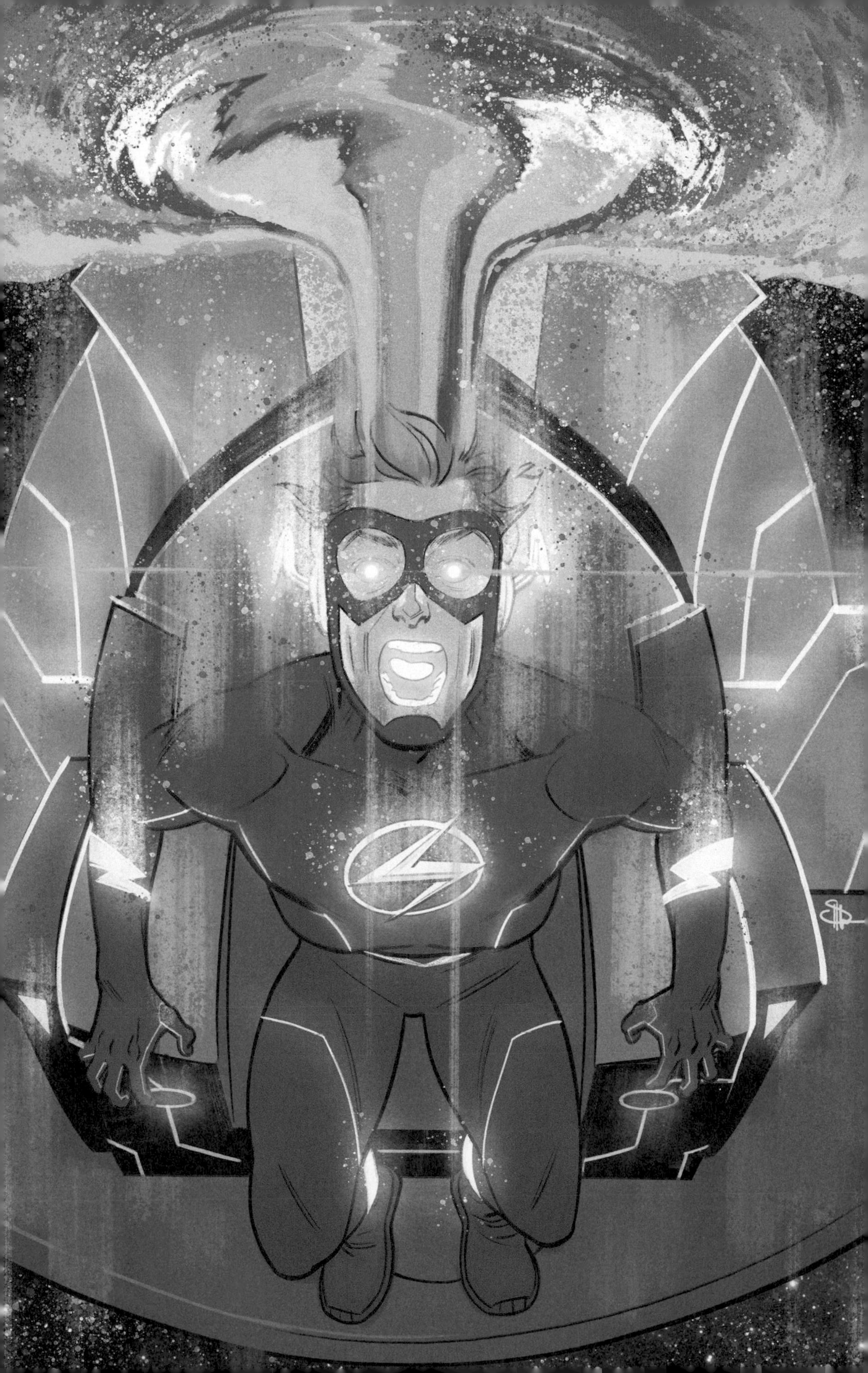

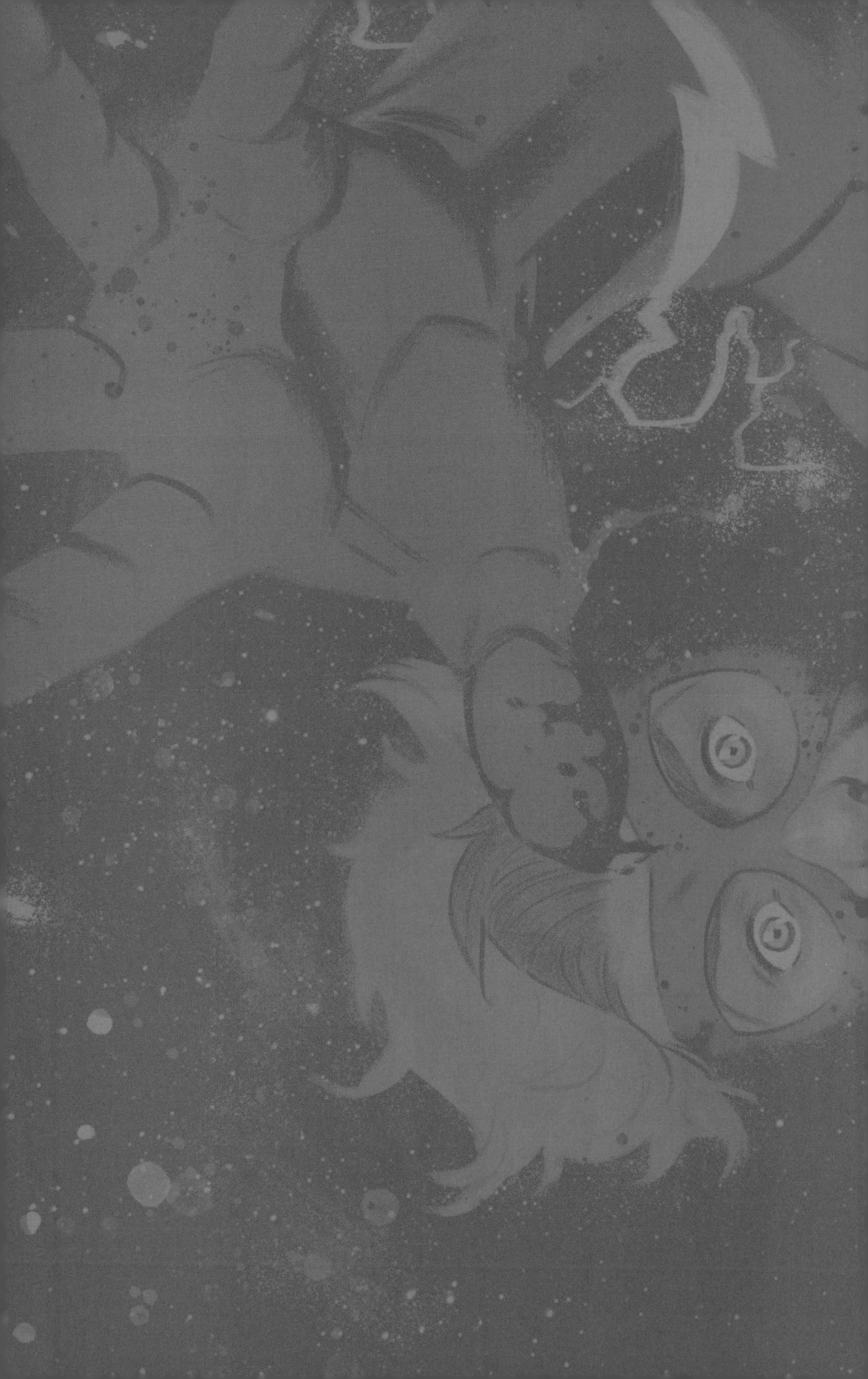

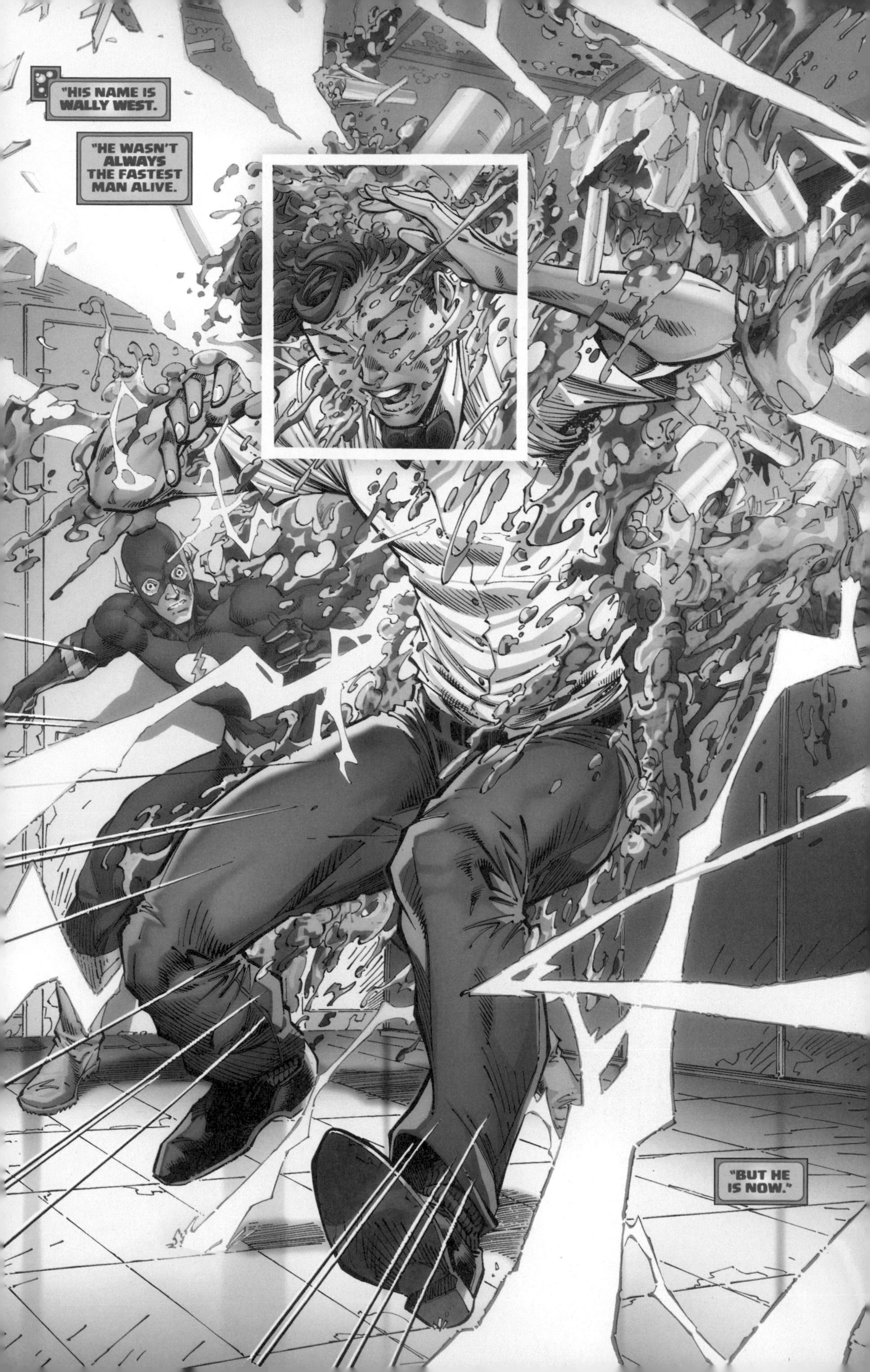
"HIS NAME IS WALLY WEST.
"HE WASN'T ALWAYS THE FASTEST MAN ALIVE.
"BUT HE IS NOW."

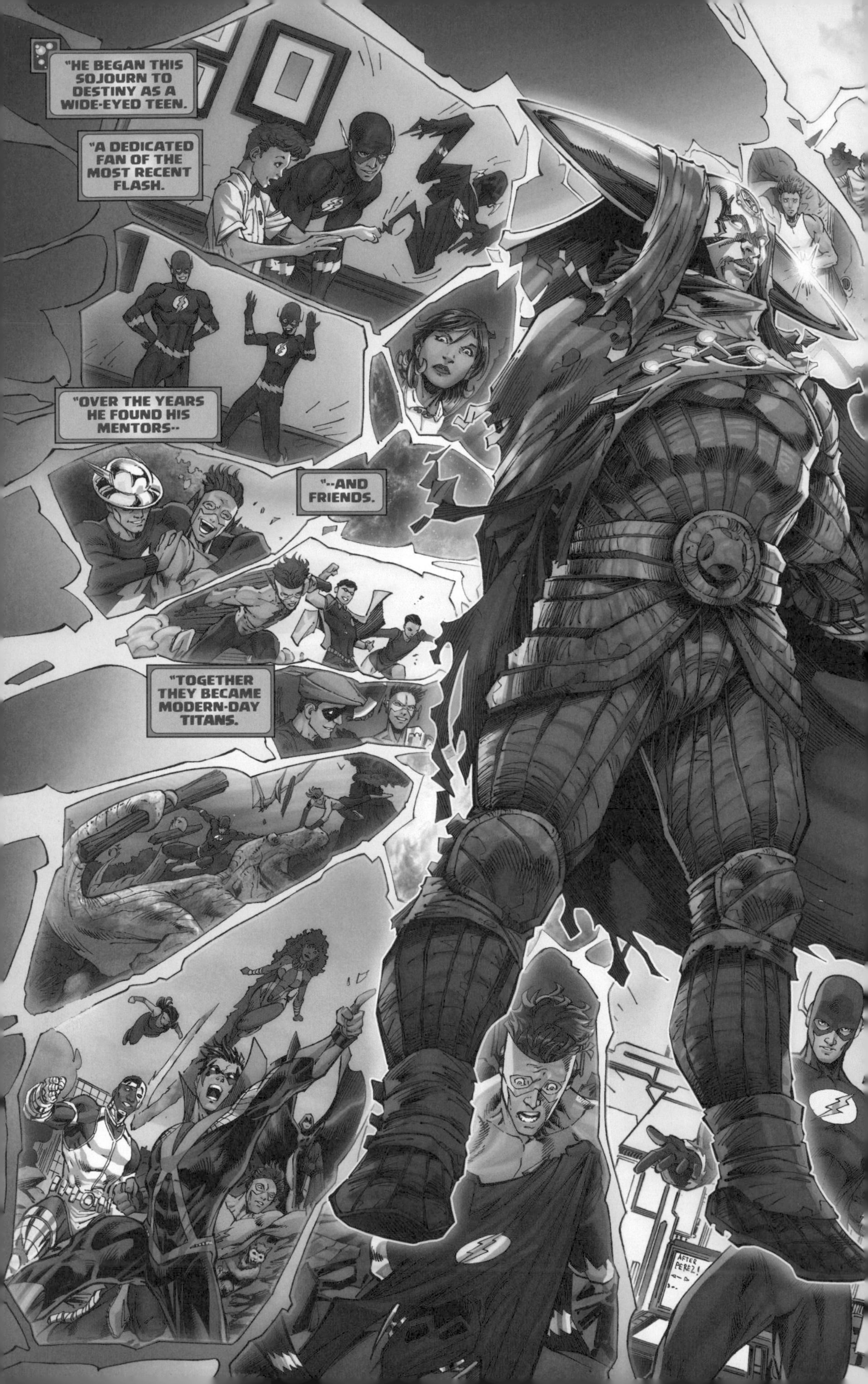
"HE BEGAN THIS SOJOURN TO DESTINY AS A WIDE-EYED TEEN.
"A DEDICATED FAN OF THE MOST RECENT FLASH.
"OVER THE YEARS HE FOUND HIS MENTORS--
"--AND FRIENDS.
"TOGETHER THEY BECAME MODERN-DAY TITANS.
AFTER PEREZ!

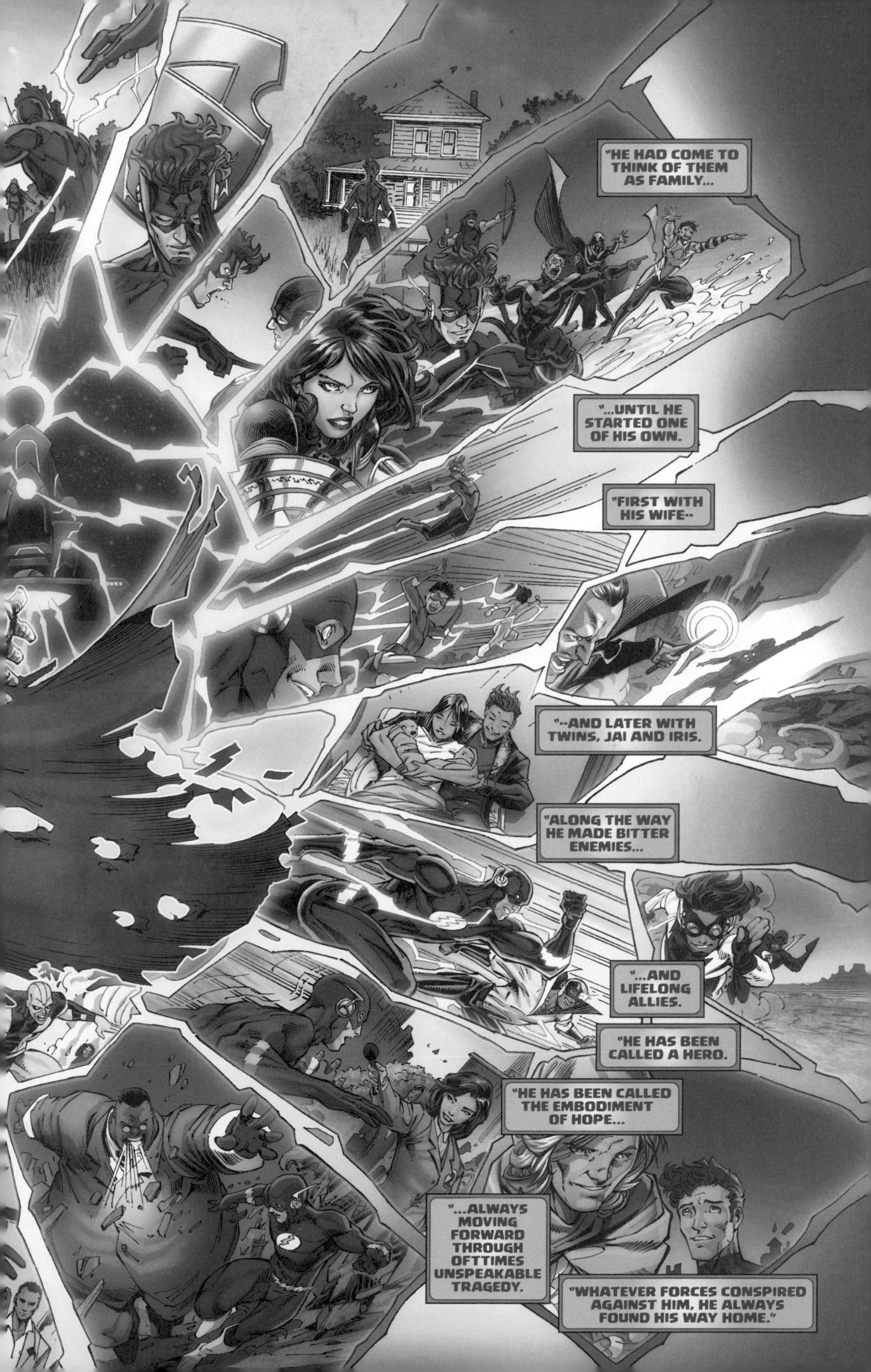
"HE HAD COME TO THINK OF THEM AS FAMILY...
"...UNTIL HE STARTED ONE OF HIS OWN.
"FIRST WITH HIS WIFE--
"--AND LATER WITH TWINS, JAI AND IRIS.
"ALONG THE WAY HE MADE BITTER ENEMIES...
"...AND LIFELONG ALLIES.
"HE HAS BEEN CALLED A HERO.
"HE HAS BEEN CALLED THE EMBODIMENT OF HOPE...
"...ALWAYS MOVING FORWARD THROUGH OFTTIMES UNSPEAKABLE TRAGEDY.
"WHATEVER FORCES CONSPIRED AGAINST HIM, HE ALWAYS FOUND HIS WAY HOME."

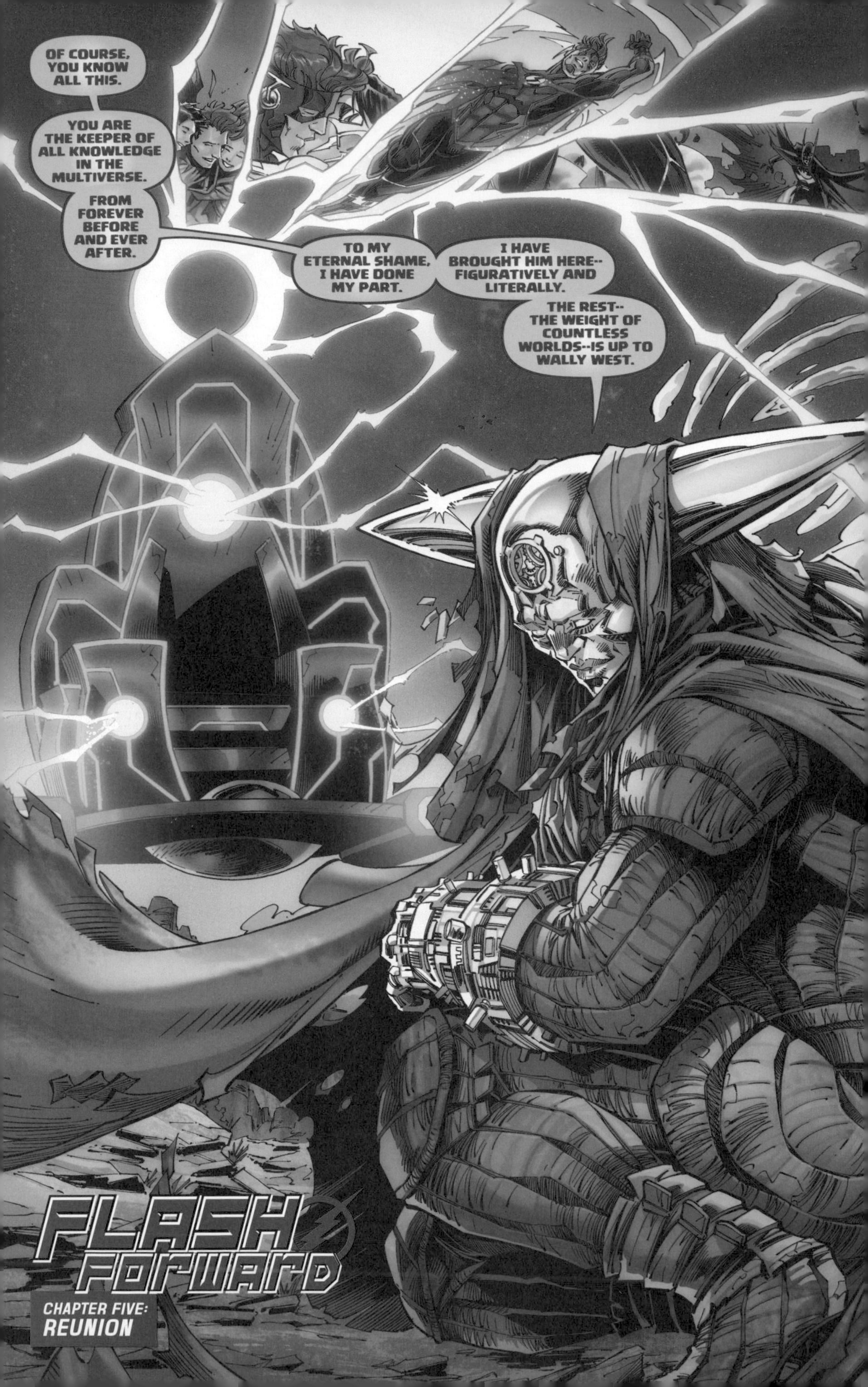

OF COURSE, YOU KNOW ALL THIS.
YOU ARE THE KEEPER OF ALL KNOWLEDGE IN THE MULTIVERSE.
FROM FOREVER BEFORE AND EVER AFTER.
TO MY ETERNAL SHAME, I HAVE DONE MY PART.
I HAVE BROUGHT HIM HERE--FIGURATIVELY AND LITERALLY.
THE REST--THE WEIGHT OF COUNTLESS WORLDS--IS UP TO WALLY WEST.
FLASH FORWARD
CHAPTER FIVE: REUNION

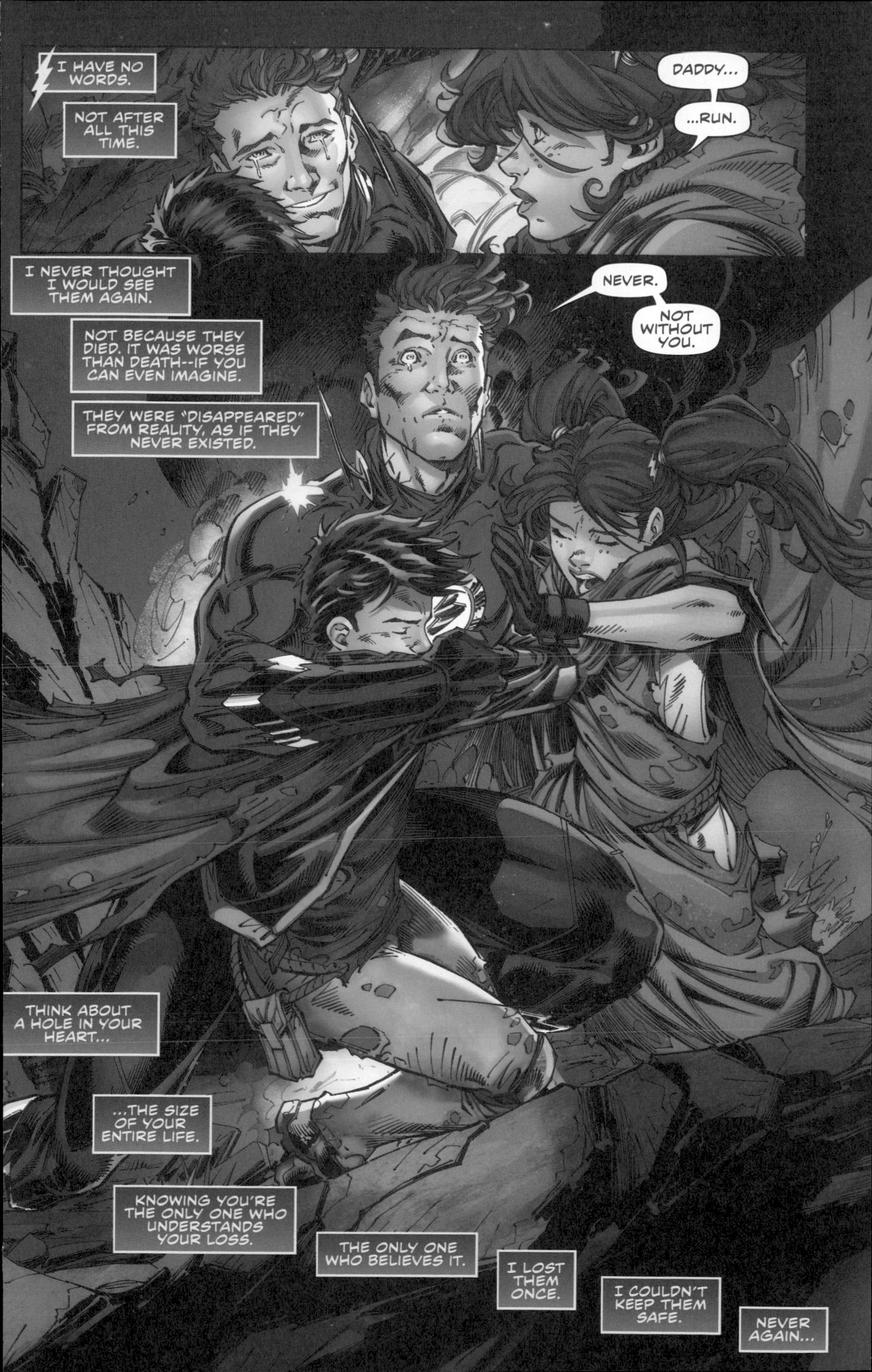
I HAVE NO WORDS.
NOT AFTER ALL THIS TIME.
DADDY...
...RUN.
I NEVER THOUGHT I WOULD SEE THEM AGAIN.
NOT BECAUSE THEY DIED. IT WAS WORSE THAN DEATH--IF YOU CAN EVEN IMAGINE.
THEY WERE "DISAPPEARED" FROM REALITY, AS IF THEY NEVER EXISTED.
NEVER.
NOT WITHOUT YOU.
THINK ABOUT A HOLE IN YOUR HEART...
...THE SIZE OF YOUR ENTIRE LIFE.
KNOWING YOU'RE THE ONLY ONE WHO UNDERSTANDS YOUR LOSS.
THE ONLY ONE WHO BELIEVES IT.
I LOST THEM ONCE.
I COULDN'T KEEP THEM SAFE.
NEVER AGAIN...

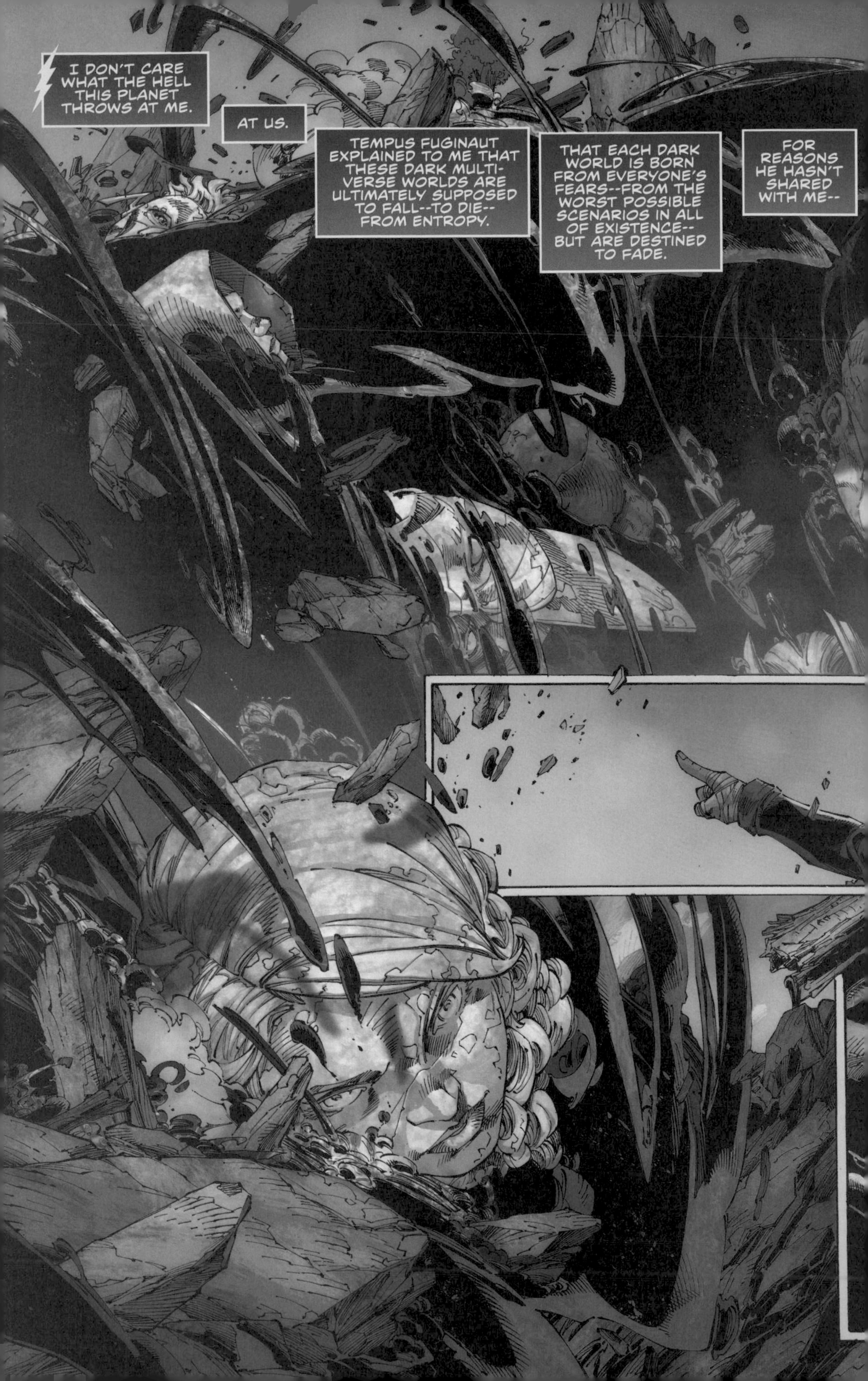
I DON'T CARE WHAT THE HELL THIS PLANET THROWS AT ME.
AT US.
TEMPUS FUGINAUT EXPLAINED TO ME THAT THESE DARK MULTI-VERSE WORLDS ARE ULTIMATELY SUPPOSED TO FALL--TO DIE--FROM ENTROPY.
THAT EACH DARK WORLD IS BORN FROM EVERYONE'S FEARS--FROM THE WORST POSSIBLE SCENARIOS IN ALL OF EXISTENCE--BUT ARE DESTINED TO FADE.
FOR REASONS HE HASN'T SHARED WITH ME--

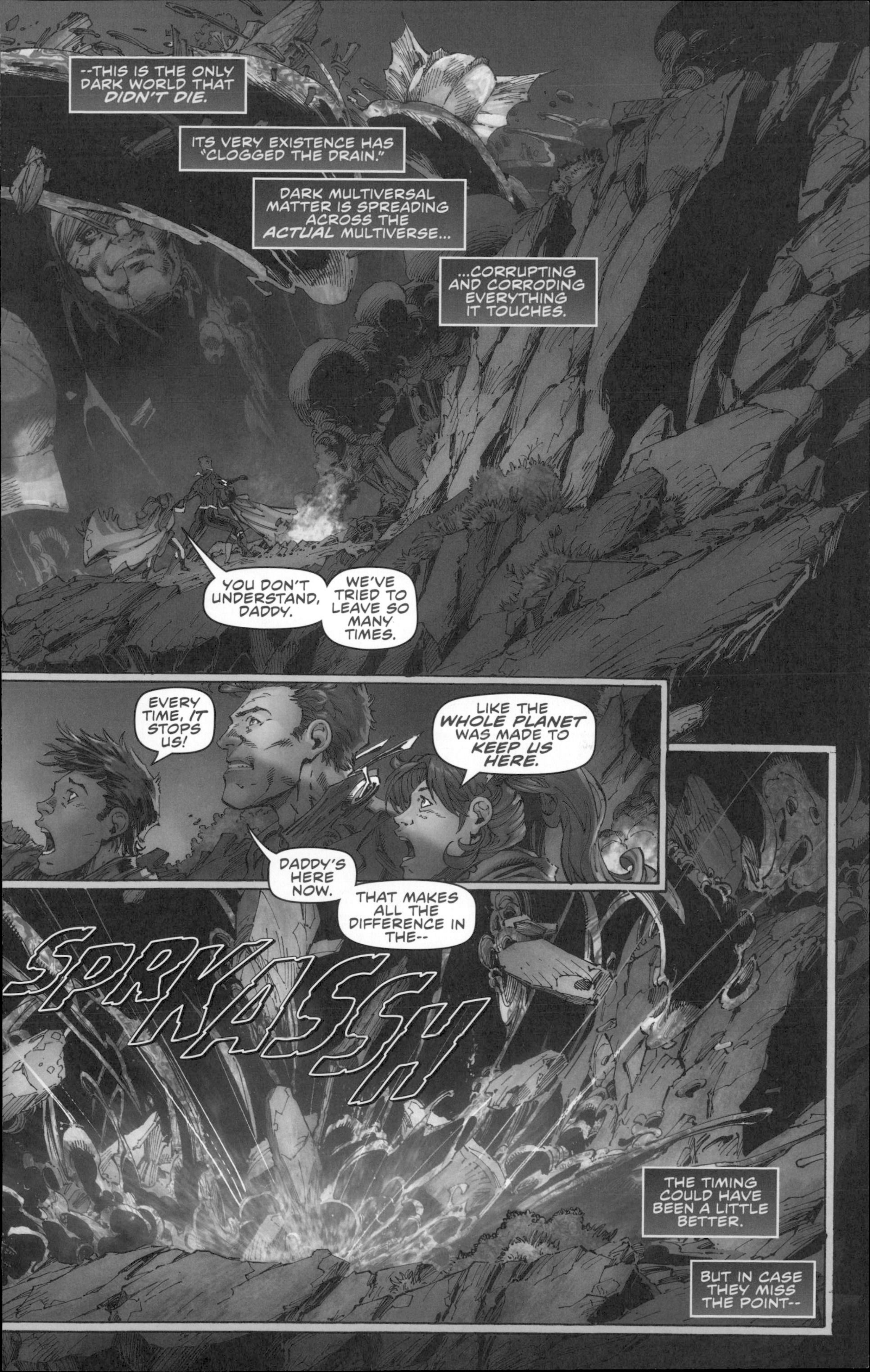
--THIS IS THE ONLY DARK WORLD THAT DIDN'T DIE.
ITS VERY EXISTENCE HAS "CLOGGED THE DRAIN."
DARK MULTIVERSAL MATTER IS SPREADING ACROSS THE ACTUAL MULTIVERSE...
...CORRUPTING AND CORRODING EVERYTHING IT TOUCHES.
YOU DON'T UNDERSTAND, DADDY.
WE'VE TRIED TO LEAVE SO MANY TIMES.
EVERY TIME, IT STOPS US!
LIKE THE WHOLE PLANET WAS MADE TO KEEP US HERE.
DADDY'S HERE NOW.
THAT MAKES ALL THE DIFFERENCE IN THE--
SPRKASSH
THE TIMING COULD HAVE BEEN A LITTLE BETTER.
BUT IN CASE THEY MISS THE POINT--

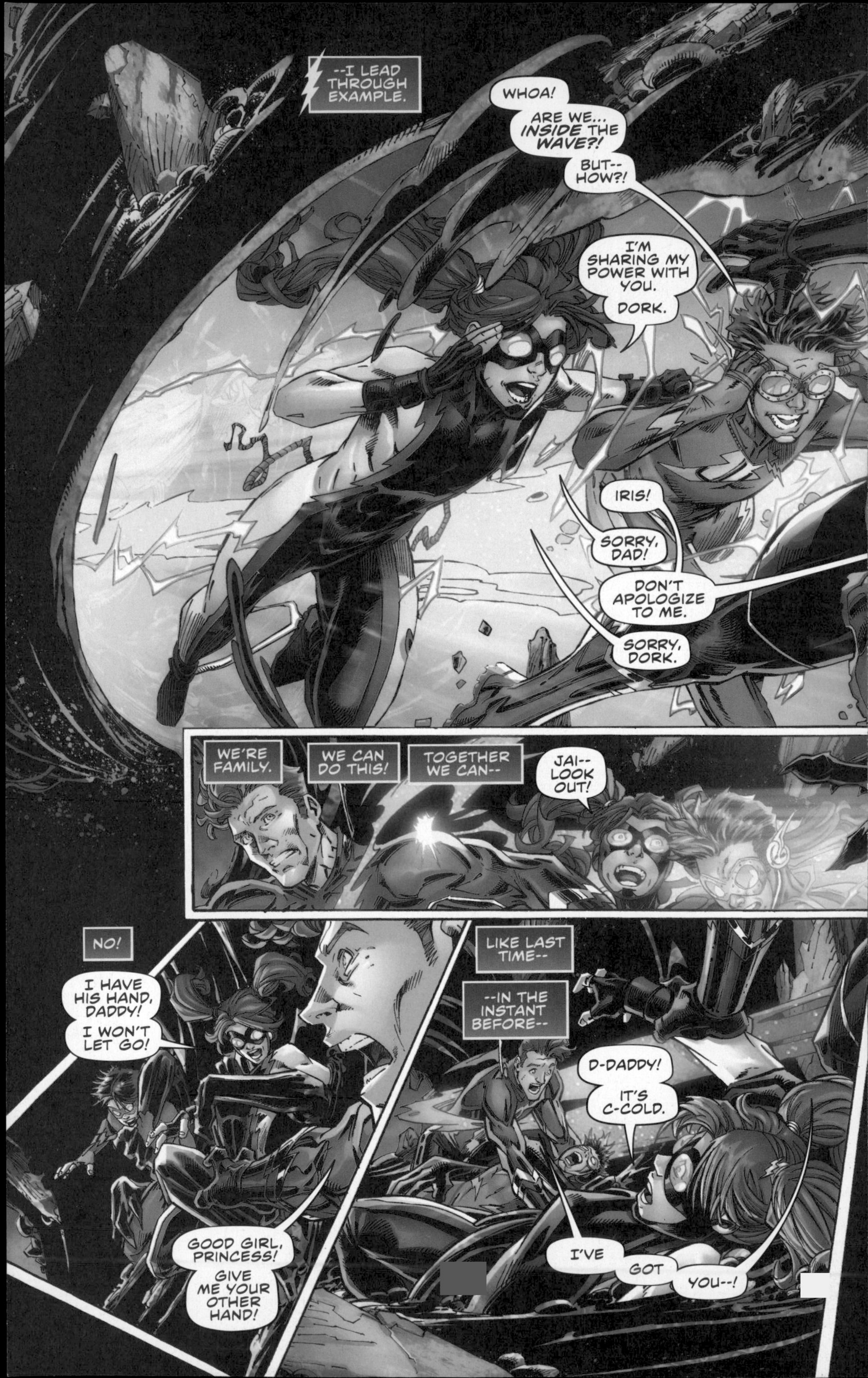
--I LEAD THROUGH EXAMPLE.
WHOA!
ARE WE... *INSIDE* THE *WAVE*?!
BUT-- HOW?!
I'M SHARING MY POWER WITH YOU.
DORK.
IRIS!
SORRY, DAD!
DON'T APOLOGIZE TO ME.
SORRY, DORK.
WE'RE FAMILY.
WE CAN DO THIS!
TOGETHER WE CAN--
JAI-- LOOK OUT!
NO!
I HAVE HIS HAND, DADDY!
I WON'T LET GO!
GOOD GIRL, PRINCESS!
GIVE ME YOUR OTHER HAND!
LIKE LAST TIME--
--IN THE INSTANT BEFORE--
D-DADDY!
IT'S C-COLD.
I'VE
GOT
YOU--!

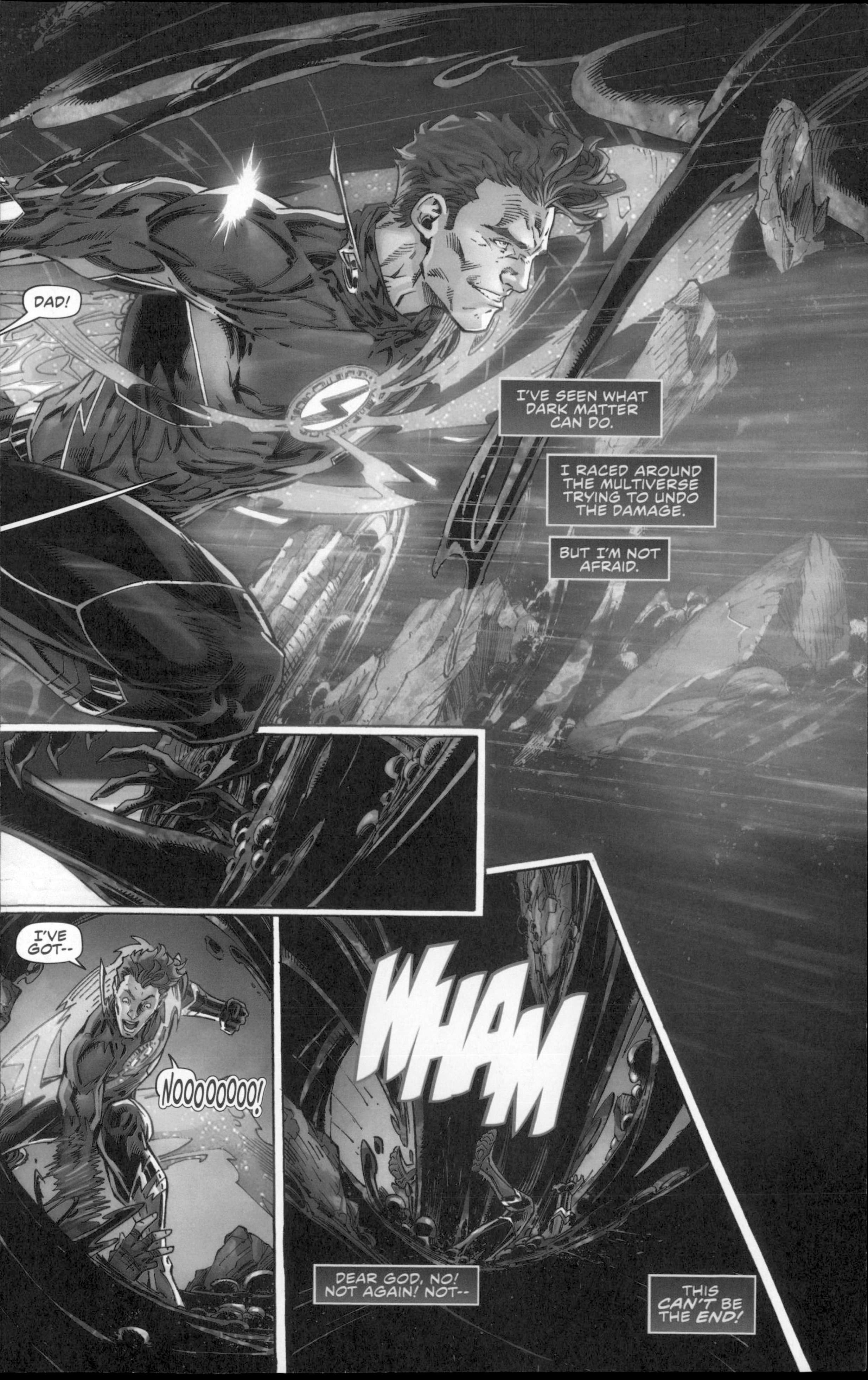
DAD!
I'VE SEEN WHAT DARK MATTER CAN DO.
I RACED AROUND THE MULTIVERSE TRYING TO UNDO THE DAMAGE.
BUT I'M NOT AFRAID.
I'VE GOT--
NOOOOOOOO!
WHAM
DEAR GOD, NO! NOT AGAIN! NOT--
THIS CAN'T BE THE END!

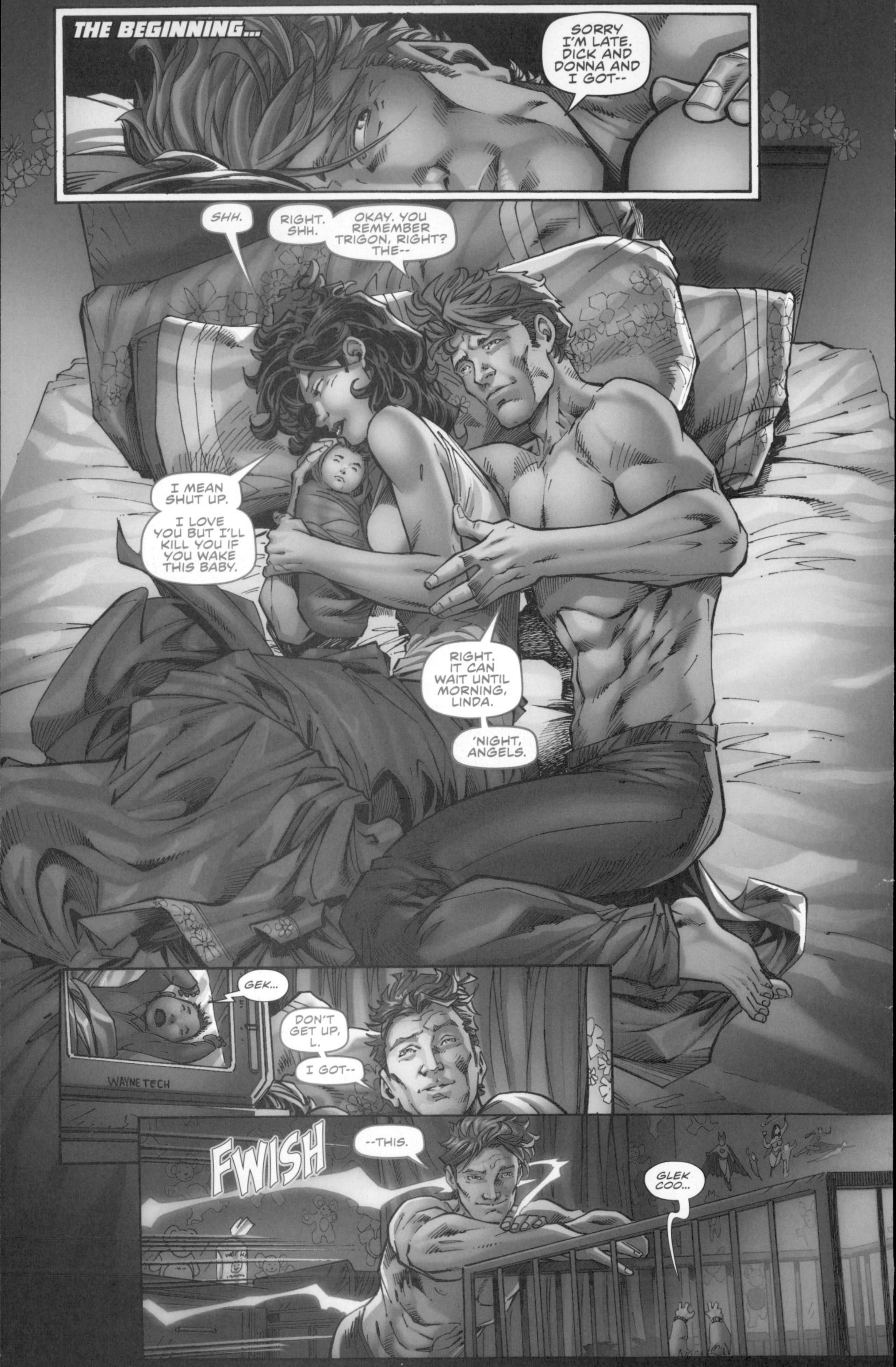
THE BEGINNING...
SORRY I'M LATE. DICK AND DONNA AND I GOT--
SHH.
RIGHT. SHH.
OKAY. YOU REMEMBER TRIGON, RIGHT? THE--
I MEAN SHUT UP.
I LOVE YOU BUT I'LL KILL YOU IF YOU WAKE THIS BABY.
RIGHT. IT CAN WAIT UNTIL MORNING, LINDA.
'NIGHT, ANGELS.
GEK...
DON'T GET UP, L.
I GOT--
WAYNE TECH
FWISH
--THIS.
GLEK COO...

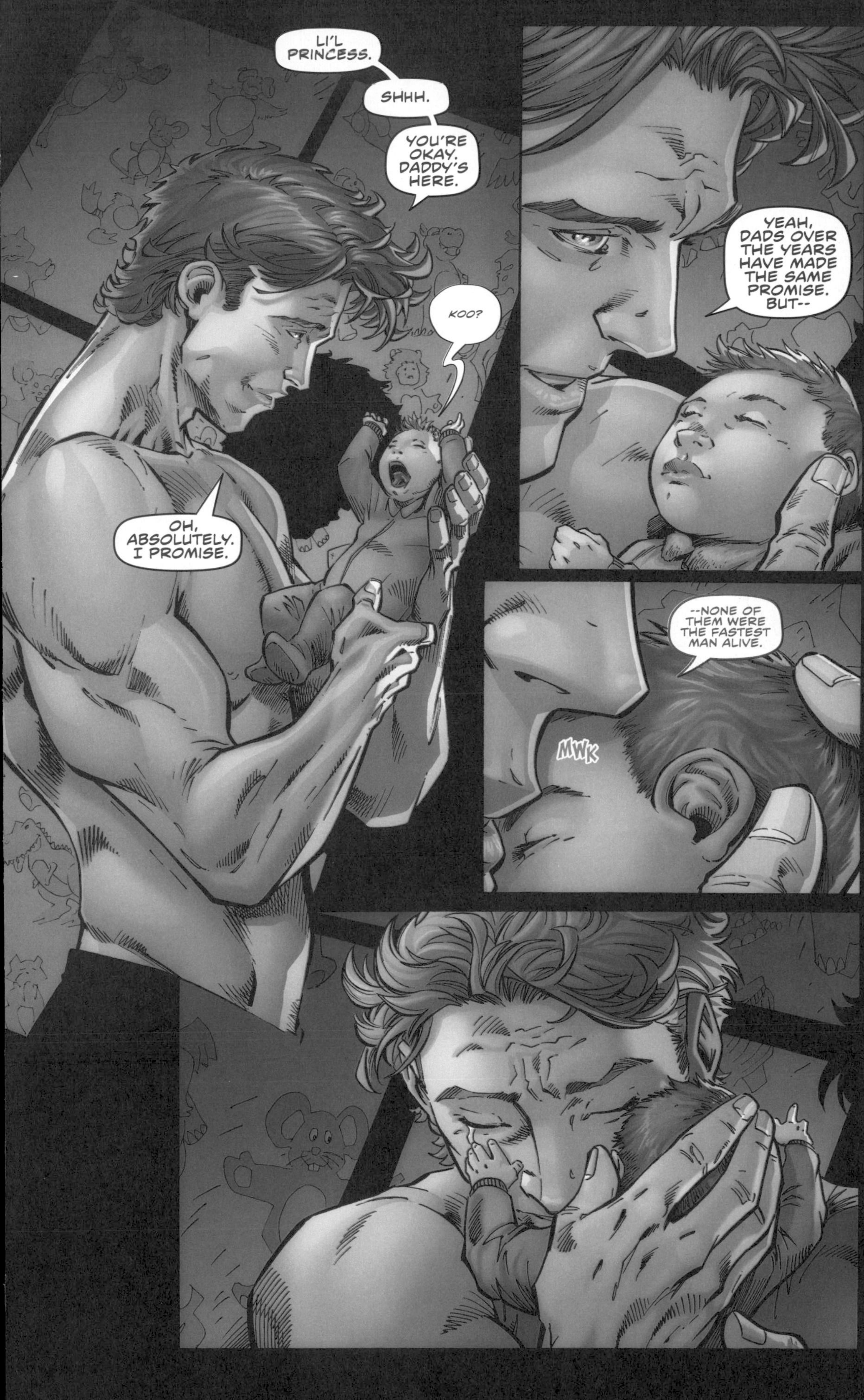
LI'L PRINCESS.
SHHH.
YOU'RE OKAY. DADDY'S HERE.
KOO?
OH, ABSOLUTELY. I PROMISE.
YEAH, DADS OVER THE YEARS HAVE MADE THE SAME PROMISE. BUT--
--NONE OF THEM WERE THE FASTEST MAN ALIVE.
MWK

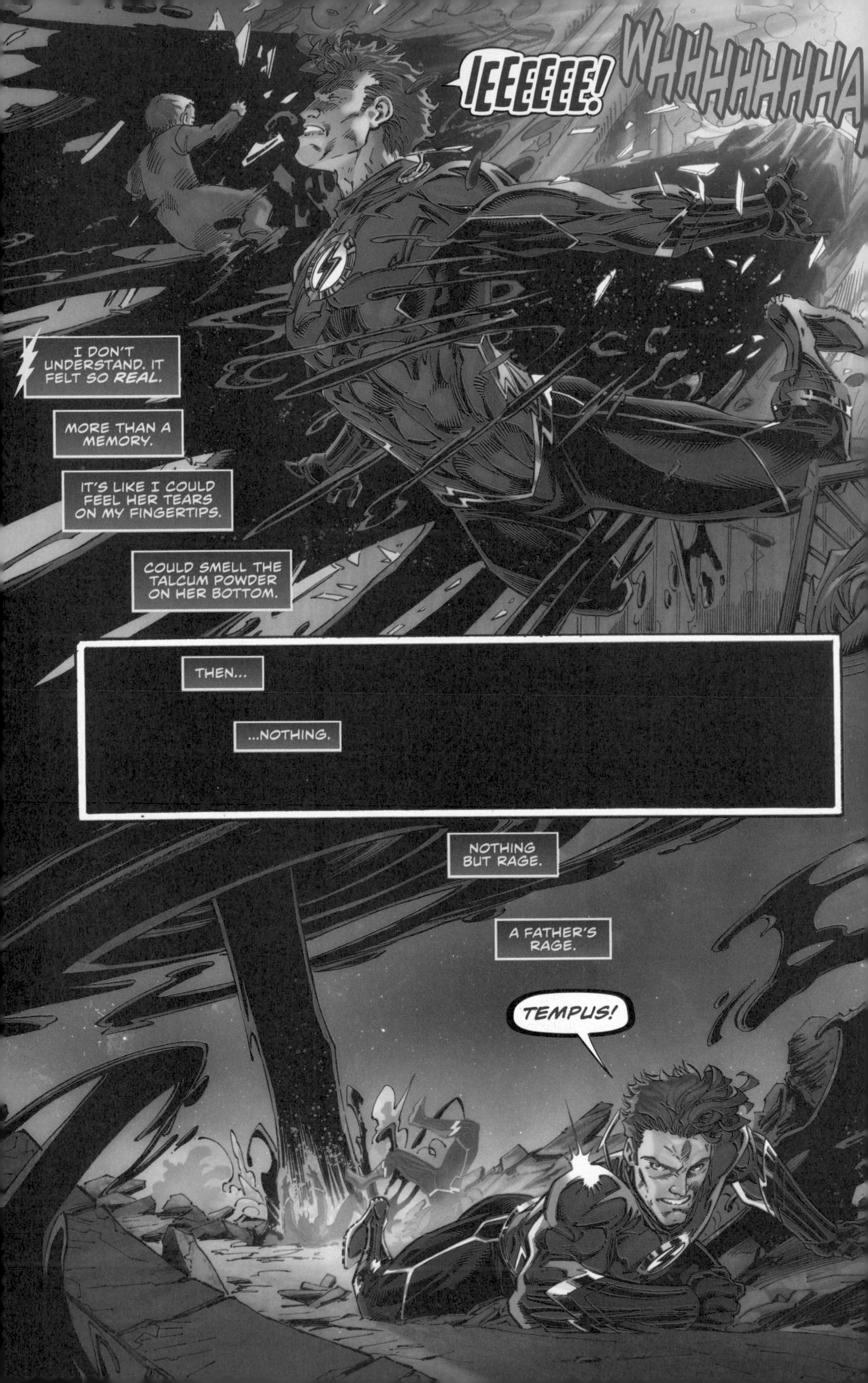
IEEEEEE!
WHHHHHHA
I DON'T UNDERSTAND. IT FELT SO *REAL*.
MORE THAN A MEMORY.
IT'S LIKE I COULD FEEL HER TEARS ON MY FINGERTIPS.
COULD SMELL THE TALCUM POWDER ON HER BOTTOM.
THEN...
...NOTHING.
NOTHING BUT RAGE.
A FATHER'S RAGE.
TEMPUS!

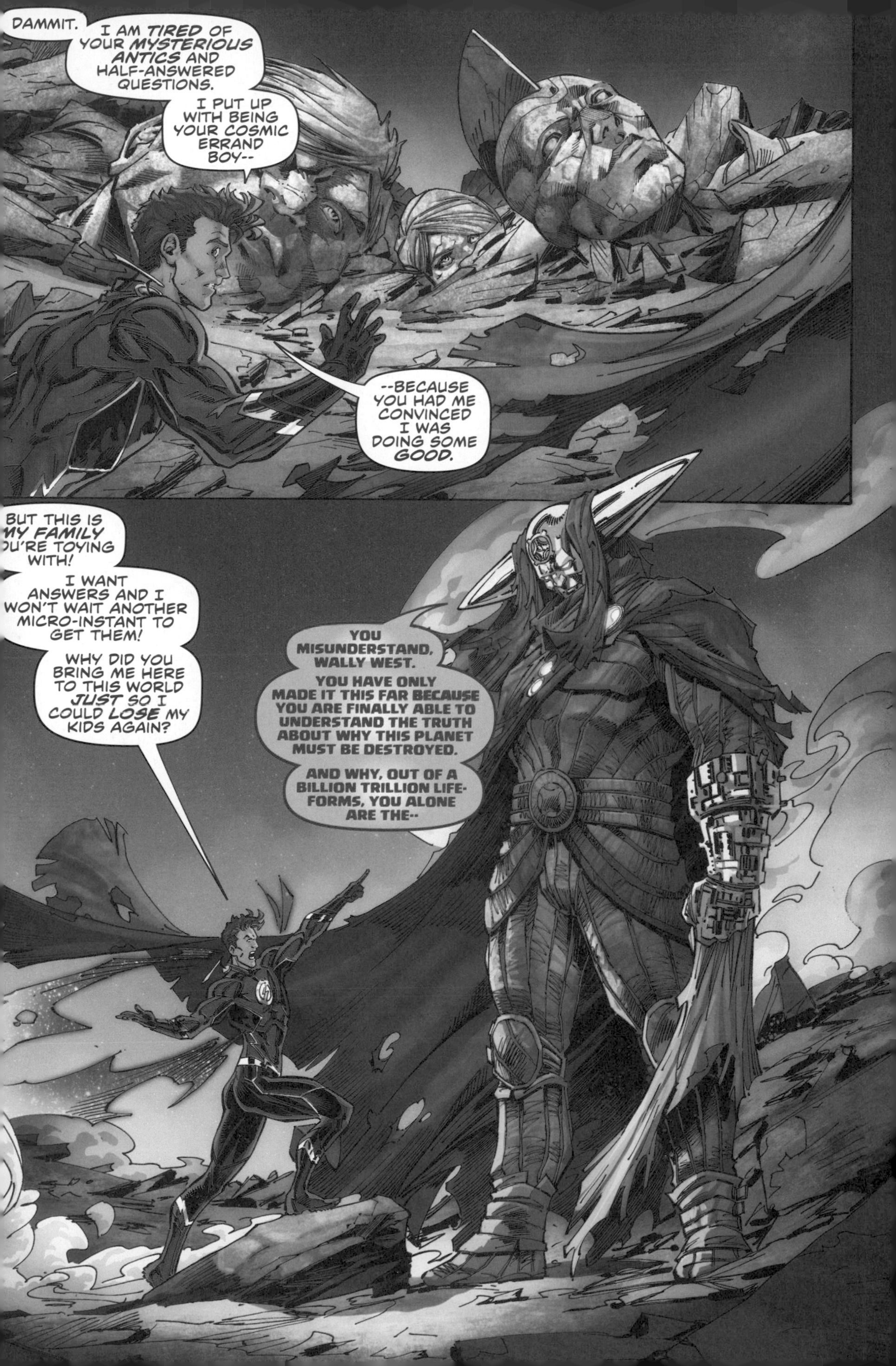

DAMMIT.
I AM TIRED OF YOUR MYSTERIOUS ANTICS AND HALF-ANSWERED QUESTIONS.
I PUT UP WITH BEING YOUR COSMIC ERRAND BOY--
--BECAUSE YOU HAD ME CONVINCED I WAS DOING SOME GOOD.
BUT THIS IS MY FAMILY U'RE TOYING WITH!
I WANT ANSWERS AND I WON'T WAIT ANOTHER MICRO-INSTANT TO GET THEM!
WHY DID YOU BRING ME HERE TO THIS WORLD JUST SO I COULD LOSE MY KIDS AGAIN?
YOU MISUNDERSTAND, WALLY WEST.
YOU HAVE ONLY MADE IT THIS FAR BECAUSE YOU ARE FINALLY ABLE TO UNDERSTAND THE TRUTH ABOUT WHY THIS PLANET MUST BE DESTROYED.
AND WHY, OUT OF A BILLION TRILLION LIFE-FORMS, YOU ALONE ARE THE--

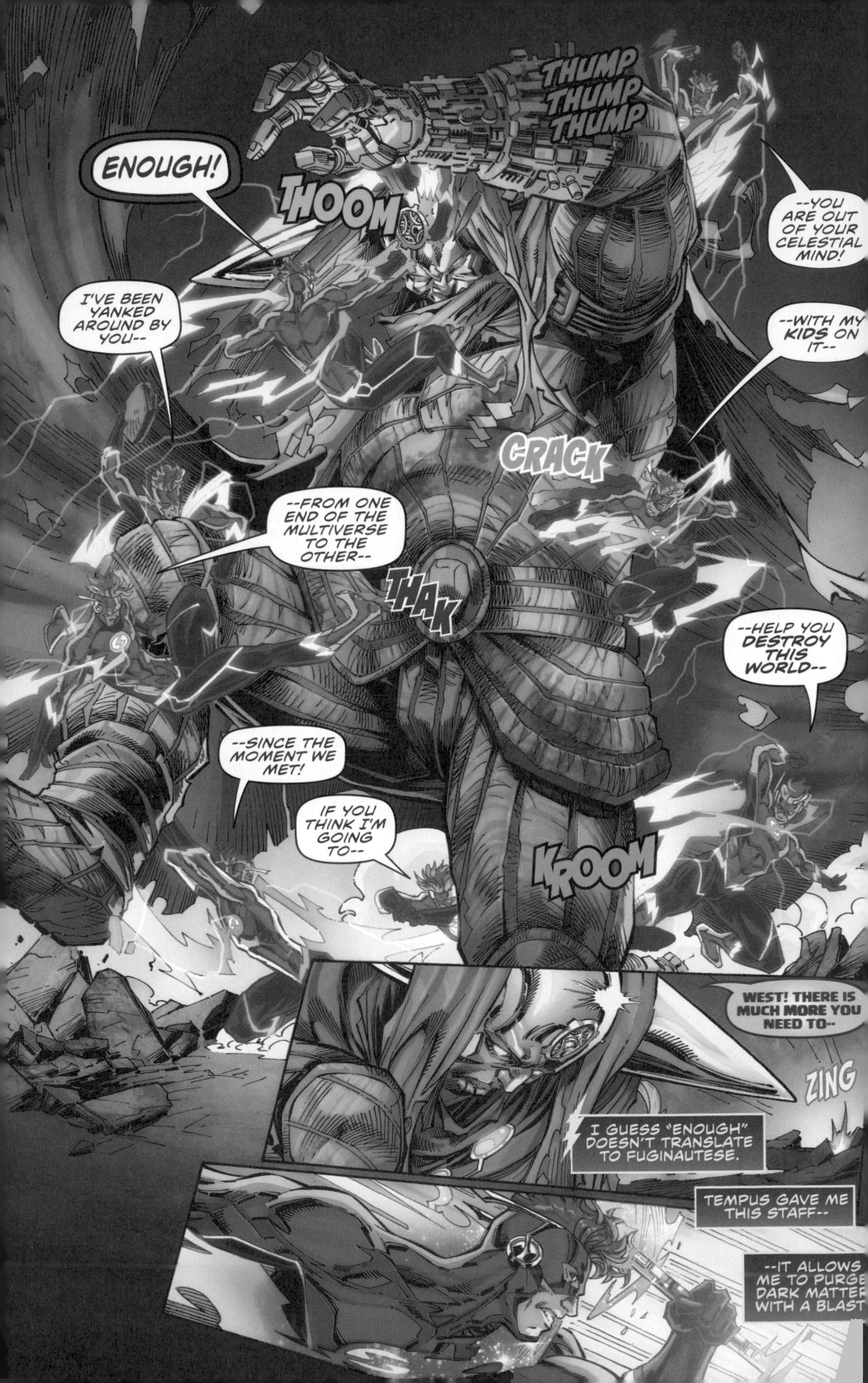
THUMP THUMP THUMP
ENOUGH!
THOOM
--YOU ARE OUT OF YOUR CELESTIAL MIND!
I'VE BEEN YANKED AROUND BY YOU--
--WITH MY KIDS ON IT--
CRACK
--FROM ONE END OF THE MULTIVERSE TO THE OTHER--
THAK
--HELP YOU DESTROY THIS WORLD--
--SINCE THE MOMENT WE MET!
IF YOU THINK I'M GOING TO--
KROOM
WEST! THERE IS MUCH MORE YOU NEED TO--
ZING
I GUESS "ENOUGH" DOESN'T TRANSLATE TO FUGINAUTESE.
TEMPUS GAVE ME THIS STAFF--
--IT ALLOWS ME TO PURGE DARK MATTER WITH A BLAST

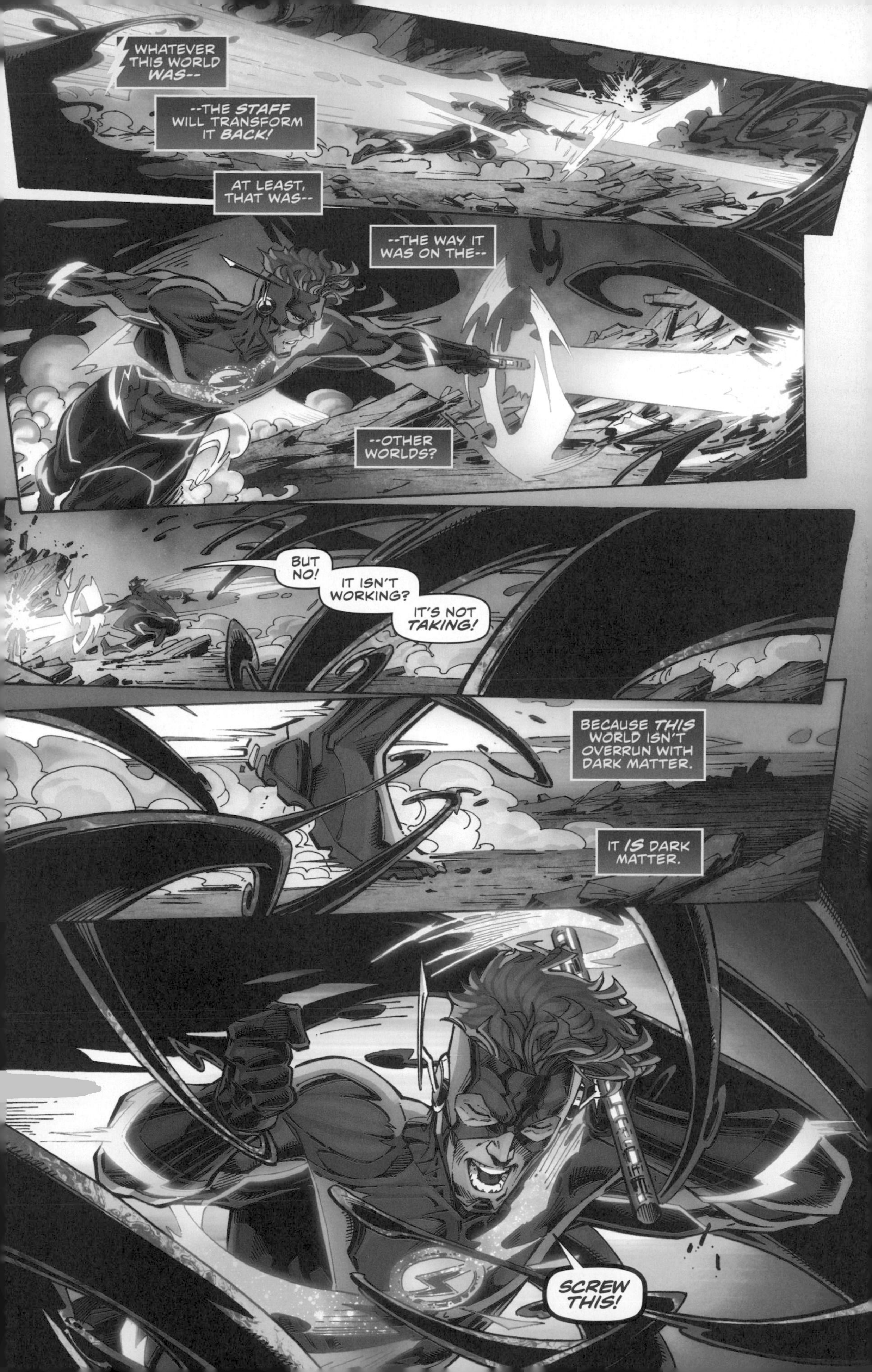
WHATEVER THIS WORLD WAS--
--THE STAFF WILL TRANSFORM IT BACK!
AT LEAST, THAT WAS--
--THE WAY IT WAS ON THE--
--OTHER WORLDS?
BUT NO!
IT ISN'T WORKING?
IT'S NOT TAKING!
BECAUSE THIS WORLD ISN'T OVERRUN WITH DARK MATTER.
IT IS DARK MATTER.
SCREW THIS!

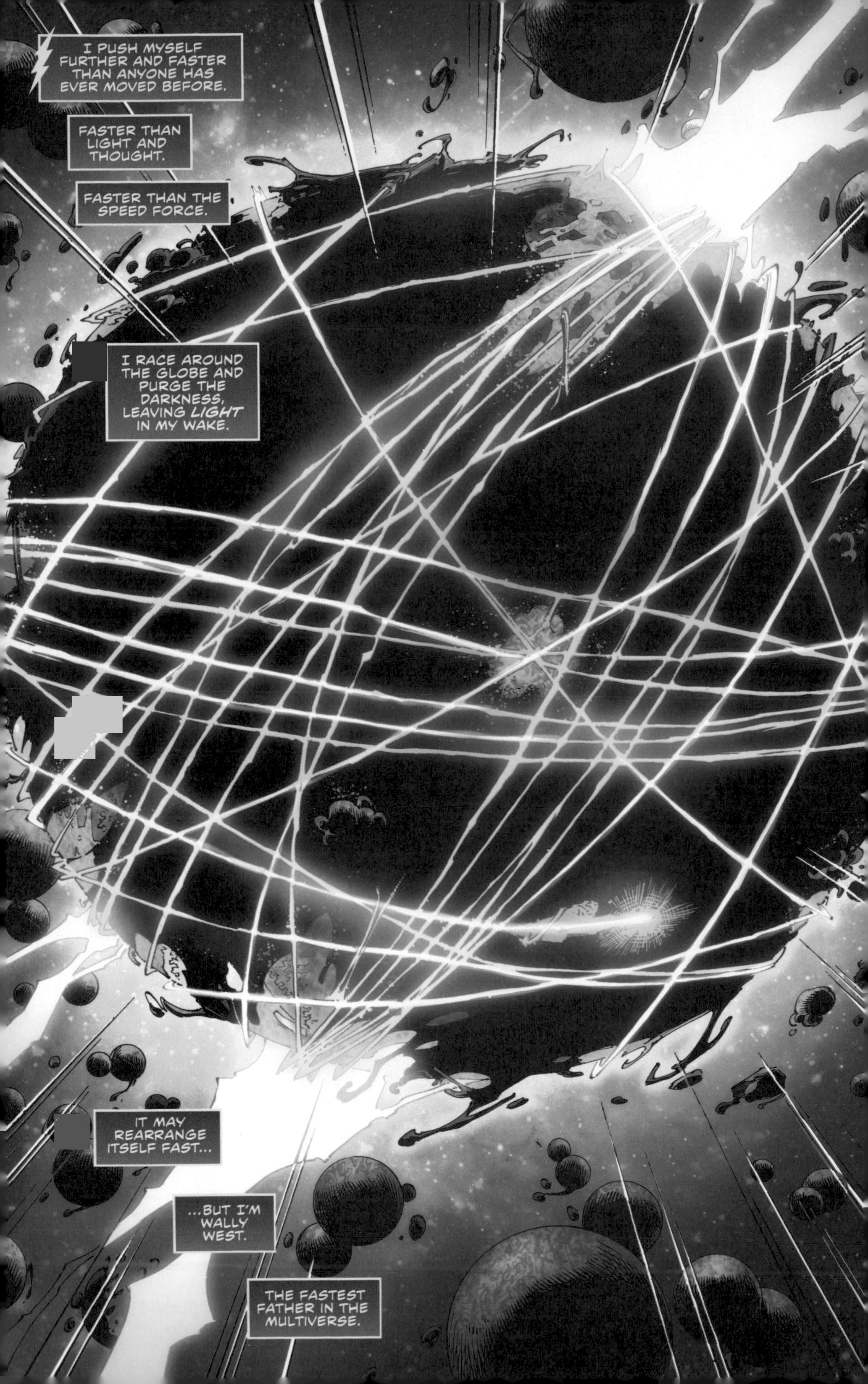
I PUSH MYSELF FURTHER AND FASTER THAN ANYONE HAS EVER MOVED BEFORE.
FASTER THAN LIGHT AND THOUGHT.
FASTER THAN THE SPEED FORCE.
I RACE AROUND THE GLOBE AND PURGE THE DARKNESS, LEAVING *LIGHT* IN MY WAKE.
IT MAY REARRANGE ITSELF FAST...
...BUT I'M WALLY WEST.
THE FASTEST FATHER IN THE MULTIVERSE.

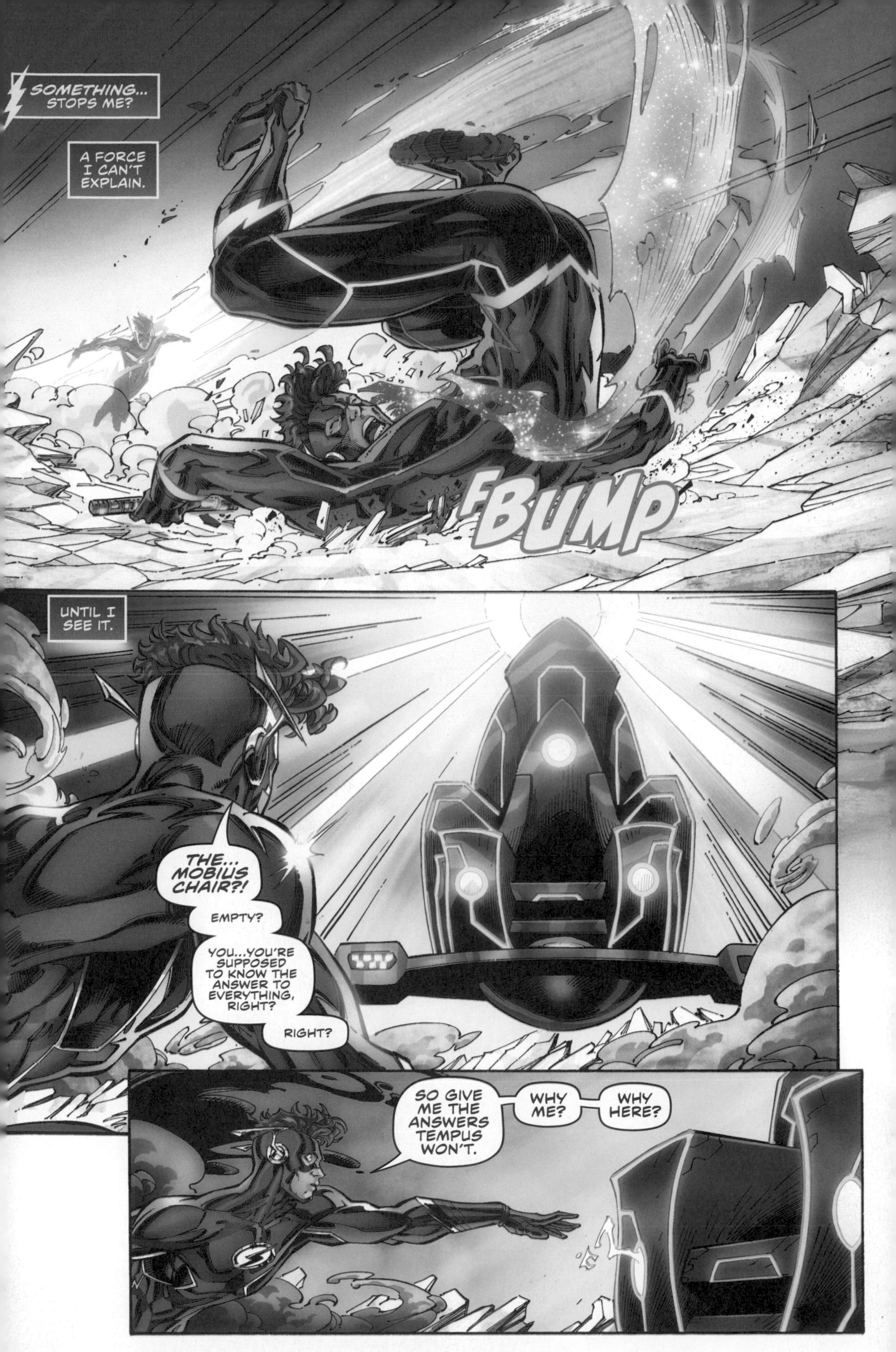
SOMETHING... STOPS ME?
A FORCE I CAN'T EXPLAIN.
FBUMP
UNTIL I SEE IT.
THE... MOBIUS CHAIR?!
EMPTY?
YOU...YOU'RE SUPPOSED TO KNOW THE ANSWER TO EVERYTHING, RIGHT?
RIGHT?
SO GIVE ME THE ANSWERS TEMPUS WON'T.
WHY ME?
WHY HERE?

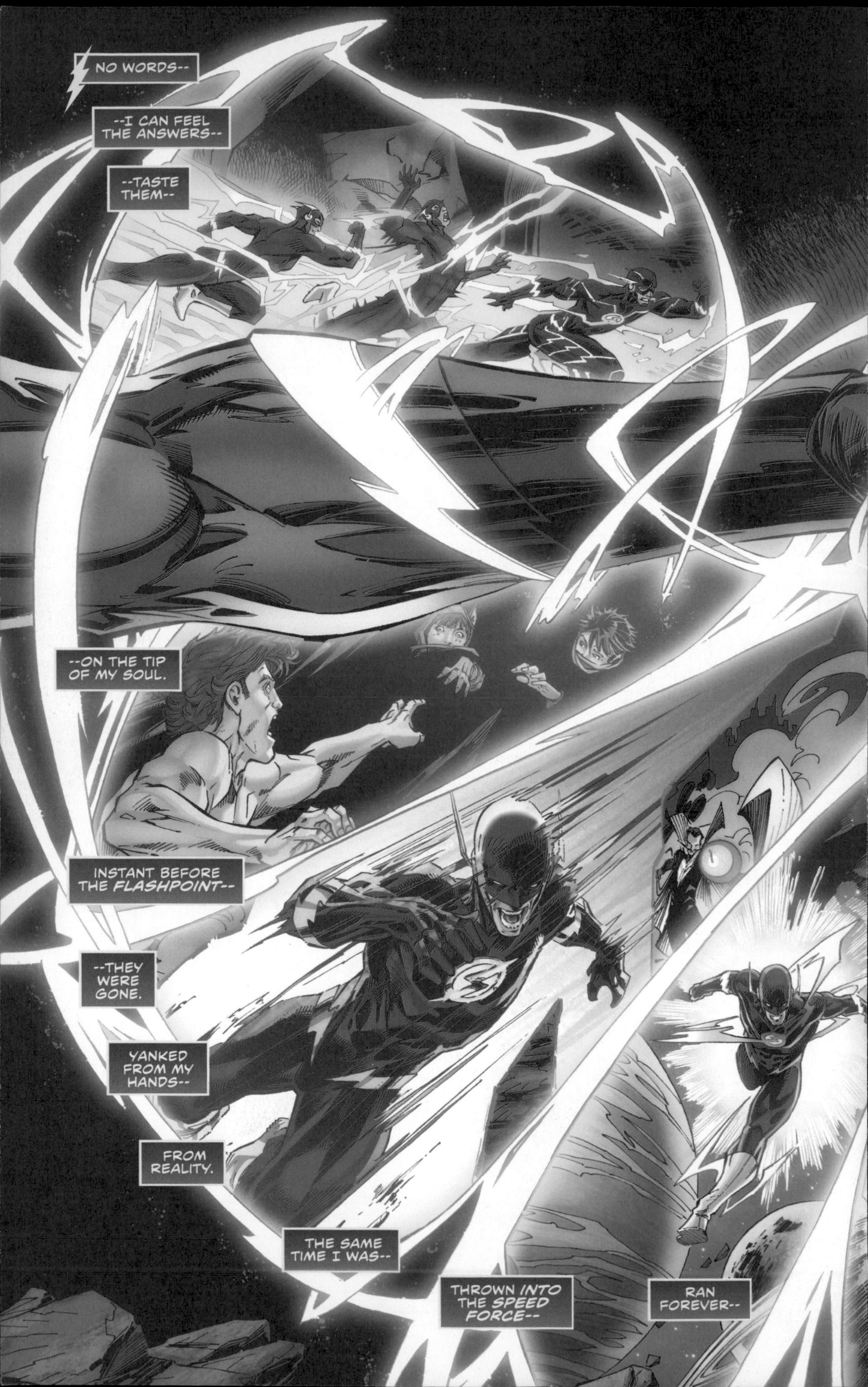
NO WORDS--
--I CAN FEEL THE ANSWERS--
--TASTE THEM--
--ON THE TIP OF MY SOUL.
INSTANT BEFORE THE *FLASHPOINT*--
--THEY WERE GONE.
YANKED FROM MY HANDS--
FROM REALITY.
THE SAME TIME I WAS--
THROWN *INTO* THE *SPEED FORCE*--
RAN FOREVER--

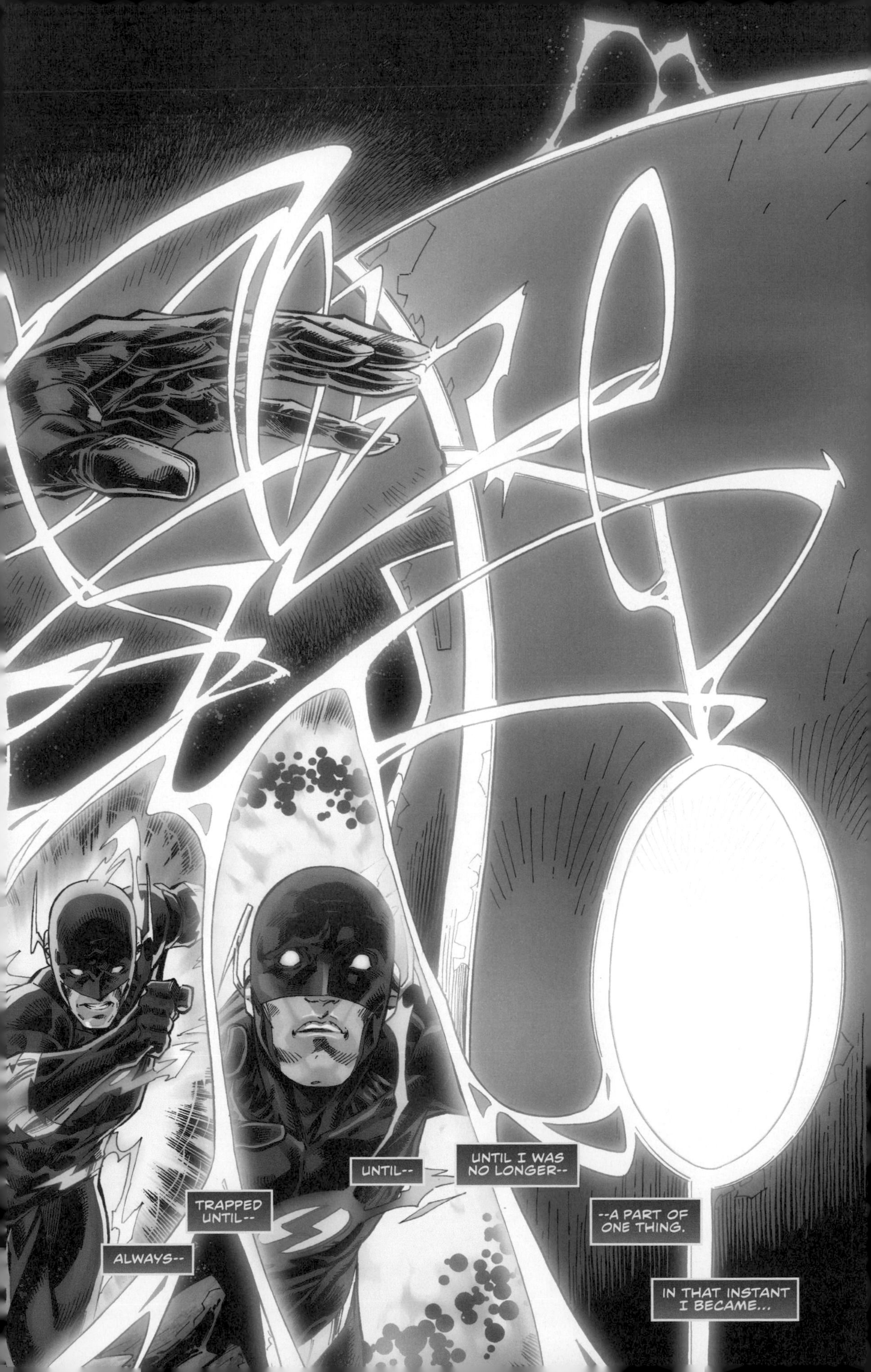
ALWAYS--
TRAPPED UNTIL--
UNTIL--
UNTIL I WAS NO LONGER--
--A PART OF ONE THING.
IN THAT INSTANT I BECAME...

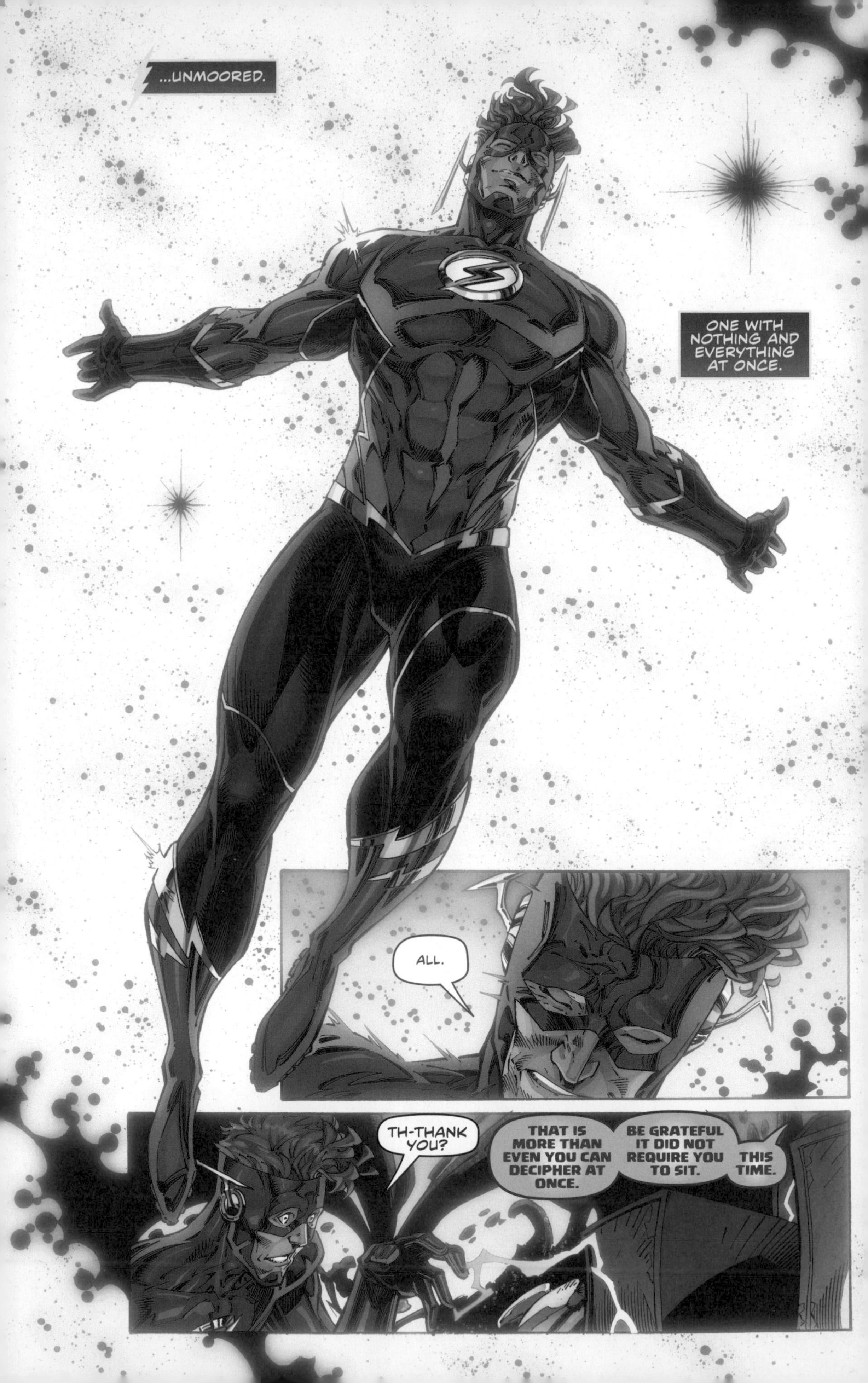
...UNMOORED.
ONE WITH NOTHING AND EVERYTHING AT ONCE.
ALL.
TH-THANK YOU?
THAT IS MORE THAN EVEN YOU CAN DECIPHER AT ONCE.
BE GRATEFUL IT DID NOT REQUIRE YOU TO SIT.
THIS TIME.

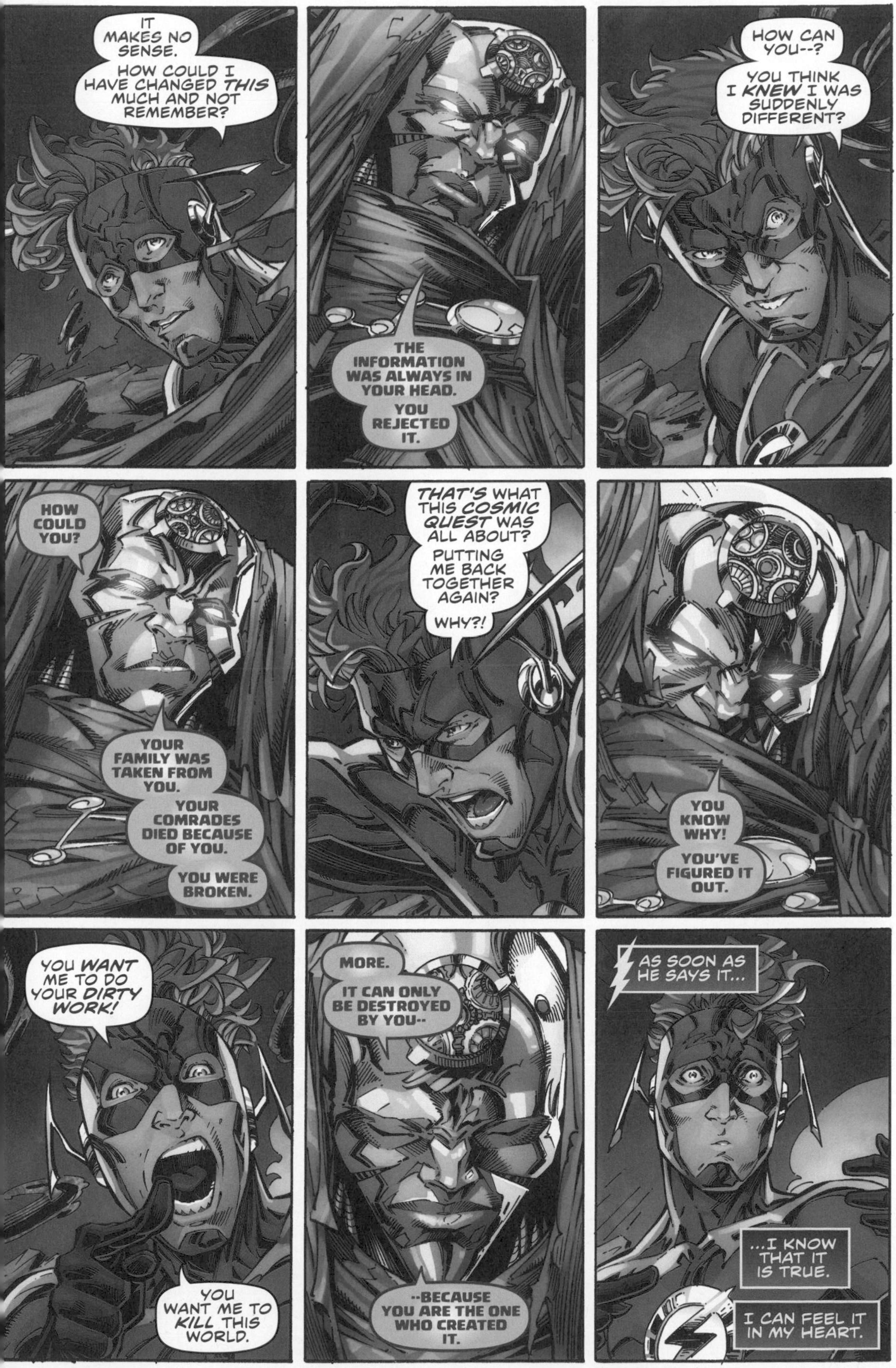
IT MAKES NO SENSE.
HOW COULD I HAVE CHANGED *THIS* MUCH AND NOT REMEMBER?
THE INFORMATION WAS ALWAYS IN YOUR HEAD.
YOU REJECTED IT.
HOW CAN YOU--?
YOU THINK I *KNEW* I WAS SUDDENLY DIFFERENT?
HOW COULD YOU?
YOUR FAMILY WAS TAKEN FROM YOU.
YOUR COMRADES DIED BECAUSE OF YOU.
YOU WERE BROKEN.
THAT'S WHAT THIS *COSMIC QUEST* WAS ALL ABOUT?
PUTTING ME BACK TOGETHER AGAIN?
WHY?!
YOU KNOW WHY!
YOU'VE FIGURED IT OUT.
YOU *WANT* ME TO DO YOUR *DIRTY WORK!*
YOU WANT ME TO *KILL* THIS WORLD.
MORE.
IT CAN ONLY BE DESTROYED BY YOU--
--BECAUSE YOU ARE THE ONE WHO CREATED IT.
AS SOON AS HE SAYS IT...
...I KNOW THAT IT IS TRUE.
I CAN FEEL IT IN MY HEART.

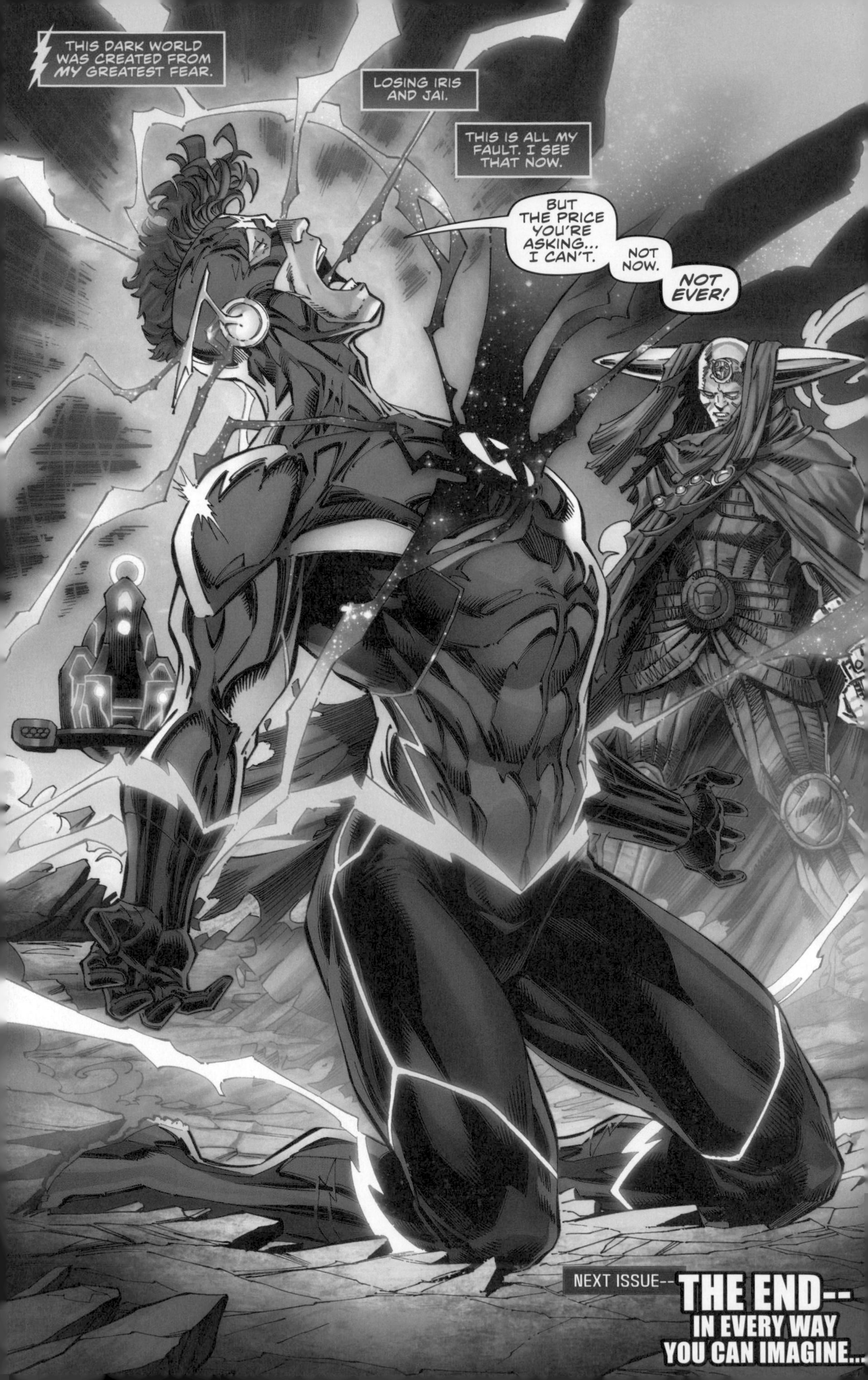
THIS DARK WORLD WAS CREATED FROM MY GREATEST FEAR.
LOSING IRIS AND JAI.
THIS IS ALL MY FAULT. I SEE THAT NOW.
BUT THE PRICE YOU'RE ASKING... I CAN'T.
NOT NOW.
NOT EVER!
NEXT ISSUE--
THE END--
IN EVERY WAY YOU CAN IMAGINE...

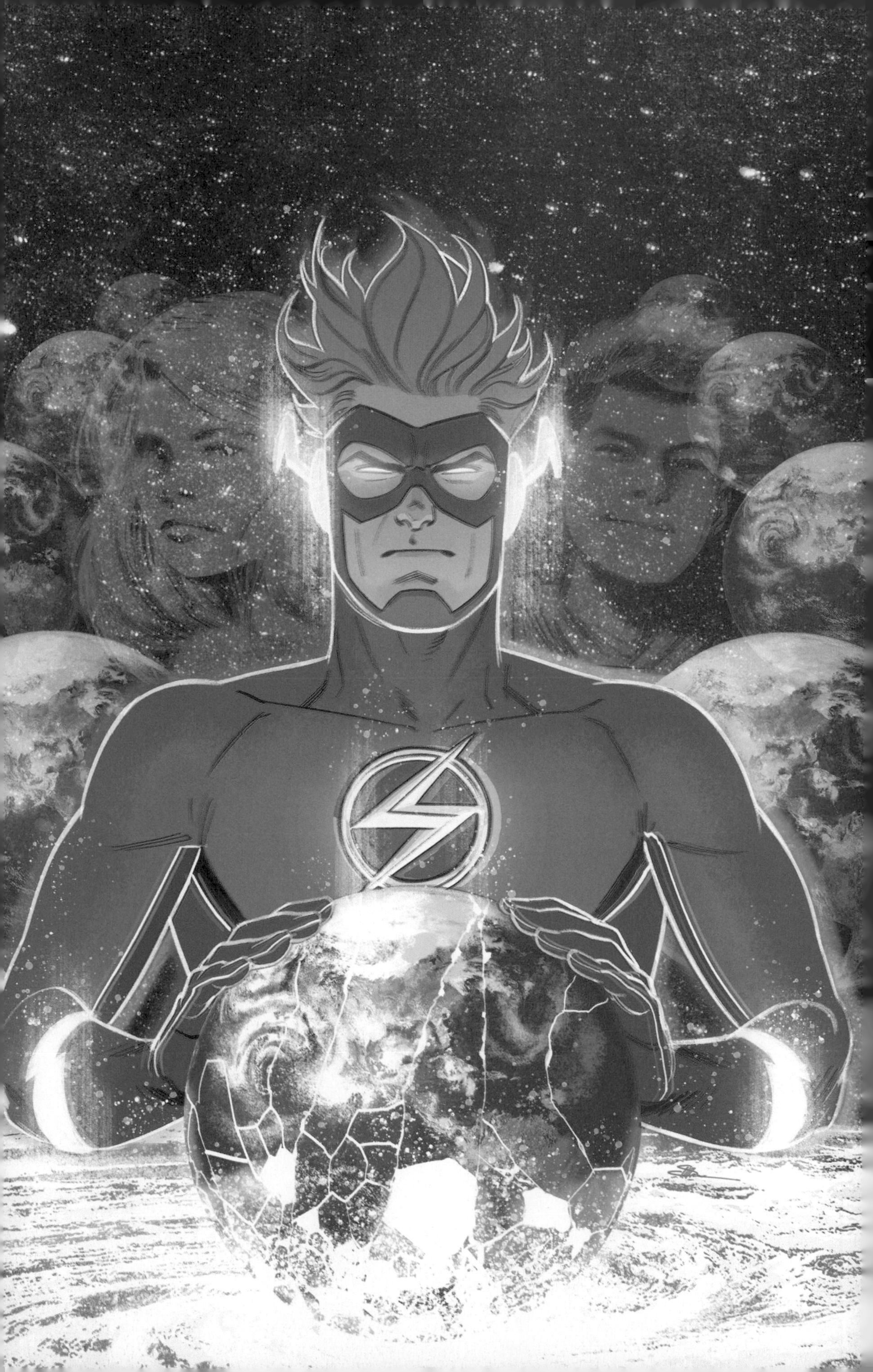

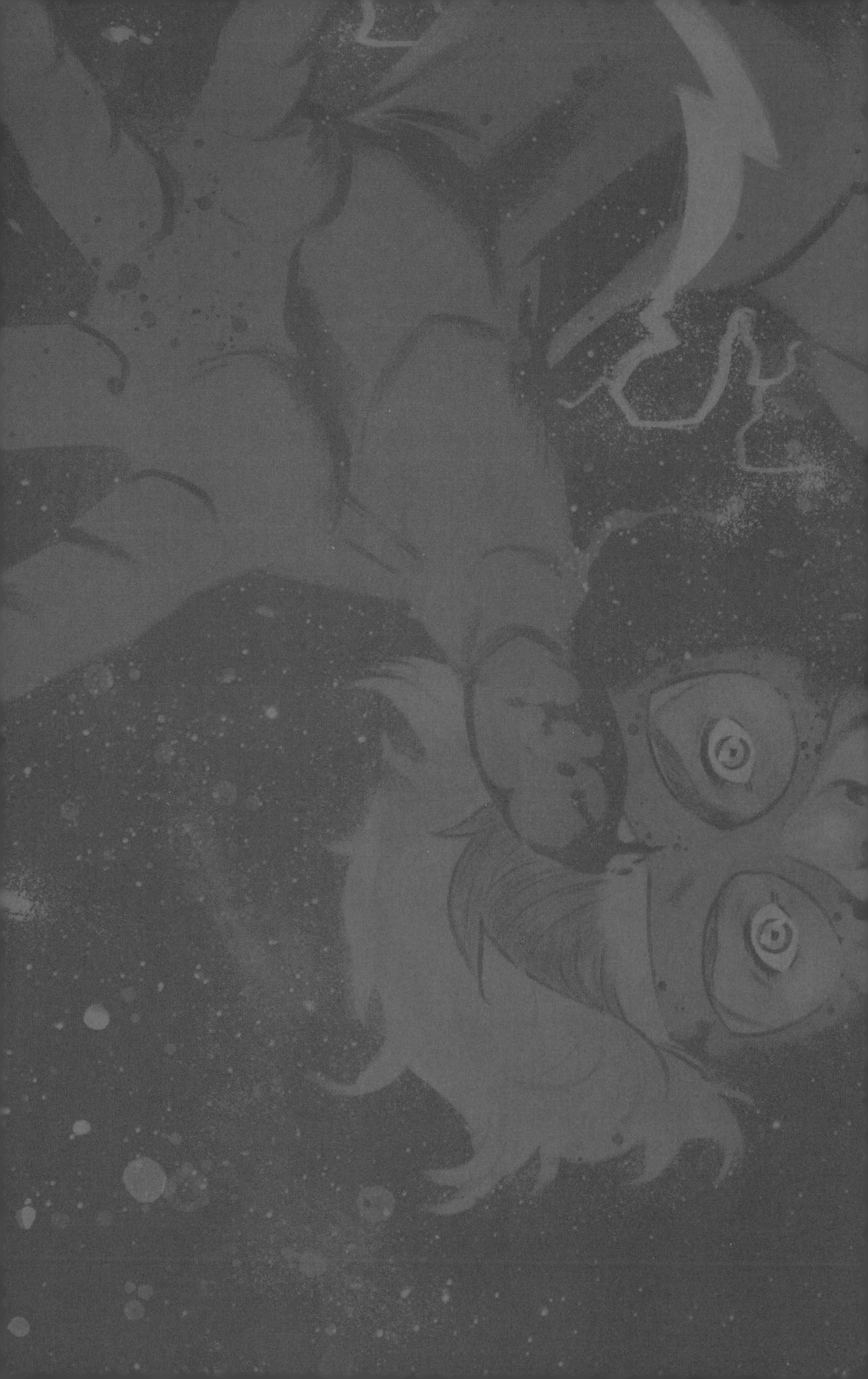

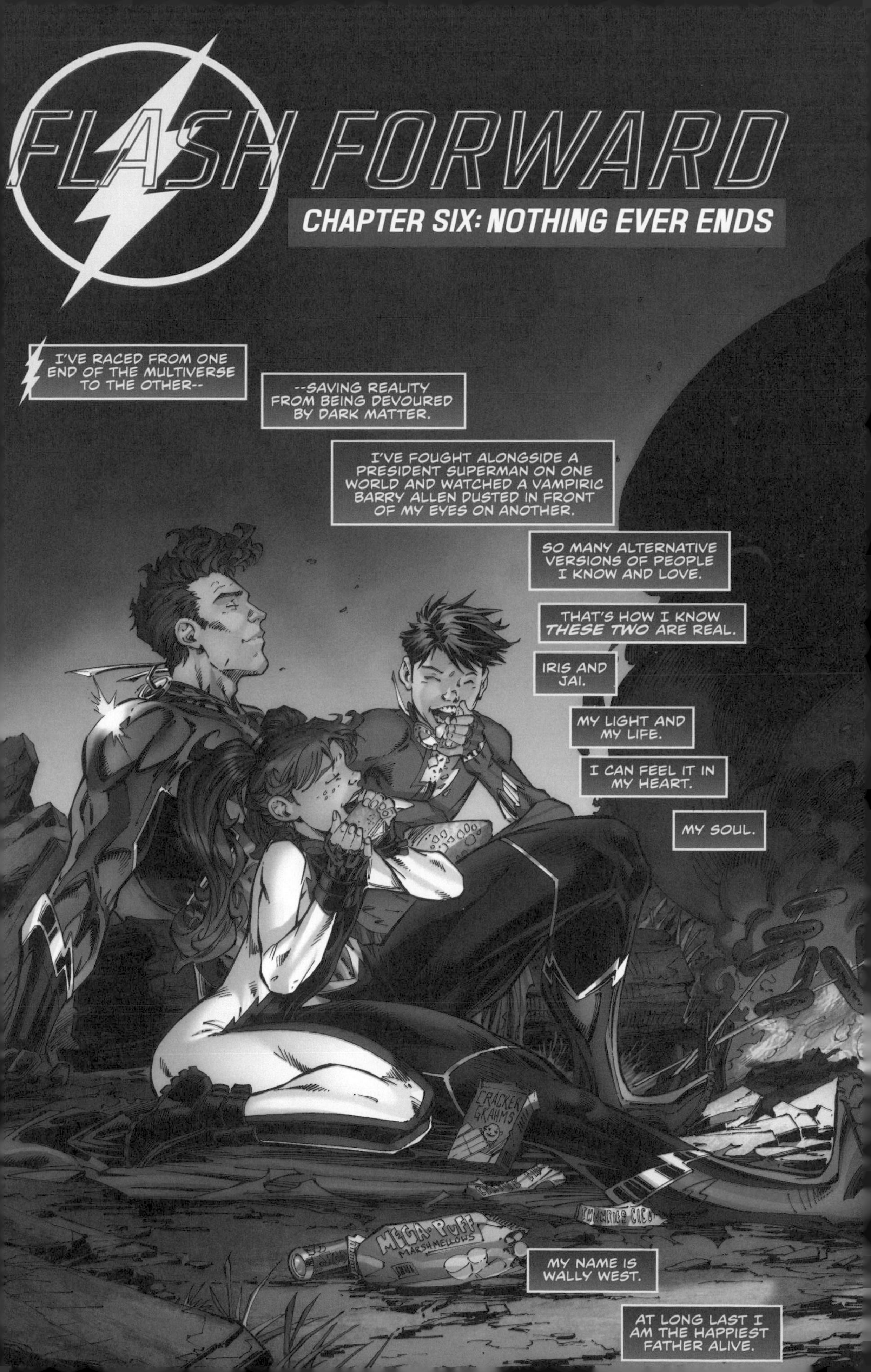
FLASH FORWARD
CHAPTER SIX: NOTHING EVER ENDS
I'VE RACED FROM ONE END OF THE MULTIVERSE TO THE OTHER--
--SAVING REALITY FROM BEING DEVOURED BY DARK MATTER.
I'VE FOUGHT ALONGSIDE A PRESIDENT SUPERMAN ON ONE WORLD AND WATCHED A VAMPIRIC BARRY ALLEN DUSTED IN FRONT OF MY EYES ON ANOTHER.
SO MANY ALTERNATIVE VERSIONS OF PEOPLE I KNOW AND LOVE.
THAT'S HOW I KNOW THESE TWO ARE REAL.
IRIS AND JAI.
MY LIGHT AND MY LIFE.
I CAN FEEL IT IN MY HEART.
MY SOUL.
CRACKER GRAHMS
MEGA-PUFF MARSHMELLOWS
MY NAME IS WALLY WEST.
AT LONG LAST I AM THE HAPPIEST FATHER ALIVE.

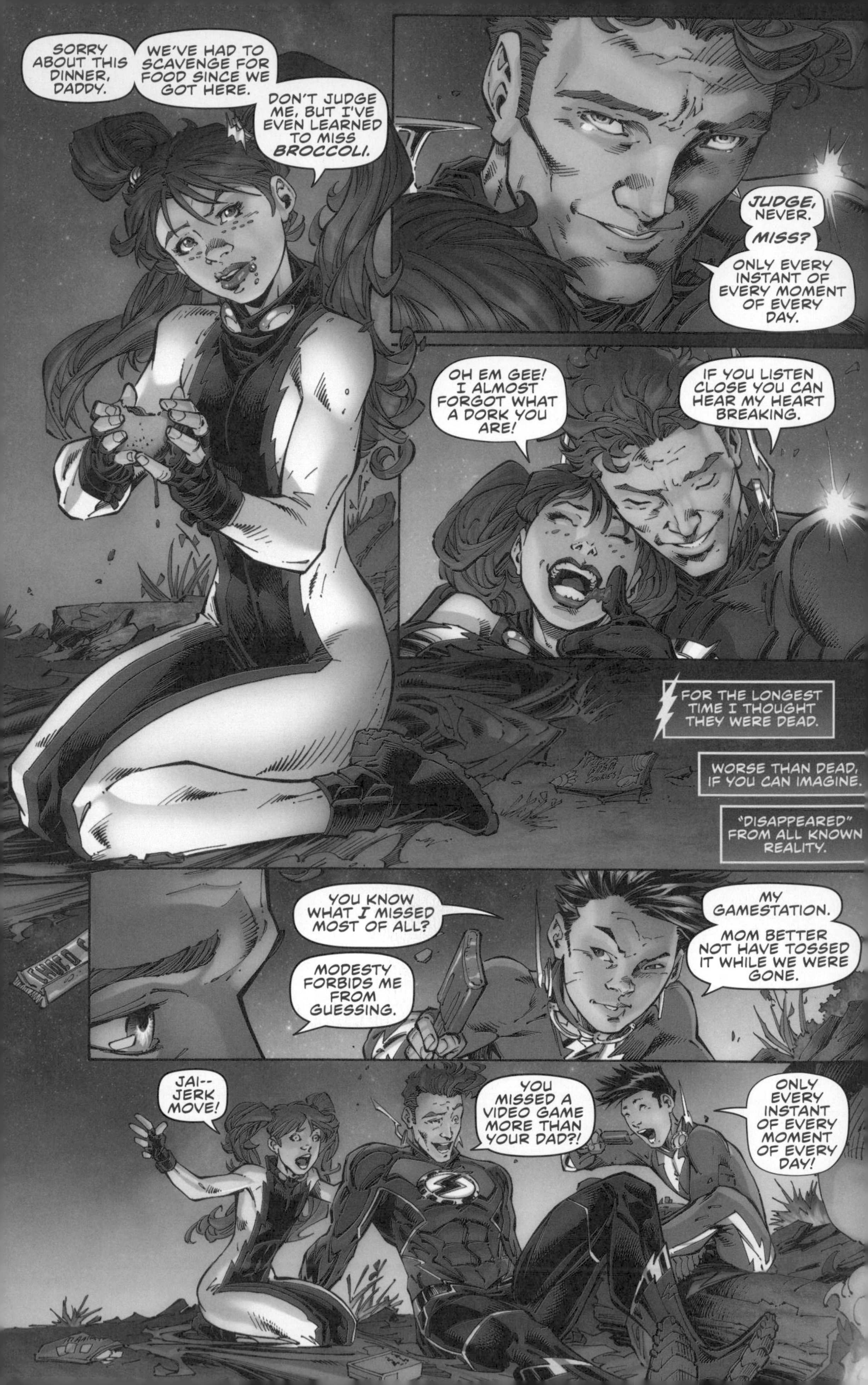
SORRY ABOUT THIS DINNER, DADDY.
WE'VE HAD TO SCAVENGE FOR FOOD SINCE WE GOT HERE.
DON'T JUDGE ME, BUT I'VE EVEN LEARNED TO MISS BROCCOLI.
JUDGE, NEVER.
MISS?
ONLY EVERY INSTANT OF EVERY MOMENT OF EVERY DAY.
OH EM GEE! I ALMOST FORGOT WHAT A DORK YOU ARE!
IF YOU LISTEN CLOSE YOU CAN HEAR MY HEART BREAKING.
FOR THE LONGEST TIME I THOUGHT THEY WERE DEAD.
WORSE THAN DEAD, IF YOU CAN IMAGINE.
"DISAPPEARED" FROM ALL KNOWN REALITY.
YOU KNOW WHAT I MISSED MOST OF ALL?
MODESTY FORBIDS ME FROM GUESSING.
MY GAMESTATION.
MOM BETTER NOT HAVE TOSSED IT WHILE WE WERE GONE.
JAI-- JERK MOVE!
YOU MISSED A VIDEO GAME MORE THAN YOUR DAD?!
ONLY EVERY INSTANT OF EVERY MOMENT OF EVERY DAY!

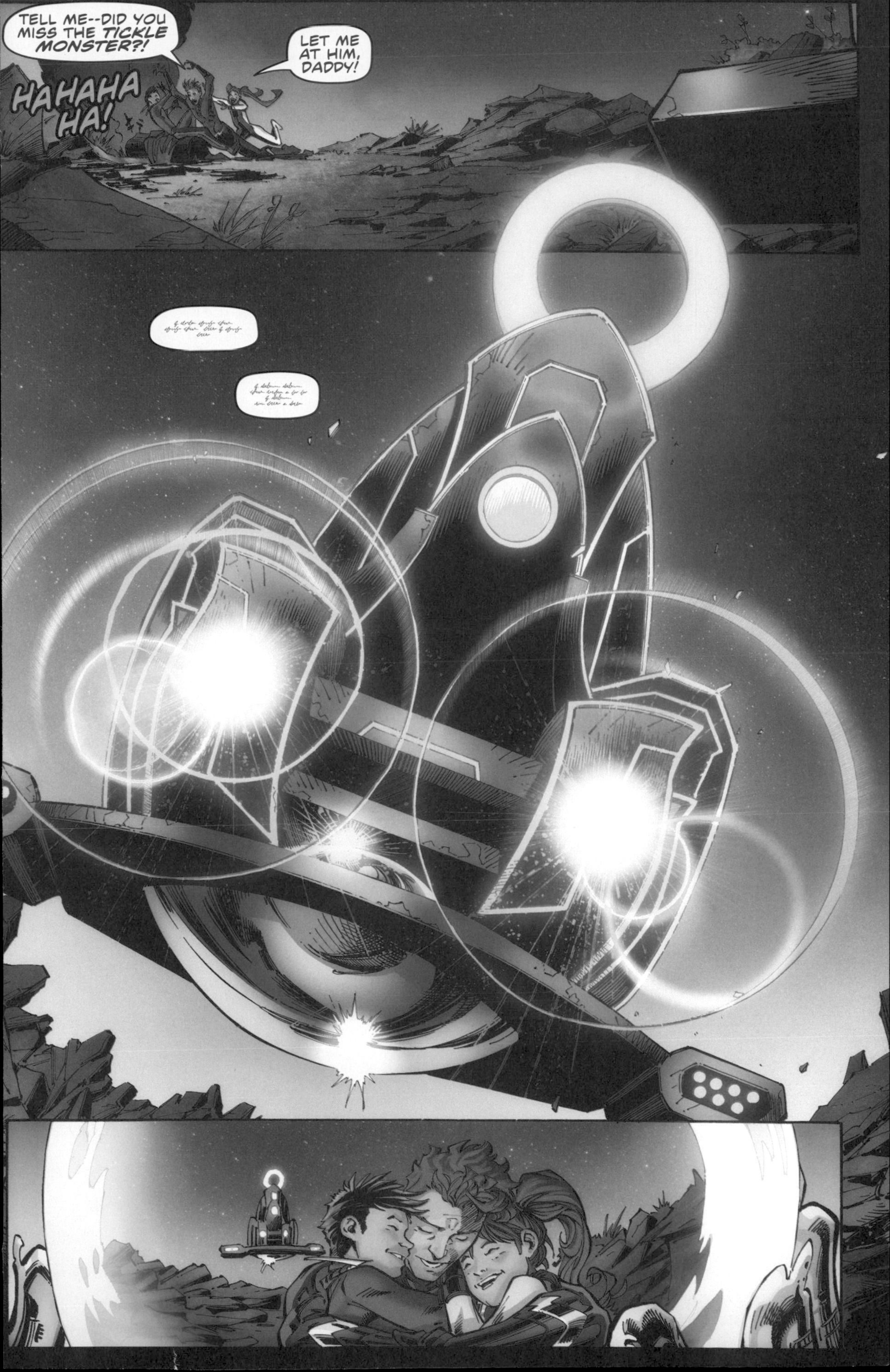
TELL ME--DID YOU MISS THE TICKLE MONSTER?!
LET ME AT HIM, DADDY!
HAHAHA HA!

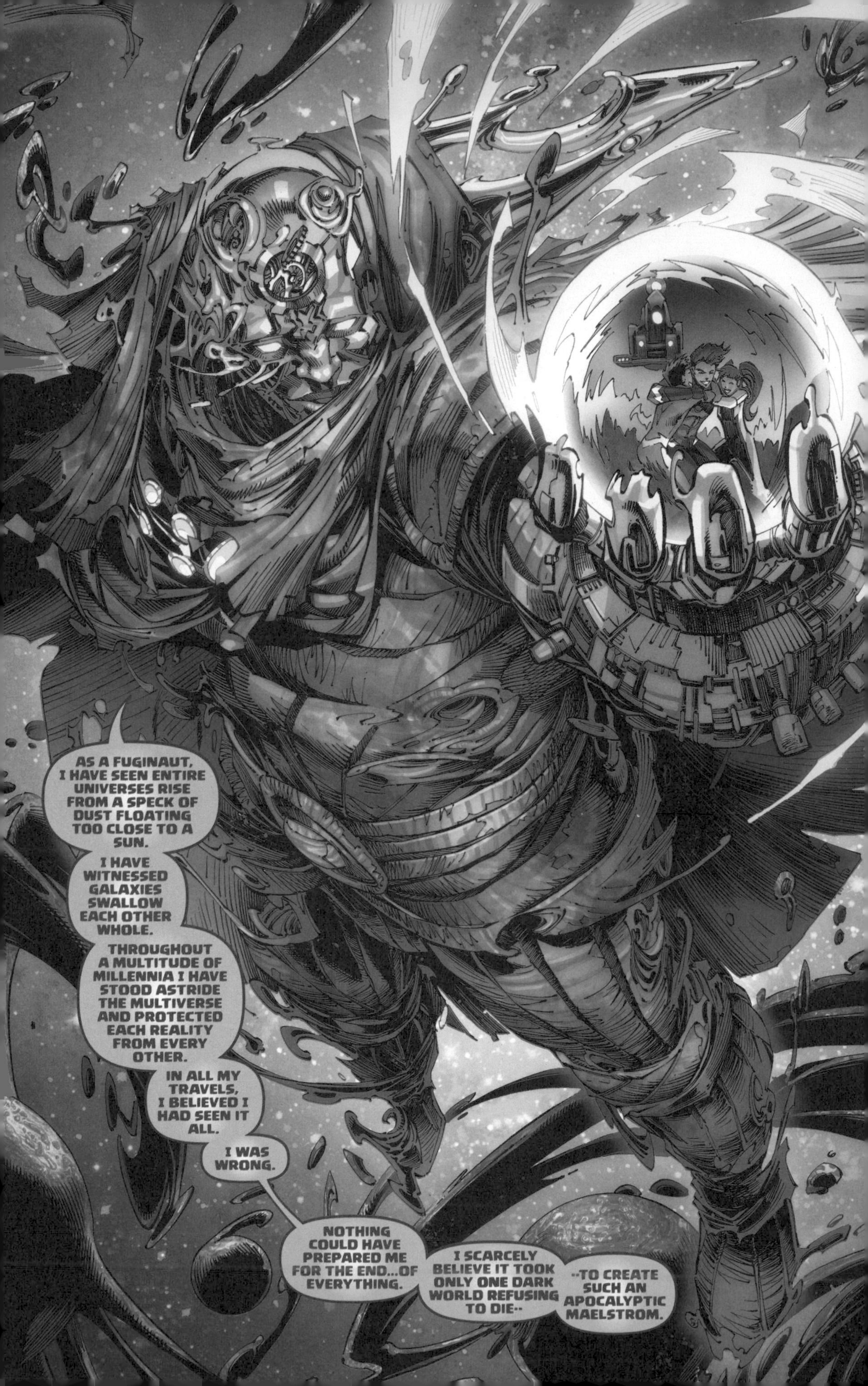
AS A FUGINAUT, I HAVE SEEN ENTIRE UNIVERSES RISE FROM A SPECK OF DUST FLOATING TOO CLOSE TO A SUN.
I HAVE WITNESSED GALAXIES SWALLOW EACH OTHER WHOLE.
THROUGHOUT A MULTITUDE OF MILLENNIA I HAVE STOOD ASTRIDE THE MULTIVERSE AND PROTECTED EACH REALITY FROM EVERY OTHER.
IN ALL MY TRAVELS, I BELIEVED I HAD SEEN IT ALL.
I WAS WRONG.
NOTHING COULD HAVE PREPARED ME FOR THE END...OF EVERYTHING.
I SCARCELY BELIEVE IT TOOK ONLY ONE DARK WORLD REFUSING TO DIE--
--TO CREATE SUCH AN APOCALYPTIC MAELSTROM.

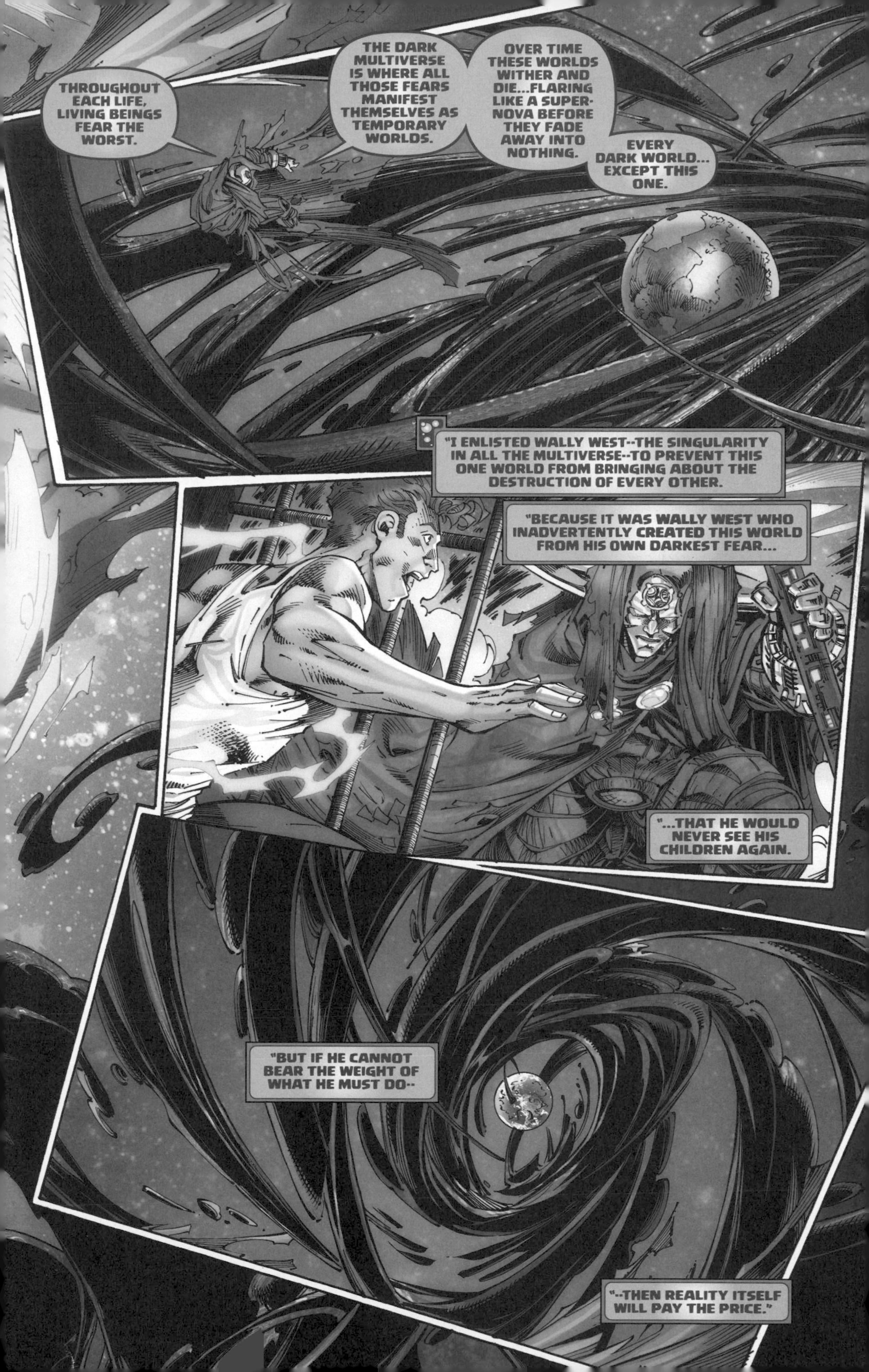
THROUGHOUT EACH LIFE, LIVING BEINGS FEAR THE WORST.
THE DARK MULTIVERSE IS WHERE ALL THOSE FEARS MANIFEST THEMSELVES AS TEMPORARY WORLDS.
OVER TIME THESE WORLDS WITHER AND DIE...FLARING LIKE A SUPER-NOVA BEFORE THEY FADE AWAY INTO NOTHING.
EVERY DARK WORLD... EXCEPT THIS ONE.
"I ENLISTED WALLY WEST--THE SINGULARITY IN ALL THE MULTIVERSE--TO PREVENT THIS ONE WORLD FROM BRINGING ABOUT THE DESTRUCTION OF EVERY OTHER.
"BECAUSE IT WAS WALLY WEST WHO INADVERTENTLY CREATED THIS WORLD FROM HIS OWN DARKEST FEAR...
"...THAT HE WOULD NEVER SEE HIS CHILDREN AGAIN.
"BUT IF HE CANNOT BEAR THE WEIGHT OF WHAT HE MUST DO--
"--THEN REALITY ITSELF WILL PAY THE PRICE."

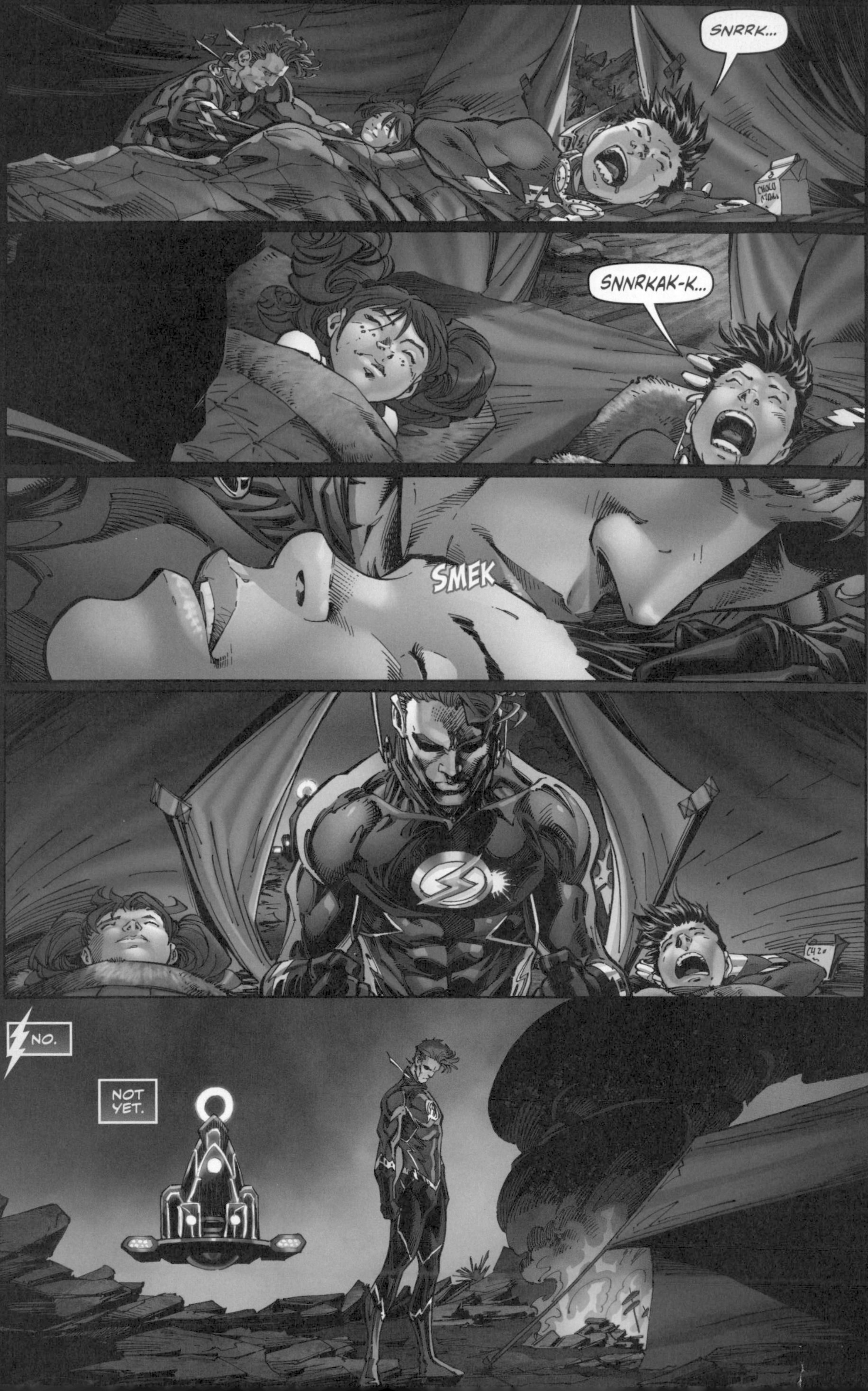

SNRRK...
SNNRKAK-K...
SMEK
NO.
NOT YET.

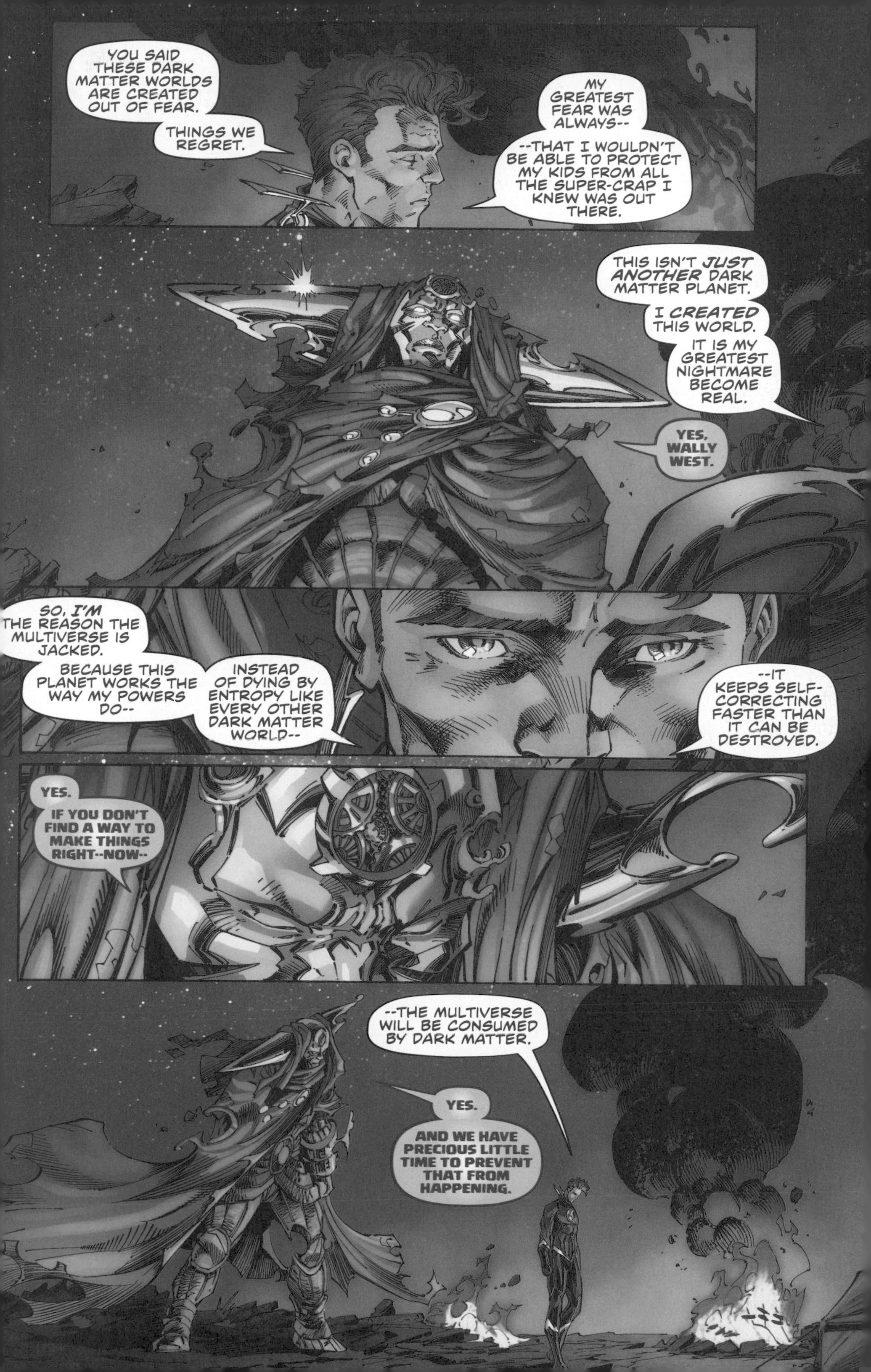

YOU SAID THESE DARK MATTER WORLDS ARE CREATED OUT OF FEAR.
THINGS WE REGRET.
MY GREATEST FEAR WAS ALWAYS--
--THAT I WOULDN'T BE ABLE TO PROTECT MY KIDS FROM ALL THE SUPER-CRAP I KNEW WAS OUT THERE.
THIS ISN'T JUST ANOTHER DARK MATTER PLANET.
I CREATED THIS WORLD.
IT IS MY GREATEST NIGHTMARE BECOME REAL.
YES, WALLY WEST.
SO, I'M THE REASON THE MULTIVERSE IS JACKED.
BECAUSE THIS PLANET WORKS THE WAY MY POWERS DO--
INSTEAD OF DYING BY ENTROPY LIKE EVERY OTHER DARK MATTER WORLD--
--IT KEEPS SELF-CORRECTING FASTER THAN IT CAN BE DESTROYED.
YES.
IF YOU DON'T FIND A WAY TO MAKE THINGS RIGHT--NOW--
--THE MULTIVERSE WILL BE CONSUMED BY DARK MATTER.
YES.
AND WE HAVE PRECIOUS LITTLE TIME TO PREVENT THAT FROM HAPPENING.

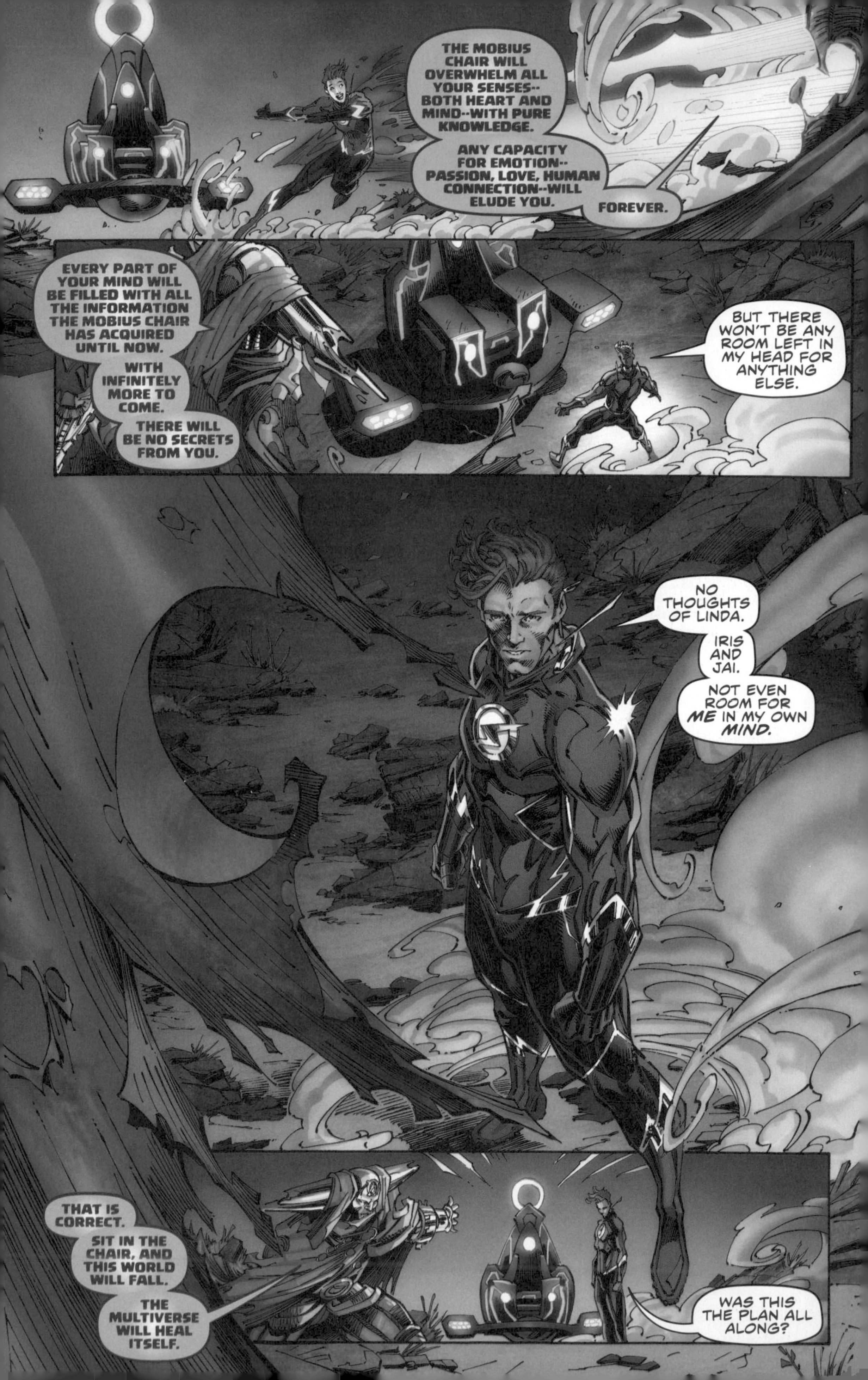
THE MOBIUS CHAIR WILL OVERWHELM ALL YOUR SENSES-- BOTH HEART AND MIND--WITH PURE KNOWLEDGE.
ANY CAPACITY FOR EMOTION-- PASSION, LOVE, HUMAN CONNECTION--WILL ELUDE YOU.
FOREVER.
EVERY PART OF YOUR MIND WILL BE FILLED WITH ALL THE INFORMATION THE MOBIUS CHAIR HAS ACQUIRED UNTIL NOW.
WITH INFINITELY MORE TO COME.
THERE WILL BE NO SECRETS FROM YOU.
BUT THERE WON'T BE ANY ROOM LEFT IN MY HEAD FOR ANYTHING ELSE.
NO THOUGHTS OF LINDA.
IRIS AND JAI.
NOT EVEN ROOM FOR *ME* IN MY OWN *MIND.*
THAT IS CORRECT.
SIT IN THE CHAIR, AND THIS WORLD WILL FALL.
THE MULTIVERSE WILL HEAL ITSELF.
WAS THIS THE PLAN ALL ALONG?

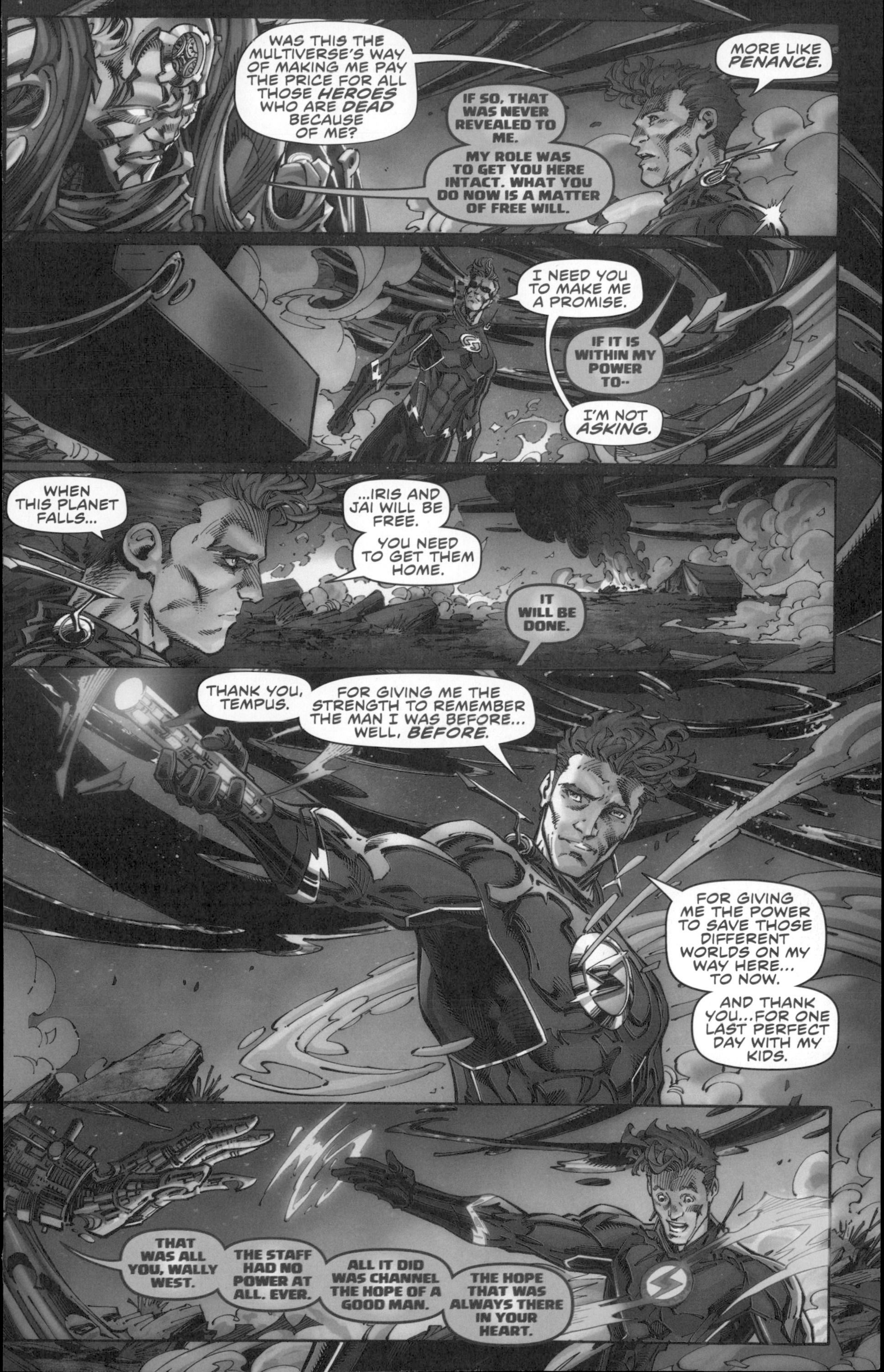
WAS THIS THE MULTIVERSE'S WAY OF MAKING ME PAY THE PRICE FOR ALL THOSE *HEROES* WHO ARE *DEAD* BECAUSE OF ME?
IF SO, THAT WAS NEVER REVEALED TO ME.
MY ROLE WAS TO GET YOU HERE INTACT. WHAT YOU DO NOW IS A MATTER OF FREE WILL.
MORE LIKE *PENANCE.*
I NEED YOU TO MAKE ME A PROMISE.
IF IT IS WITHIN MY POWER TO--
I'M NOT *ASKING.*
WHEN THIS PLANET FALLS...
...IRIS AND JAI WILL BE FREE.
YOU NEED TO GET THEM HOME.
IT WILL BE DONE.
THANK YOU, TEMPUS.
FOR GIVING ME THE STRENGTH TO REMEMBER THE MAN I WAS BEFORE... WELL, *BEFORE.*
FOR GIVING ME THE POWER TO SAVE THOSE DIFFERENT WORLDS ON MY WAY HERE... TO NOW.
AND THANK YOU...FOR ONE LAST PERFECT DAY WITH MY KIDS.
THAT WAS ALL YOU, WALLY WEST.
THE STAFF HAD NO POWER AT ALL. EVER.
ALL IT DID WAS CHANNEL THE HOPE OF A GOOD MAN.
THE HOPE THAT WAS ALWAYS THERE IN YOUR HEART.

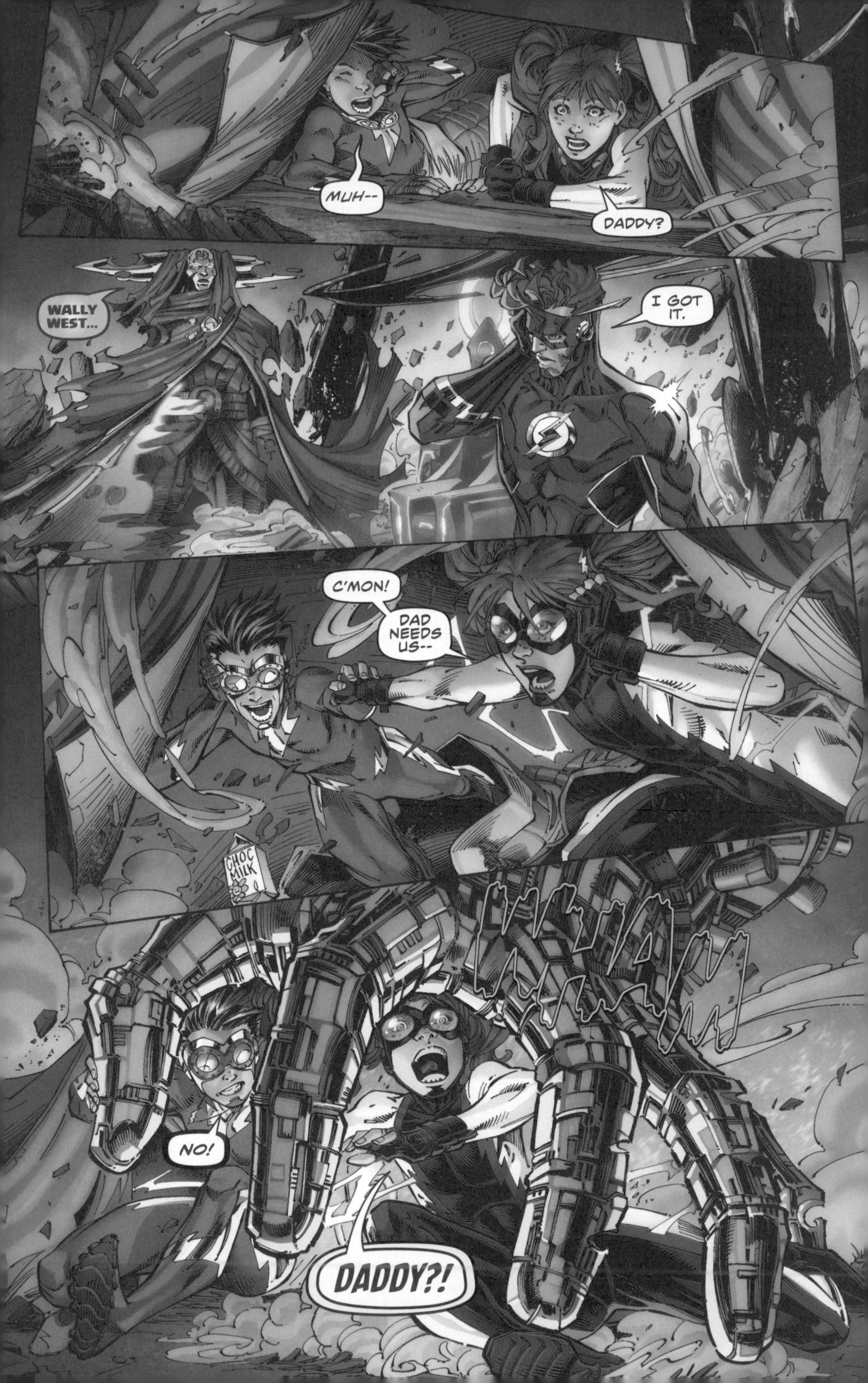
MUH--
DADDY?
WALLY WEST...
I GOT IT.
C'MON!
DAD NEEDS US--
CHOC MILK
NO!
DADDY?!

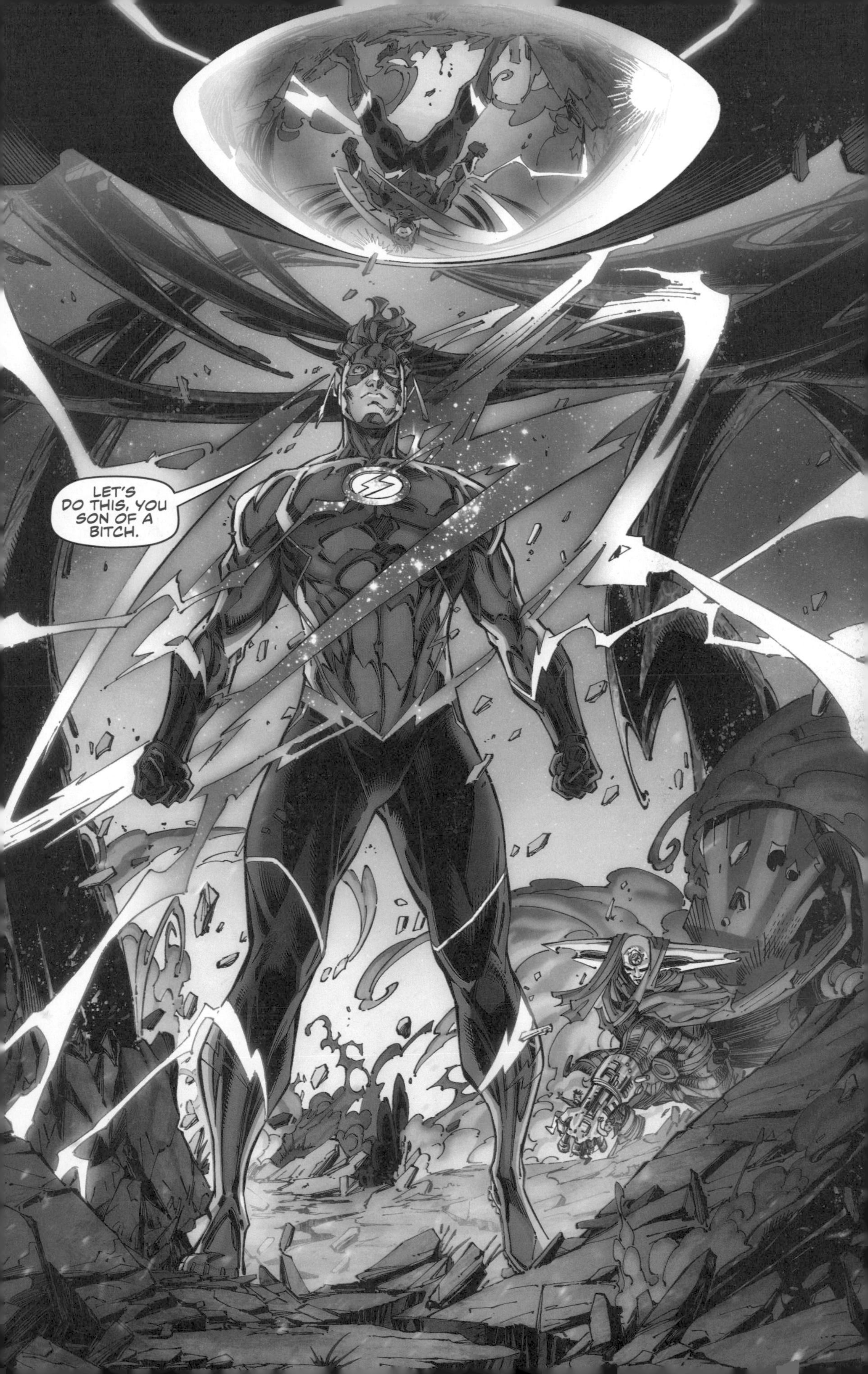
LET'S DO THIS, YOU SON OF A BITCH.

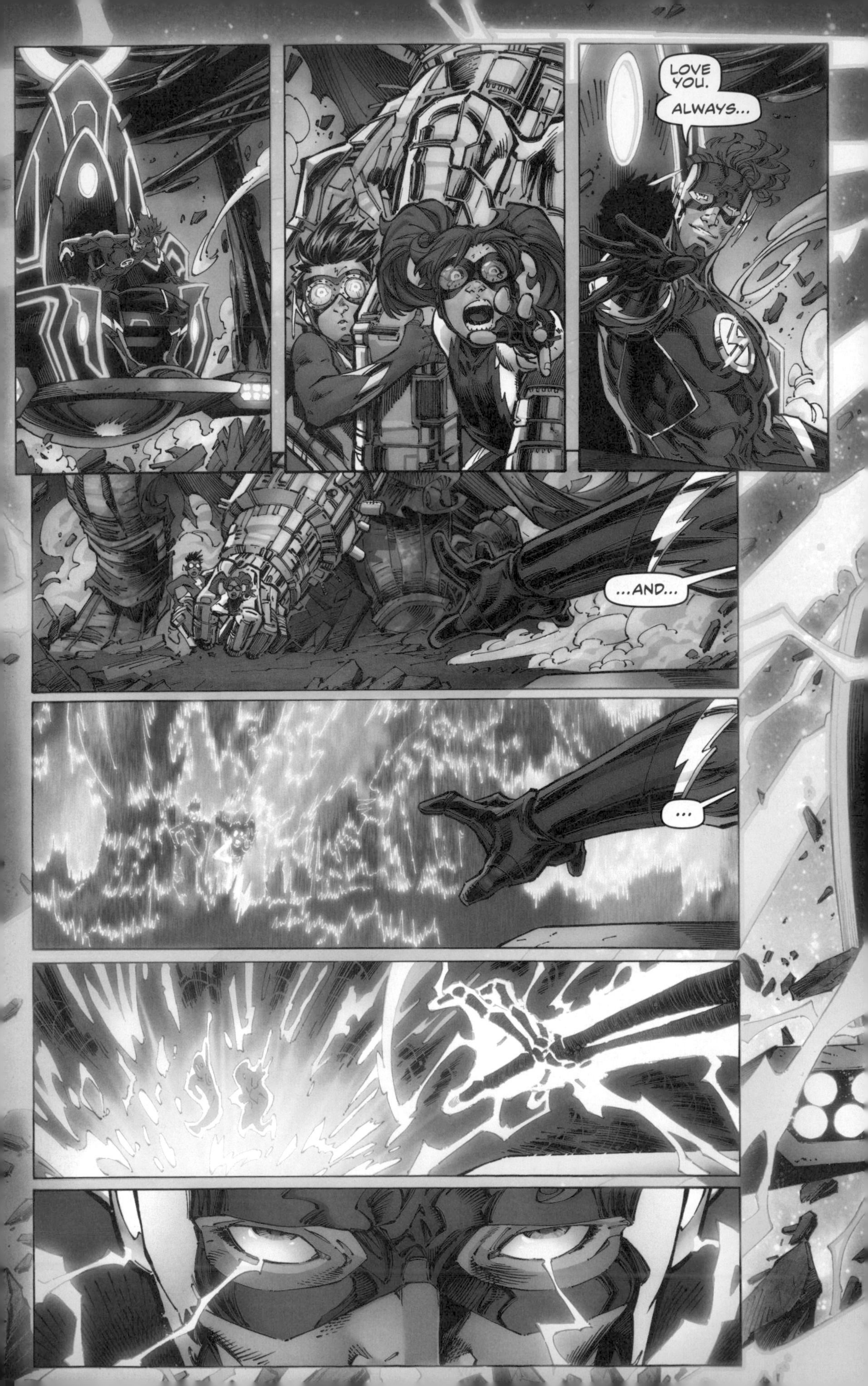
LOVE YOU.
ALWAYS...
...AND...
...

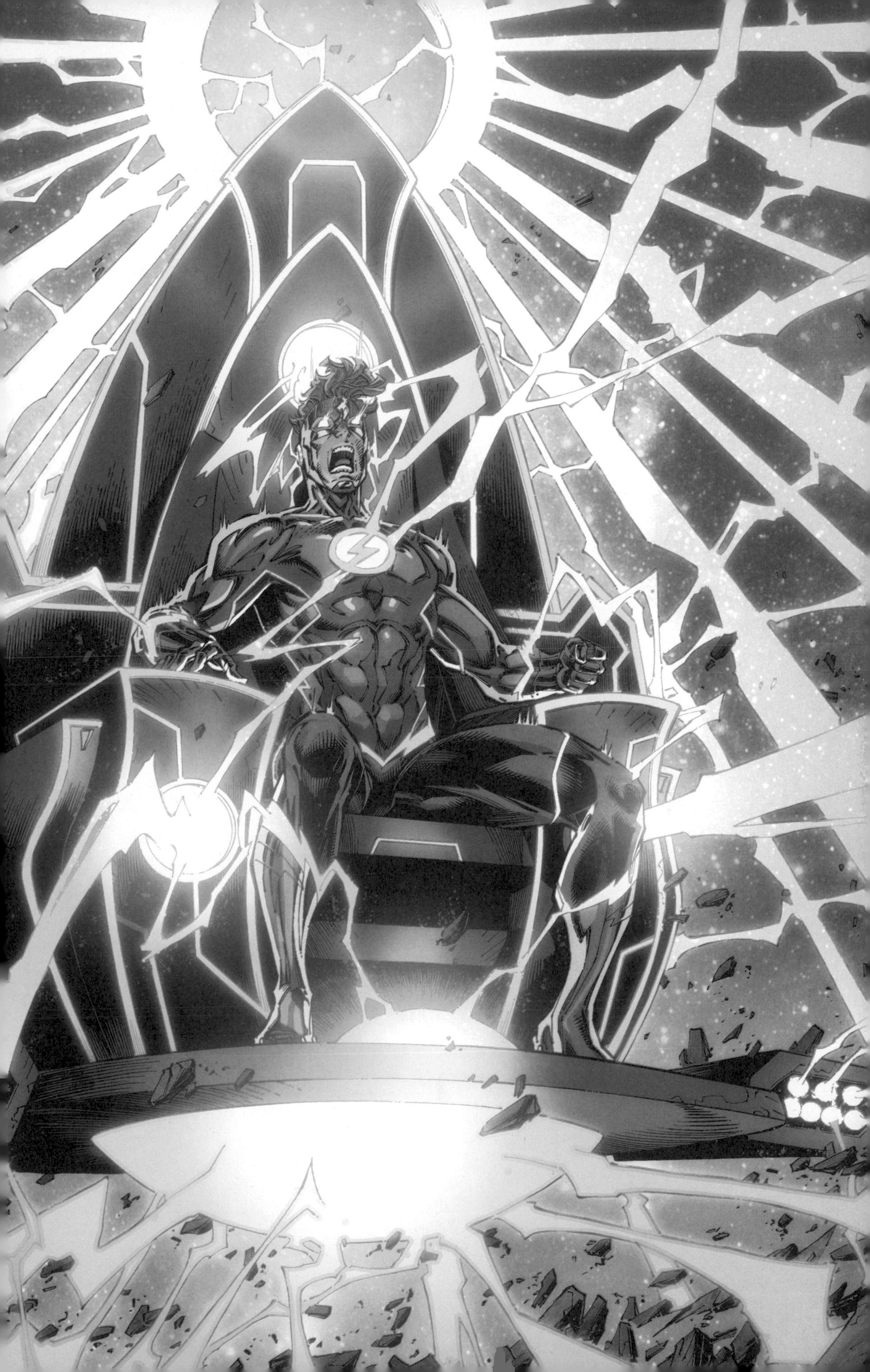

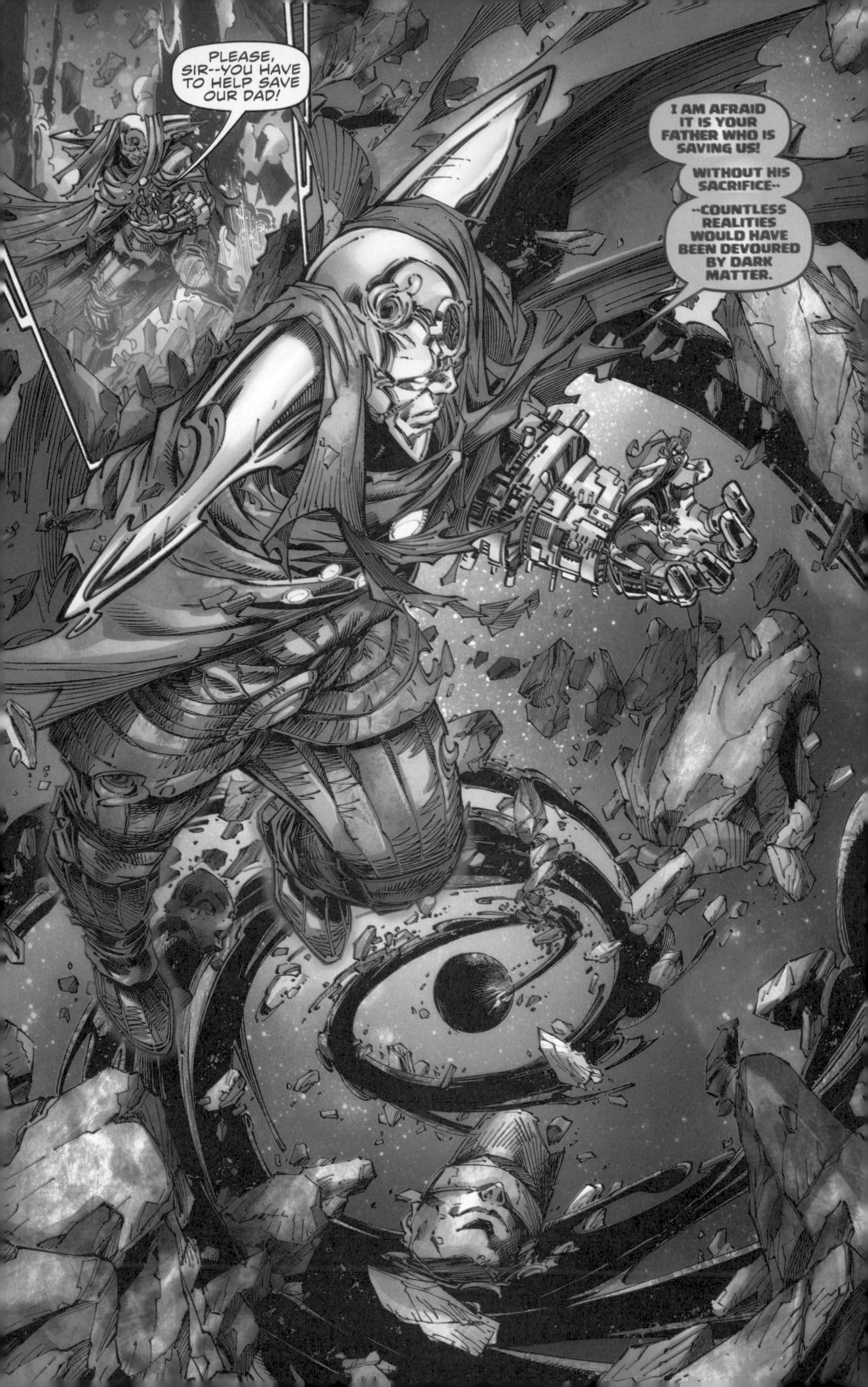
PLEASE, SIR--YOU HAVE TO HELP SAVE OUR DAD!
I AM AFRAID IT IS YOUR FATHER WHO IS SAVING US!
WITHOUT HIS SACRIFICE--
--COUNTLESS REALITIES WOULD HAVE BEEN DEVOURED BY DARK MATTER.

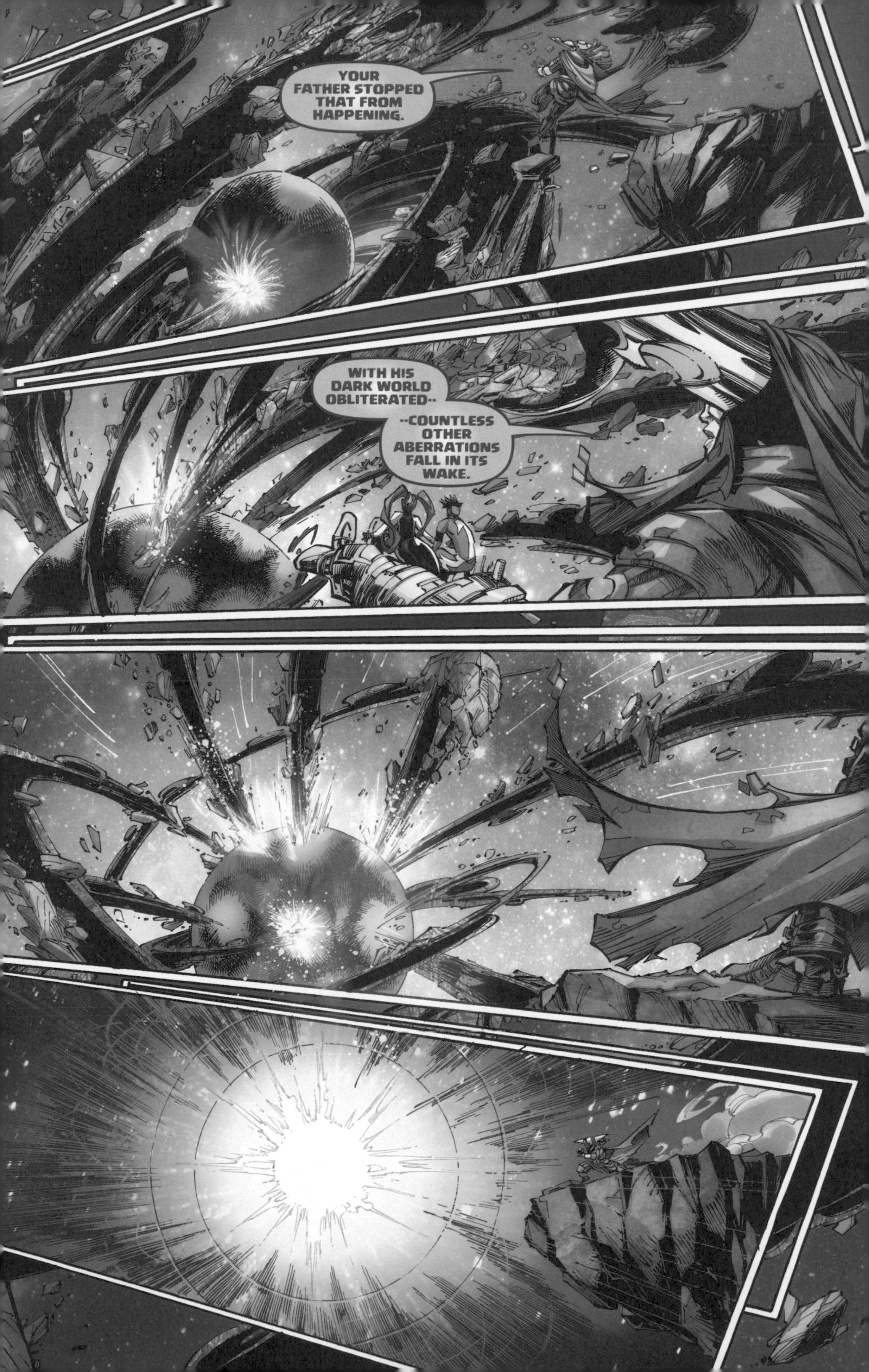
YOUR FATHER STOPPED THAT FROM HAPPENING.
WITH HIS DARK WORLD OBLITERATED--
--COUNTLESS OTHER ABERRATIONS FALL IN ITS WAKE.

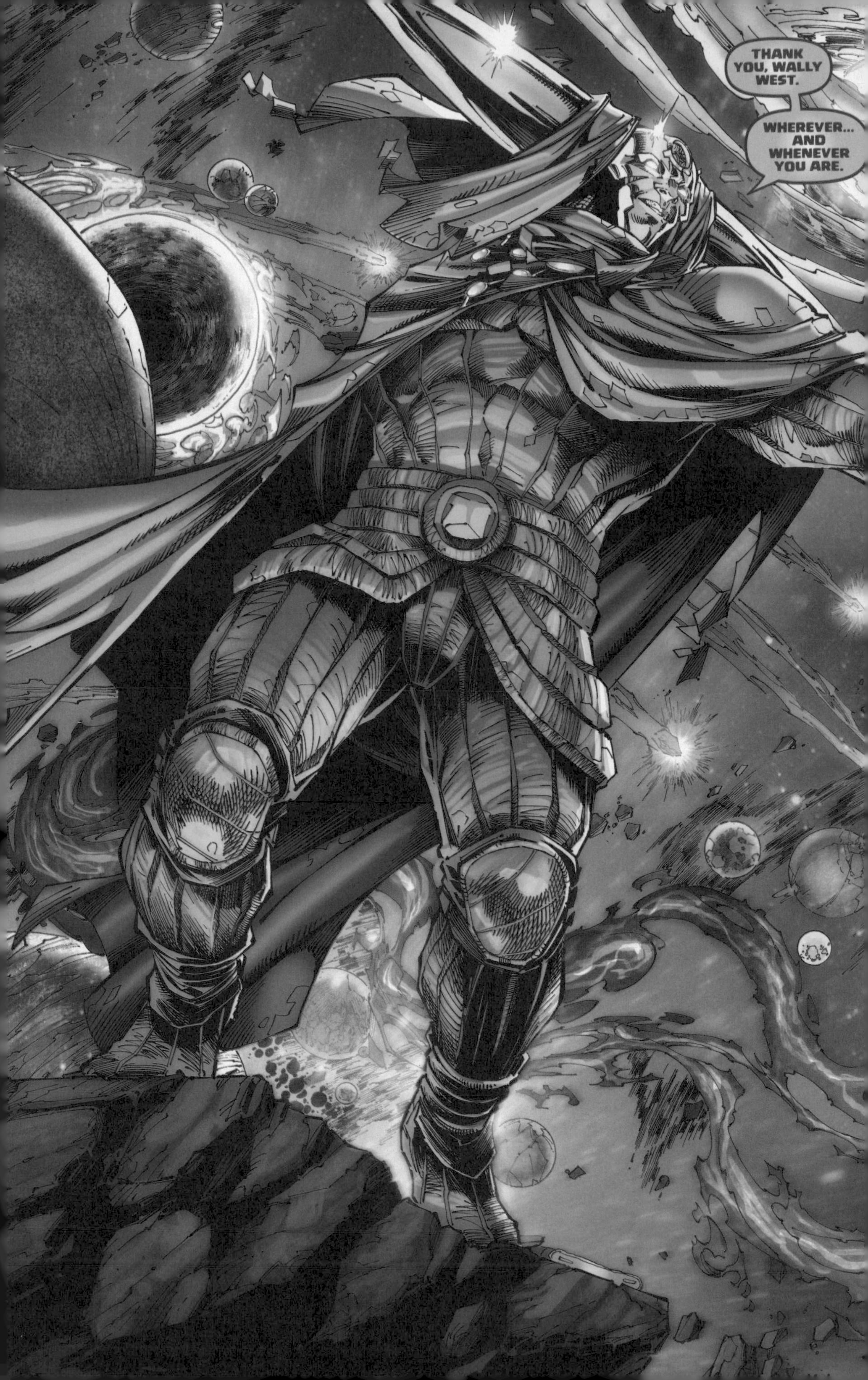
THANK YOU, WALLY WEST.
WHEREVER... AND WHENEVER YOU ARE.

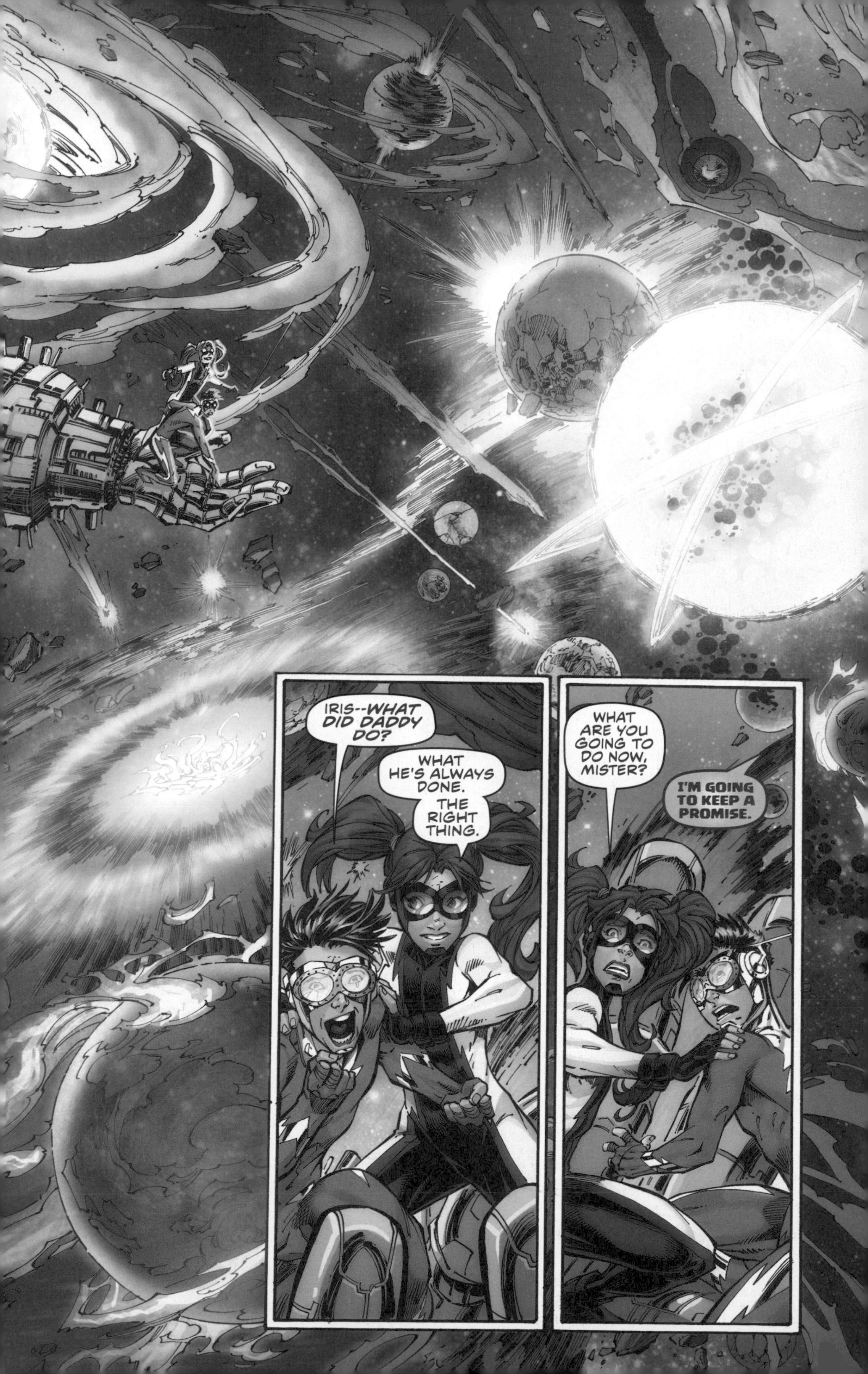
IRIS--WHAT DID DADDY DO?
WHAT HE'S ALWAYS DONE.
THE RIGHT THING.
WHAT ARE YOU GOING TO DO NOW, MISTER?
I'M GOING TO KEEP A PROMISE.

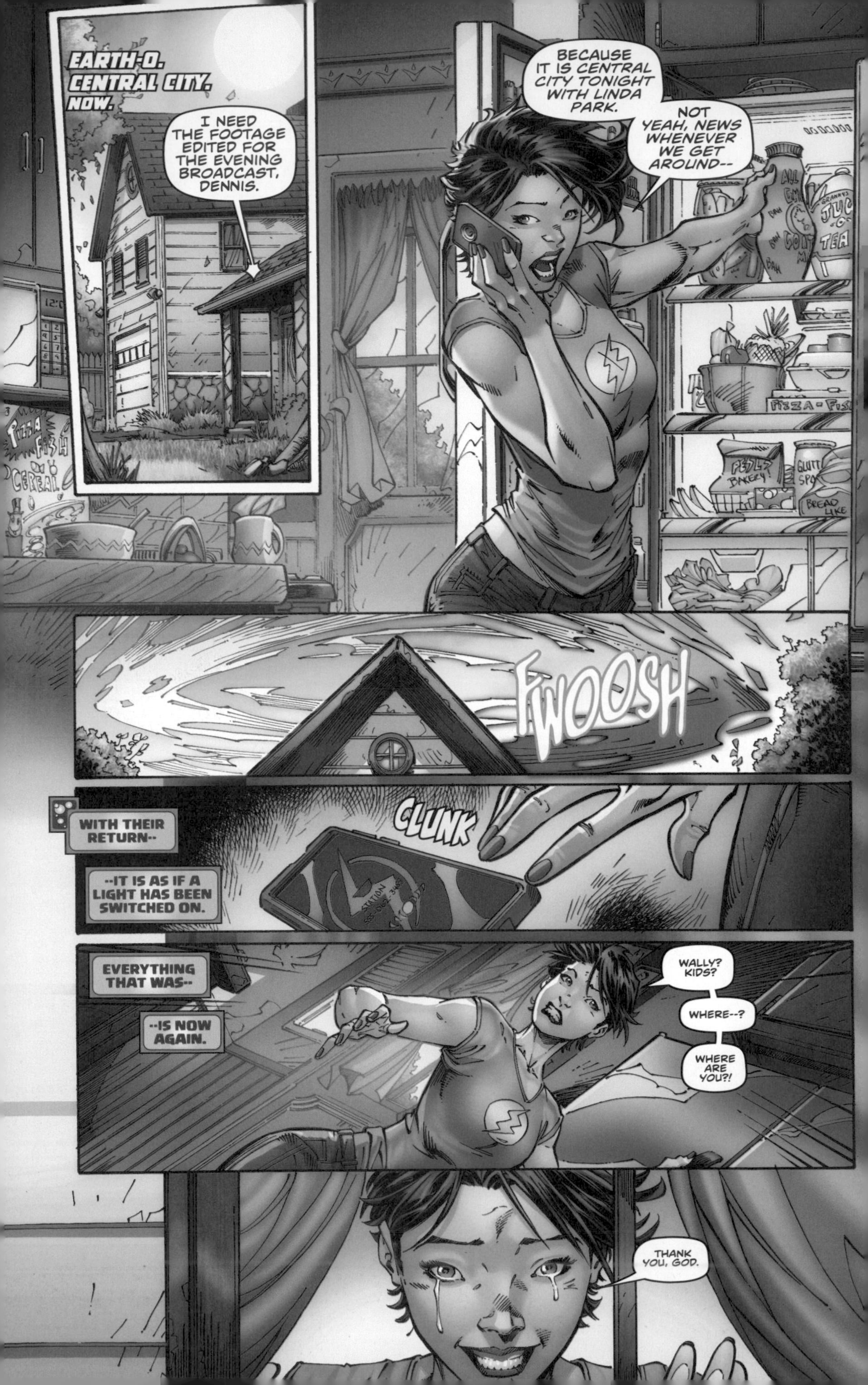
EARTH-0. CENTRAL CITY. NOW.
I NEED THE FOOTAGE EDITED FOR THE EVENING BROADCAST, DENNIS.
BECAUSE IT IS CENTRAL CITY TONIGHT WITH LINDA PARK.
NOT YEAH, NEWS WHENEVER WE GET AROUND--
FWOOSH
WITH THEIR RETURN--
CLUNK
--IT IS AS IF A LIGHT HAS BEEN SWITCHED ON.
EVERYTHING THAT WAS--
--IS NOW AGAIN.
WALLY? KIDS?
WHERE--?
WHERE ARE YOU?!
THANK YOU, GOD.

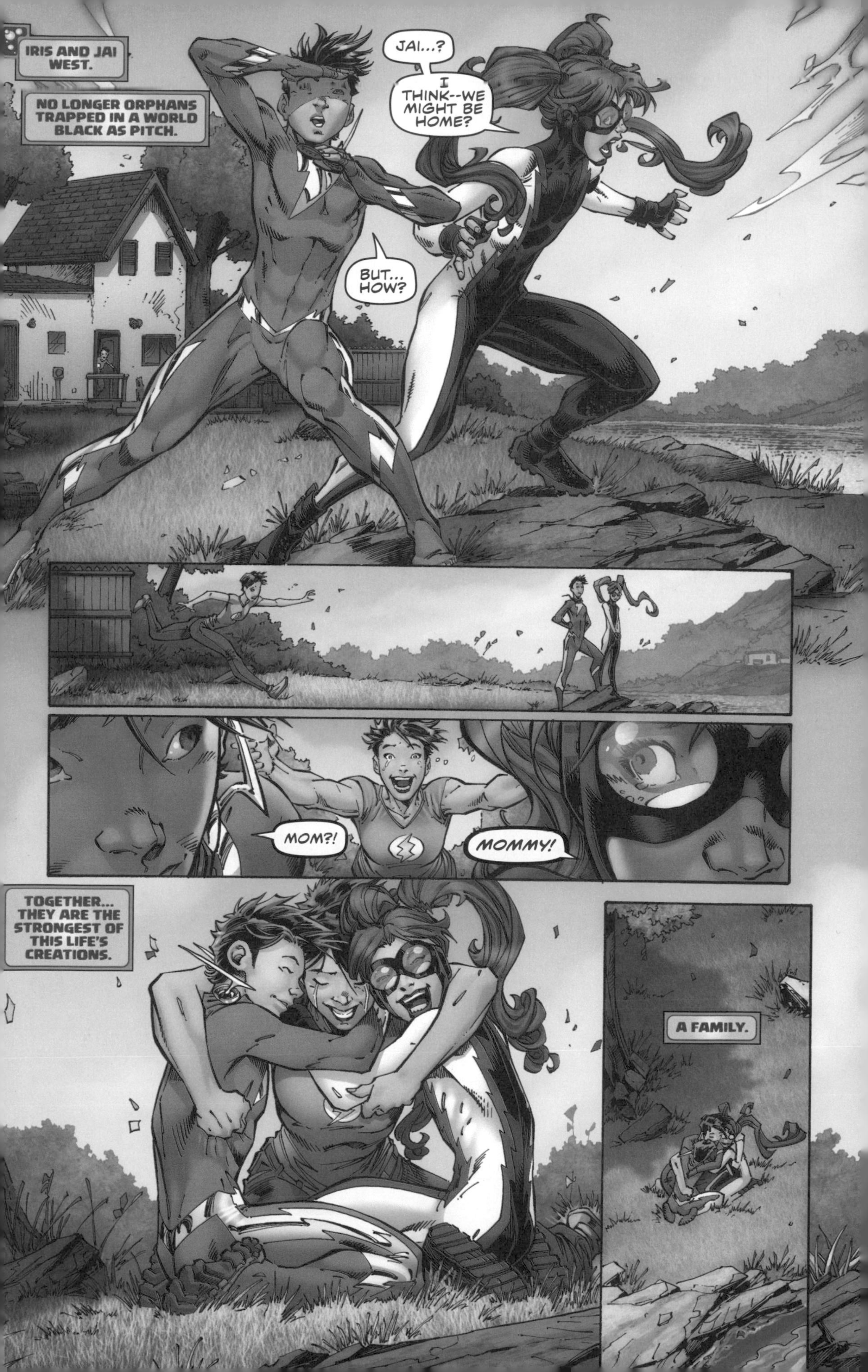
IRIS AND JAI WEST.
NO LONGER ORPHANS TRAPPED IN A WORLD BLACK AS PITCH.
JAI...?
I THINK--WE MIGHT BE HOME?
BUT... HOW?
MOM?!
MOMMY!
TOGETHER... THEY ARE THE STRONGEST OF THIS LIFE'S CREATIONS.
A FAMILY.

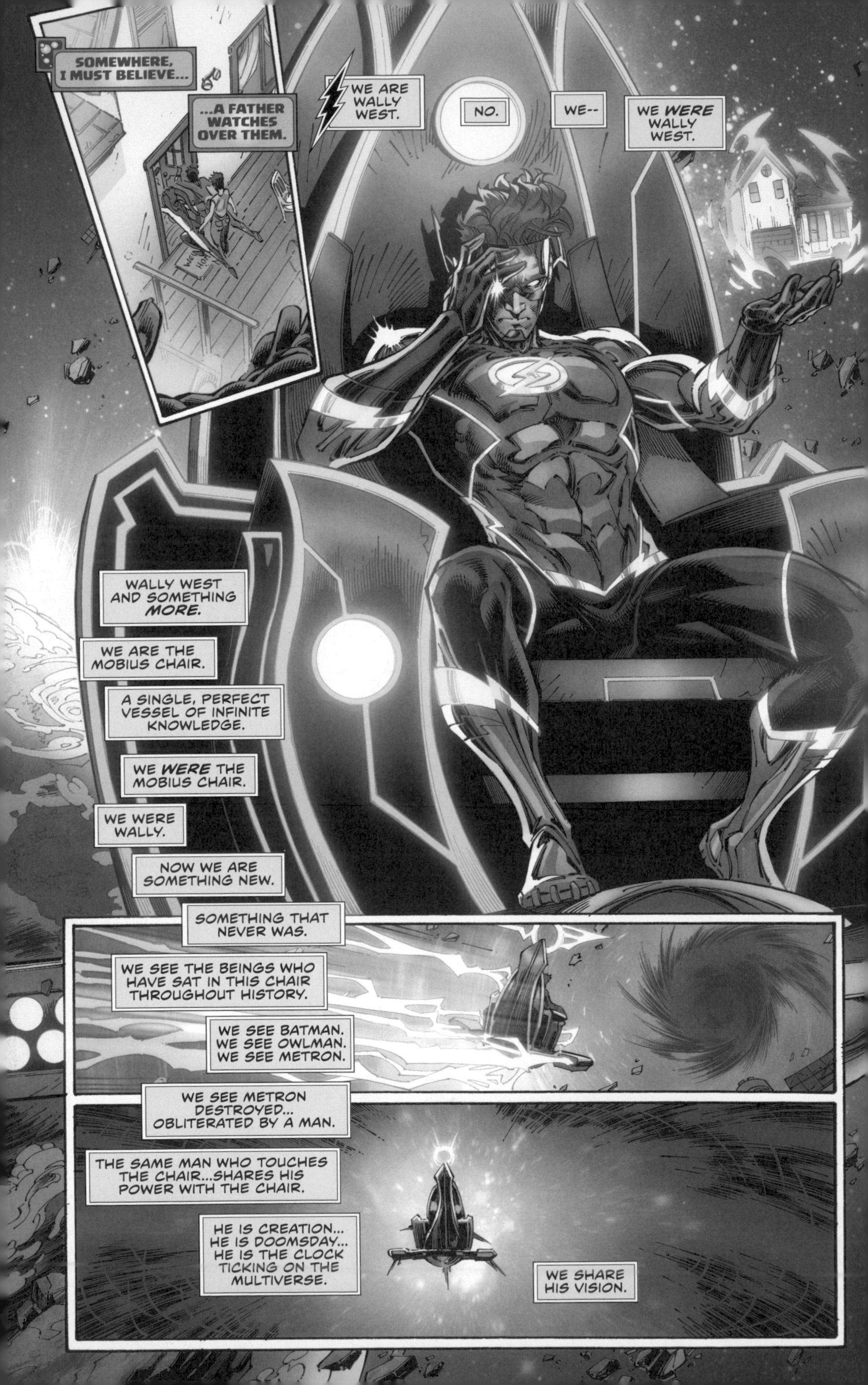
SOMEWHERE, I MUST BELIEVE...
...A FATHER WATCHES OVER THEM.
WE ARE WALLY WEST.
NO.
WE--
WE WERE WALLY WEST.
WALLY WEST AND SOMETHING MORE.
WE ARE THE MOBIUS CHAIR.
A SINGLE, PERFECT VESSEL OF INFINITE KNOWLEDGE.
WE WERE THE MOBIUS CHAIR.
WE WERE WALLY.
NOW WE ARE SOMETHING NEW.
SOMETHING THAT NEVER WAS.
WE SEE THE BEINGS WHO HAVE SAT IN THIS CHAIR THROUGHOUT HISTORY.
WE SEE BATMAN. WE SEE OWLMAN. WE SEE METRON.
WE SEE METRON DESTROYED... OBLITERATED BY A MAN.
THE SAME MAN WHO TOUCHES THE CHAIR...SHARES HIS POWER WITH THE CHAIR.
HE IS CREATION... HE IS DOOMSDAY... HE IS THE CLOCK TICKING ON THE MULTIVERSE.
WE SHARE HIS VISION.

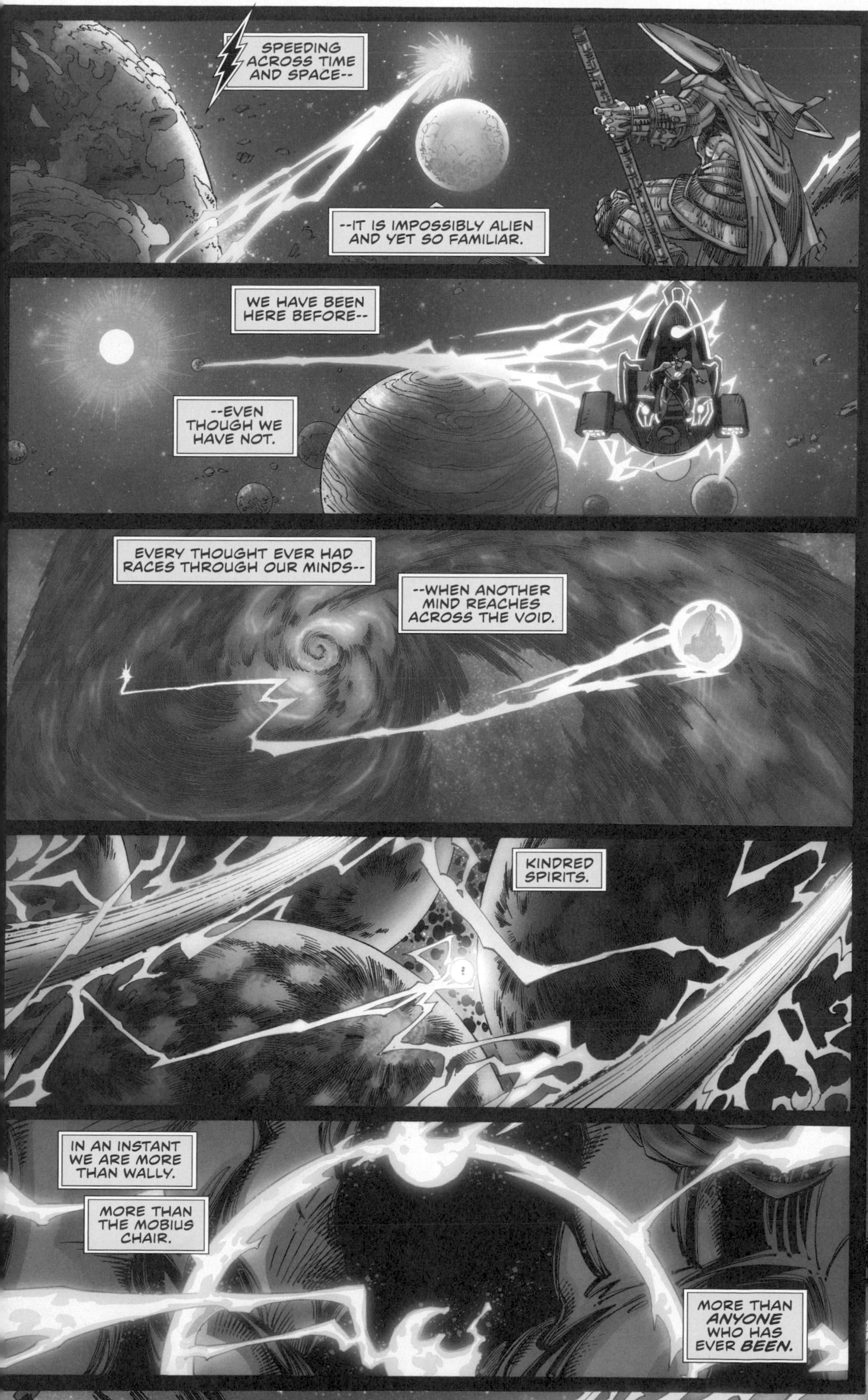
SPEEDING ACROSS TIME AND SPACE--
--IT IS IMPOSSIBLY ALIEN AND YET SO FAMILIAR.
WE HAVE BEEN HERE BEFORE--
--EVEN THOUGH WE HAVE NOT.
EVERY THOUGHT EVER HAD RACES THROUGH OUR MINDS--
--WHEN ANOTHER MIND REACHES ACROSS THE VOID.
KINDRED SPIRITS.
IN AN INSTANT WE ARE MORE THAN WALLY.
MORE THAN THE MOBIUS CHAIR.
MORE THAN *ANYONE* WHO HAS EVER *BEEN*.

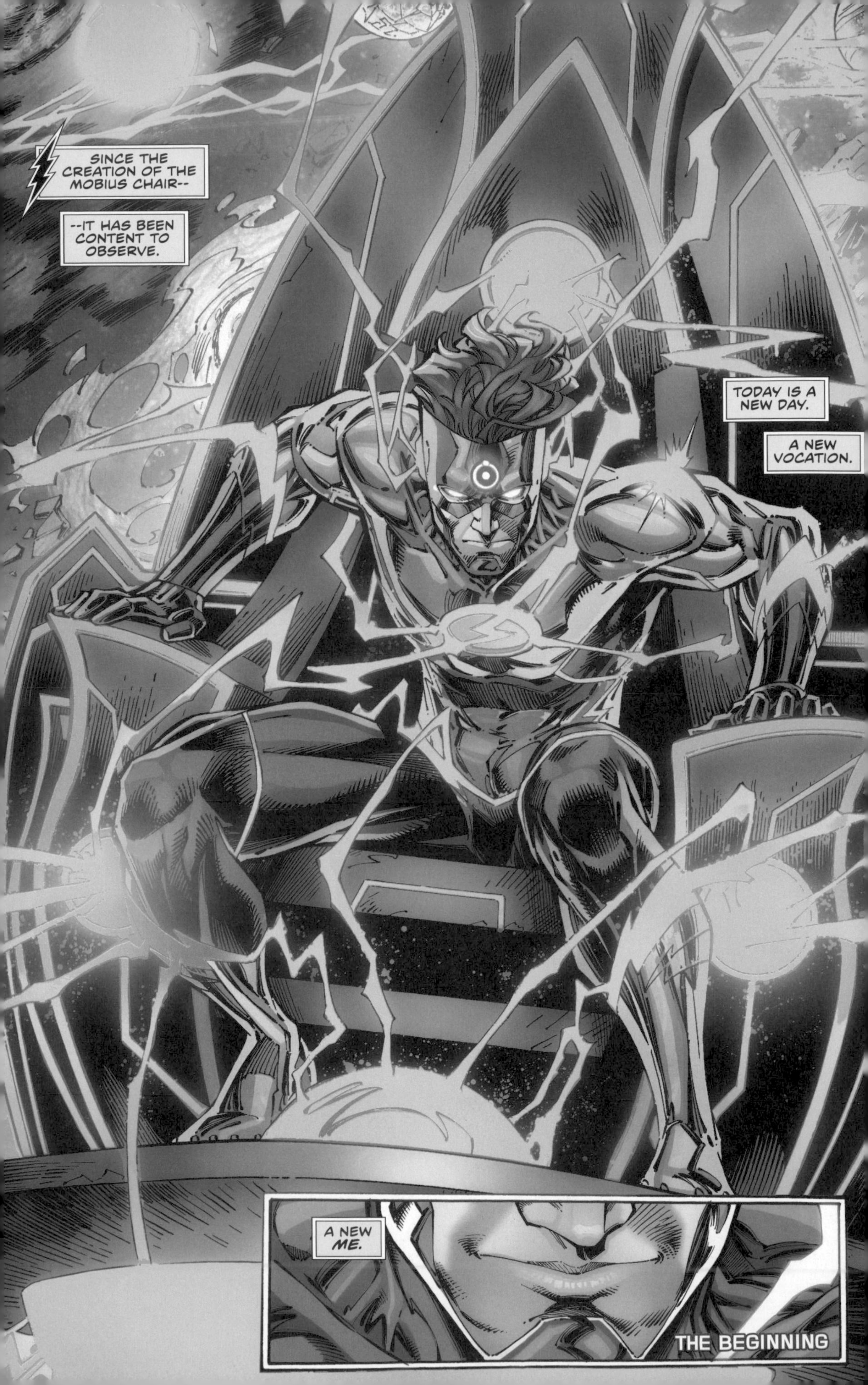
SINCE THE CREATION OF THE MOBIUS CHAIR--
--IT HAS BEEN CONTENT TO OBSERVE.
TODAY IS A NEW DAY.
A NEW VOCATION.
A NEW ME.
THE BEGINNING

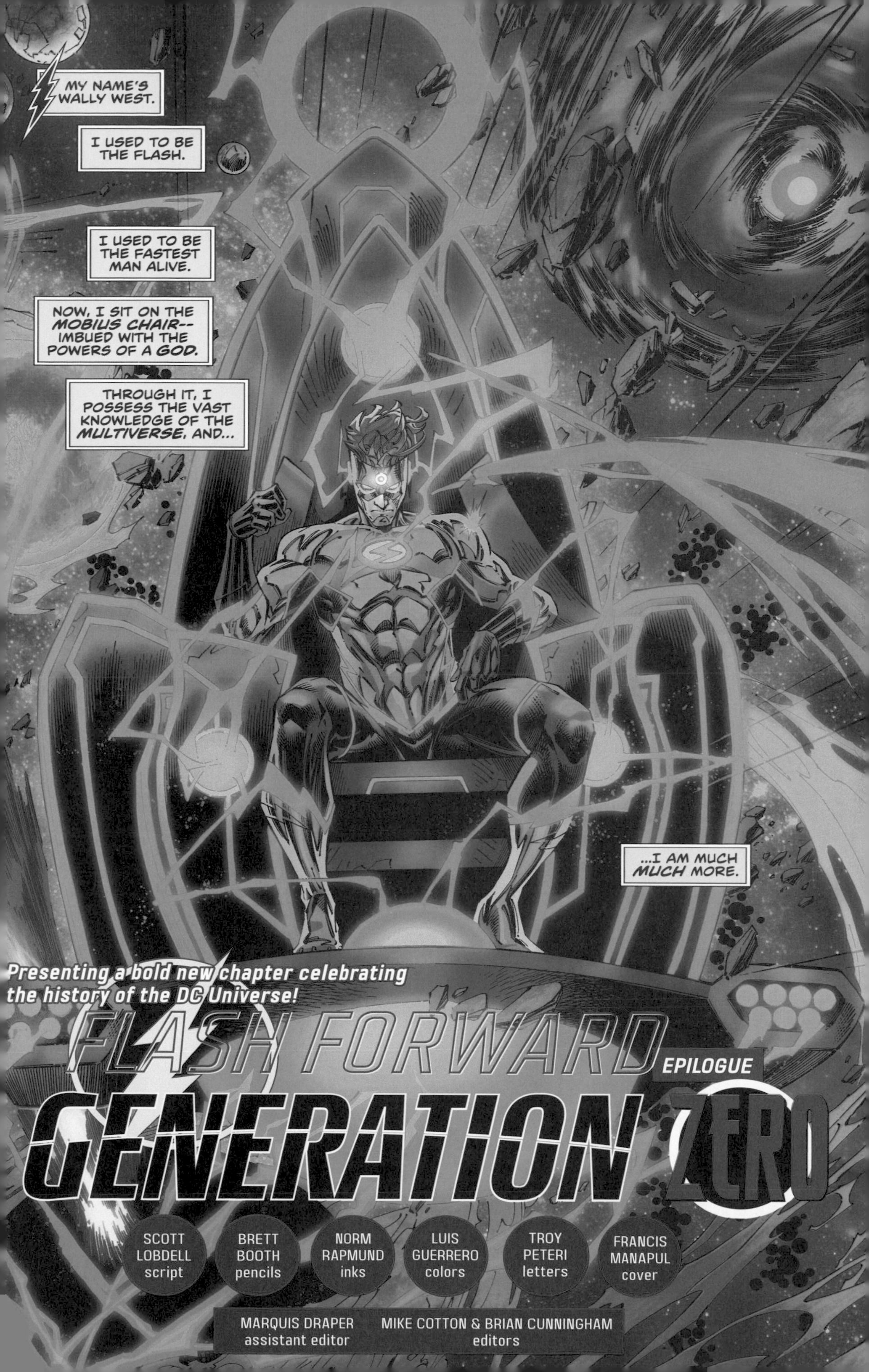

MY NAME'S WALLY WEST.
I USED TO BE THE FLASH.
I USED TO BE THE FASTEST MAN ALIVE.
NOW, I SIT ON THE MOBIUS CHAIR-- IMBUED WITH THE POWERS OF A GOD.
THROUGH IT, I POSSESS THE VAST KNOWLEDGE OF THE MULTIVERSE, AND...
...I AM MUCH MUCH MORE.
Presenting a bold new chapter celebrating the history of the DC Universe!
FLASH FORWARD EPILOGUE
GENERATION ZERO
SCOTT LOBDELL script
BRETT BOOTH pencils
NORM RAPMUND inks
LUIS GUERRERO colors
TROY PETERI letters
FRANCIS MANAPUL cover
MARQUIS DRAPER assistant editor
MIKE COTTON & BRIAN CUNNINGHAM editors

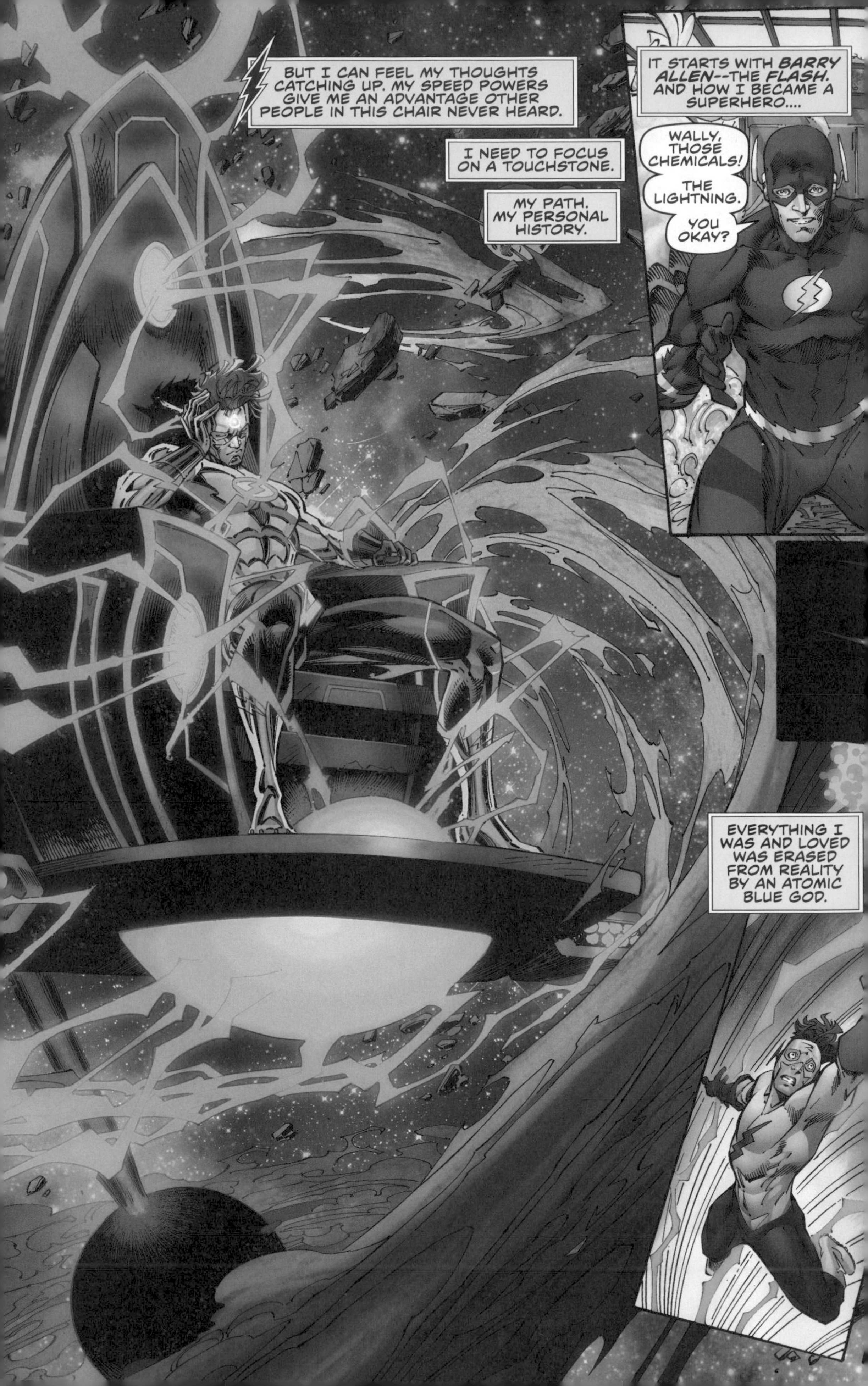

BUT I CAN FEEL MY THOUGHTS CATCHING UP. MY SPEED POWERS GIVE ME AN ADVANTAGE OTHER PEOPLE IN THIS CHAIR NEVER HEARD.
I NEED TO FOCUS ON A TOUCHSTONE.
MY PATH. MY PERSONAL HISTORY.
IT STARTS WITH BARRY ALLEN--THE FLASH. AND HOW I BECAME A SUPERHERO....
WALLY, THOSE CHEMICALS!
THE LIGHTNING.
YOU OKAY?
EVERYTHING I WAS AND LOVED WAS ERASED FROM REALITY BY AN ATOMIC BLUE GOD.

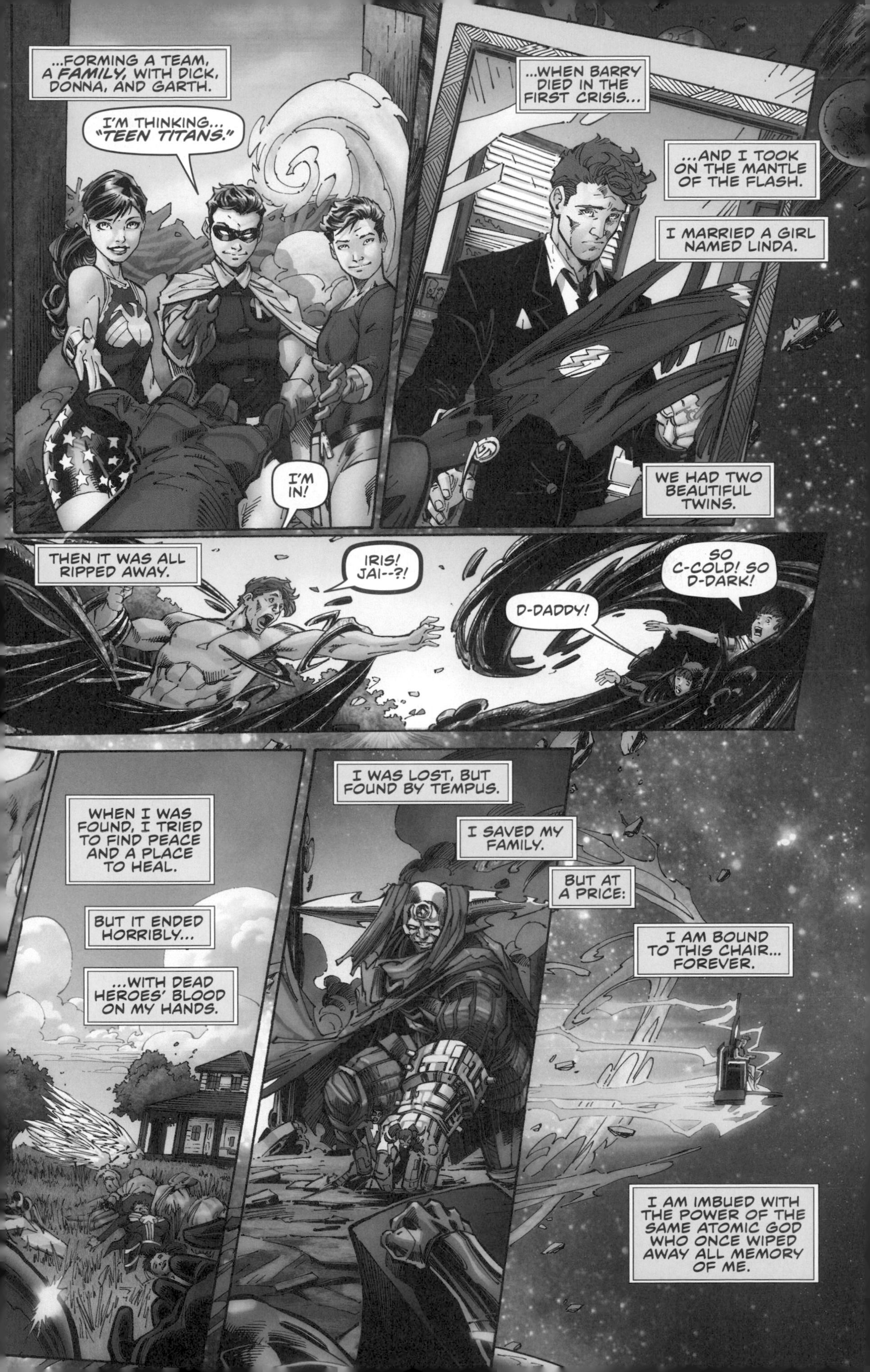
...FORMING A TEAM, A FAMILY, WITH DICK, DONNA, AND GARTH.
I'M THINKING... "TEEN TITANS."
I'M IN!
...WHEN BARRY DIED IN THE FIRST CRISIS...
...AND I TOOK ON THE MANTLE OF THE FLASH.
I MARRIED A GIRL NAMED LINDA.
WE HAD TWO BEAUTIFUL TWINS.
THEN IT WAS ALL RIPPED AWAY.
IRIS! JAI--?!
SO C-COLD! SO D-DARK!
D-DADDY!
WHEN I WAS FOUND, I TRIED TO FIND PEACE AND A PLACE TO HEAL.
BUT IT ENDED HORRIBLY...
...WITH DEAD HEROES' BLOOD ON MY HANDS.
I WAS LOST, BUT FOUND BY TEMPUS.
I SAVED MY FAMILY.
BUT AT A PRICE:
I AM BOUND TO THIS CHAIR... FOREVER.
I AM IMBUED WITH THE POWER OF THE SAME ATOMIC GOD WHO ONCE WIPED AWAY ALL MEMORY OF ME.

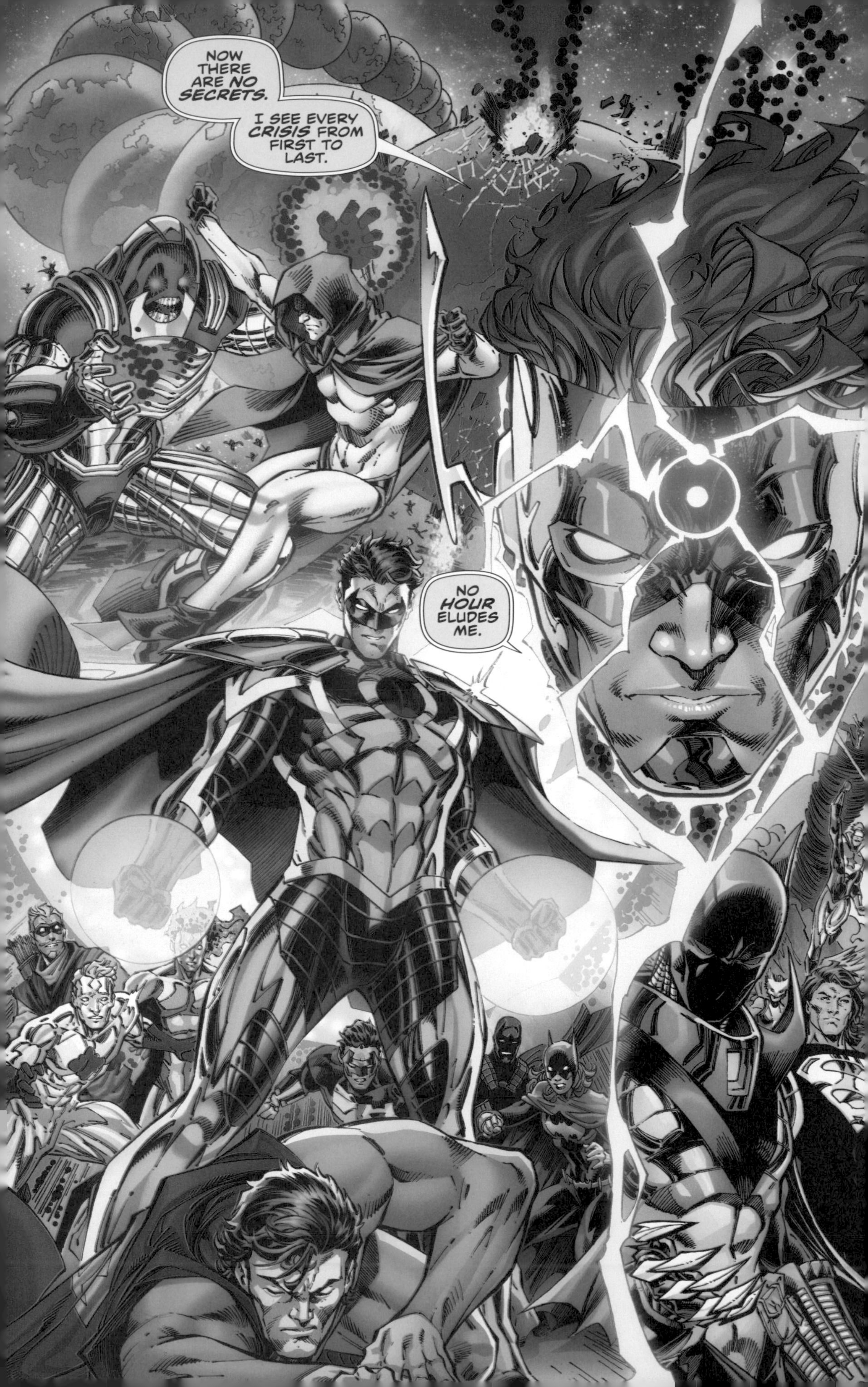
NOW THERE ARE NO SECRETS.
I SEE EVERY CRISIS FROM FIRST TO LAST.
NO HOUR ELUDES ME.

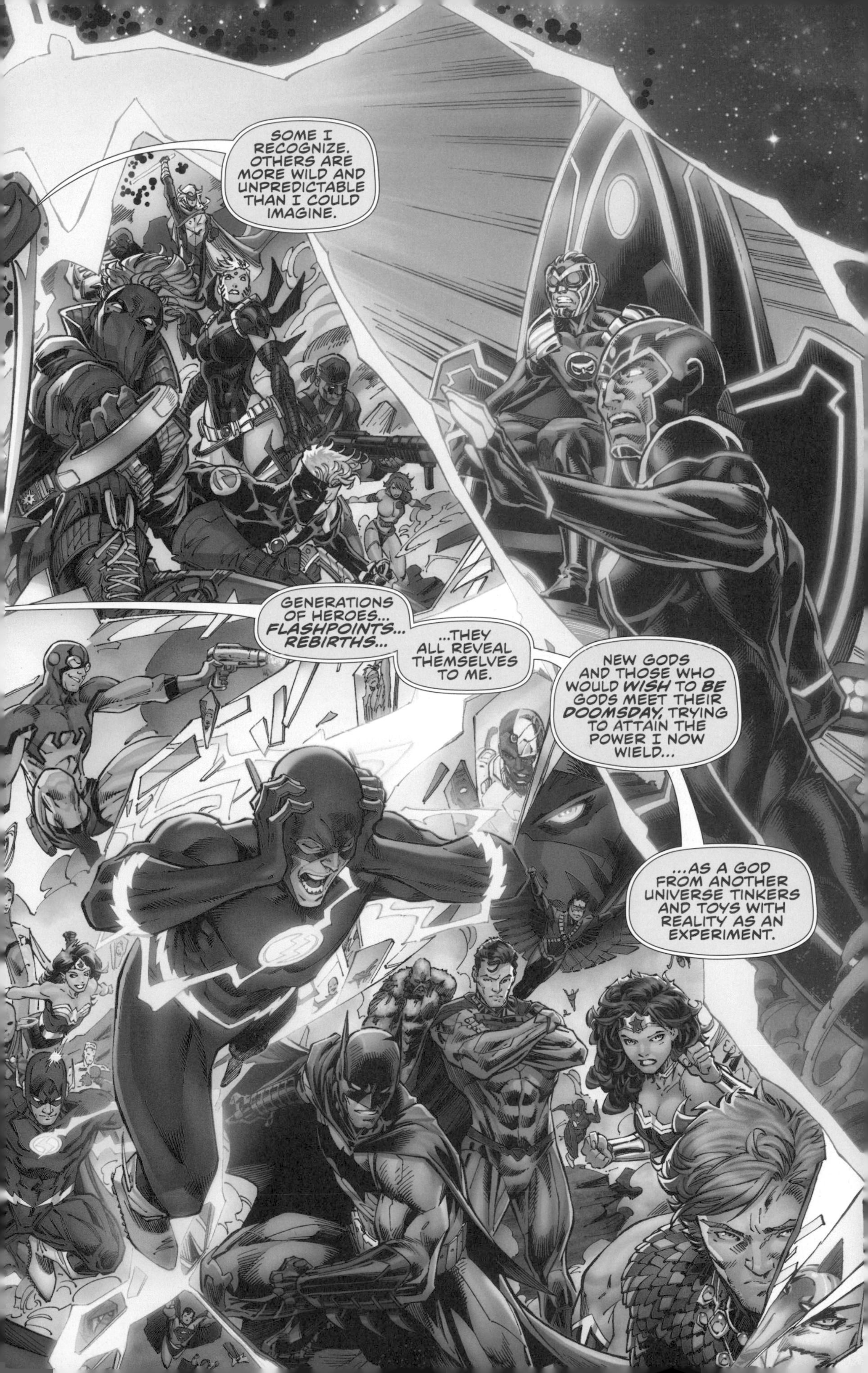
SOME I RECOGNIZE. OTHERS ARE MORE WILD AND UNPREDICTABLE THAN I COULD IMAGINE.
GENERATIONS OF HEROES... FLASHPOINTS... REBIRTHS...
...THEY ALL REVEAL THEMSELVES TO ME.
NEW GODS AND THOSE WHO WOULD WISH TO BE GODS MEET THEIR DOOMSDAY, TRYING TO ATTAIN THE POWER I NOW WIELD...
...AS A GOD FROM ANOTHER UNIVERSE TINKERS AND TOYS WITH REALITY AS AN EXPERIMENT.

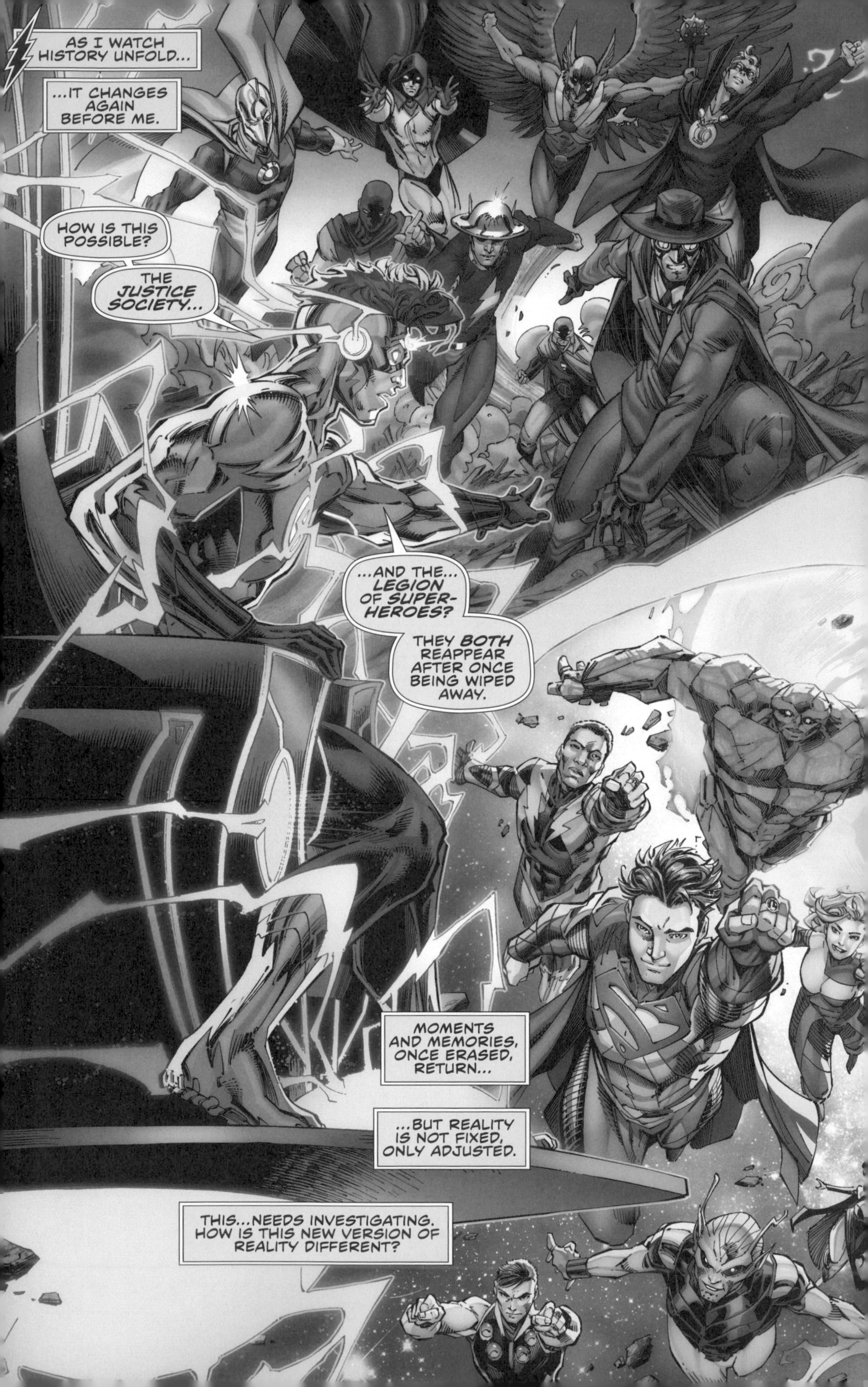

AS I WATCH HISTORY UNFOLD...
...IT CHANGES AGAIN BEFORE ME.
HOW IS THIS POSSIBLE?
THE JUSTICE SOCIETY...
...AND THE... LEGION OF SUPER-HEROES?
THEY BOTH REAPPEAR AFTER ONCE BEING WIPED AWAY.
MOMENTS AND MEMORIES, ONCE ERASED, RETURN...
...BUT REALITY IS NOT FIXED, ONLY ADJUSTED.
THIS...NEEDS INVESTIGATING. HOW IS THIS NEW VERSION OF REALITY DIFFERENT?

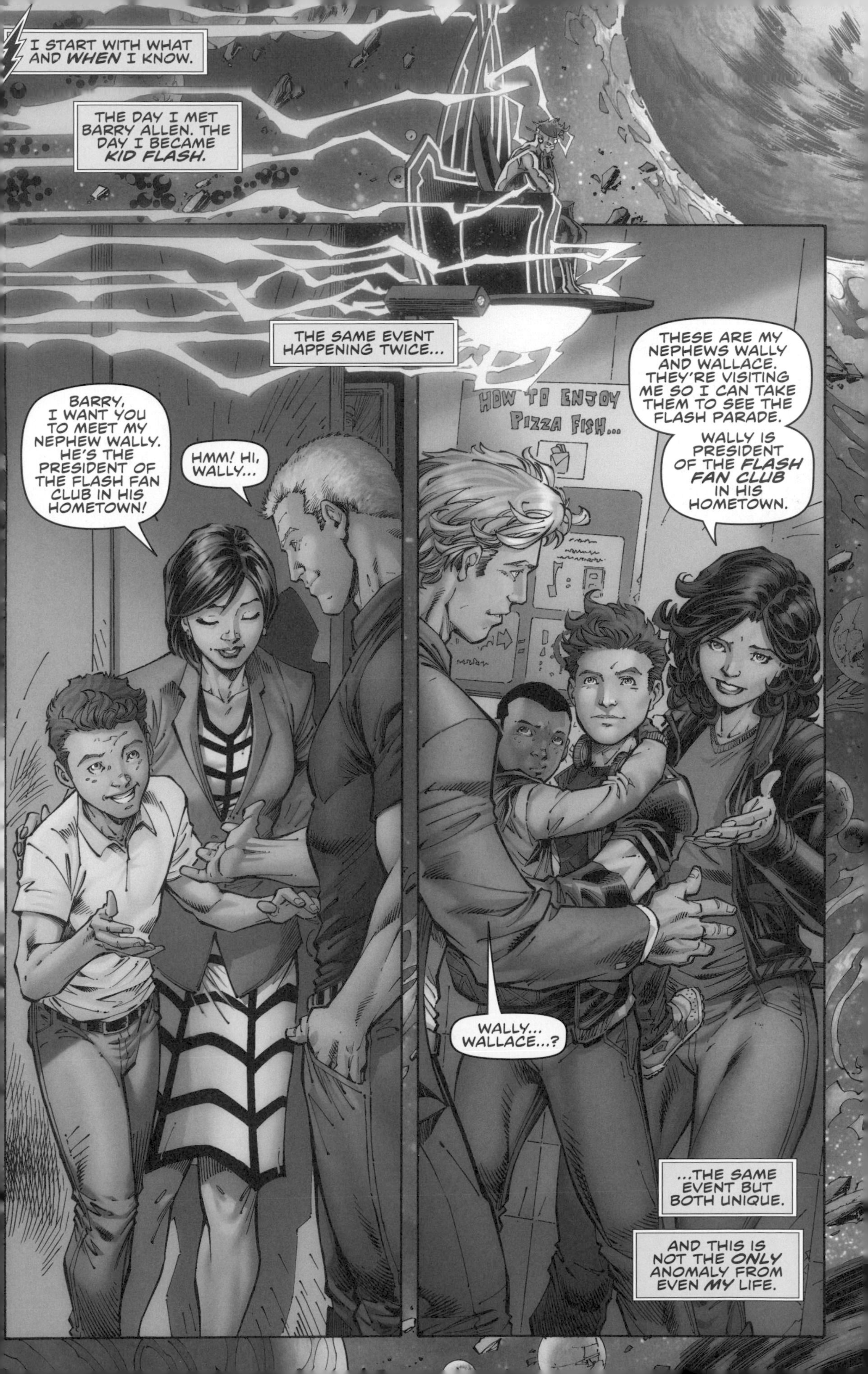
I START WITH WHAT AND *WHEN* I KNOW.
THE DAY I MET BARRY ALLEN. THE DAY I BECAME *KID FLASH.*
THE SAME EVENT HAPPENING TWICE...
BARRY, I WANT YOU TO MEET MY NEPHEW WALLY. HE'S THE PRESIDENT OF THE FLASH FAN CLUB IN HIS HOMETOWN!
HMM! HI, WALLY...
HOW TO ENJOY PIZZA FISH...
THESE ARE MY NEPHEWS WALLY AND WALLACE. THEY'RE VISITING ME SO I CAN TAKE THEM TO SEE THE FLASH PARADE.
WALLY IS PRESIDENT OF THE *FLASH FAN CLUB* IN HIS HOMETOWN.
WALLY... WALLACE...?
...THE SAME EVENT BUT BOTH UNIQUE.
AND THIS IS NOT THE *ONLY* ANOMALY FROM EVEN *MY* LIFE.

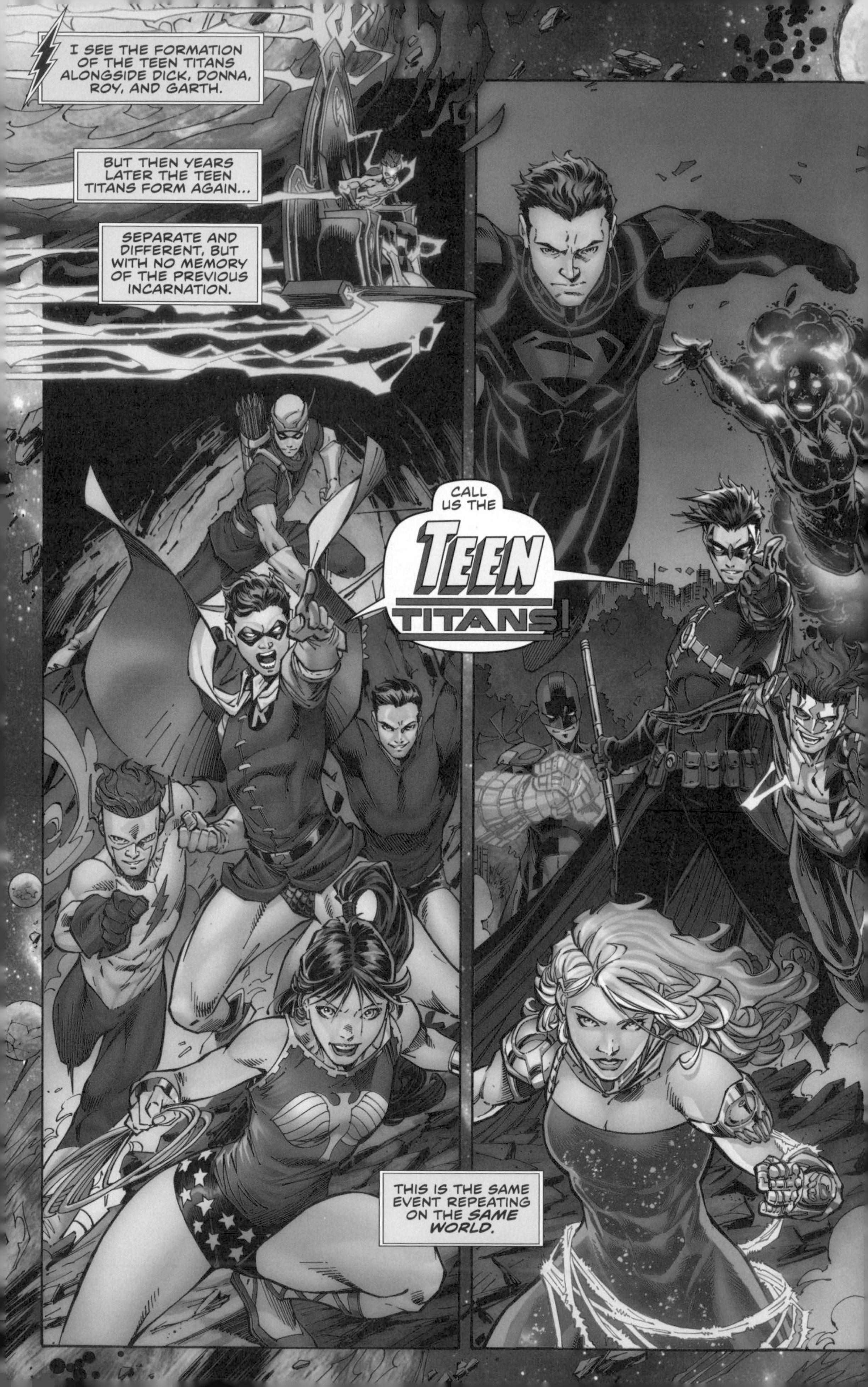
I SEE THE FORMATION OF THE TEEN TITANS ALONGSIDE DICK, DONNA, ROY, AND GARTH.
BUT THEN YEARS LATER THE TEEN TITANS FORM AGAIN...
SEPARATE AND DIFFERENT, BUT WITH NO MEMORY OF THE PREVIOUS INCARNATION.
CALL US THE TEEN TITANS!
THIS IS THE SAME EVENT REPEATING ON THE SAME WORLD.

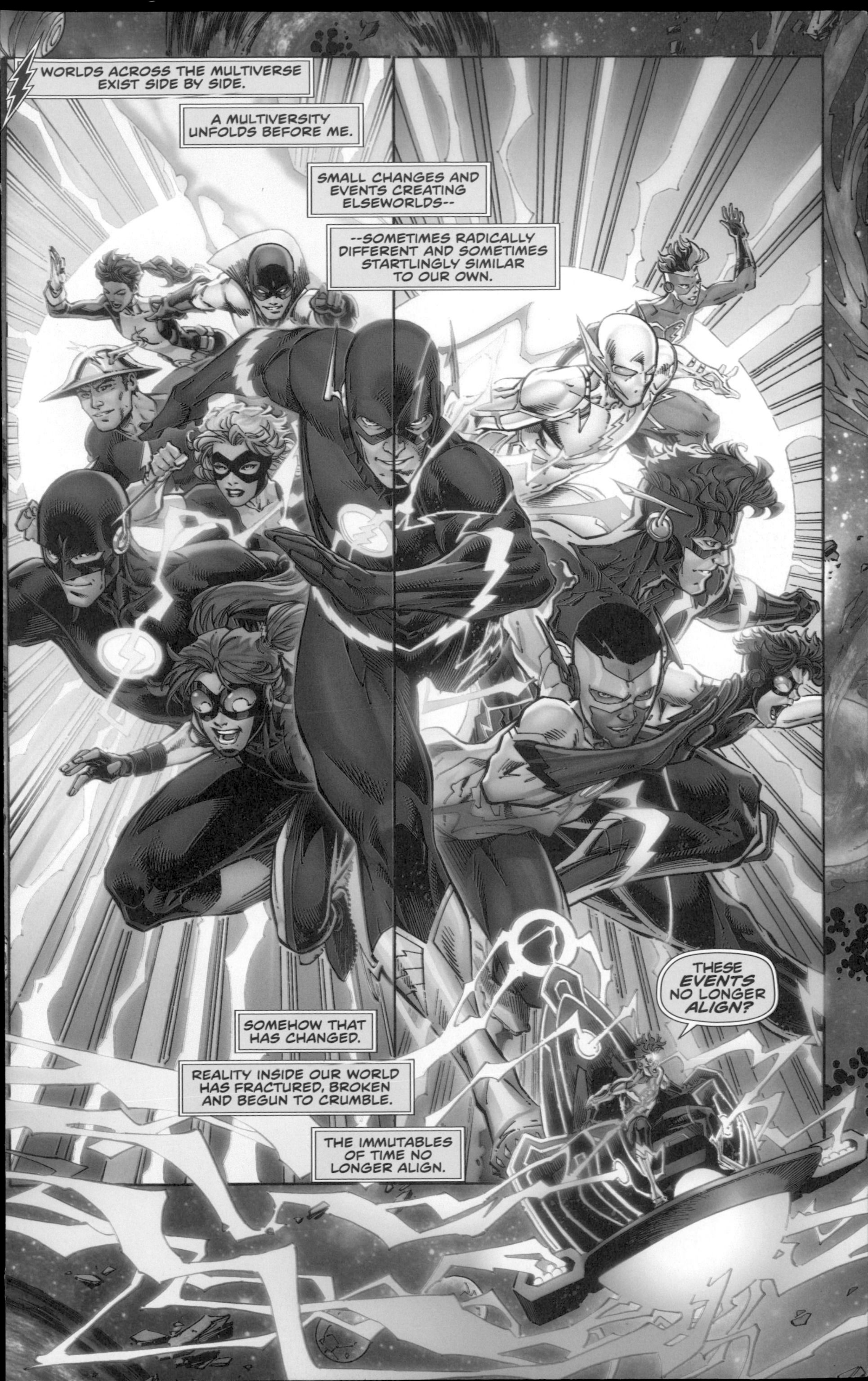
WORLDS ACROSS THE MULTIVERSE EXIST SIDE BY SIDE.
A MULTIVERSITY UNFOLDS BEFORE ME.
SMALL CHANGES AND EVENTS CREATING ELSEWORLDS--
--SOMETIMES RADICALLY DIFFERENT AND SOMETIMES STARTLINGLY SIMILAR TO OUR OWN.
SOMEHOW THAT HAS CHANGED.
REALITY INSIDE OUR WORLD HAS FRACTURED, BROKEN AND BEGUN TO CRUMBLE.
THE IMMUTABLES OF TIME NO LONGER ALIGN.
THESE EVENTS NO LONGER ALIGN?

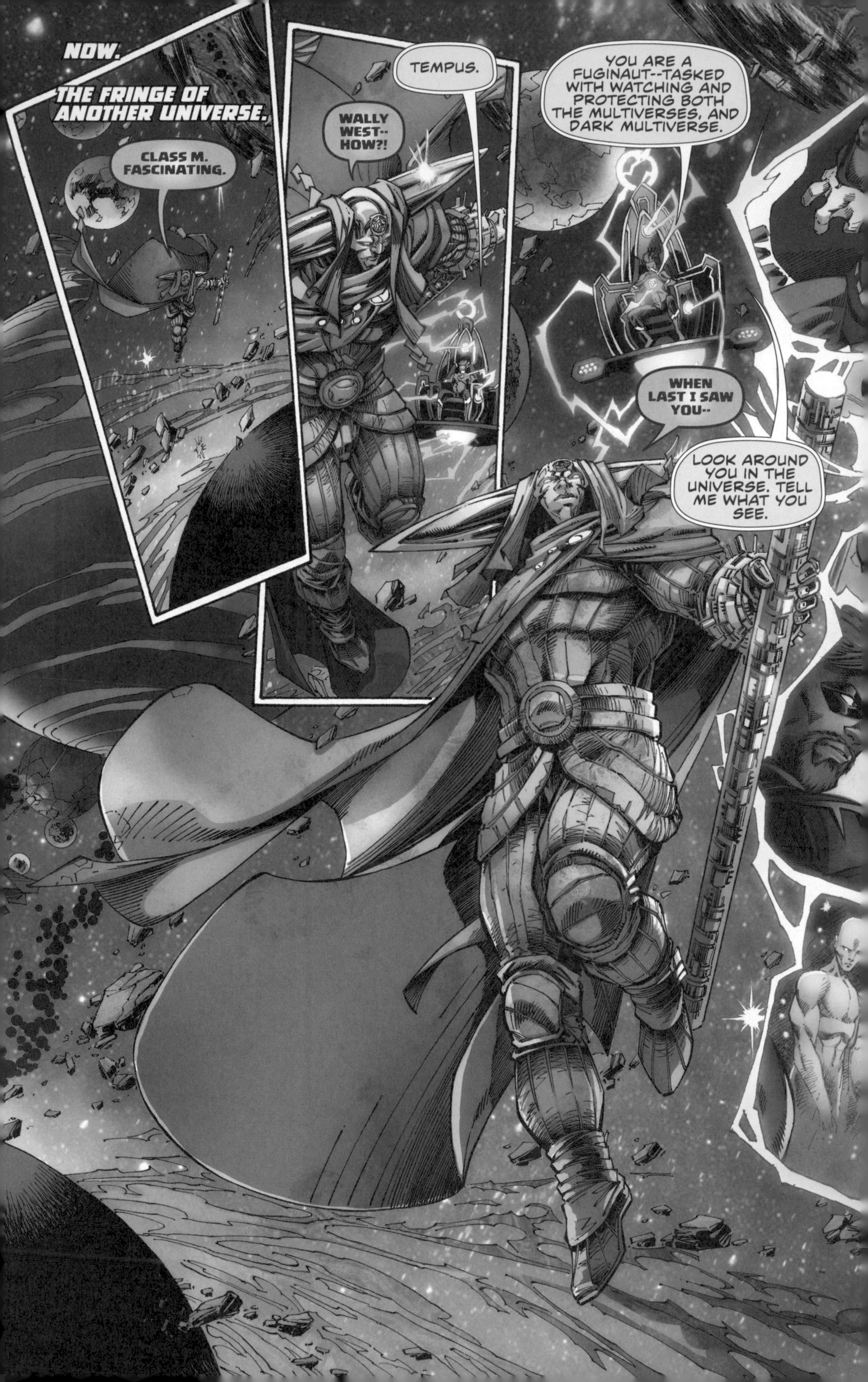
NOW.
THE FRINGE OF ANOTHER UNIVERSE.
CLASS M. FASCINATING.
TEMPUS.
WALLY WEST-- HOW?!
YOU ARE A FUGINAUT--TASKED WITH WATCHING AND PROTECTING BOTH THE MULTIVERSES, AND DARK MULTIVERSE.
WHEN LAST I SAW YOU--
LOOK AROUND YOU IN THE UNIVERSE. TELL ME WHAT YOU SEE.

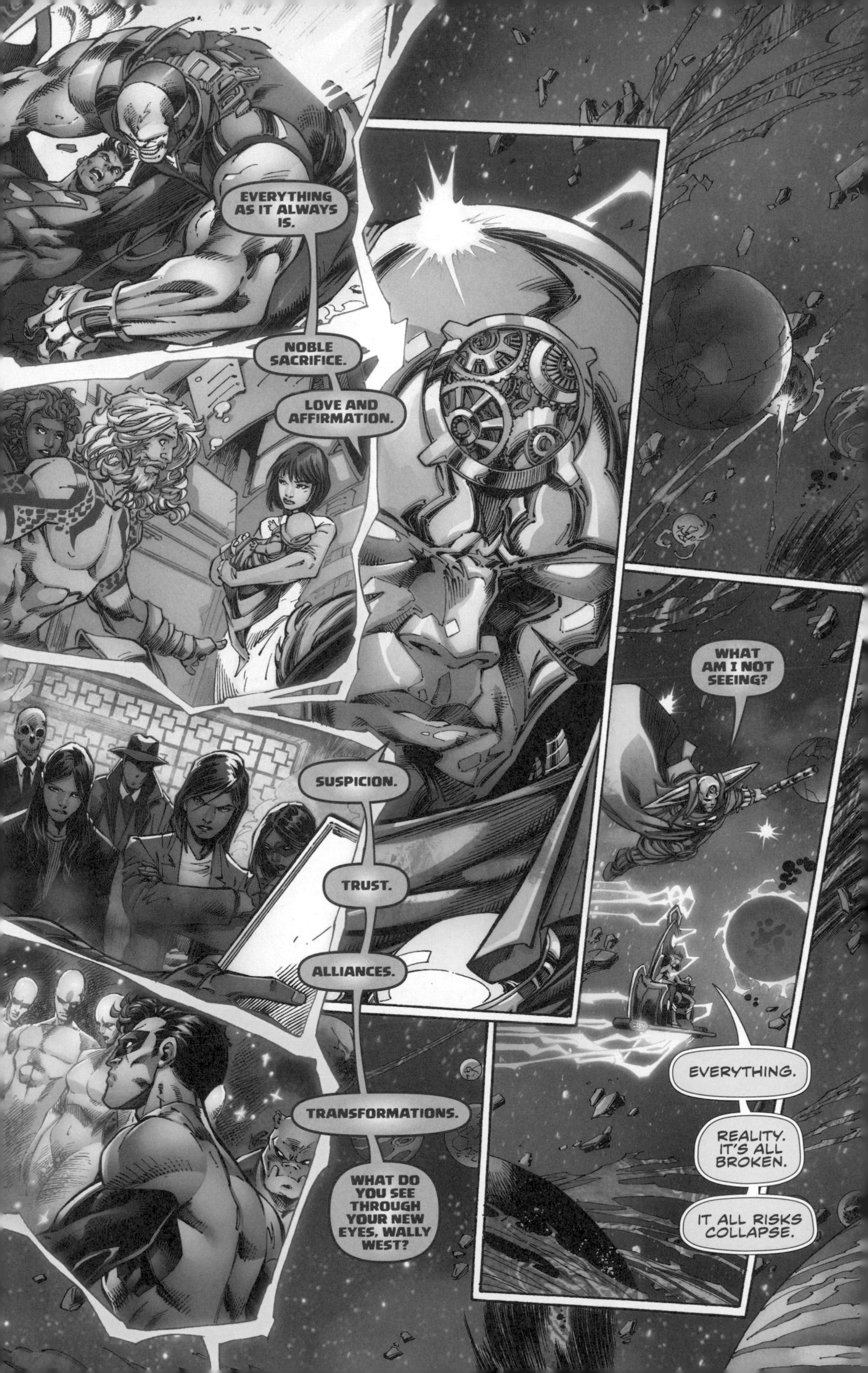
EVERYTHING AS IT ALWAYS IS.
NOBLE SACRIFICE.
LOVE AND AFFIRMATION.
SUSPICION.
TRUST.
ALLIANCES.
TRANSFORMATIONS.
WHAT DO YOU SEE THROUGH YOUR NEW EYES, WALLY WEST?
WHAT AM I NOT SEEING?
EVERYTHING.
REALITY. IT'S ALL BROKEN.
IT ALL RISKS COLLAPSE.

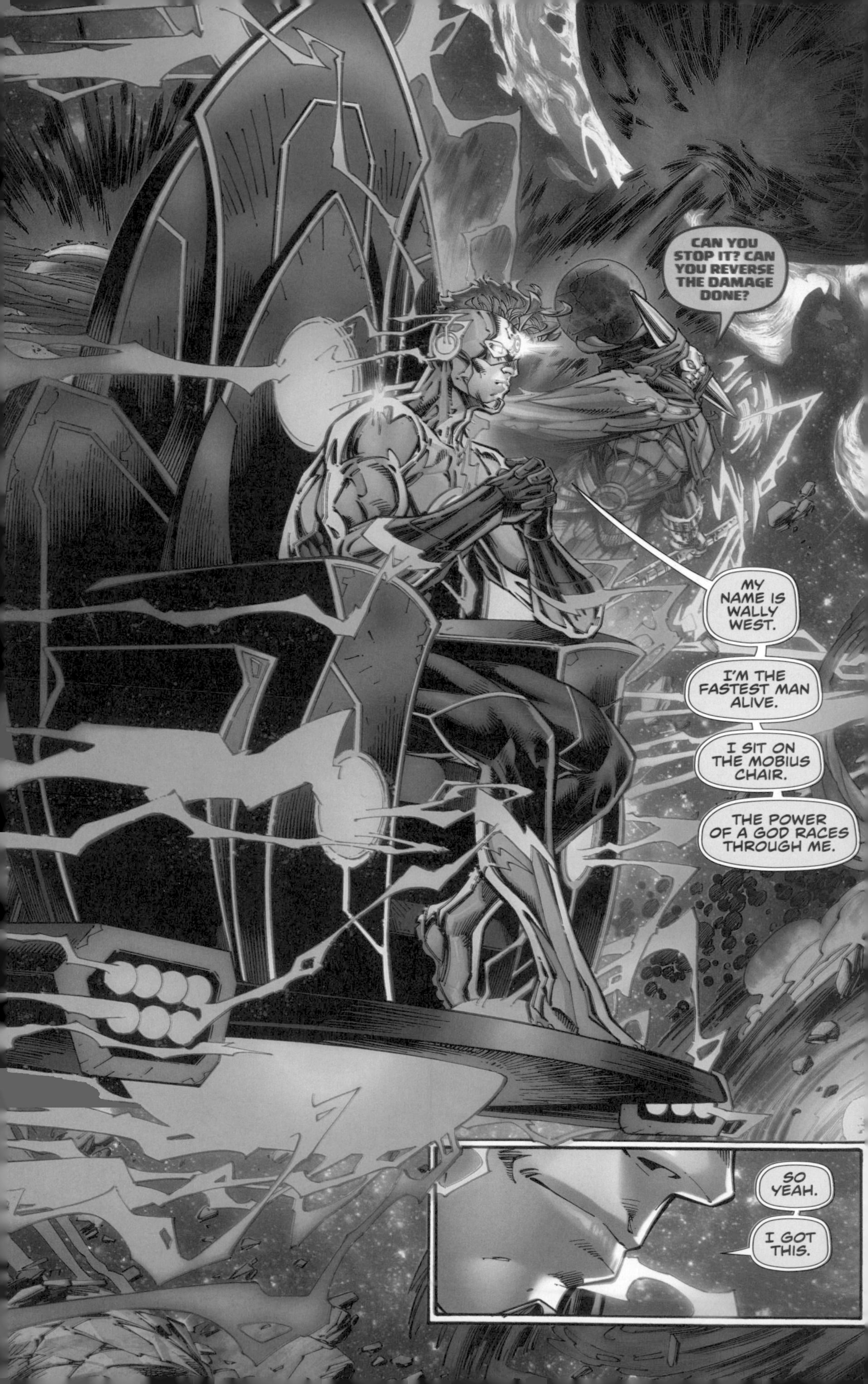
CAN YOU STOP IT? CAN YOU REVERSE THE DAMAGE DONE?
MY NAME IS WALLY WEST.
I'M THE FASTEST MAN ALIVE.
I SIT ON THE MOBIUS CHAIR.
THE POWER OF A GOD RACES THROUGH ME.
SO YEAH.
I GOT THIS.

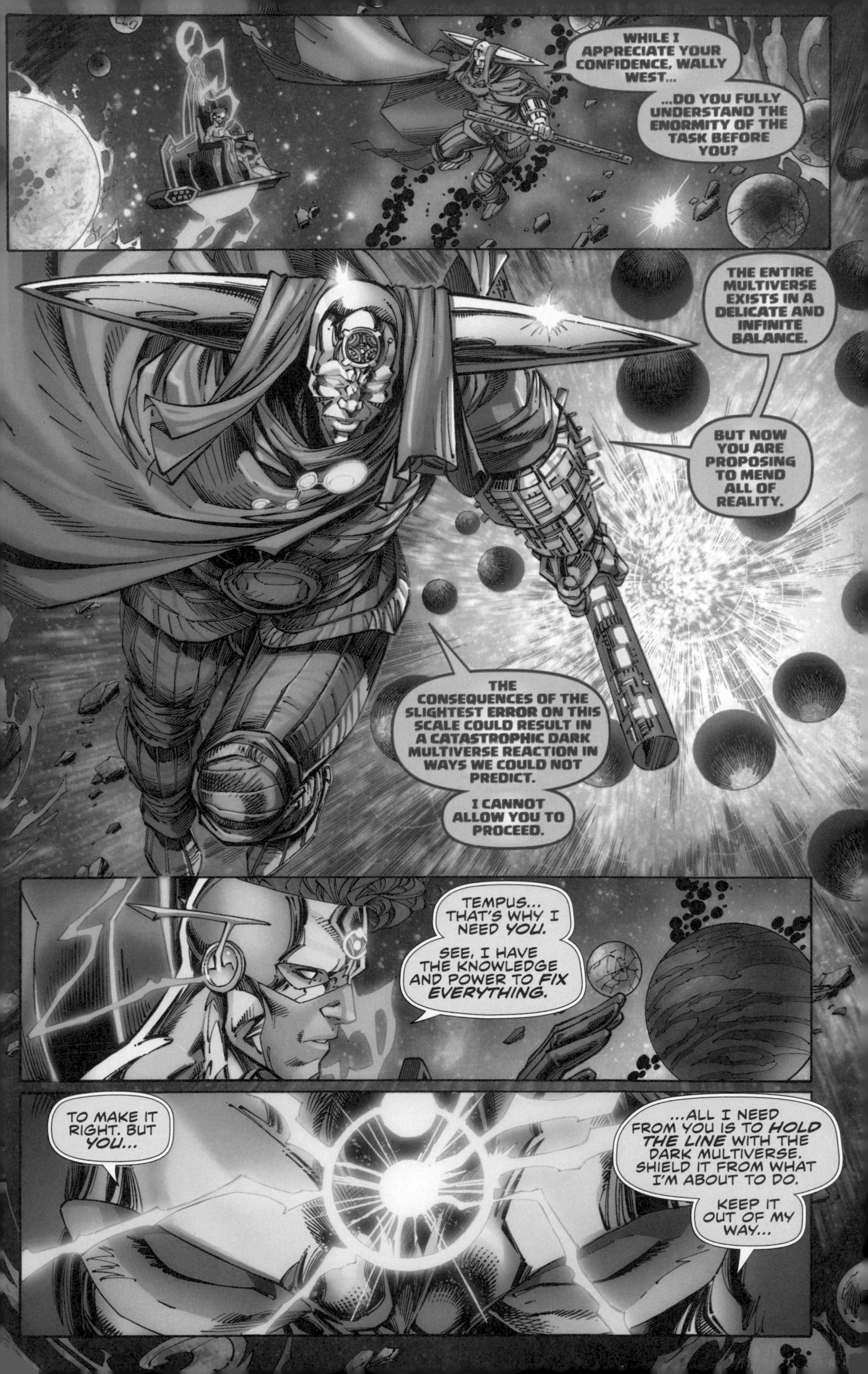
WHILE I APPRECIATE YOUR CONFIDENCE, WALLY WEST...
...DO YOU FULLY UNDERSTAND THE ENORMITY OF THE TASK BEFORE YOU?
THE ENTIRE MULTIVERSE EXISTS IN A DELICATE AND INFINITE BALANCE.
BUT NOW YOU ARE PROPOSING TO MEND ALL OF REALITY.
THE CONSEQUENCES OF THE SLIGHTEST ERROR ON THIS SCALE COULD RESULT IN A CATASTROPHIC DARK MULTIVERSE REACTION IN WAYS WE COULD NOT PREDICT.
I CANNOT ALLOW YOU TO PROCEED.
TEMPUS... THAT'S WHY I NEED YOU.
SEE, I HAVE THE KNOWLEDGE AND POWER TO FIX EVERYTHING.
TO MAKE IT RIGHT. BUT YOU...
...ALL I NEED FROM YOU IS TO HOLD THE LINE WITH THE DARK MULTIVERSE. SHIELD IT FROM WHAT I'M ABOUT TO DO.
KEEP IT OUT OF MY WAY...

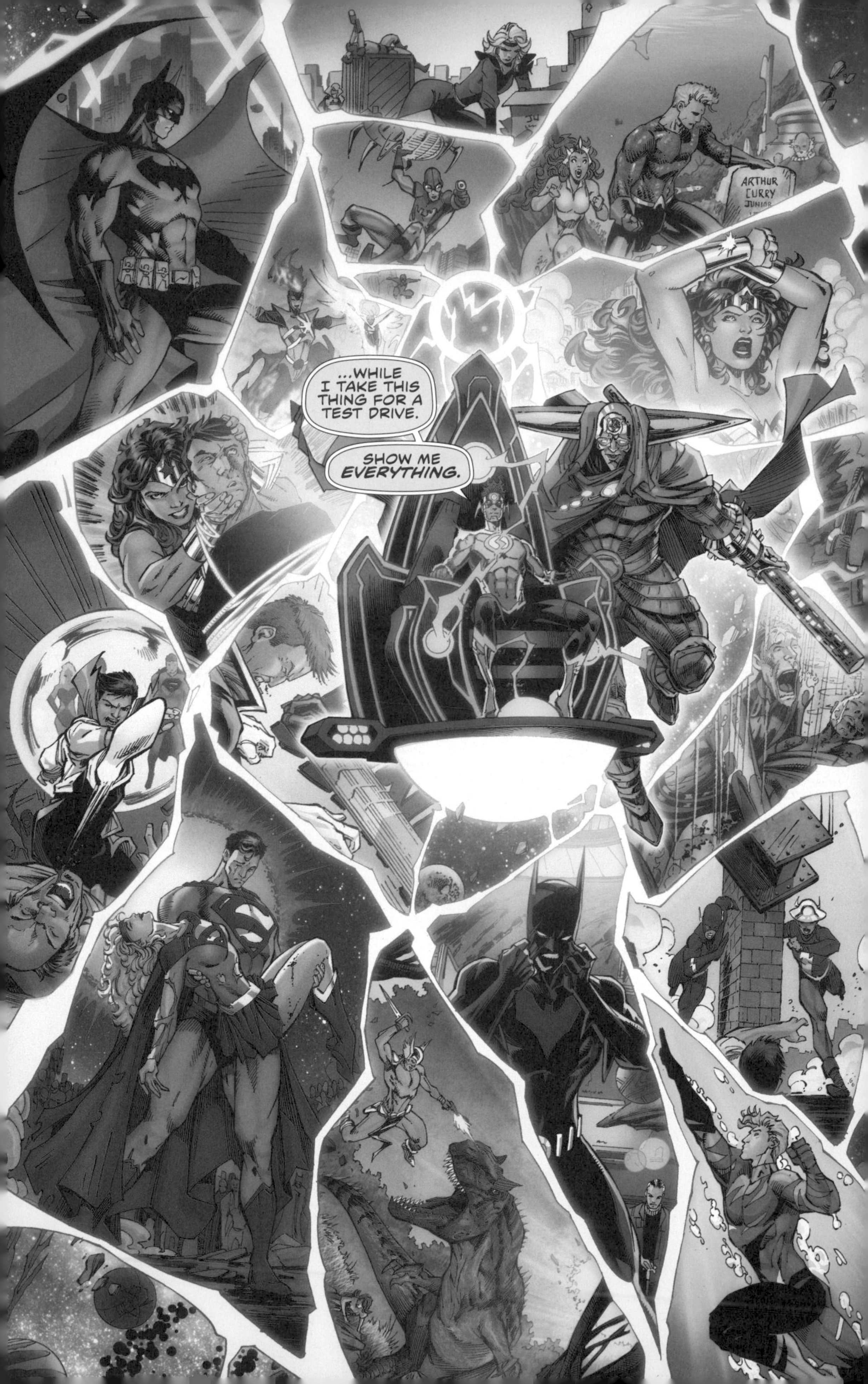
ARTHUR CURRY JUNIOR
...WHILE I TAKE THIS THING FOR A TEST DRIVE.
SHOW ME *EVERYTHING.*

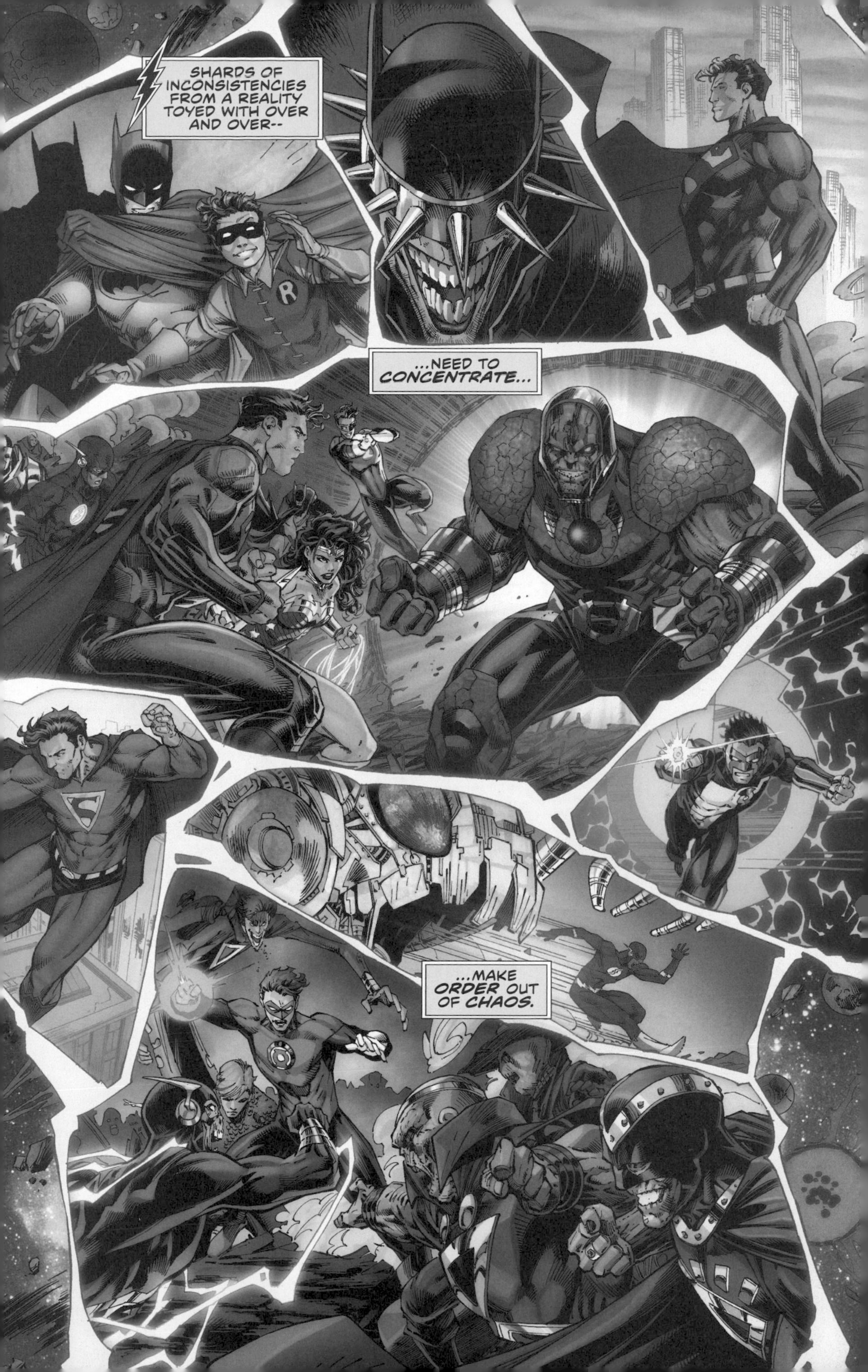
SHARDS OF INCONSISTENCIES FROM A REALITY TOYED WITH OVER AND OVER--
...NEED TO CONCENTRATE...
...MAKE ORDER OUT OF CHAOS.

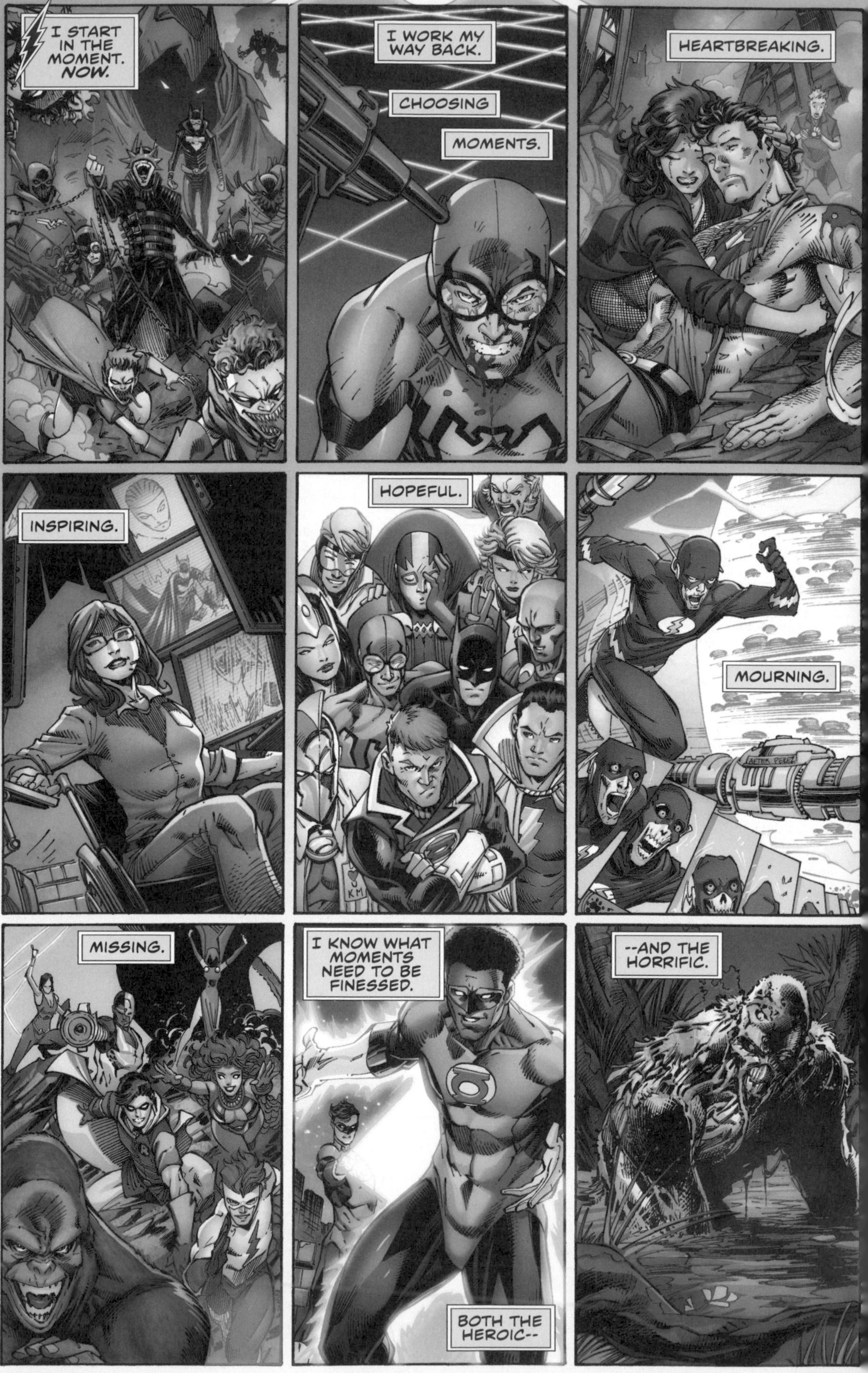
I START IN THE MOMENT. NOW.
I WORK MY WAY BACK.
CHOOSING
MOMENTS.
HEARTBREAKING.
INSPIRING.
HOPEFUL.
MOURNING.
MISSING.
I KNOW WHAT MOMENTS NEED TO BE FINESSED.
BOTH THE HEROIC--
--AND THE HORRIFIC.

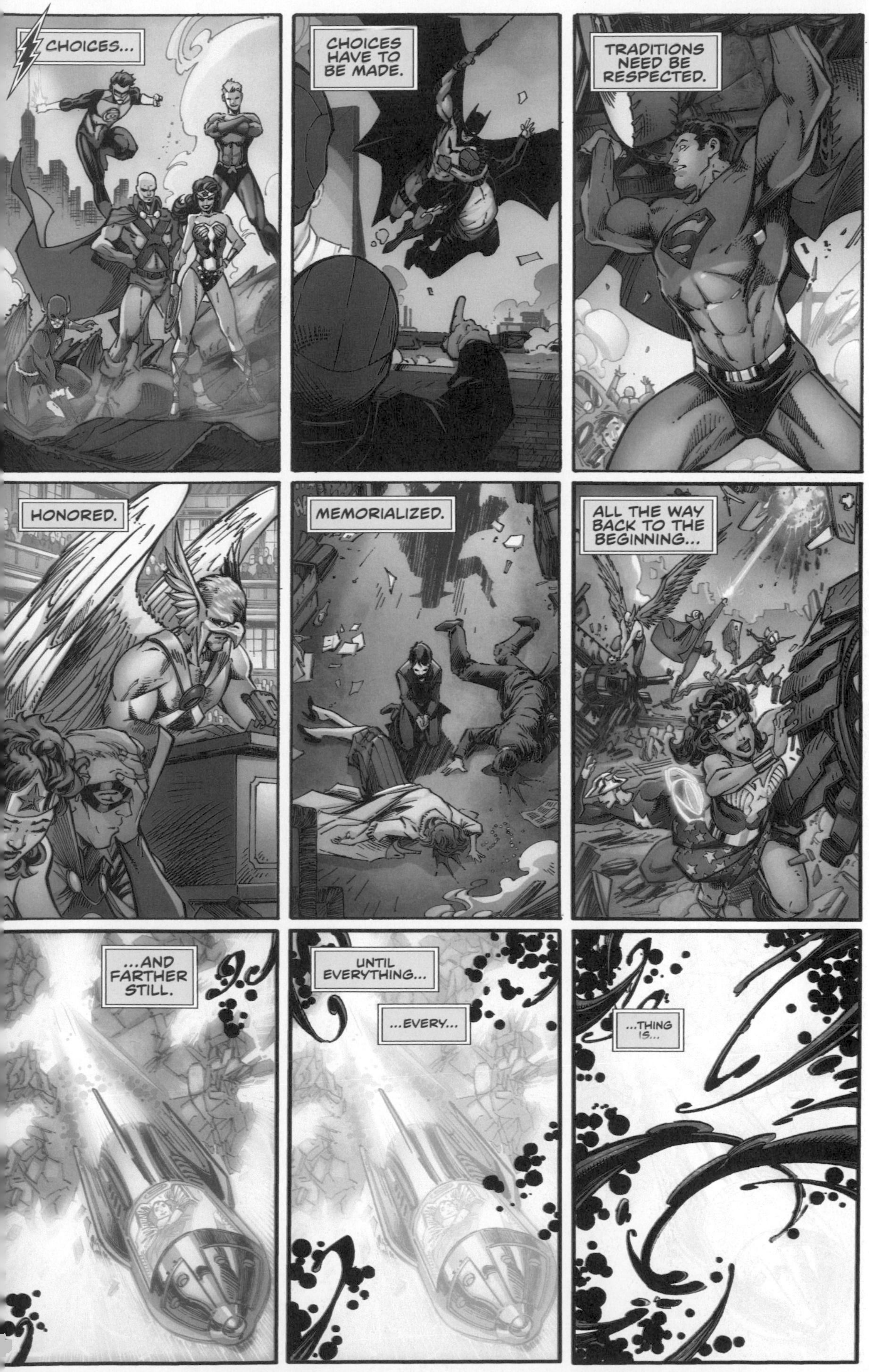
CHOICES...
CHOICES HAVE TO BE MADE.
TRADITIONS NEED BE RESPECTED.
HONORED.
MEMORIALIZED.
ALL THE WAY BACK TO THE BEGINNING...
...AND FARTHER STILL.
UNTIL EVERYTHING...
...EVERY...
...THING IS...

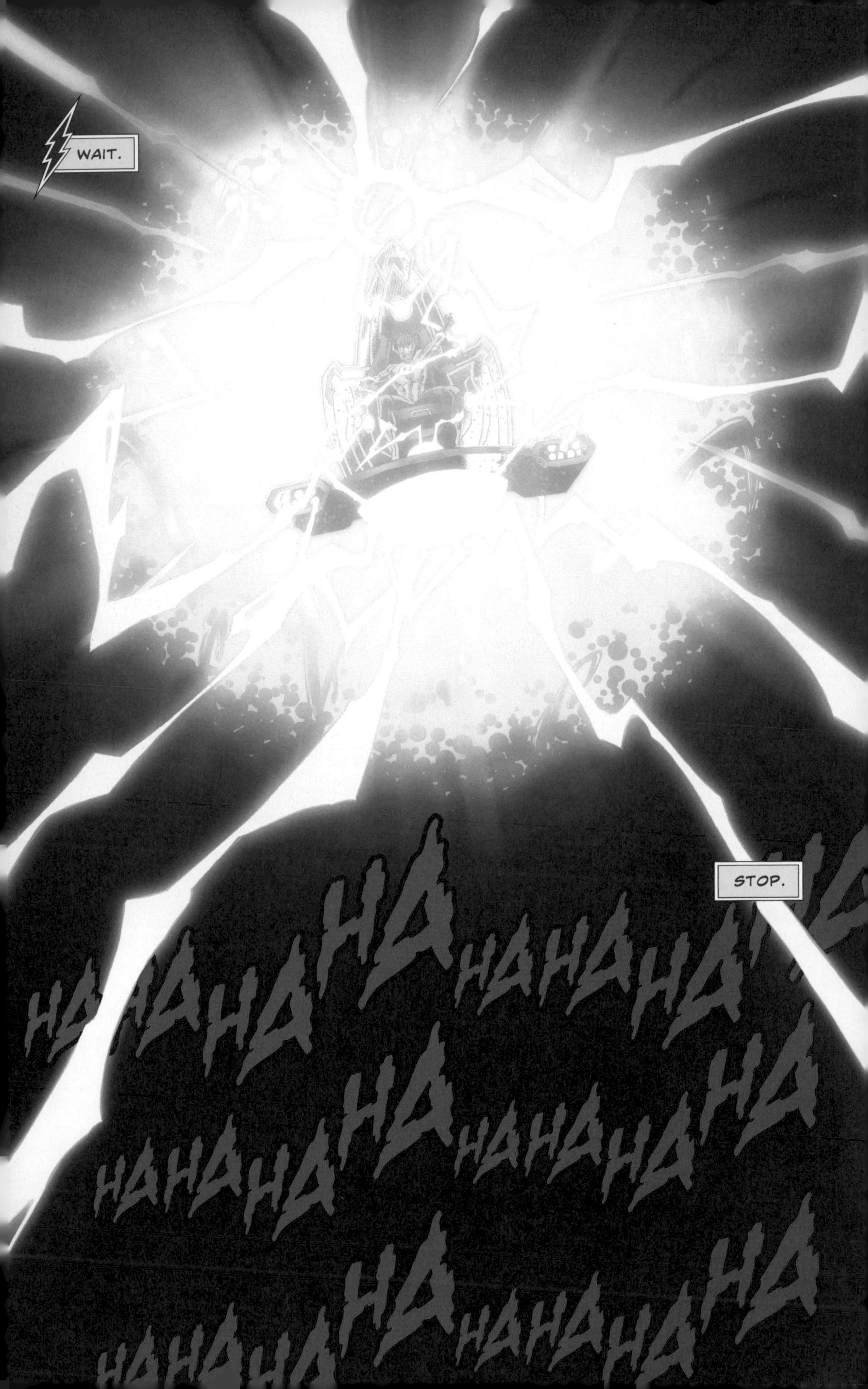
WAIT.
STOP.
HAHAHAHAHAHAHAHA
HAHAHAHAHAHAHAHA
HAHAHAHAHAHAHAHA

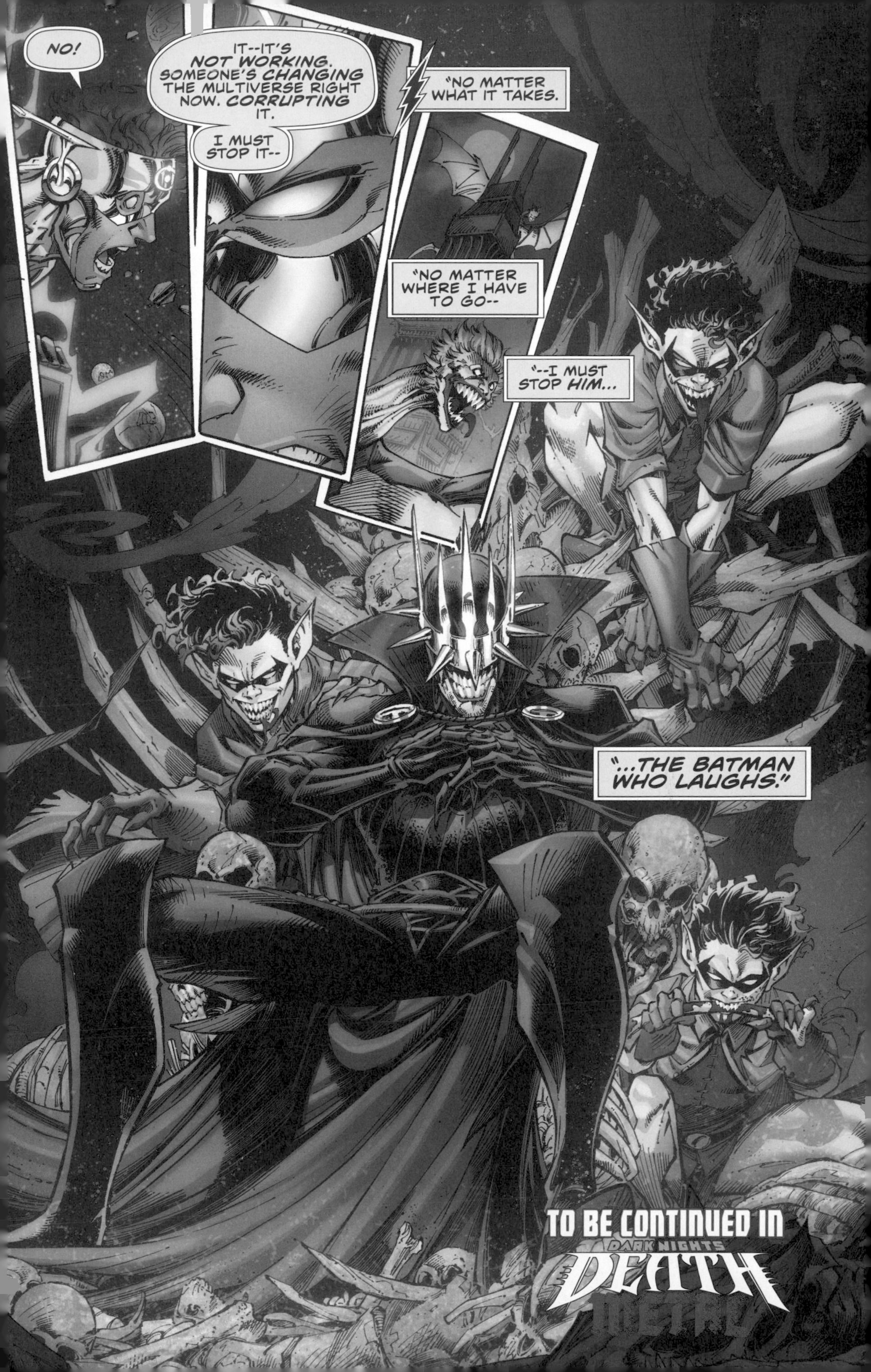
NO!
IT--IT'S NOT WORKING. SOMEONE'S CHANGING THE MULTIVERSE RIGHT NOW. CORRUPTING IT.
I MUST STOP IT--
"NO MATTER WHAT IT TAKES.
"NO MATTER WHERE I HAVE TO GO--
"--I MUST STOP HIM...
"...THE BATMAN WHO LAUGHS."
TO BE CONTINUED IN
DARK NIGHTS DEATH METAL

Flash Forward **#1** variant cover by INHYUK LEE

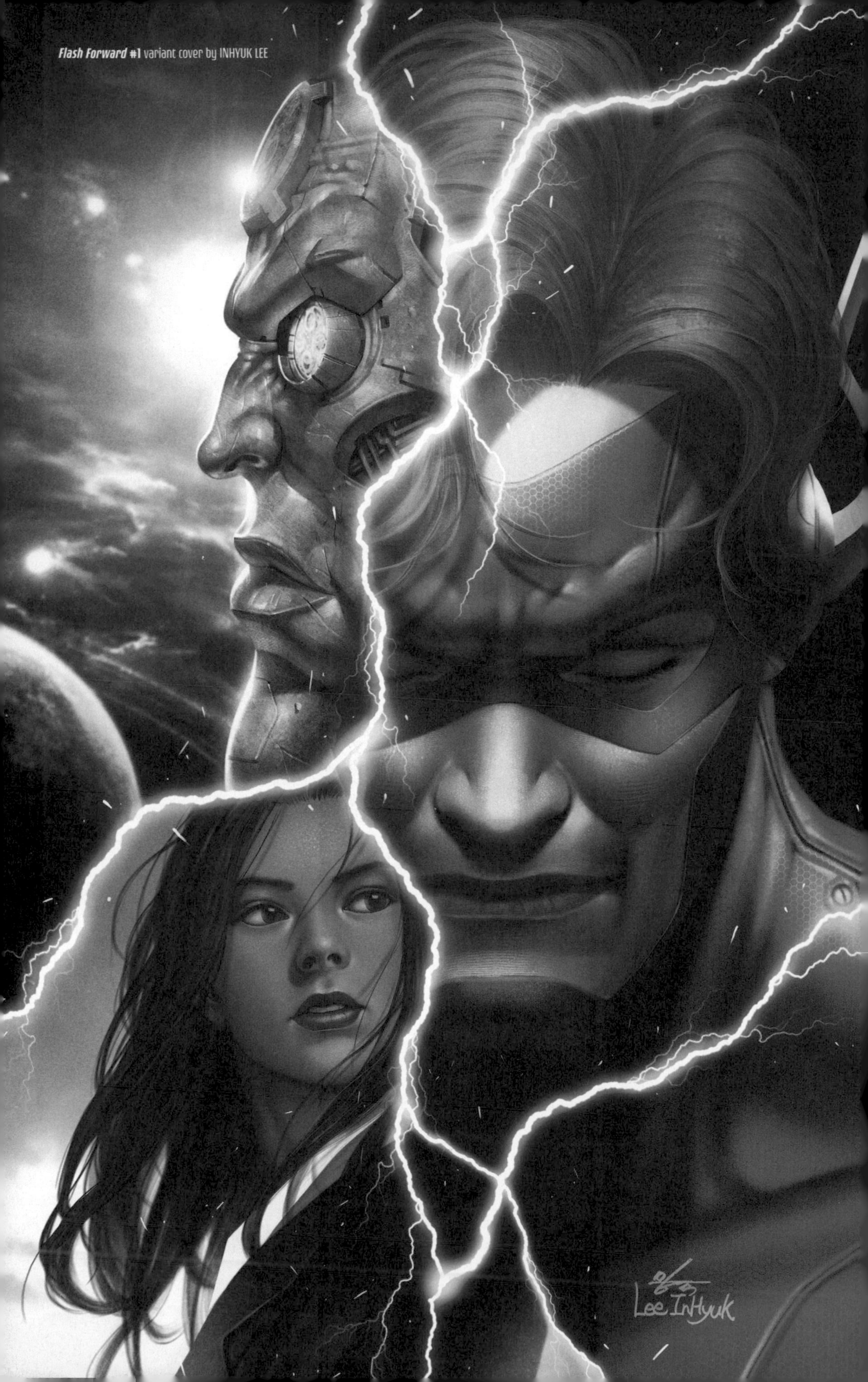
Lee InHyuk

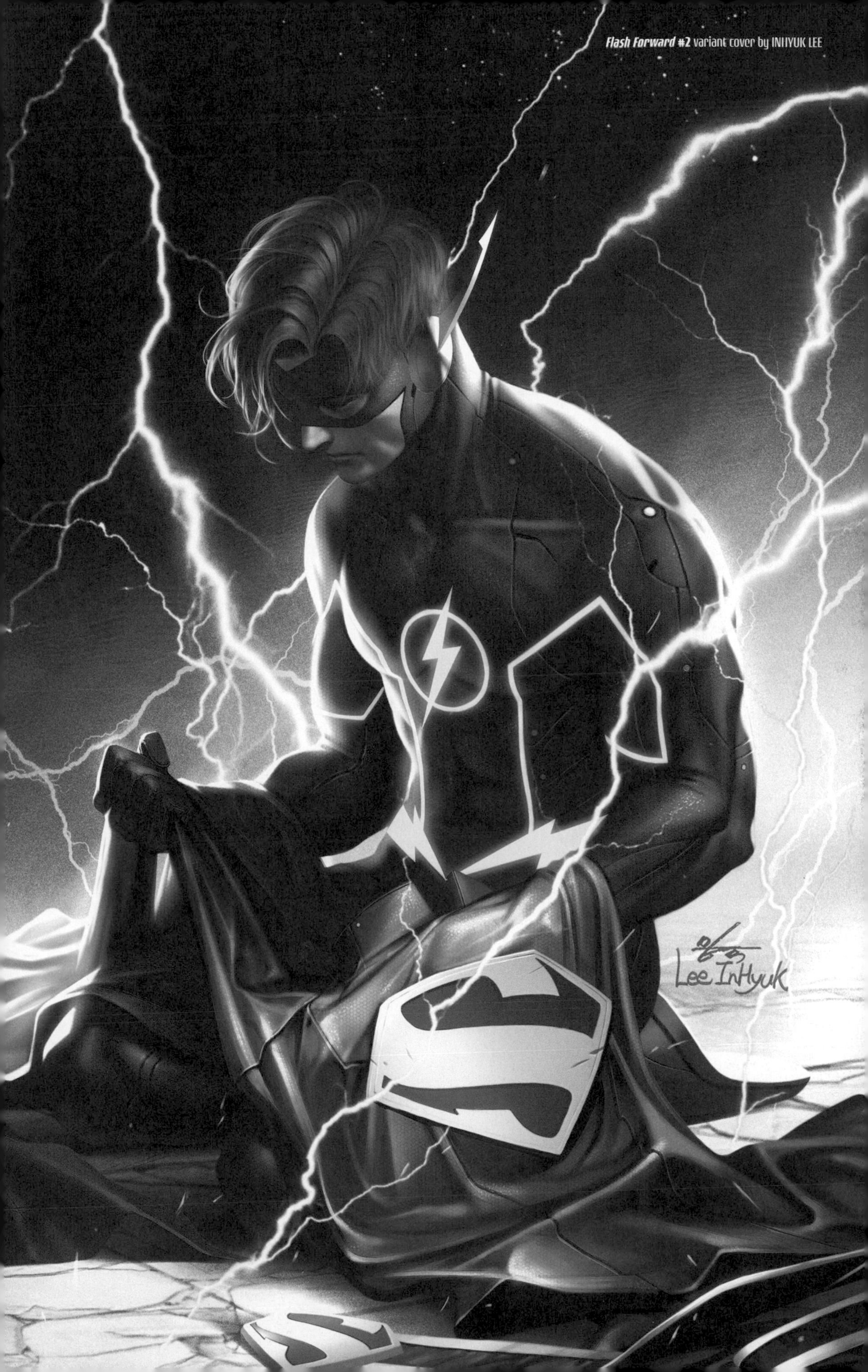
Lee InHyuk
Flash Forward #2 variant cover by INHYUK LEE

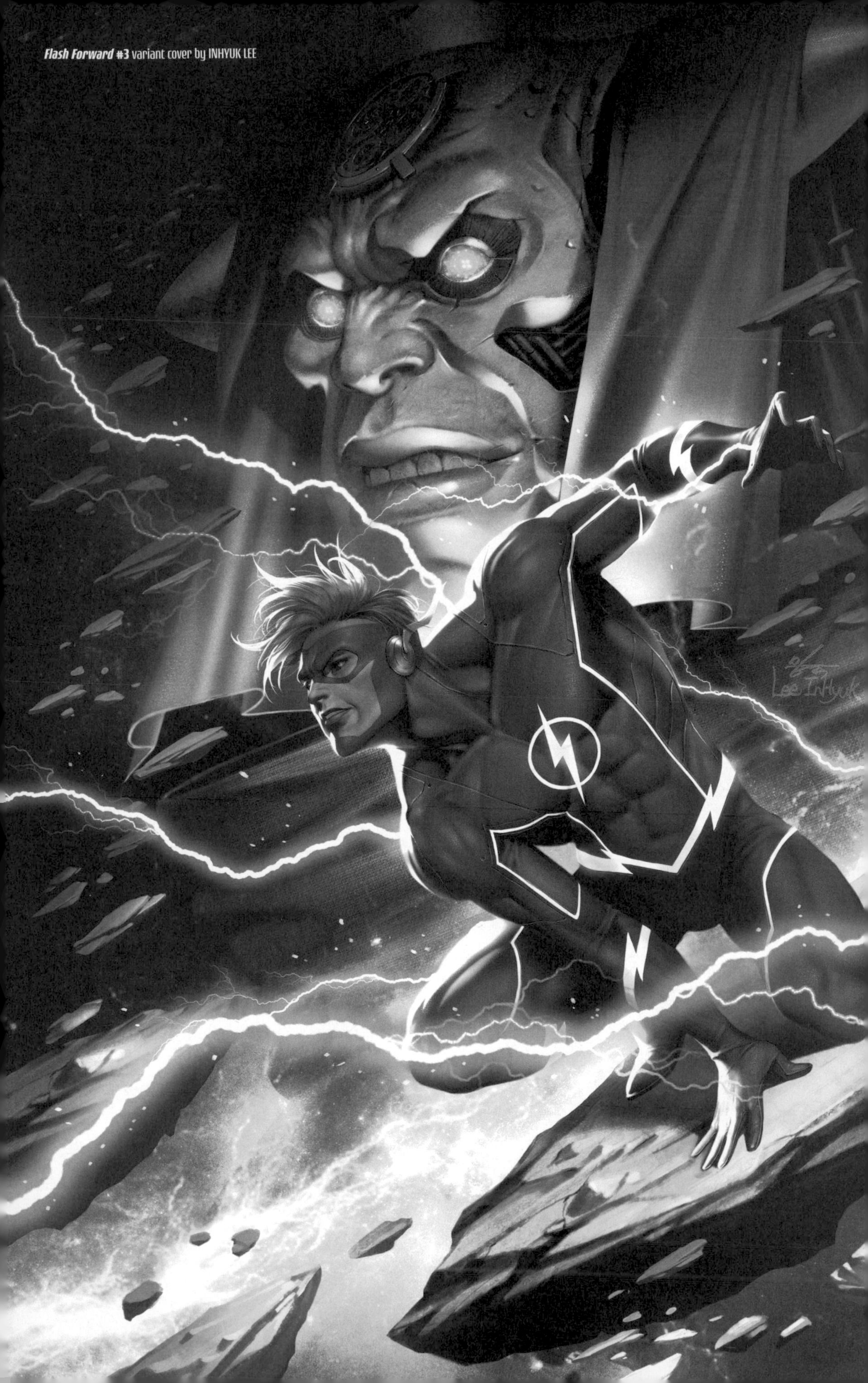
Lee InHyuk

Flash Forward #3 variant cover by INHYUK LEE

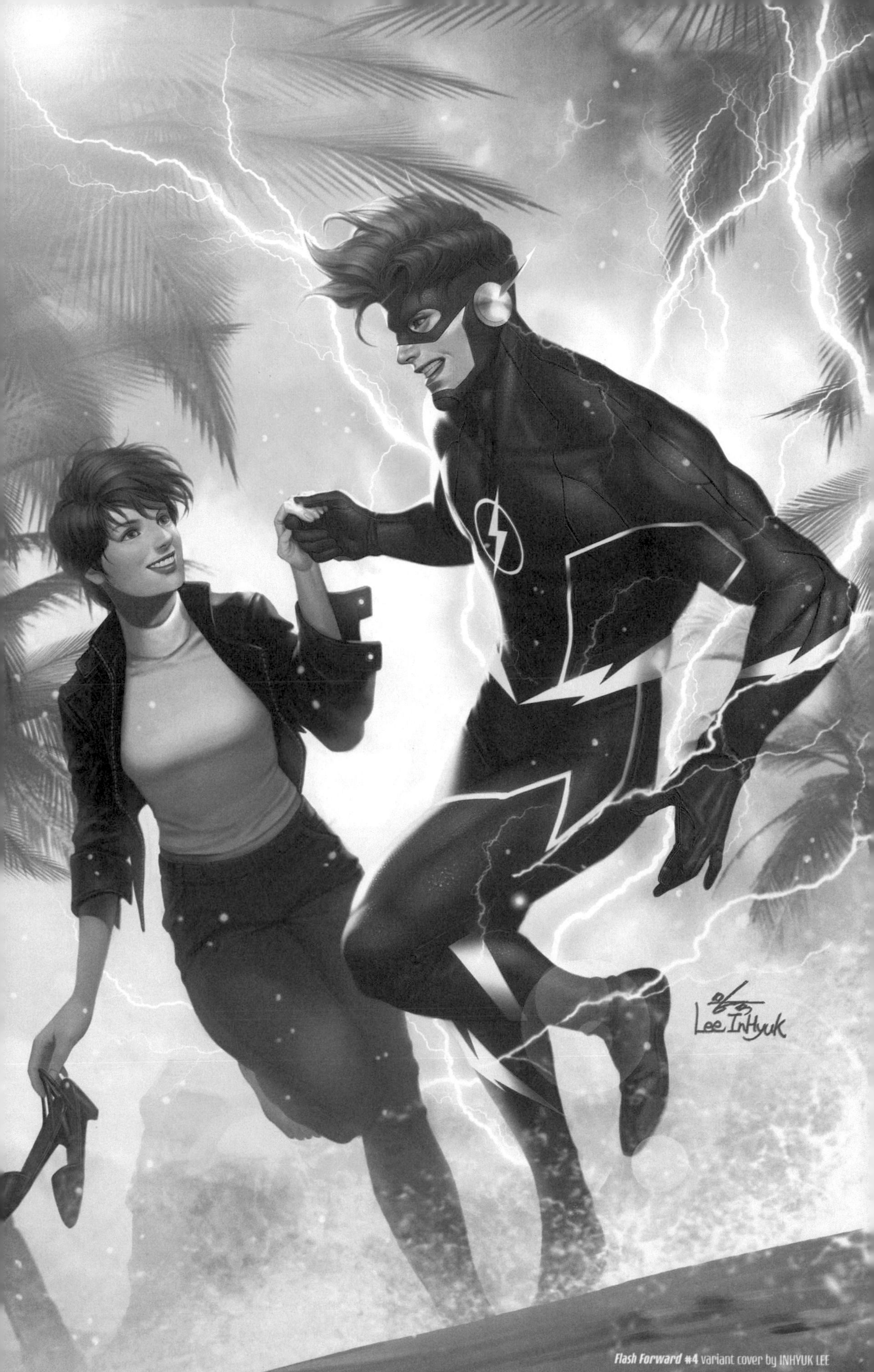
Lee InHyuk

Flash Forward #4 variant cover by INHYUK LEE

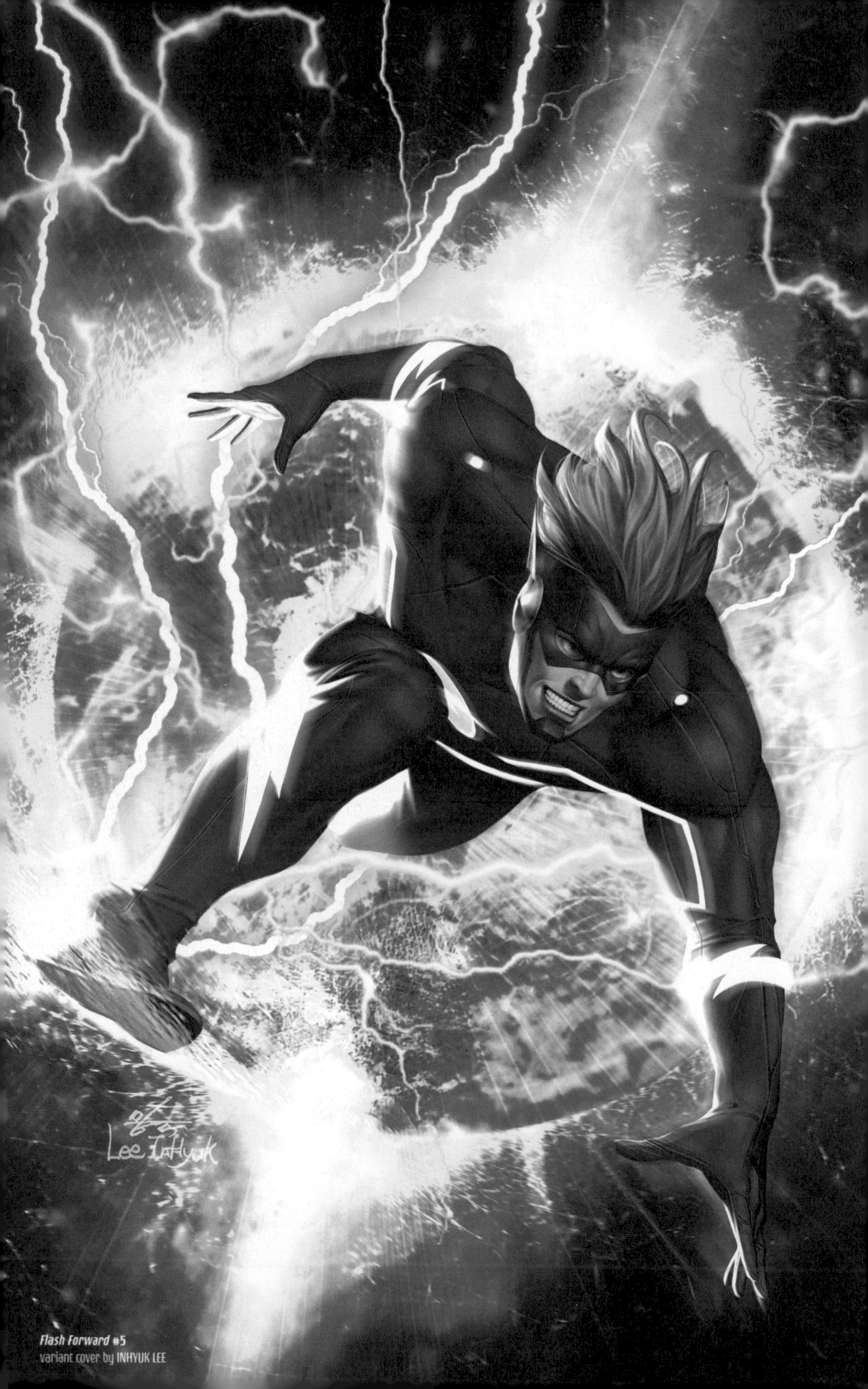
Lee InHyuk

***Flash Forward* #5**
variant cover by INHYUK LEE

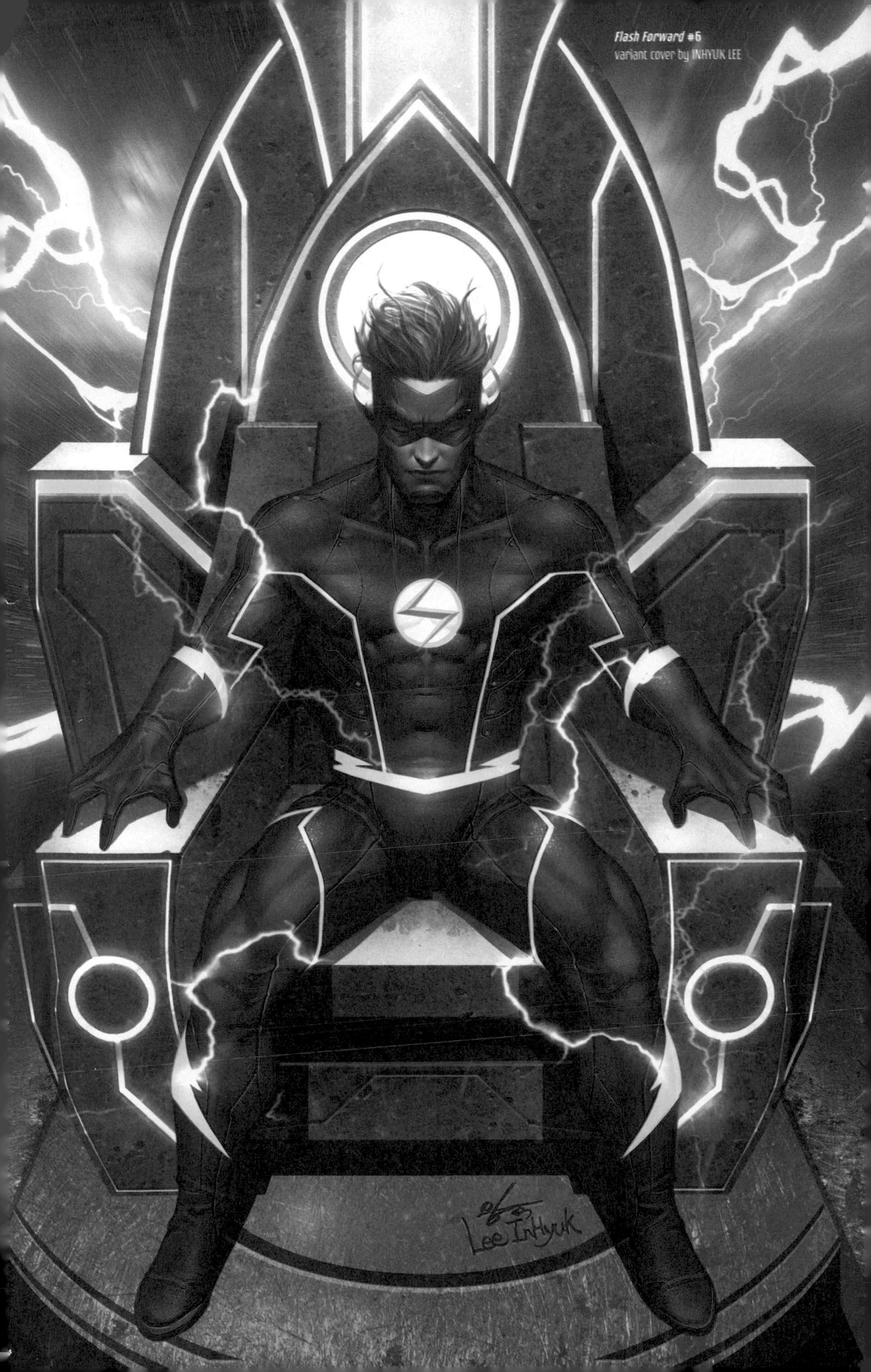
Lee InHyuk

Flash Forward #6
variant cover by INHYUK LEE

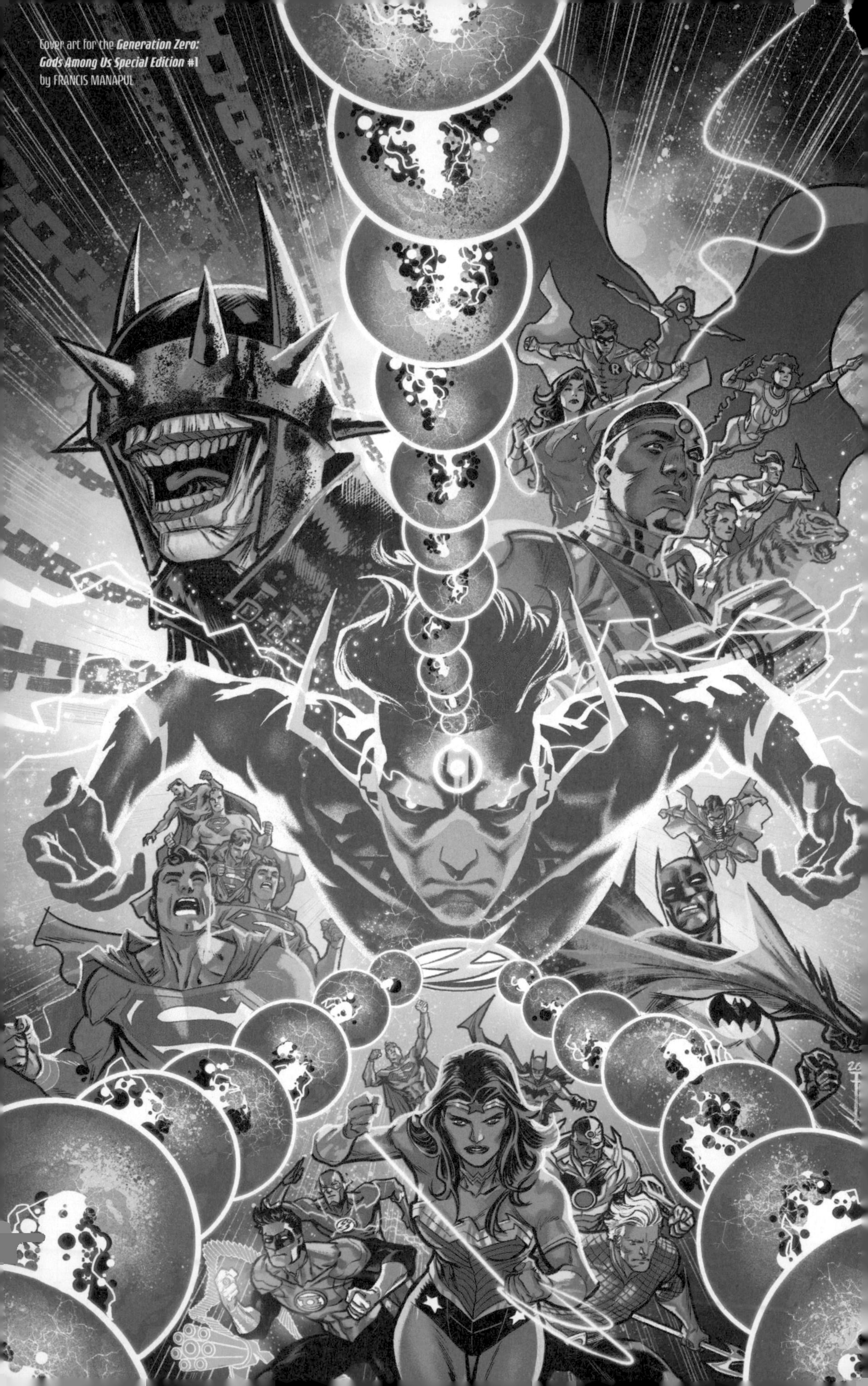

Cover art for the ***Generation Zero: Gods Among Us Special Edition* #1**
by FRANCIS MANAPUL